Strategic and
Critical Materials

Also of Interest

National Security and Strategic Minerals: U.S. Dependence on Foreign Sources of Cobalt, Barry Blechman

International Minerals: A National Perspective, edited by Allen F. Agnew

National Security and Technology Transfer: The Strategic Dimensions of East-West Trade, edited by Gary K. Bertsch and John R. McIntyre

The Politics of East-West Trade, edited by Gordon B. Smith

Economic Warfare or Détente: An Assessment of East-West Relations in the 1980s, edited by Reinhard Rode and Hanns-D. Jacobsen

The U.S. and the World Economy: Policy Alternatives for New Realities, edited by John Yochelson

The Politics of Resource Allocation in the U.S. Department of Defense, Alex Mintz

†*Defense Facts of Life: The Plans/Reality Mismatch*, Franklin C. Spinney, edited and with commentary by James Clay Thompson

†Available in hardcover and paperback.

About the Book and Authors

Much attention has been focused on U.S. dependency on imports for supplies of strategic minerals and materials. There is alarm about the extent of that dependency and about the possibility that U.S. economic, political, and strategic decisions might be unduly influenced by arbitrary actions of foreign suppliers. In addition, there is concern that the Soviet Union may be pursuing a so-called "resources war" with the West to restrict the flow of certain strategic and critical materials from producer nations to the United States and its allies. A wide range of expert opinion has developed concerning the degree to which such fears are justified.

The authors of this book examine these controversies and stress the need to consider basic resources, foreign policy, industry, and technical issues in an interrelated fashion. They trace the role of strategic materials in the U.S. economy, discuss the global distribution of supplies, and make recommendations for more effectively coping with the problem in the future.

L. Harold Bullis, formerly a specialist in science and technology and head of the Geosciences, Materials, and Industrial Technology Section of the Science Policy Research Division of the Congressional Research Service, is currently a private consultant. **James E. Mielke** is a specialist in earth and marine sciences and is head of the Geosciences, Materials, and Industrial Technology Section of the Science Policy Research Division of the Congressional Research Service, U.S. Library of Congress.

In memory of Franklin P. Huddle

Strategic and Critical Materials

L. Harold Bullis
and James E. Mielke

Westview Press / Boulder and London

A Westview Special Study

Published in 1985 in the United States of America by Westview Press, Inc.; Frederick A. Praeger, Publisher; 5500 Central Avenue, Boulder, CO 80301

Library of Congress Cataloging in Publication Data
Bullis, L. Harold.
  Strategic and critical materials.
  Includes index.
  1. Strategic materials—United States. I. Mielke,
James E. II. Title.
HC110.S8B85 1985   333.8′5   85-713
ISBN 0-86531-637-6

Printed and bound in the United States of America

10   9   8   7   6   5   4   3   2   1

Contents

Figures and Tables

Preface

As rapid growth in world population continues to increase the pressures on maintaining adequate supplies of every major commodity, the United States and other nations can expect to encounter serious problems of materials supply in the years ahead. These problems will arise not from a lack of sufficient materials on a global basis, but rather from a combination of many factors—international, political, social, economic, and technological—that may restrict the future availability and flow of materials and impede their customary use. Yet very little is now being done by the federal government to anticipate or prevent such potential materials disruptions from taking place. Hence, the primary purpose of this book is to draw attention to how serious these problems have become, how they originated, and what can be done about them.

These problems are so internationally complex that the private sector—including industry, academe, and the general public—cannot hope to solve them alone but can only alleviate them. Definitive solutions require that a major role be played by the federal government, and for the most part the government has yet to act. In recent years Congress has taken the initiative in attempting to promote federal action, but the executive branch has generally resisted these overtures. And even Congress has not been monolithic in recognizing the serious nature of these problems among a multitude of other concerns.

What can be done? The authors believe that only the general public and the rest of the private sector—which ultimately will bear the full brunt of future materials disruptions—can effectively stimulate federal action toward coordinated long-term materials policy planning. Thus, an early step toward assuring future materials availability must be the emergence of a concerned constituency, fully informed of the nature of the problem. We strongly agree that "citizens without an informed view of the basic resource choices have taken themselves out of the democratic process."[1]

Authorship has been divided mainly along the lines of the individual writers' background experience and expertise. Thus, Harold Bullis is largely responsible for Chapters 1, 5, 6, 7, and 8, and James Mielke[2] for Chapters 2, 3, and 4. Both authors owe thanks to many colleagues who have helped with various portions of the manuscript. Special acknowledgment is due to John G. Ellis for much of the discussion on the changing structure and behavior of international minerals trade in Chapter 3; to Langdon T. Crane for some of the discussion of materials conservation in industry in Chapter 6; and to David E. Lockwood for much of the historical material on stockpiling, also in Chapter 6. Thanks are also due to Paul F. Rothberg for information dealing with economic and regulatory constraints facing the U.S. materials industries, which forms part of Chapter 8. We are also deeply indebted to the late Franklin P. Huddle for much of the spirit and discussion, in Chapter 8, of the need for a national materials policy.

Errors in a work of this magnitude are virtually unavoidable. It is our hope that they will be minimal and that we have managed to avoid any really serious ones. If not, we apologize and trust that any inconvenience to the reader will be forgiven.

As this book goes to press, new developments on the national scene— as discussed in Chapter 8—provide at least some cause for modest optimism regarding possibilities for dealing successfully with the materials-related problems described herein. We will be pleased if the present work helps contribute to that future success.

L. Harold Bullis
James E. Mielke

Notes

1. Richard J. Barnet, *The Lean Years—Politics in the Age of Scarcity* (New York: Simon and Schuster, 1980), p. 3.

2. The views expressed are those of the authors and do not necessarily represent positions of the Congressional Research Service or the Library of Congress.

Introduction

For the greater part of our country's relatively short history, we who live in the United States have taken for granted the abundance of minerals and materials. Only rarely have we encountered situations in which whatever we wanted was not readily available, usually at a quite affordable price. The vast array of consumer goods at our disposal—almost unparalleled in quantity and diversity in any other major, technologically oriented society—has led us to believe that this immense flow of materials will always be available in the future to the same extent that it has been in the past. By and large, we have given little thought to the origin of the materials from which this prodigious variety of consumer products flows, or to the processes by which materials are shaped into these products we consider so essential to a comfortable, civilized life.

Until recently, a similar attitude existed toward minerals and materials used not as materials but as fuels: wood, coal, natural gas, and petroleum. That attitude, at least with respect to petroleum, was abruptly shattered in October 1973 when the Arab oil-producing nations instituted a collective petroleum boycott of the United States. Soon gasoline shortages developed, exacerbated by hasty, ill-advised, and poorly planned government allocation policies that largely made matters worse. Long lines formed at gasoline stations throughout much of the nation, consumers often were limited to the quantity of gasoline they could buy, and tempers sometimes flared. As the petroleum shortage swept through the petrochemical industry it multiplied into shortages of everything from dental tooth amalgams to plastic for phonograph records. For perhaps the first time, U.S. consumers were forced to recognize the reality of being dependent or partly dependent on foreign sources for a vital mineral commodity.

In retrospect, the 1973–1974 experience, however traumatic it may have seemed at the time, would have proved a blessing in disguise had it fully awakened our national consciousness to our growing dependence upon imported materials. For these materials include not only those used as fuels, like petroleum and natural gas, but—more importantly for the purposes of this book—the large number of basic industrial raw materials upon which the health and strength of the U.S. economy depend. Unfortunately, when the shortages disappeared, most consumers simply assumed that the problems had been solved and that steps would be taken to prevent any future

1

occurrences. Increased prices quickly became accepted, and life settled down to the usual routine of taking materials pretty much for granted. Such complacency, however, could be highly dangerous to our future comfort and security. As this book will document, the United States already is heavily dependent upon foreign nations—some of doubtful reliability—for many of the nonfuel minerals and materials required as feedstocks for our industrial establishment. Worse, this dependency is rapidly increasing.

Articles on this subject now appear from time to time in daily newspapers, popular magazines, and trade and professional journals. On rare occasions, time on television is devoted to it. Yet despite this growing media attention, little interest appears to have been ignited in the general public. Their lack of interest is not surprising in view of the current widespread availability of consumer goods of all kinds, as well as the highly publicized existence of a mineral fuels "glut" that is expected to continue for some time, possibly for a decade or more. Under such circumstances, it is difficult to generate much concern over materials shortages that may not occur until some unspecified time in the future.

U.S. consumers are fortunate to be given this time, when virtually all evidence to date points to the need for some form of mechanism to deal constructively with the nation's materials problems. This book attempts to define these problems explicitly, to show how they arose, and to describe various approaches that may be taken to help resolve them. Subjectively, the book can be said to consist of three sections. The first section— comprising Chapters 1, 2, and 3—deals with the practical and economic aspects of materials. Thus, Chapter 1 discusses the importance of materials in everyday life, how materials may be categorized or classified, the historical and current role played by materials in the economy, and the primary uses of the basic industrial raw materials. Chapter 2 describes the global distribution of materials, their nature and extent, and the particular materials postures of the United States, the Soviet Union, Australia, Canada, and the Republic of South Africa. Chapter 3 then emphasizes the global nature of materials production and use, focusing upon the international flow of materials among primary producer and user nations.

The second section of the book—essentially Chapters 4, 5, and 6— focuses upon those relatively few materials that can truly be considered most strategic and critical. Chapter 4 defines what strategic and critical materials are in terms of specific criteria, Chapter 5 discusses why existing conditions of supply and usage of these materials represents a dependency or vulnerability of the nation to potential supply interruptions, and Chapter 6 delineates measures that could be taken to help alleviate this dependency or vulnerability.

The third section—Chapters 7 and 8—treats the national policy implications of materials import dependency. Thus, Chapter 7 discusses the various problems that should be solved and the issues that require consideration, and Chapter 8 proposes the need for a national policy to help in these considerations. Of particular importance is the discussion of how the private sector can exert leadership in helping to alleviate materials problems, rather than simply waiting for the federal government to do its part. Indeed, stimulating such private sector activity is one of the major purposes of this book.

1
Materials and the Economy

The Importance of Materials

Materials have been essential to mankind ever since Adam and Eve first fashioned clothing from fig leaves in the Garden of Eden. Since that time, major uses for materials have become increasingly more sophisticated. For at least 8,000 years, metals have been extracted from various ores to make both useful and decorative objects. By 3000 B.C., relatively advanced metallurgical techniques already were being practiced in ancient Anatolia, Egypt, and Mesopotamia for the smelting and alloying of copper, lead, silver, and tin. By 1500 B.C., man-made iron—as contrasted to iron obtained from meteorites—was coming into use in the Hittite Empire.[1] Silver and gold soon became established as symbols of beauty and wealth. Minerals naturally present in soils have been essential from earliest times for the growth of crops to feed expanding populations, and in modern times have been augmented with unparalleled success by the widespread use of chemical fertilizers. Wood, peat, coal, natural gas, and petroleum have provided life-saving heat and energy. Today, materials of all kinds are manipulated to satisfy an incredible variety of physical and chemical requirements for an almost endless number of uses.

The manipulation of materials to serve their needs is not unique to human beings. Birds and squirrels build nests, termites build their mounds, beavers build dams and huts, and sea creatures secrete shells and build reefs. But humans remain unique in their ability to discover where the richest deposits of the most useful materials occur and in their ability to exploit these materials effectively. The enormous material wealth thus discovered, and the human desire to develop and utilize this wealth, has helped shape—for better or worse—the economic, social, and political institutions that govern the way in which we live. And underlying the growth of these institutions is the assumption, now increasingly questioned, that this material wealth is inexhaustible, either in itself or because of the belief that technology will always permit materials production to outpace consumption.

In brief, materials have been and will no doubt continue to be one of the most vital forces affecting mankind. Their pervasive influence has been summarized as follows:

Materials are all about us; they are engrained in our culture and thinking as well as in our very existence. In fact, materials have been so intimately related to the emergence and ascent of man that they have given names to the Stone, Bronze, and Iron ages of civilization. Naturally-occurring and man-made materials have become such an integral part of our lives that we often take them for granted, and yet materials rank with food, living space, energy, and information as basic resources of mankind. Materials are indeed the working substance of our society; they play a crucial role not only in our way of life but also in the well-being and security of nations.[2]

Thus, every age of civilization has been identified with the dominant use of a particular class of materials. Today, it is sometimes said that the United States and other post-industrial nations are entering the "Age of Quantum Materials"—that is, an age in which minute bits of semiconducting materials are utilized in sophisticated ways for transmitting, storing, analyzing, and displaying vast quantities of information.[3]

This book focuses primarily upon the importance of materials to the nation's economic health and strategic security.

Definition and Classification of Materials

Despite the enormous importance of materials in everyday life, most individuals rarely think about what materials consist of and, indeed, what exactly is meant by the term "materials." Materials may be defined broadly as those substances of which physical things are composed or made, or simply as "the stuff that things are made with."[4] Thus, materials include such diverse categories as metals, glasses, woods, fibers, ceramics, plastics, superconductors, semiconductors, sand, stone, dielectrics, and many other substances whose properties make them useful to human beings in everyday life. Indeed, the term "materials" may be extended to include virtually all substances, in whatever form, that can be perceived by the human senses.

The term "minerals" is sometimes used as a synonym for materials, although minerals actually represent a subset of materials. Classically, the typical scientific or engineering definition of a mineral is "a naturally occurring inorganic solid crystalline substance with a definite chemical composition and a characteristic crystal structure."[5] Over time, however, the criteria of being inorganic, crystalline, and solid have become blurred so that today many materials having none of these characteristics are commonly referred to as being minerals. The situation becomes even less clear, and more complex, when considering mineral ores and ore bodies.

Typically the terms "minerals" and "materials" have been used quite loosely, and frequently they are used together as a compound term. In most instances no real harm is likely to result from following this somewhat untidy practice, which occurs in this book from time to time. However, at other times it may prove useful—and occasionally essential—to be somewhat more specific, restricting minerals in their definition; hence, they will be defined here as naturally occurring substances, whatever their form, composition, or structure, that have not yet been altered in any substantial way by man. Thus, the igneous and sedimentary rock ores from which copper is usually obtained will be considered as minerals (hence also materials), whereas the extracted and refined copper itself will be considered a material (but not a mineral). Minerals as so defined are a relatively small but important subset of the much larger set of raw or processed materials.

Major Categories of Engineering Materials

The number of materials available to a modern civilization is staggering. It has been estimated that there are at least 2,000 types of steel, 5,000 types of plastics, and possibly 10,000 types of glass.[6] Numerous attempts have been made to classify materials into a limited number of readily recognizable categories. One such attempt, shown in Table 1.1, classifies materials as minerals, forest products, paper materials, nonfood agricultural products, plastics, and ceramics.[7] Although such a classification has operational usefulness in commerce, it is unnecessarily complex for the purposes of the present discussion. For example, "paper materials," which are derived from "forest products," are listed in the table as a separate category.

A somewhat more common practice is to classify engineering materials into three major groups: metals, organics (polymers or plastics), and ceramics. Although not all materials fall neatly into these three major categories (the most significant example being forest products), this classification is useful because major processing procedures differ for each of the three categories, especially with regard to the initial steps of raw materials processing and the primary refining operations.[8] These three categories, of course, refer primarily to engineering materials. By and large they do not include such materials as foods, drugs, biomatter, fertilizers, fossil fuels, water, and even air—materials typically in the domains of the life and agricultural sciences. However, the scope of this book encompasses virtually all materials other than food, drugs, and energy materials used specifically as fuels.

Metals. Metals are perhaps the simplest kind of material to be easily recognized, although some complex organics and ceramics may look and feel like metals at first acquaintance. Metals are elemental substances, as distinguished from chemical compounds, but may be combined with one another to form a wide variety of metal alloys. The most distinguishing characteristic of a metal is that it readily conducts both heat and electricity. It is easy to recognize the high thermal conductivity of a metal because it quickly conducts heat to or from one's hand. Most metals also exhibit such properties as opaqueness to light, hardness, stiffness, lustrousness, and ductility. Their most valuable engineering characteristics include hardness, physical strength, rigidity, formability, machinability, thermal and electrical conductivity, and dimensional stability. These useful properties are related to the crystalline structure of metals, and also—especially for electrical, thermal, and optical properties—to the fact that electrons in metals have much greater freedom of movement than they have in organic or ceramic materials.

Table 1.1 A System for the Classification of Materials

MINERALS

Iron and Ferroalloy Ores

Iron	Cobalt
Manganese	Molybdenum
Tungsten	Nickel
Chromium	

Other Metal Ores

Gold	Antimony
Silver	Cadmium
Copper	Magnesium
Lead	Platinum—group metals
Zinc	Selenium
Bauxite	Tellurium
Titanium	Tin
Uranium—radium—vanadium	

Mineral Fuels

Anthracite	Natural gas
Bituminous coal and	Natural gasoline
lignite	Liquefied petroleum gases
Crude petroleum	

Construction Minerals

Dimension stone:	Sand and gravel:
Limestone	Construction sand
Granite	Gravel
Slate	Glass sand
Marble	Other industrial sand

Abrasives and Miscellaneous Minerals

Fuller's earth	Grinding pebbles and tube-mill liners
High-grade clay:	Grindstone, pulpstones, and other special silica stone products
Bentonite	Quartz, ground sand, and sandstone for abrasive purposes
Kaolin	
Ball clay	
Miscellaneous high-grade clay	
Feldspar	Tripoli and rottenstone
Mica sheet	Peat
Mica scrap	Diatomite
Pumice and pumicite	Graphite
Talc and soapstone	Greensand
Emery and garnet	Vermiculite

FOREST PRODUCTS

Saw logs	Pulpwood
Veneer logs	Miscellaneous products
Fuel wood	

PAPER MATERIALS

Paper	Paperboard

NONFOOD AGRICULTURAL PRODUCTS

Cotton	Oil crops and others

continued

Basalt
Sandstone
Miscellaneous stone   except for abrasives

Crushed and broken stone:
For cement manufacture   Fire clay
For lime manufacture   Magnesite
Other limestone   Common clay and shale
Granite   Gypsum
Slate   Native asphalt and
Marble   bitumens
Basalt   Asbestos
Sandstone   Perlite
                            Shell

Chemical and Fertilizer Minerals

Barite   Bromine
Fluorspar   Calcium and calcium—
Potash   magnesium chloride
Borates   Magnesium compounds
Phosphate rock   Sodium carbonate
Sodium chloride   Sodium sulfate
Sulfur and pyrites   Iodine
Arsenious oxide

Wool
Fish products   Rubber

PLASTICS

Polymers   Synthetic fibers
Elastomers   Other plastic materials

CERAMICS

Glass   Construction Ceramics
Brick   Cement
Clay products   Tile
                                 Mineral wool

Glass containers   Consumer Ceramics
China   Pressed glass
Pottery   Earthenware
                                 Porcelain materials

Pigments   Industrial Ceramics
Refractories   Oxides
Abrasive products   Asbestos products

                             Electronic Ceramics
Transistors   Semi-conductors
Capacitors   Ferrites and magnets

Source: National Commission on Materials Policy, *Materials Needs and the Environment Today and Tomorrow* (Washington, D.C.: U.S. Government Printing Office, 1973), p. 2-4.

Metals are the materials most often thought of as being strategic and critical, and often exclusively so. This viewpoint is too narrow, however, and should be enlarged to include other kinds of materials as discussed below.

Organics. Organic materials are largely a development of the twentieth century. They are based primarily upon different combinations of carbon and hydrogen, typically supplemented by various amounts of chlorine, fluorine, oxygen, nitrogen, or sulfur. Most are characterized by their low density as well as by their poor electrical and thermal conductivity, properties that make them excellent for use as insulators. Typical of their behavior is the formation of long, chainlike molecules or macromolecules having large numbers of identical repeating units or monomers. Small molecules made of up to about a dozen such monomers are called oligomers. Macromolecules formed by the linking together of large numbers of monomers are called polymers.

The development of polymers has resulted in the production of a broad range of new synthetic industrial and consumer products, including adhesives, detergents, elastomers, epoxies, explosives, fibers, lubricants, paints and finishes, refrigerants, resins, rubbers, and textiles. Many polymers possess structures that readily deform; that is, they exhibit a high degree of plasticity— hence the term plastics. They, with other structural organic materials, share a number of characteristics: light weight, good electrical and thermal insulation, high combustibility, softness and ductility, dimensional instability, and poor temperature resistance.

It is useful to distinguish between two major kinds of plastics: *thermoplastics* and *thermosetting* plastics. Thermoplastics may be repeatedly softened by heating and, upon cooling, will harden again. Among the most commonly known thermoplastics are polystyrene, polyethylene, nylon, plexiglas, and Teflon™. In general, thermoplastics will not withstand high temperatures, with the exception of Teflon, and will melt if heated to sufficiently high temperatures. Thermosetting plastics, on the other hand, will harden upon heating and take a permanent set; they cannot be made soft again by additional heating. Among the most commonly known thermosetting plastics are bakelite, rubber, silicones, and epoxies. They tend to be brittle and, if heated to high temperatures, to char and disintegrate rather than burn.

At one time it was thought that organic polymers and plastics were completely amorphous, that is, totally lacking any orderly, crystalline structure such as that shown by metals. More recently, however, it has been found that if these materials are properly annealed—that is, heated slowly below their melting point—a high degree of crystallinity can be induced, the basis for which is much more complex than in metals. Likewise, composites of polymers can be said to form "alloys" consisting of various combinations of chemically different polymers. Thus, much of the classical distinction between metals and polymers has become somewhat blurred.

One reason for including these kinds of organic materials as relevant to the subject of strategic and critical materials is that many of them, including plastics, are derived from petrochemical feedstocks produced primarily from petroleum and natural gas. These latter two materials customarily are not thought of as "materials" by most consumers, but rather as fuels for the production of energy. Another reason some organic materials are of strategic importance is that they are useful components of certain composite materials that also include metals of major strategic concern.

Ceramics. A ceramic material, most simply, is a compound formed by a metal and a nonmetallic material. Historically, ceramic materials are known to have been employed considerably before metals, with glass and bricks being among the earliest materials used. No sharp boundaries exist between ceramics and metals or between ceramics and organics. As a class, ceramics are poorer electrical and thermal conductors than are metals, are more stable than metals in both thermal and chemical environments, and exhibit much greater temperature stability than do organics. Both ceramics and organics crystallize less easily than do metals, with ceramics not only forming single crystals but also assemblages of small crystals called "grains."

Ceramics consist primarily of rocks or clays and include brick, cement, concrete, fiberglass insulation, grinding wheels, plaster, and sparkplug bodies, to mention just a few familiar ones. Ceramics also include a wide variety of both natural and synthetic materials. Natural ceramics, including the ores from which almost all metals are extracted, are simply dug out of the ground and may require little or no further processing. Synthetic ceramics, which may be quite complex, consist mainly of various borides, carbides, nitrides, oxides, and silicates. A few examples of ceramics of major industrial importance are boron nitrides, silicon carbides, and tungsten carbides.

Ceramics may be rocklike in appearance, relatively hard and brittle as compared with most other materials, and opaque to light. They are typically very poor conductors of heat and electricity. Their good tolerance of very high temperatures and highly corrosive environments have made them the preferred materials for applications in nuclear engineering and chemical processing.

Other Categories of Materials

In addition to the engineering materials described above, three other categories of materials are worth noting: composite materials, renewable materials, and energy resources used as materials. These categories are not exclusive, in that such materials may also be used for engineering purposes, but in general the materials in these categories differ markedly in their major characteristics from engineering materials.

Composite Materials. The term "composite material" is often used to describe a combination of materials in which one material is distributed more or less uniformly throughout a second, "matrix" material. More properly, such combinations should be called "reinforced materials," which constitute only one class of composite materials, albeit a very important one. In the broadest sense, it might be argued that almost all of the materials in use today are composites because few materials are used in their most pure forms. However, it is useful in classifying materials to consider composites as those materials that meet the following criteria:

1. Materials that are manufactured. (Composite materials such as wood can be found in nature, but are not considered here.)
2. Materials that consist of a combination of at least two chemically distinct materials with a distinct interface separating the components.
3. Materials for which the separate components are combined three-dimensionally. (Thus, laminates such as clad metals or honeycomb sandwiches are not considered to be basic composite materials.)
4. Materials that are created to obtain properties that would not be achievable by use of any of the components acting alone.[9]

Some forms of composite materials have been used since ancient times. The early Chinese, Egyptians, and Israelites used mixtures of straw embedded in clay to form bricks with improved structural capabilities over plain clay bricks. The Incas—sometimes cited as the first to use composite materials—dispersed platinum in gold and silver because they lacked the technology to achieve the high furnace temperatures necessary to work platinum alone. Some of these early uses of composite materials closely parallel functions for which much more complex composites are used today.

Modern composite technology is sometimes dated from the use of glass-filament reinforcement in a variety of organic matrices. Recent advances include the use of metal, graphite, or alumina fibers embedded in both metal and ceramic matrices for high temperature use, as well as plastics reinforced with graphite, glass, or metallic fibers for the replacement of stainless steel and other metals in applications requiring light weight and good corrosion resistance. The current use of composites ranges from inexpensive materials for low-cost housing to high-performance aircraft wing structures and such jet engine parts as fan blades, ducting, thrust beams, and shrouds.

The development of composite materials has done much to help achieve a major materials engineering objective of "tailoring" the properties of materials to meet the precise physical and chemical requirements of specific materials applications. Such tailoring has helped close the historic gap that existed between metals and nonmetals, for it is now the nonmetals that frequently offer some of the best combinations of both lightness and physical strength. For example, at present up to 90 percent of all medium or large containers for liquids or other bulk materials are made from fiber-reinforced plastics rather than from the steel or aluminum previously used.[10]

Renewable Materials. Most of the engineering materials discussed above fall into the category of fixed, nondestructible nonrenewable resources: they are essentially inherited physical components of the world and for the most part remain constant in quantity because inevitable losses take place relatively slowly. They may become too dispersed through use to be economically recoverable, or may be discarded as waste, but their essential physical identity remains largely unchanged. Other nonrenewable resources—like petroleum, natural gas, and uranium—are generally consumed in use. At present, the bulk of our materials and energy needs are derived largely from these nonrenewable resources. As demands upon these resources have become greater, increased attention is being directed toward the possibility of enlarging our use of renewable resources, which are derived largely from plants and animals.

This increased attention to renewable resources follows from the recognition that many of the world's most highly concentrated, high-quality, nonrenewable resources already have been depleted, and that with the passage of time it becomes increasingly unlikely that equally rich discoveries will be made in the future. As it becomes necessary to turn to less concentrated and less accessible resource deposits, increasingly larger amounts of energy will be required both to extract these less desirable ores and to process them into useful materials. Indeed, the 1970s witnessed a steep rise in the price of energy derived from nonrenewable sources, and serious questions remain unanswered about both the cost and the availability of such energy in the future. It is likely, therefore, that in many cases energy costs alone may prevent the utilization of these dilute, low-grade, or relatively inaccessible nonrenewable resources. Such considerations make the increased use of renewable resources even more attractive.[11]

Energy Resources as Materials. Interest in strategic and critical materials typically has been limited to those metals—especially chromium, cobalt, manganese, and molybdenum—required for making the specialty steels and complex superalloys needed by the defense and aerospace industries. Metals, however, comprise only one part of the overall materials picture, as noted earlier in this chapter. Also important are the uses of energy materials, especially petroleum and natural gas, as feedstocks in the production of a wide variety of nonmetallic industrial raw materials. In passing, it is interesting to note that the Energy Security Act of 1980 designates "energy" itself, at least within the context of synthetic fuels, as a strategic and critical material for defense purposes.[12]

At present, only a relatively small proportion of the energy materials consumed in the United States is used for the production of materials. Typically, the U.S. petrochemical industry accounts for about 7 percent of total U.S. energy consumption, with somewhat less than half of this 7 percent used for feedstocks and somewhat more than half for fuel. In 1982, petrochemical feedstocks accounted for about one-third of natural gas consumption, somewhat more than 3 percent of crude petroleum consumption, and about one-fifth of natural gas liquids consumption.[13] Historically, the preferred petrochemical feedstocks in the United States have been natural gas and natural gas liquids because of their widespread availability, low price, and relative cleanliness. More recently, however, the largest source of petrochemical feedstocks has been petroleum, a situation unlikely to change in the near future.

The U.S. petrochemical industry produces a vast number and variety of chemicals that are either marketed as finished products or utilized in the manufacturing operations of other industries. These chemicals are used in a wide variety of products including antifreeze, dyes, glues, paints, photographic film, pharmaceuticals, cosmetics, solvents, ink, insecticides, herbicides, plastics, clothing, sports equipment, electrical insulation, automobiles, and airplanes. Many also can be categorized as strategic and critical materials because they are essential to the production of numerous weapons systems of strategic importance to national defense.

Resources and Reserves

It is not uncommon when discussing minerals and materials to confuse the terms "resources" and "reserves," and not infrequently the two terms are used synonymously. This confusion arises at times from ignorance in use of the terms, and at other times because accepted definitions vary significantly among various disciplines. Thus economists, lawyers, mining industry executives, geologists, and physical scientists and engineers all view the terms from somewhat different perspectives.

To an economist, for example, a natural resource may be "anything in the material universe that someone considers useful or beneficial, or potentially beneficial," provided that its utilization is profitable.[14] Another, similar economic definition is noted elsewhere:

> Natural resources could refer to all the living and nonliving endowment of the earth, but traditional usage confines the term to naturally occurring resources and systems that are useful to humans or could be under plausible technological, economic, and social circumstances. Today, however, we must augment this definition to include environmental and sociological systems.[15]

A mining geologist, on the other hand, may take a much more restricted view—similar to that of a physical scientist or engineer—in considering a mineral resource to be a "naturally occurring crystalline substance with a specific set of properties and a chemical composition which varies only within well defined limits."[16] In the extreme, a 1970 United Nations survey of world iron resources included a glossary of terms listing no less than sixteen definitions for "reserves" and a further thirteen definitions of terms used exclusively to describe iron ore.[17] Understandably, these differences in usage at times have produced serious misunderstandings among economists and policymakers concerning the real meaning of the resource and reserve estimates provided by scientists and engineers.

From the point of view of strategic and critical materials, it is essential to distinguish clearly between resources and reserves, because it is primarily reserves, rather than other resources, that can contribute to providing near-term relief in the event of a critical materials emergency.

Terminology and Definitions. In discussing resources and reserves, it will be useful to adopt the terminology of Table 1.2. This terminology, which has received widespread support and acceptance within the scientific, engineering, and mining communities, is due largely to the U.S. Bureau of

14

Table 1.2 A Classification of Mineral Resources

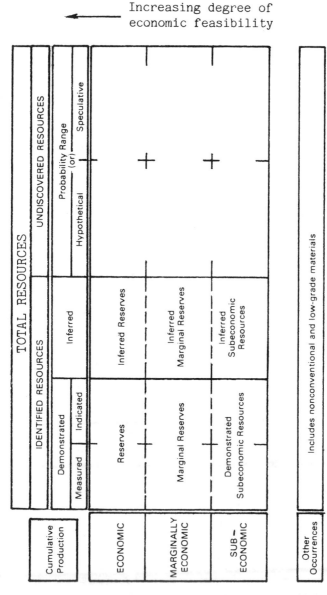

Increasing degree of economic feasibility

Decreasing degree of geologic assurance ➝

Source: Derived from U.S. Bureau of Mines, *Mineral Commodity Summaries 1985* (Washington, D.C.: U.S. Department of the Interior, 1985), p. 183. Definitions of terms that follow are based on pages 180–182 of *Mineral Commodity Summaries 1985* and pages 16–18 of G.J.S. Govett and M. H. Govett, ed., *World Mineral Supplies, Assessment and Perspective* (New York: Elsevier, 1976).

DEFINITIONS OF TERMS:

Total Resources. All deposits of mineral-bearing rock and other concentrations of materials in or near the earth's crust, whether already identified or yet to be discovered, that ultimately may provide materials useful to humankind.

Identified Resources. Specific resource deposits whose existence, location, grade, quality, and quantity are known or estimated from specific geological evidence.

    Economic Resources or Reserves. Known, identified resource deposits from which minerals or materials can be extracted profitably with existing technology and under present economic circumstances.

        Measured. Deposits for which quantity and quality estimates are within a margin of error of 20 percent or less, from geologically well known sample sites. (Proved or assured ores.)

        Indicated. Deposits for which quantity and quality have been estimated partly from sample analyses and partly from reasonable geologic projections. (Probable or semiproved ores.)

        Inferred. Deposits highly likely to exist in unexplored extensions of demonstrated resources based upon geologic projections. (Possible ores.)

    Marginally Economic Resources. Deposits that border on being economically producible, whose essential characteristic is economic uncertainty. Included are resources that would be producible, given postulated changes in economic or technologic factors. Measured, indicated, and inferred terms apply, as defined above.

    Subeconomic Resources. Identified resources that do not yet meet the economic criteria of reserves or marginal resources. Include deposits that are not profitably or technologically mineable at present but that may eventually become reserves when suitable conditions of economics and technology are met. (Conditional resources.) Measured, indicated, and inferred terms apply, as defined above.

Undiscovered Resources. Unspecified bodies of mineral-bearing materials surmised to exist on the basis of broad geologic knowledge and theory.

    Hypothetical Resources. Undiscovered resources that are similar to known mineral bodies and that may be reasonably expected to exist in the same producing district or region undergoing analogous geologic conditions.

    Speculative Resources. Undiscovered resources that may occur in either known types of deposits in favorable geologic settings where mineral discoveries have not yet been made or in types of deposits as yet unrecognized for their economic potential.

Other Occurrences. Materials resources that are too low in grade, or that for other reasons are not now considered potentially economic, although their extent may be recognized and their magnitude estimated. (Not currently classified as resources by the Bureau of Mines.)

Mines and the U.S. Geological Survey, the two federal agencies having primary responsibility for mining and materials.

The first observation to be noted from the table is that "total resources" represents a very broad term. It includes the sum total of all naturally occurring concentrations of materials, whether they exist in such form that extraction of usable commodities from them is either currently or potentially feasible, or whether they exist in such low grade or poor location that economic extraction at present is unlikely. These concentrations of materials, for which our interest lies chiefly in those that are U.S.-owned or claimable, may be located in or on the earth's crust, in the oceans, or on the deep seabeds. They may consist of elemental materials like iron or aluminum, chemical compounds like salt or borax, minerals like emerald or asbestos, or rocks like marble or gypsum.[18] It should be emphasized that the concern here is with *concentrations* of materials, not the *abundance* of these materials in the earth's crust. Estimates of crustal abundance of materials, made from time to time and used prominently in discussions of "limits to growth," are sometimes confused with resource estimates, which are much smaller. Terrestrial abundance estimates include all materials currently thought to exist on the planet Earth, whereas resource estimates are limited to concentrations of materials that conceivably may be utilized in the foreseeable future. Thus, a resource represents the total amount of a material in the earth's crust down to some grade higher than average crustal abundance but lower than what currently can be economically mined. Crustal abundances of materials are discussed at greater length in Chapter 2.

It is sometimes noted that an element of *need* or *desire* exists in defining resources. This qualification arises because enormous quantities of materials exist everywhere—materials that nobody wants or thinks useful at present. Consequently, it would seem somewhat pointless to consider these currently unwanted or useless materials to be resources. However, a use for such materials may be found some day, at which time they will become legitimate resources. One benefit of considering this point in defining what is meant by resources is that it emphasizes the fact that technology and the human needs and desires promoted by that technology determine or even create materials resources.

Total resources are classified in terms of two major criteria, one geologic and the other economic. In terms of the geologic parameter, resources are first classified according to whether they actually have been identified or discovered, or instead remain to be discovered. This distinction is plausible in that large areas of the earth's surface, not to mention its seabeds, have yet to be explored, and it is reasonable to expect that many such unexplored areas may contain useful concentrations of materials. Thus, the abscissa of Table 1.2 represents the degree of geologic certainty that a resource concentration does indeed exist. This parameter ranges from absolute certainty at the extreme left of the figure to a high degree of uncertainty at the extreme right.

The other major parameter in classifying resources is the feasibility of economically recovering a material from an ore concentration, whether identified or undiscovered. This parameter, represented by the ordinate of Table 1.2, ranges from uneconomic recovery at the bottom of the figure to economic recovery at the top. This concept of classifying resources is intended to highlight the long-range potential of resources that have not yet been discovered, rather than to emphasize economic recoverability, which has been more common in the past. The rationale for this change in emphasis is that, clearly, resources must first be discovered before their economic recoverability can be ascertained.

Categories of Reserves. As shown in Table 1.2, identified resources consist of three categories distinguished according to their potential for economic exploitation: economic, marginally economic, and subeconomic. The first category is that represented by resources that have been identified and demonstrated (both "Measured" and "Indicated" in the table) as economically extractable at the present time. In terms of national resources only these materials, represented by the upper left-hand box in the table, are true *reserves*, and as such they are the materials of paramount importance in considering strategic and critical materials. These reserves represent the rather small portion of total resources that definitely have been discovered and identified, "whose extent and grade are known to a greater or lesser degree and whose grade and physical nature are such that they may be extracted at a profit with existing technology and at present prices."[19] Thus these reserves represent a form of national domestic inventory from which U.S. industries draw needed materials as required. It is the extent of these reserves at a given time, as compared with the nation's consumption of these materials at that same time, that determines the degree to which materials must be imported from abroad (without regard to price). Such imports, in turn, determine the nation's import dependency/vulnerability condition.

Reserves, as indicated in the table, can be categorized as "Measured" or "Indicated," terms that are qualitative indices of the degree of certainty with which these resources are known to exist and have been examined geologically.[20] Measured reserves are those that have been most thoroughly determined. They consist of ore bodies blocked out in three dimensions, either by drilling or by actual underground mining operations. Tonnage figures are compiled from drill holes, trenches, workings, and outcrops, and grades are computed from detailed sampling. The useful content, size, and shape of the deposits is well established, with an error no greater than 20 percent, which has tended to become the rule. Also included are minor extensions beyond actual drill test holes and openings where ore extension is almost certain. Measured reserves essentially represent the "proved or assured ores" category once widely used by industry.

Indicated reserves are those that have yet to be completely measured but, because they are located adjacent to measured ores, are highly likely to exist in the suggested quantities. Tonnage and grade figures are computed partly from specific measurements, as for measured reserves, and partly from projections made for reasonable distances. The size and shape of the deposits are not fully determined, nor is the grade precisely established; that is, the error is likely to be larger than the 20 percent for measured reserves. Indicated reserves correspond roughly to the "probable or semi-proved ore" category previously used by industry.

Also part of this first category of economic, identified resources are inferred reserves located near known ore bodies and in geologic structures such that their presence may reasonably be presumed. However, insufficient exploration and development work have been carried out to confirm their existence. Thus, tonnage and grade figures must be estimated on the basis of broad geological knowledge and may include a representation of concealed deposits where sufficient geological evidence so warrants. The error is almost certainly larger than 20 percent. Inferred reserves essentially correspond to industry's "possible ore" category. Thus, although inferred reserves are not definitely known to exist because the effort and expense to prove them out have not been undertaken, the geologic likelihood of their existence is judged very high. Equally important, the economic likelihood of their profitable extraction is also judged very high.

In summary, these "identified economic" resources—that is, measured, indicated, and inferred reserves—essentially represent the domestic materials base currently available for economic exploitation by U.S. industries.

The second category of identified resources is that represented by resources that are only marginally economic at the present time, represented by the middle left portion of Table 1.2. These resources are sometimes called "conditional reserves" because at some point they may become reserves, if conditions of economics and technology become suitable for their exploitation.[21] Their foremost characteristic, therefore, is economic rather than geologic uncertainty. Marginally economic resources consist of marginal reserves, both measured and indicated, and inferred marginal reserves; terms are as defined above and in Table 1.2 for economic resources. Essentially, these resources have the most immediate potential for future development and provide a primary target for research into new, improved, or more economic extraction and processing technologies. They are especially important within the context of strategic and critical materials because they represent a significant pool of domestic resources that, during an emergency, conceivably could be drawn upon if needed, despite the additional cost associated with their extraction.

The third and remaining category of identified resources is that represented by resources that do not yet meet the economic criteria of reserves and marginal reserves, but possibly may do so at some future date if rising prices and/or developing technology make their exploitation economically possible. These subeconomic identified resources, represented by the lower left-hand portion of Table 1.2, also encompass both demonstrated and inferred resources.

When reference is made to *reserves* in this book, the definition will follow the practice of the Bureau of Mines in referring only to those specific resources that have been identified, have been demonstrated either as measured or indicated resources, and have been shown to be economically exploitable at prevailing prices using current technology. Thus, such commonly used terms as "exploitable reserves" or "recoverable reserves" are redundant and will be avoided.

Some materials deposits, which do not fit any of the three categories of resources discussed above, are classified as "other occurrences," as shown at the bottom of Table 1.2. They represent materials deposits that are of too low a grade to be considered potentially exploitable economically, or they may be uneconomic for other reasons. Clearly, the boundary between such materials deposits and the three categories of resources discussed above is uncertain; determinants of this boundary may include grade, quality, thickness, depth, percent extractable, or other variables related to economic exploitation. The Bureau of Mines does not at present consider materials classified as "other occurrences" to be resources.

Dynamic Nature of Reserves. It should be clear from the above that the nation's reserve status is dynamic, not static, and that changes can take place in either direction depending upon changes in economic and technological conditions. Thus, resources become reserves, a shift in a technologically desirable direction, when raw materials prices increase and/or technological developments make mining operations less costly. With few exceptions, the case historically has been that reserves have tended to increase with time and—especially for the most important materials—have increased at a faster rate than that at which they have been depleted.[22] However, reserves can become resources—a change in the less desirable direction—if rising production costs make mining uneconomic or if prices fall sufficiently to deter new investment in exploration and development. Without exploration and development, reserves theoretically could decline to zero.

Problems in Reserve Estimation. Whether domestic reserves will continue to increase (or will decrease) in the future is an important question that is difficult to answer. It has been pointed out that many quantitative predictions made during the past three decades have been grossly in error and that in a period of unprecedented change it is virtually impossible to picture the world even one generation ahead.[23] Resource estimation is further complicated by the fact that certain conditions are often imposed upon the exercise, either by the requesting authority or by the participants themselves, a situation that leads to estimates that will differ from one another depending upon these constraints. Estimates always include assumptions—not always clearly or completely specified, or at times not even mentioned—involving future technology, physical barriers, general economic conditions, and predictions that may not turn out as projected. Furthermore, mineral deposits— natural concentrations of minerals—are geochemically rare and abnormal events. The total volume in or near the earth's crust where such anomalies occur is relatively small, and mineral deposits located within such areas are essentially fixed in quantity because the formation of new deposits occurs so slowly on a geologic time scale. Consequently, some analysts argue that with fewer discoveries of rich ore bodies being made today despite more intensive efforts and the use of more scientific and sophisticated exploration techniques, the world must be running out of such deposits. Others maintain a more optimistic outlook and suggest that the reserve picture should continue to increase in the future much as it has done in the past.

It should be emphasized in discussing resources that estimates are indeed *estimates,* not *measurements,* and typically tend to be optimistic. As noted earlier, even the best-evaluated reserve deposits may reflect error by as much as 20 percent. Moreover, each mineral deposit is unique in some way. Most lie hidden beneath the earth's surface, making it difficult to locate and examine them in a way that yields accurate knowledge of their extent and quality. Although large quantities of empirical data can be obtained about mineral deposits—including their physical and chemical state, their structural features, large- and small-scale geological associations, and many other geological variables—no method exists at present for combining this store of information into precise resource estimates. Perhaps even more important, no agreement exists as to what weights these quantifiable factors of geological occurrence should have relative to one another. Additionally, changes in technology, exploration and development, price, production costs, availability of public lands for exploration and development, tax incentives, and environmental restrictions all have definite and often unpredictable effects upon reserve figures.

A final comment regarding the status of domestic reserves is that mining firms have a tendency not to explore and prove reserves any further than actually necessary for immediate planning and development purposes. Since proving an ore body is both costly and time consuming, companies often are reluctant to map out more than a few years' worth of reserves at a time. Obviously there is little point in spending money to develop reserves too long in advance of when they may be needed; such money can be spent much more profitably elsewhere. Furthermore, companies often are unwilling to publish data concerning their reserves, especially if taxes on measured reserves are greater than they are on other classes of resources. Consequently, known reserves at any one point in time may be considered as a conservative estimate; that is, an unknown fraction of current reserves undoubtedly remains classified as nonreserve resources for the reasons given above.

The right-hand portion of Table 1.2 represents resources that have not yet been discovered but that scientific evidence suggests may exist. Such resources, both hypothetical and speculative, are of little concern here as they have no bearing on the nation's near-term strategic materials posture. However, such resources do have long-range significance regarding the nation's potential for ultimately reducing its materials import dependency. Clearly, their true extent will remain unknown pending adequate exploration of domestic land areas for which the materials content has not yet been determined. Pending such exploration, debate will undoubtedly continue over the extent to which domestic resources, as yet undeveloped, could satisfy a larger percentage of U.S. requirements for strategic and critical materials.

The Reserve Base. To aid in long-range materials contingency planning, the U.S. Bureau of Mines recently introduced the concept of the "reserve base."[24] As defined by the bureau, the reserve base includes all reserves, all marginal reserves, and a variable uppermost portion of demonstrated subeconomic resources, as identified in Table 1.2. This uppermost portion of subeconomic resources encompasses those resources with a reasonable potential for becoming economically available within planning horizons extending somewhat beyond those of proven technology and current economic conditions. Thus, the portion of subeconomic resources to be included within the reserve base is flexible and is dependent upon a particular time frame or plan. By analogy, the bureau also has defined an "inferred reserve base" consisting of corresponding portions of identified, inferred resources.

The value of the reserve base concept lies in its application to long-range planning. Such planning necessarily is based upon the extent of current known resources, the probability of discovering new resources, the development of new technology to promote the exploitation of currently unworkable materials deposits, and detailed knowledge concerning the status of current resources. Consequently, such planning requires a continuous reassessment of the nation's resource posture in the light of new geologic knowledge, progress in science and technology, and changing economic and political conditions. Such reassessment, as is clear from the discussion of resources above, has two primary components, one geologic and one economic. The geologic component consists essentially of detailed technical knowledge regarding known materials deposits, especially concerning their physical and chemical characteristics, including grade, quality, tonnage, thickness, and depth. Given sufficient time and money, the geologic component can be determined to whatever extent may be desired or required and, once established, represents a relatively stable scientific foundation. The economic component, consisting largely of profitability analyses based upon estimated costs of extracting and marketing materials in a given economy at a given time, is less easily and accurately determinable and is subject to constantly changing economic and political conditions. This relative instability in the economic component has made it difficult in the past to achieve agreement upon what resources should be considered marginally economic rather than subeconomic.

In effect, the reserve base concept removes the above difficulty by recognizing the arbitrary nature of the line separating marginal reserves from demonstrated subeconomic resources. Thus, for any given deposit or area, or indeed for the nation as a whole, the position of the lower boundary of the reserve base, and hence the extent to which it extends into the subeconomic category, depends upon the specific objectives of those who are doing the planning and estimating. The goal is to define a definite quantity of in-place material, any part of which may become economically exploitable depending upon the specific extractive plans made and the economic assumptions used. Because the size of the reserve base will therefore depend upon these plans and assumptions, the latter will be specified as known quantities; they will be explicitly identified. This practice contrasts strongly with past ones in which the plans and assumptions underlying reserve calculations frequently were unspecified or altogether unknown.

The Role of Materials in the U.S. Economy

The role of materials in the U.S. economy can best be illustrated in terms of population growth and industrialization. In just over 200 years, the United States has grown from a struggling group of colonies to a powerful, industrialized nation. Over that time, the pattern of materials use has changed dramatically, increasing both absolutely and per capita. Overall growth has been surprisingly steady despite two world wars, a world depression, and several more limited wars and recessions. Although certain finished products have become obsolete, no major material has become so. Indeed, the longevity of some materials is dramatic: of the six metals recognized by primitive metallurgists thousands of years ago—gold, silver, copper, iron, lead, and tin—all have retained key roles throughout world and U.S. history and today in modern industrial civilization. Furthermore, materials that were largely unknown earlier—beryllium, germanium, hafnium, selenium, silicon, tellurium, titanium, zirconium, and the rare-earth metals—have become important for new industrial processes requiring materials with special properties; in all, a host of new products are made today that were not even dreamed of in colonial times. In response to a national materials system that has had the capacity to develop, grow, and on occasion to contract in response to market demand for goods and services, there have been substantial—and in some cases, striking—increases in such principal indicators of personal and national wealth as personal income, disposable income, housing, education, highways, and consumer goods.[25] Thus, the orderly flow of materials through the U.S. economy has provided a virtually infallible index of U.S. economic health, productivity, and employment.

General Historical Overview

Roughly, the industrial development of the United States can be characterized by three major periods:[26] the extractive period, extending from the earliest colonial times to about 1900; the manufacturing period, extending from about 1900 to 1960; and the services period, which began about 1950 and continues today.

The Extractive Period. Prior to the American Revolution, the major output of the colonies was agricultural, primarily consisting of cotton, dairy products, fish, flour, grains, indigo, livestock, rice, timber, and tobacco. The major manufacturing industry was shipbuilding, but despite efforts on the part of Alexander Hamilton to promote increased manufacturing activity, factory workers remained heavily outnumbered by farm, forest, and mining workers until well toward the close of the nineteenth century. Total annual per capita usage of materials at the time of the Revolutionary War is estimated at about 1,200 pounds as follows:

Sand and gravel	1,000 lbs
Brick and lime	112 lbs
Coal	40 lbs
Iron	20 lbs
All other	28 lbs
	1,200 lbs

The "all other" category consisted primarily of copper, glass, lead, potash, salt, nitrates, sulfur, and zinc.[27]

The extractive period was characterized by the fact that society at that time, as an agrarian system, depended largely upon renewable resources—plants, animals, water, air, sunshine, and land—rather than upon nonrenewable resources. Within this context, resources are considered to have been renewable in the sense that an appropriate improvement in conservation measures could maintain and even increase the productive capacity of the resources.[28] During this early period, most of the power required to run the economy was still supplied by wind, water, animals, and people. Even as late as 1850, coal supplied only about 10 percent as much of society's fuel energy as did wood. Indeed, annual production of wood for fuel continued to increase until about 1870, when it peaked and then declined as coal became increasingly popular.[29] Coal, in turn, was gradually displaced by petroleum as a fuel during the twentieth century.

During the latter part of the nineteenth century, the young nation was not only able to satisfy its own materials needs, but was also able to export sizable quantities of coal, metals, and even petroleum. This early period of abundant resources helped initiate the unfortunately lasting impression that, through the application of knowledge, ingenuity, and technological capabilities, the nation would always have essentially unlimited materials resources at its disposal.

The Manufacturing Period. During the early 1900s, imports consisted primarily of those relatively few materials that could not be produced domestically, particularly asbestos and rubber. However, also imported were relatively small quantities of chromite, cobalt, columbium, manganese, platinum, tin, and a few other materials that foreshadowed the deluge of imports of such materials that would eventually follow. Even so, the net export surplus of domestic materials amounted to about 3 percent of domestic consumption until about 1910, when the surplus began to disappear. After about 1920, imports of raw materials consistently exceeded exports.[30]

Upon the entry of the United States into World War I, sharply increased demands for certain materials caused shortages in some parts of the country from 1917 to 1918, although much of the difficulty was due to confusion resulting from inexperience with planning for a major conflict. The war itself served to accelerate the shift in emphasis from the extractive to the manufacturing industries that was already evident toward the close of the nineteenth century. By the 1920s manufacturing clearly was dominant and, despite management emphasis upon increasing labor productivity, employment in the manufacturing sector continued to rise. By contrast, even though increased quantities of an ever-widening list of industrial materials necessitated increased production of fiber, fuels, and minerals, employment in the extractive industries steadily declined.

New post–World War I discoveries of petroleum and the continuing exploration of the mineral resources of the western United States further enhanced the impression of limitless natural wealth. With the advent of the Great Depression, however, demand for products and materials dropped sharply, and many factories, steel mills, copper refineries, and coal mines fell idle.

At about this time, technologists in the developed countries were searching for ways to enhance the properties of such basic materials as copper, aluminum, and steel by adding relatively small amounts of nickel, chromium, manganese, molybdenum, zirconium, and tungsten to form various alloys having characteristics very much superior to those of the basic metals as previously used. Additionally, other metals long considered rather exotic by comparison with the major industrial metals—especially beryllium, uranium, and columbium—were beginning to find specialized industrial uses, as were such nonmetallic materials as asbestos, graphite, mica, quartz crystal, and talc. Uses of such nonferrous metals as lead, magnesium, tin, and zinc were expanding. Furthermore, new or increased uses were being found for such organic materials as copra, kapok, palm oil, and pyrethrum. All these materials, and many others, found increased applications in the new kinds of hardware and sophisticated technology employed during World War II.

The new war brought with it a radical change in the nation's use of materials. A large fraction of industrial capacity was put to work on the production of materials and products for war. Mines, mills, and smelters worked overtime, and new petroleum pipelines were built to fuel war-created or expanded industries. Among such industries were the $750 million synthetic rubber industry, built during the war from scratch; the aluminum- and magnesium-refining industries, greatly enlarged to provide materials for military aircraft; specialty industries producing beryllium, high-purity graphite, and stainless steel for the $2 billion nuclear Manhattan Project; and industries producing materials for radio, radar, sonar, and primitive gas turbine engines. Thus World War II was a conflict in which materials played an unprecedented role.

After the war, pent-up consumer demand created requirements for materials without parallel in a peacetime economy. These needs had hardly been satisfied when the outbreak of the Korean War created requirements for additional quantities of strategic and critical materials, especially for use in artillery, combat aircraft, and helicopters. Following this war, materials usage remained high due to the need for the United States to retain a strong defense capability and to help rebuild the war-devastated European nations under the Marshall Plan. By 1952, the United States was producing about half the world total of manufactured goods and consuming about half the world's annual production of industrial raw materials.

The Services Period. The rapid expansion of employment in institutions specializing in services rather than goods began between 1940 and 1950 and accelerated after 1960, giving rise to what is now called the services period. Indeed, the shift from industry to services may be considered as a second Industrial Revolution, following the shift from agriculture to industry in the first Industrial Revolution. The United States was the first industrialized nation to enter this brave new age of the service economy.[31]

Major sectors of the service economy include personal services (beauty and barbershops, eating and lodging places, entertainment, and repair services), business services (accounting, advertising, banking, insurance, and legal services), social services (education, government, medical, and welfare), and various transportation and communication services (for the latter, computerized information storage and retrieval, data processing, electronic "mailing," and so on). These services, combined, have overtaken the goods sector of the economy in size, whether measured by the number of persons employed or by their contribution to the gross national product (GNP). Among the factors that have probably contributed most strongly to the growth of the services sector are: increased concern with education and health; the rapid growth of technology, especially in the computer and data-processing fields; the need for business specialists in such fields as accounting, advertising, marketing, and personnel management; increased expectations and demands for a wide variety of government services; and the growing affluence necessary to pay for this high level of services.

The growth of the services sector has brought about several important and long-lasting changes in the U.S. economy. First, expansion in services has meant that the extractive and manufacturing sectors of the economy, which produce, process, and fabricate materials, are becoming a declining fraction of the total economy. Second, expanded services have increasingly skewed the nation's tax base because much of the services sector is tax-supported. Third, the services period has ushered in an era of high technology calling for items characterized by high cost, frequent design change, small production volume, and relatively small quantities of a greatly expanded variety of essential materials having special properties. The high-technology, services-oriented industries include aircraft, cable television, computers, electronics, medical equipment, photocopiers, and many others. And fourth, a service economy has meant that materials requirements for the expanding services industries have had to be met at the same time that materials requirements for an increasing variety of basic consumer goods for a growing population have also had to be met.

In giving adequate recognition to the growth of the services sector, one should recognize that it is not always easy to distinguish between a goods sector and a services sector in the economy. Although services are typically indispensable in the process of marketing goods, conversely the services sector itself heavily depends upon inputs and outputs of various material goods. Hence, a substantial materials base supports the services industries. Transportation and utilities, for example, represent services that at least in part are highly materials-intensive. Heavy materials usage also extends to such rapidly growing nonmaterial categories as recreation, medical services, and entertainment. Indeed, it has been pointed out that the most pronounced and significant trend toward services is seen to exist not from evidence of materials usage but largely when shifts in employment are considered.[32] This observation does not detract from the growing role of the services sector in the economy but rather serves to underscore the fact that materials remain a vital and important requirement in the services period.

To summarize, during the extractive period the primary emphasis was upon the discovery, extraction, processing, and fabrication of materials for use in a relatively unsophisticated economy. Emphasis during the manufacturing period was upon maintaining and increasing sources of domestic and foreign supply, upon increased production of a large and rapidly growing variety of manufactured products, and upon further improving the technology of materials use and performance. Today, in the services period, the role of materials has become vastly more complex and difficult to understand and manage, both domestically and internationally. We have graduated from horses to tractors, trucks, and automobiles; from animal manure to chemically manufactured fertilizers; from wooden tools and implements to iron and steel; from wood, clay, and stone to steel, concrete, glass, and aluminum; and from natural fibers and rubber to petroleum-derived synthetics and plastics. All of these changes in materials usage have had profound effects upon our lives.

Current Extent of U.S. Materials Usage

The U.S. economy, like that of all other highly industrialized nations, is heavily dependent upon a reliable flow of raw materials. Yet it is clear that there is no *absolute* need for particular materials, other than food, water, and air. Man's need for materials is largely self-imposed and is closely related to such factors as the methods of production used in any given society, the closely related habits of consumption that society has formed, and the size of the population that must be supported. Clearly, the plains Indians of North America depended upon buffalo hides and pipestone clay but managed to live quite comfortably without chromium and manganese for alloy steels, or tin and aluminum for food containers, or rubber for tires. As noted in one of the early twentieth-century studies of materials usage, "It is an important characteristic of modern industrial civilization that it has made itself dependent upon such an array of raw materials, and upon such enormous quantities of them, as to dwarf by comparison the raw material needs of all previous civilizations in human history."[33]

Not only have those materials requirements been enormous, but over much of recent human history they have accelerated at a very rapid pace. The world's major industrialized nations, with less than 30 percent of the world's population, now consume more than 80 percent of the total world production of the major industrial metals: aluminum, chromium, cobalt, copper, iron, manganese, nickel, the platinum-group metals, tin, tungsten, and zinc. It has been estimated that the economies of the United States, the major European nations, and Japan have together consumed more materials since 1950 than were actually produced in the entire world prior to that date.

Because of the diversity of materials and the complex ways in which they are used, it is difficult to obtain an accurate overall view of the current extent of domestic materials usage. Although statistics on materials are compiled by such federal agencies as the U.S. Bureau of Mines and the Department of Commerce and are summarized annually by the Bureau of Statistics and the Commodity Research Bureau,[34] aggregating such statistics in terms of either total weight or value is a formidable undertaking. Despite this difficulty, the National Commission on Materials Policy has estimated that for the period 1900 to 1969 the total annual domestic consumption of materials increased by a factor of almost thirty-four, from about $6.7 billion to more than $220 billion (in 1967 constant dollars), and that annual per capita consumption of materials more than doubled, from about $70 to about $180 (also in 1967 constant dollars).[35]

Although per capita materials usage today unquestionably is much greater than it was in 1969—the cutoff year for the commission's effort—the rate of overall domestic materials usage has been declining over the past several decades. Much of this decline has resulted from increased efficiency in materials processing and use, as well as from the growth of the services-oriented economy. Indeed, the U.S. share of total world materials use in 1975 was about half as great as in 1950, and the tendency for it to decline is expected to persist over future decades.[36] Clearly, considerable success has been achieved in reducing materials rates of consumption relative to both the quantity of final goods and the level of services desired by society.

Despite this improvement, U.S. consumption of materials, whether measured totally or per capita, continues to be by far the largest of any nation in the world. With just over 5 percent of the world's population and not quite 7 percent of its land area, the United States at present consumes about 23 percent of the world's nonenergy minerals production. It has been estimated that in the last thirty-five years alone, the United States has consumed more minerals than did all mankind from the beginning of time up to about 1940.[37] Present per capita consumption of mineral materials is about 40,000 pounds per year, including about 22,000 pounds of nonfuel materials, as shown in Figure 1.1. It is interesting to compare this current dependence with the 1,200 pounds of consumption per capita that existed at about the time of the American Revolution, as discussed earlier.

It has been estimated that of roughly 2,000 different mineral materials, only about 100 are of economic significance.[38] In general, the consumption of any material is not proportional to its geologic occurrence but rather dependent upon technological developments that require or promote its

Figure 1.1 Current per capita consumption of nonfuel materials in the United States

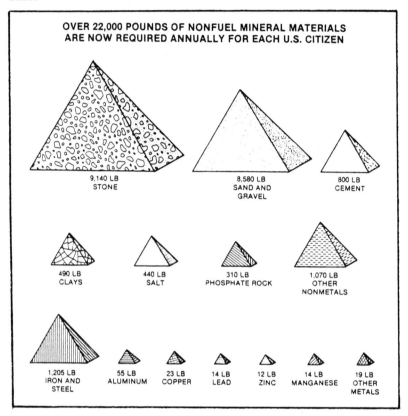

OVER 22,000 POUNDS OF NONFUEL MINERAL MATERIALS ARE NOW REQUIRED ANNUALLY FOR EACH U.S. CITIZEN

9,140 LB
STONE

8,580 LB
SAND AND
GRAVEL

800 LB
CEMENT

490 LB
CLAYS

440 LB
SALT

310 LB
PHOSPHATE ROCK

1,070 LB
OTHER
NONMETALS

1,205 LB
IRON AND
STEEL

55 LB
ALUMINUM

23 LB
COPPER

14 LB
LEAD

12 LB
ZINC

14 LB
MANGANESE

19 LB
OTHER
METALS

Source: U.S. Bureau of Mines.

use. As technology develops and changes, so do requirements for different kinds of materials, some declining in importance as others, previously not much used, gain in importance. An excellent example of such technological change has occurred in the automobile industry, which, in reducing the weight of vehicles to conserve fuel, has shifted dramatically to greater use of new high-strength steels, fiber-reinforced composites, structural plastics, and high-technology ceramics. It has been estimated that from the late 1970s to the mid-1980s, the use of cast iron alone in automobiles has decreased by as much as 40 to 50 percent.[39]

Despite such changes, however, it is rare for a major material actually to fall into relative disuse. Indeed, the growth in production of many of the key basic metals including copper, nickel, iron, lead, aluminum, and zinc has been exponential over the period from 1850 to 1970.[40] Because of this rapid growth in production and consumption, many of the richest known concentrations of domestic reserves have now been exhausted, and it is necessary in the United States to mine increasingly lower concentrations of ores. For example, copper ore in the early 1900s ran about 2 to 3 percent copper but currently averages less than 0.7 percent copper. The leanest copper ore now being mined, in Arizona, runs as low as about 0.4 percent.[41] Likewise, deposits of iron ore in the Lake Superior districts, which long served as the major source of iron ore for the U.S. steel industry, typically contained about 55 percent iron. When these richer deposits gave out, it became necessary to use taconite ores that contain only about 35 percent iron.[42]

From such examples it is clear that a choice must be made between reliance upon leaner materials ores for the bulk of U.S. materials needs (recognizing the additional costs in labor and energy in mining and processing such ores) and the alternative of increasing our imports of richer ores or even processed materials from abroad, thereby increasing U.S dependence upon foreign sources of supply. A further consideration is how long U.S. domestic materials reserves will last at current projected usage rates. These concerns regarding our present and future domestic materials posture are discussed at greater length in the following chapter.

Some Economic Aspects of Materials Usage

It is sometimes argued that because nonenergy materials are not a dominant feature of the nation's aggregate production of goods and services, their role in the economy warrants less attention as the services period of national growth develops. For example, in 1982 the output (at the mine) of mineral raw materials was estimated at about $27 billion, as contrasted with $90 billion for petroleum, $45 billion for natural gas, and about $25 billion for coal, for a total energy materials value of about $160 billion. Consequently, some analysts minimize the importance of nonfuel materials to the economy.

Nonetheless, it is clear that even an energy-oriented, increasingly services-dominated economy must rest upon a materials base. As often pointed out by materials scientists, plumbers would be hard put to provide their services without wrenches, or carpenters without hammers or saws, or for that matter dentists without amalgams and drills. Some economists tend to find this rationale for the underlying importance of materials less than persuasive. Yet it is difficult to overlook the fact that materials contribute substantially to the national economy in a number of important ways: as a basic source of income or wealth, as cargo to be hauled by many different carriers, as a source of jobs, as a source of taxes, and as a "mother" industry for a myriad of satellite industries.[43] However, it is difficult to measure accurately the effects of materials upon the economy, other than the initial contributions made by the extractive and materials-processing segments of the materials industries. The difficulty is that materials products flow into the manufacturing, chemical, agricultural, energy, and other industries in complex ways and their ultimate contributions to the economy, through these industries, are relatively concealed and hence seldom credited directly to the materials industries.

The Multiplier Effect. A further argument for the importance of materials to the economy can be made in terms of the so-called "multiplier effect" that materials usage exerts upon the GNP, defined as the dollar value of the nation's output of goods and services each year.[44] This multiplier effect essentially recognizes that each dollar's worth of raw materials produced in the economy is effectively multiplied many times over as its influence is felt throughout the economy as a whole. Statistics show that on the average each $10 million worth of materials put into a technologically based economy contributes about $250 million worth of total economic activity, thus providing an average multiplier effect of twenty-five. For specific industries, the effect is much larger. For example, it is estimated that each $4 billion worth of petrochemical materials forms the basis for approximately $430 billion worth of industrial and consumer products, for a multiplier effect of more than 100.[45]

The current role of nonfuel materials in the U.S. economy is illustrated in Figure 1.2, which shows that the estimated value of raw materials produced by the domestic extractive industries was about $23 billion in 1984. These raw materials, after being processed and augmented by about $5 billion in raw materials imports and an additional $4 billion worth of recovered scrap, formed the basis for about $253 billion worth of processed materials of mineral origin. Thus, about $32 billion worth of raw materials and scrap were "multiplied" into about $253 billion worth of processed materials, which, augmented by about $34 billion worth of imported processed materials, formed the materials basis for the nation's $3,660 billion economy.

The Balance of Payments. Another parameter sometimes used to assess the role of materials in the economy is the effect of materials exports and imports upon the U.S. balance of payments. Briefly, the balance of payments of a nation is a systematic record of all economic transactions between the residents of that nation and the residents of all foreign nations during a given period of time. Thus, the balance of payments is a measure of the relative economic activity between nations: a positive balance indicates that a country has more export economic transactions than import transactions, and a negative balance indicates more import transactions than export. The United States has a negative balance of payments, indicating that it is spending more dollars abroad for all purposes than are being returned by foreign countries for various goods and services. Since a chronic negative balance of payments may suggest a weak or deteriorating economy, considerable psychological pressure exists to maintain, over time, a positive balance or at least a limit to negative excursions.

As is clear from Figure 1.2, exports of raw and processed nonfuel materials amounted to about $20 billion in 1984, substantially less than the $34 billion of imported processed materials and the $5 billion of imported raw materials. Thus, strictly in terms of raw and processed materials of mineral origin, materials usage contributed about $19 billion to the 1984 U.S. negative

Figure 1.2 Materials and the economy

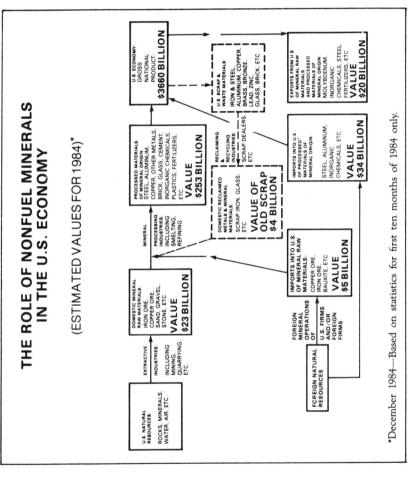

THE ROLE OF NONFUEL MINERALS IN THE U.S. ECONOMY

(ESTIMATED VALUES FOR 1984)*

U.S. NATURAL RESOURCES:
ROCKS, MINERALS, WATER, AIR, ETC.

EXTRACTIVE INDUSTRIES:
INCLUDING MINING, QUARRYING, ETC.

DOMESTIC MINERAL RAW MATERIALS:
IRON ORE, COPPER ORE, SAND, GRAVEL, STONE, ETC.
VALUE $23 BILLION

MINERAL PROCESSING INDUSTRIES:
SMELTING, REFINING

PROCESSED MATERIALS OF MINERAL ORIGIN:
STEEL, ALUMINUM, COPPER, OTHER METALS, BRICK, GLASS, CEMENT, INORGANIC CHEMICALS, PLASTICS, FERTILIZERS, ETC.
VALUE $253 BILLION

U.S. ECONOMY: GROSS NATIONAL PRODUCT: $3660 BILLION

U.S. SCRAP & WASTE MATERIALS:
IRON & STEEL, ALUMINUM, COPPER, BRASS, BRONZE, LEAD, ZINC, GLASS, BRICK, ETC.

RECLAIMING & RECYCLING INDUSTRIES:
SCRAP DEALERS, ETC.

DOMESTIC RECLAIMED METALS & MINERAL MATERIALS:
SCRAP IRON, GLASS, ETC
VALUE OF OLD SCRAP $4 BILLION

EXPORTS FROM U.S. OF PROCESSED MATERIALS AND PROCESSED MATERIALS OF MINERAL ORIGIN:
MOLYBDENUM, INORGANIC CHEMICALS, STEEL, FERTILIZERS, ETC
VALUE $20 BILLION

IMPORTS INTO U.S. OF PROCESSED MATERIALS OF MINERAL ORIGIN:
STEEL, ALUMINUM, INORGANIC CHEMICALS, ETC.
VALUE $34 BILLION

IMPORTS INTO U.S. OF MINERAL RAW MATERIALS:
COPPER ORE, IRON ORE, BAUXITE, ETC
VALUE $5 BILLION

FOREIGN MINERAL OPERATIONS OF U.S. FIRMS AND/OR FOREIGN FIRMS

FOREIGN NATURAL RESOURCES

*December 1984—Based on statistics for first ten months of 1984 only.

Source: U.S. Bureau of Mines, *Mineral Commodity Summaries 1985* (Washington, D.C.: U.S. Department of the Interior, 1985), p. ii.

balance of payments (which amounted to approximately $110 billion). This tells only part of the story, however, because the materials component of many of the high-technology goods exported by the United States is significant; without these materials, the negative balance of payments might have been even larger. However, if imports of raw and processed materials continue to increase in the future and if domestic materials production continues to decline—events that are not at all unlikely—then materials could well contribute even more significantly to a continuing negative U.S. balance of payments in the future.

The Materials Cycle. Mankind's dependence upon materials has been discussed at some length and, correspondingly, the enormous quantities of materials that have been extracted over time from the earth. But what has happened to these materials over the span of many years? Some, like gold, are virtually indestructible and, once mined and processed, last almost forever. Others, like iron, gradually form oxides that eventually return to the earth. Over a much shorter time frame, however, most materials tend to move in a cycle that has considerable immediate economic significance. One way of illustrating this materials cycle is shown in Figure 1.3.

The materials cycle begins with the exploration of the earth to locate concentrations of materials that have potential for exploitation—that is, to discover resources, as discussed earlier in this chapter. It continues with the extraction of those resources that are economically recoverable—that is, reserves—from their location of origin through mining, drilling, and harvesting. Mineral raw materials at this stage of the cycle may primarily resemble rock or stone. The raw materials thus obtained are subjected to various beneficiation, processing, and refining operations to remove unwanted matter and to concentrate further the desired materials. At this stage, the bulk materials may be in the form of metal ingots, crushed stone, petrochemicals, or lumber. These bulk materials are then fabricated into engineering materials—for example, structural steel, concrete, plastics, alloys, ceramics, plywood, or textiles. These engineering materials, through various stages of design, manufacture, and assembly, then are used for the production of consumer products of all kinds. When such products have completed their useful life, having provided their intended performance and service, they become "waste junk" that may be recycled as bulk material for reprocessing into new engineering materials and consumer products, or that may be disposed of in dumps or landfills or simply left to disintegrate wherever abandoned.

Although this brief introduction is a highly oversimplified description of the materials cycle, it serves to illustrate two major points of economic importance. The first is that when materials that have served their initial purpose are recovered or returned for reprocessing and refabrication—that is, recycling and reuse—the materials cycle for such materials becomes a closed loop in which, at least theoretically, the materials could circulate indefinitely. Such recirculation should result in a net economic gain because the costs of the initial stages of exploration, extraction, and the original

Figure 1.3 The total materials cycle

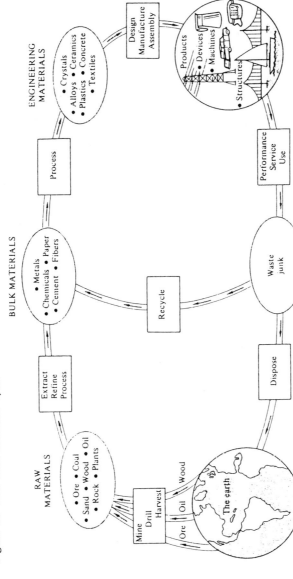

Source: Committee on Resources and the Environment, *Mineral Resources and the Environment* (Washington, D.C.: National Academy of Sciences, 1975), p. 30.

processing are not repeated. In practice, however, the costs of collecting and transporting these used materials from where they are located to where they can be reprocessed and refabricated often exceeds the potential saving.

The second point is that when used or waste materials escape from an otherwise closed cycle, many costs are incurred that are not usually included in the direct cost of goods and services, but that nonetheless must be paid by society. These include such real costs as waste disposal charges and cleanup charges due to pollution caused by toxic or hazardous wastes, as well as such intangible costs as the presence of unsightly dumps, poor land utilization for dumping purposes, and air pollution caused by open burning or incineration of refuse. If these costs, to be discussed in Chapter 6, were included in the overall cost of goods, the economic feasibility of greater levels of recycling would be much enhanced.

In practice, even though the maximum possible recycling of used materials might somehow be accomplished, it is highly unlikely that an almost closed materials cycle for all materials could be achieved. This is because some materials inevitably are removed from the cycle by the very nature of their use. For example, the steel and concrete in bridges and buildings is for all practical purposes removed from the cycle by long-term use; the rubber in automobile tires and the lead in gasoline is dispersed beyond any real possibility of collection and recycling; and food and fuel materials are actually consumed in use. Nonetheless, the achievement of a near-closed cycle of materials use remains a goal of considerable economic and environmental significance.

Major Industrial Uses of Materials

The major materials of industrial significance and their primary industrial uses are listed below, as compiled from data of the U.S. Bureau of Mines.[46] Together, these materials form the primary base upon which the nation's economy rests. An adequate examination of the importance and varied uses of these materials is beyond the scope of the present discussion but can be found elsewhere. For example, an overview of current materials requirements for more than three hundred fifty major industries can be found in the annual editions of the *U.S. Industrial Outlook.*[47]

As the data below make clear, the concentration of use for some materials in certain industries and for certain purposes is quite high. For example, steelmaking consumes very large fractions of the total use of the following materials (in percentages): iron ore, 98.5; molybdenum, 75; tellurium, 55; nickel, 44; and fluorspar, 33. About 60 percent of all antimony and 35 percent of all bromine consumed is used in the manufacture of flame retardants. The nation's transportation sector consumes large quantities (in percentages) of lead, 75; vanadium, 41; the platinum-group metals, 35; silicon, 31; iron and steel, 27; nickel, 24; zinc, 25; columbium, 26; sand and gravel, 22; and chromium and salt, 20 each. Likewise, the use of some materials is heavily concentrated in the electronics and electrical industries (in percentages): gallium, 90; thallium, 60 to 70; mercury, 61; tantalum, 62; indium, 10; gold, 34; and copper, 24.

The major uses of the principal industrial raw materials are as follows (the figures are percentages).

Aluminum	Packaging (35), transportation (20), building (18), electrical (9), consumer durables (8), other (10)
Antimony	Flame retardants (60), transportation (15), ceramics and glass (10), chemicals (10), other (5)
Arsenic	Industrial chemicals (55), agricultural chemicals (35), ceramics and glass (5), nonferrous alloys (3), other (2)
Asbestos	Friction products (22), flooring products (21), asbestos-cement pipe (12), coatings and compounds (11), packaging and gaskets (6), asbestos-cement sheets (8), roofing products (3), paper and textiles (1), other (16)
Barite	Weighting agent in oil and gas well drilling (90), paints, glass, rubber, and chemicals (10)
Bauxite	Alumina (89), refractories, chemicals, and abrasives (11)
Beryllium	Metal in nuclear reactors and aerospace (40), alloy and oxide in electrical equipment (36), electronic components (17), other (7)
Bismuth	Pharmaceuticals and chemicals (48), manufacturing of parts for machinery (27), primary metal industries (23), other (2)
Boron	Textile-grade glass fibers and cellulosic insulation (100)
Bromine	Gasoline additives (24), flame retardants (35), oil and gas drilling fluids (15), chemicals (26)
Cadmium	Coating and plating (35), batteries (25), pigments (20), plastics and synthetics (15), other (5)
Cement	Ready-mixed concrete (69), concrete products (12), buildings (6), highways (4), other (9)
Cesium	Compounds for magnetohydrodynamic electric power generators, thermionic energy converters, electronic, photoelectric, and medical applications (100)
Chromium	As chromite for the chemical and metallurgical industry (79) and the refractory industry (21). End uses: stainless and heat-resisting steel (81); full-alloy steel (9); superalloys (3), and other alloys (7)
Clays	Paper, refractories, dinnerware and pottery, foundry sand bond, drilling mud, iron ore pelletizing, absorbants and filters, construction materials (100)

Cobalt	Superalloys (34), magnetic materials (19), driers (10), catalysts (10), metal cutting and mining tool bits (6), other (21)
Columbium	Construction (40), transportation (26), oil and gas industries (13), machinery (12), other (9)
Copper	Construction (34), electrical and electronic (24), industrial machinery and equipment (16), transportation (12), consumer and general products (14)
Corundum	Optical grinding and polishing (60), metal products (25), other (15)
Diamond (industrial)	Machinery (27), mineral services (18), stone and ceramic products (17), abrasives (16), construction (13), transportation (6), other (3)
Diatomite	Filter aid (62), industrial fillers (34), other (4)
Feldspar	Glass (58), pottery (38), porcelain enamel and other applications (4)
Fluorspar	Hydrofluoric acid (66), steelmaking flux (33), glass manufacture, coatings, enamels, and other (1)
Gallium	Electronics (90), other (10)
Garnet	Abrasives (49), water filtration (29), finishing wood furniture (9), electronics (7), ceramics and glass (3), other (3)
Gemstones	Jewelry, mineral collections, and industrial uses (100)
Germanium	Infrared optics (50), fiber optics (15), semiconductors (15), detectors (10), other (10)
Gold	Jewelry and arts (54), electronic (34), dental (11), other (1)
Graphite (natural)	Steel (8), refractories (25), foundry (20), lubricants (10), brake linings (9), crucibles (5), other (23)
Gypsum	Crude and calcined gypsum products, cement retarders, agricultural land plasters (100)
Hafnium	Naval nuclear reactors (50), ceramics, refractories, alloys, carbide and cutting tool alloys (50)
Helium	Cryogenics (33), welding (19), pressurizing and purging (18), synthetic breathing gases (8), other (22)
Ilmenite	Titanium pigment (99), coatings, alloys, chemicals, carbides (1)

Indium	Electrical and electronic components (40), solders, alloys, and coatings (40), other (20)
Iodine	Catalysts, animal feed additives, pharmaceuticals, disinfectants, stabilizers, inks and colorants, photographic equipment, other (100)
Iron ore	Blast furnaces (98.5), steel furnaces (0.5), cement, heavy media materials and other products (1)
Iron and steel	Construction (31), transportation (27), machinery (19), appliances and equipment (7), other (16)
Iron and steel scrap	Steel (78), ferrous castings (21), ferroalloys, chemical industry, other (1)
Iron and steel slag	Roadbuilding (42), fill (16), asphaltic concrete aggregate (11), railroad ballast (10), other (21)
Kyanite and related materials	Ferrous metal smelting and processing (55), nonferrous metals (20), glassmaking (15), boiler furnaces and nonrefractory uses (10)
Lead	Batteries, gasoline additives, and other transportation uses (75), construction, paint, ammunition, and electrical (22), ceramics, glass, type metal (3)
Lime	Iron and steel (38), environmental (27), other chemical and industrial uses (21), construction (10), refractories and agriculture (4)
Lithium	Aluminum potlines (35), glass and ceramics manufacture and lubricants (50), other (15)
Magnesium metal	Aluminum-base alloys (56), magnesium castings and wrought products (18), cathodic protection (7), reducing agents (6), cast iron manufacture (3), other (10)
Magnesium compounds	Refractories (80), caustic-calcined and specified magnesias and other compounds (20)
Manganese	Primarily manganese ferroalloys for steel production, also pig iron, batteries, chemicals: construction (23), transportation (19), machinery (14), other (44)
Mercury	Electrical apparatus (64), production of chlorine and caustic soda (14), mildew-proofing paint (9), industrial and control instruments (6), other (7)
Mica flake (natural)	Joint cement, paint, roofing, oil well drilling, and rubber products (100)

Mica sheet (natural)	Electrical and electronic equipment (100)
Molybdenum	Ferromolybdenum, metal powder, and chemicals; iron and steel producers (75). End uses: machinery (35), oil and gas industry (20), transportation (15), chemicals (15), electrical (10), other (5)
Nickel	Stainless and alloy steel (44), nonferrous alloys (34), electroplating (18). End uses: transportation (24), chemicals (16), electrical (11), construction (10), metal products (9), petroleum (8), appliances (8), machinery (7), other (7)
Nitrogen (fixed)	Fertilizers (80), plastics, fibers, and resins (10), explosives (4), other chemicals (6)
Peat	Soil improvement and potting soils (100)
Perlite	Building construction (69), filter aid (17), other (14)
Phosphate rock	Fertilizer (90), chemicals (10)
Platinum-group metals	Catalysts for automotive, chemical, and petroleum industries. End uses: automotive (35), electrical (25), chemical (10), dental and medical (20), other (10)
Potash	Fertilizer (95), chemicals (5)
Pumice and pumicite	Concrete admixtures and aggregates (92), other (8)
Quartz crystal, industrial	Oscillator plates; filter, resonator, and transducer plates; optical applications (100)
Rare-earth metals	Petroleum catalysts (65), metallurgical (20), glass and ceramics (12), other (3)
Rhenium	Catalysts (90), thermocouples, heating elements, X-ray tubes, flashbulbs, vacuum tubes, electrical contacts, metallic coatings (10)
Rubidium	Chemicals, electronics, medical applications (100)
Rutile	Titanium dioxide pigment (84), titanium metal and glass fibers, welding rod coatings (16)
Salt	Chemical industry (55), highway use (20), other (25)
Sand and gravel	Concrete (38), roadbases and coverings (22), construction fill (17), bituminous mixtures and aggregates (14), other (9)

Selenium	Electronics and photocopying (35), glass manufacturing (30), chemicals and pigments (25), other (10)
Silicon	Ferrosilicon for the ferrous foundry and steel industries, silicon metal for aluminum producers. End uses: transportation (31), machinery (17), construction (14), chemicals (18), other (20)
Silver	Photography (48), electrical and electronics (25), sterlingware, jewelry, and electroplated ware (11), brazing alloys and solders (5), other (11)
Sodium carbonate	Glass manufacture (51), chemicals (20), soaps and detergents (9), water treatment (3), pulp and paper (3), other (14)
Sodium sulfate	Pulp and paper (36), detergents (47), glass and other (17)
Stone (crushed)	Road construction and maintenance (65), cement and lime manufacture (12), agriculture (2), metallurgical processing (1), other (20)
Stone (dimension)	Buildings (42), monuments (27), rubble (13), flagging (4), curbing (4), other (10)
Strontium	Glass television tube faceplates (64), pyrotechnics and signals (14), magnets (5), other (17)
Sulfur	Fertilizers (65), chemicals (10), petroleum refining (7), metal mining (3), other (15)
Talc and pyrophyllite	Ground talc in ceramics (35), paints (18), roofing (11), paper (9), plastics (6), cosmetics (5), rubber (3), other (13); pyrophyllite in refractories (27), ceramics (32), insecticides (14), roofing (8), other (19)
Tantalum	Electronic components (62), machinery (20), transportation (14), other (4)
Tellurium	Primary use as alloying material in producing free-machining steels, copper and lead alloys, accelerator in rubber compounding, semiconductor in thermoelectric, thermal imaging, and photoelectric applications. End uses: iron and steel products (55), nonferrous metals (22), chemicals (15), other (8)
Thallium	Electronics industry (60 to 70), pharmaceuticals, alloys and glass manufacturing (30 to 40)
Thorium	Nuclear fuels, incandescent lamp mantles, alloys, refractories, welding rods (100)

Tin	Cans and containers (21), electrical (18), construction (14), transportation (14), other (33)
Titanium and titanium dioxide	Jet engines, airframes, and space and missile applications (60), chemical processing, power generation, and marine applications (20), steel and other alloys (20); titanium dioxide in paints, varnishes, and lacquers (50), paper (26), plastics (13), rubber (2), ceramics (1), other (8)
Tungsten	Metalworking and construction machinery (75), transportation (5), lamps and lighting (7), electrical machinery and equipment (9), other (4)
Vanadium	Alloying agent for iron and steel, titanium alloys, and catalyst for production of sulfuric acid. End uses: transportation (41), construction (20), machinery (25), other (14)
Vermiculite	Agriculture (25), insulation (28), plaster and cement premixes (24), lightweight concrete aggregate (21), other (2)
Yttrium	Phosphors and garnets, rare-earth alloys and compounds (100)
Zinc	Galvanizing (45), zinc-base alloys (27), brass and bronze (16), other (12). End uses: construction (45), transportation (25), machinery (11), electrical (9), other (10)
Zirconium	Foundry sands (45), refractories (20), ceramics (12), abrasives (6), chemicals, alloys for nuclear applications and chemical processing equipment (17)

The Economic Importance of Some Strategic and Critical Materials

As noted earlier, it is difficult to obtain an accurate overview of the role of materials in the U.S. economy because of the complex flow of materials products and derivatives throughout the various industries that utilize them. However, an example of the economic role played by some strategic and critical materials is afforded by a recent analysis of the importance of six such materials—aluminum, chromium, cobalt, manganese, the platinum-group metals, and titanium.[48] Although the analysis did not include columbium and tantalum—two additional materials emphasized in the present work—the general conclusions reached by the study should not differ markedly for these two materials as well.

The methodology employed in the study was to focus upon only those industries that comprise the major first-order users of the materials studied. First-order user industries were defined as those that consume the processed

Table 1.3   Economic Importance of Selected Strategic and Critical
Materials

Material	Number of First-Order User Industries[a]	Percentage of Total Domestic Consumption	Percentage of U.S. Gross National Product[b]	Percentage of Defense Industry Use[c]
Aluminum	20	83	8.1	4
Chromium	32	75	16.1	7
Cobalt	10	78	2.6	17
Manganese	20	75	12.1	5
Platinum- group metals	5	85	2.5	3
Titanium	4	100	0.8	44

a. Includes number of first-order user industries that account for 75
percent or more of the material's total domestic consumption for 1979.
b. Data for 1980.
c. Data for 1979.

Source: Senate Committee on Banking, Finance, and Urban Affairs, U.S.
Economic Dependence on Six Imported Strategic Nonfuel Minerals
(Washington, D.C.: U.S. Government Printing Office, July 1982), p. 11.

metal for the manufacture of industrial and consumer products. Thus, the
mining and smelting industries, which extract and process raw materials
ores, were not included in the analysis. Since it would be extremely difficult
to include all first-order users, however small, only those industries that
collectively account for 75 percent or more of each material's total annual
consumption were considered in the economic analysis. These industries
were considered the key first-order user industries. For the six materials
studied, the number of first-order user industries ranged from four for
titanium to thirty-two for chromium, as shown in the second column of
Table 1.3. The percentage of the total annual domestic consumption of
these materials, as shown in column three of the table, ranged from 75
percent for chromium and manganese to 100 percent for titanium.

Of particular interest to the present discussion is the estimate of the
percentage contribution of these first-order industries to the nation's GNP.
This contribution, as shown in column four of the table, ranged as high
as 12 percent for manganese and 16 percent for chromium. In considering
these figures, it is important to appreciate that they do not include the
remaining 25 percent of smaller first-order users, the mining and processing
industries, and the second-order and later downstream consuming industries.
Thus, the table understates to an undetermined extent the economic
importance of these strategic and critical materials. Even so, this conservative
estimate clearly shows the major economic significance of these materials
to the U.S. economy.

It is clear from Table 1.3 that each of these six strategic and critical
materials exerts a different level of impact upon the economy. For example,
chromium and manganese—used primarily in steelmaking—exert a much

greater impact than do the others. Because of the wide variety of its consumer and industrial applications, aluminum also exerts a considerable impact. On the other hand, those strategic and critical materials that have a much lower impact upon the economy as a whole—especially cobalt and titanium—have a relatively large effect upon the critical defense industries.

Notes

1. C. S. Smith, "Materials and the Development of Civilization and Science." *Science*, 14 May 1965, p. 913.

2. Morris Cohen, "Materials in Human Affairs." In *Elements of Materials Science and Engineering*, by Lawrence H. Van Vlack, 4th ed. (Reading, Mass.: Addison-Wesley, 1980), p. xi.

3. U.S. Congress, House Committee on Science and Technology, Subcommittee on Science, Research, and Technology, *Legislative Issues of Materials Research and Technology* (Washington, D.C.: U.S. Government Printing Office, June 1977), p. 45.

4. Franklin P. Huddle, "The Evolving National Policy for Materials." *Science*, 20 February 1976, p. 654.

5. Peter T. Flawn, *Mineral Resources* (Chicago: Rand McNally, 1966), p. 1.

6. Lawrence H. Van Vlack, *Materials for Engineering: Concepts and Applications* (Reading, Mass.: Addison-Wesley, 1982), p. 4.

7. National Commission on Materials Policy, *Materials Needs and the Environment Today and Tomorrow* (Washington, D.C.: U.S. Government Printing Office, 1973), p. 2-4.

8. Van Vlack, *Materials for Engineering: Concepts and Applications*, p. 7.

9. The discussion of composite materials draws heavily upon Lawrence J. Broutman and Richard H. Krock, *Modern Composite Materials* (Reading, Mass.: Addison-Wesley, 1967), p. 7.

10. D. G. Altenpohl, *Materials in World Perspective* (Berlin: Springer-Verlag, 1980), p. 119.

11. For a discussion of the future potential of renewable resources, see Alden D. Hinckley, *Renewable Resources in Our Future* (New York: Pergamon Press, 1980), pp. 111–112; see also Irving S. Goldstein, "The Conversion of Renewable Resources Into Chemical Feedstocks," in *Renewable Resources—A Systematic Approach*, ed. Enrique Campos-Lopez (New York: Academic Press, 1980), p. 282.

12. Energy Security Act, Title I, Part A, of the Defense Production Act Amendments of 1980 (Public Law 96–294, enacted 30 June 1980).

13. *Basic Petroleum Data Book: Petroleum Industry Statistics* (Washington, D.C.: American Petroleum Institute, January 1984), unpaginated.

14. Peter Dorner, "Natural Resource Issues in Economic Development: The International Setting." In *Resources and Development: Natural Resource Policies and Economic Development in an Interdependent World*, by Peter Dorner and Mahmoud A. El-Shafie (Madison, Wisc.: University of Wisconsin Press, 1980), p. 25.

15. Charles W. Howe, *Natural Resource Economics—Issues, Analysis, and Policy* (New York: John Wiley and Sons, 1979), p. 1.

16. G.J.S. Govett and M. H. Govett, "Defining and Measuring World Mineral Supplies." In *World Mineral Supplies, Assessment and Perspective*, ed. Govett and Govett (New York: Elsevier, 1976), p. 14.

17. Ibid., p. 13.

18. Donald A. Brobst and Walden P. Pratt, eds., *United States Mineral Resources* (Washington, D.C.: U.S. Government Printing Office, 1973), p. 3.

19. Ibid., p. 4.

20. The discussion of kinds of resources and reserves is derived from U.S. Bureau of Mines, *Mineral Commodity Summaries 1985* (Washington, D.C.: U.S. Department of the Interior, 1984), pp. 180–182, and Govett and Govett, pp. 16–18.

21. Brobst and Pratt, p. 3.

22. See, for example, the discussion in Council on International Economic Policy, *Special Report: Critical Imported Materials* (Washington, D.C.: U.S. Government Printing Office, December 1974), p. 13, and Richard J. Barnet, *The Lean Years: Politics in the Age of Scarcity* (New York: Simon and Schuster, 1980), p. 117.

23. Dorner, p. 25.

24. The discussion of the reserve base is derived from U.S. Bureau of Mines, *Mineral Commodity Summaries 1984*, p. 181.

25. National Commission on Materials Policy, p. 3-3.

26. Much of the material in this historical review has been derived from Huddle, pp. 654–657, and Dorner, pp. 19–22.

27. U.S. Bureau of Mines, *Mineral Facts and Problems* (Washington, D.C.: U.S. Government Printing Office, 1975), p. 1. For a summary of colonial and pre-federal economic activity, see *Historical Statistics of the United States, Colonial Times to 1970*, Bicentennial Edition, *Part 2* (Washington, D.C.: U.S. Government Printing Office, 1975), pp. 1152–1200.

28. Dorner, p. 21.

29. For a discussion of the early use of fuels, see Charles A. Berg, "Process Innovation and Changes in Industrial Energy Use." *Science*, 10 February 1978, p. 608.

30. National Commission on Materials Policy, p. 9-3.

31. Lester C. Thurow, "A Non-Industrial Revolution." *Newsweek*, 9 January 1984, p. 79.

32. Hans H. Landsberg, "Materials: Some Recent Trends and Issues." *Science*, 20 February 1976, p. 638.

33. Eugene Staley, *Raw Materials in Peace and War* (New York: Council on Foreign Relations, 1937), p. 4. [Reprinted by Arno Press, New York Times Company, 1976.]

34. See, for example, annual editions of the U.S. Bureau of Mines *Minerals Yearbook* (Washington, D.C.: U.S. Department of the Interior) and the *Commodity Year Book* (New York: Commodity Research Bureau).

35. National Commission on Materials Policy, p. 3-3.

36. Wilfred Malenbaum, *World Demand for Raw Materials in 1985 and 2000* (New York: McGraw-Hill, 1978), p. 2.

37. Ralph C. Kirby and Andrew S. Prokopovitsh, "Technological Insurance Against Shortages in Minerals and Metals." *Science*, 20 February 1976, p. 713.

38. Charles F. Park, Jr., *Earthbound: Minerals, Energy, and Man's Future* (San Francisco: Freeman, Cooper, 1975), p. 13.

39. Marcia J. Meermans, "U.S. Materials Policy." *Mechanical Engineering*, January 1982, p. 4.

40. Royal United Services Institute, *Will the Wells Run Dry?* (Whitstable, Kent, U.K.: Whitstable Litho, Ltd., 1979), p. 6.

41. Ibid., p. 9.

42. Kirby and Prokopovitsh, p. 714.

43. Flawn, p. 243.

44. The gross national product (GNP) is a gross measure of national expenditures: personal consumption, government purchases of goods and services, gross private domestic investment, and net exports with no deduction being made for the depreciation of capital equipment or buildings. The GNP is at times now replaced by the gross domestic product (GDP), which is defined as the value of production of goods and services within the geographical boundaries of a nation. Hence, the GDP is simply the GNP less the gross product originating outside national boundaries.

45. U.S. Congress, *Legislative Issues of Materials Research and Technology,* p. 8.

46. U.S. Bureau of Mines, *Mineral Commodity Summaries 1985.*

47. International Trade Commission, *1985 U.S. Industrial Outlook* (Washington, D.C.: U.S. Department of Commerce, January 1985).

48. U.S. Congress, Committee on Banking, Finance, and Urban Affairs, Subcommittee on Economic Stabilization, *U.S. Economic Dependence on Six Imported Strategic Nonfuel Minerals* (Washington, D.C.: U.S. Government Printing Office, July 1982), 54 pp.

2

The Global Distribution and Production of Raw Materials

Composition and Geochemistry of the Earth's Crust

The earth's crust is the primary source of all mineral and metal materials. About 100 of them form the primary feedstocks upon which civilization depends. This chapter will review the geochemical distribution of elements in the earth's crust and the distribution of materials upon which the world's industrial base is founded. From this perspective, prospects for continued discovery and development of these resources will be discussed.

The composition of the earth's crust and the distribution of elements can be based only on the best estimates and calculations that can be made with limited evidence. It has been suggested that we probably know less about the composition of the crust of the earth than about the composition of chondritic meteorites.[1] With respect to the capability for representative sampling, this is undoubtedly true. Only a fraction of the earth's crust is exposed or accessible either by drilling or inside deep mines. Estimates of the rock types at hidden depths can be made from geophysical evidence and extrapolations of deep structural features. The most easily investigated areas are the surface and near-surface portions of the continents; however, the continents account for less than one-third of the earth's surface. Seismic evidence indicates that the average thickness of the continental crust is thirty-five kilometers and of the oceanic crust five to six kilometers. Deep drilling has penetrated below nine kilometers only in a few places. The deepest mine is only 3.8 kilometers. Consequently, in terms of the total volume of the earth's crust, there is direct evidence of the composition of only a small fraction.

Small but distinct differences in bulk compositions lead geologists to distinguish between continental crust and the crust underlying the oceans. In general, the absolute abundances of many commonly sought metals is known to be greater in the oceanic crust. This has prompted some researchers to suggest that perhaps resource target maps ought to be made showing areas of the world where segments of oceanic crust are at reasonable depths for exploration.[2]

This discussion will focus primarily on the continental crust because of its current and historical accessibility. However, recent marine mineral discoveries and the emergence of commercial interest in metallic ocean minerals now suggest a long-term future potential that may be greater than recognized previously. For this reason, a separate section will be devoted to current and potential ocean mineral resources.

Crustal Abundance of the Elements

The crustal abundance of an element is the estimated content of that element in the earth's crust expressed as a percentage by volume or by weight. Eighty-eight elements have been found naturally occurring in the earth's crust. Of these, twelve elements comprise 99.23 percent of the crust by weight; eight of these twelve elements form over 98 percent of the earth's crust. The twelve elements that have a geochemical abundance of 0.1 percent or greater are listed below.

Element	Percentage by Weight
Oxygen	45.20
Silicon	27.20
Aluminum	8.00
Iron	5.80
Calcium	5.06
Magnesium	2.77
Sodium	2.32
Potassium	1.68
Titanium	0.86
Hydrogen	0.14
Manganese	0.10
Phosphorus	0.10
Total	99.23

All the rest of the elements are geochemically scarce and together account for only 0.77 percent of the crust. But these scarce elements have played a crucial technological role. As technology has grown more complex and sophisticated, most of the scarce elements have been employed in larger and larger quantities.[3]

Even a geochemical abundance of less than 0.1 percent of the earth's crust can be a staggering amount of material, and an order of magnitude decrease in estimates of crustal abundances can still represent immense amounts of material. The crustal abundance, without consideration of the role of technology and economics in processing whole rock, would obviously permit a virtually limitless supply of any mineral. However, this is not a reasonable expectation within the limitations of potential resources. Even taking into account possible quantum jumps in technology for mineral extraction, concentrations of most metals that are considerably greater than

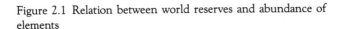

Figure 2.1 Relation between world reserves and abundance of elements

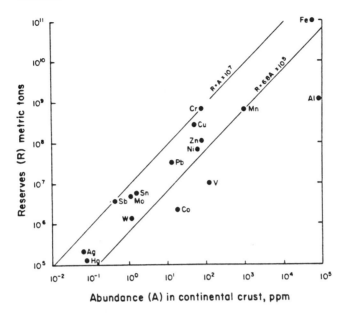

Abundance (A) in continental crust, ppm

Source: M. H. Govett and G.J.S. Govett, "Defining and Measuring World Mineral Supplies." In *World Mineral Supplies, Assessment and Perspective,* ed. G.J.S. Govett and M. H. Govett (New York: Elsevier, 1976), p. 22.

their average crustal abundance must be sought. Unfortunately, most elements are highly dispersed in nature, occasionally being concentrated only by unusual or geologically rare events. And not only physical but other, geochemical considerations involving their extraction and utilization may diminish their future availability to society.

Nevertheless, several attempts have been made to relate crustal abundance to estimates of world resources. One early attempt showed that there was a fairly close linear relationship between U.S. reserves and the abundance of elements in the earth's crust.[4] Building on that concept, other studies calculated abundance-to-resource and abundance-to-reserve relationships for a number of elements in the earth's crust.[5] It is interesting to note that for the United States those metals whose reserves most closely approach potential recoverable resources are the metals most diligently sought over the longest time (i.e., lead, molybdenum, copper, silver, gold, and zinc). The correlation between world reserves and abundance of elements in the continental crust is shown for sixteen common elements in Figure 2.1. This diagram appears to indicate that on the whole, the industrialized world has found uses for metals approximately proportional to their abundance. Within the range indicated, those metals near the upper boundary are being used at a level approaching their minimum resource potential, whereas those metals near or below the lower boundary are apparently underutilized.

Geochemical Considerations

The twelve most abundant elements combine to form the major rock-forming minerals, most of which are silicates. Silicates are combinations of silicon and oxygen in which aluminum (chemically similar to silicon) commonly substitutes for silicon in the crystal lattice. Most silicates also contain iron, calcium, and magnesium. Within the crystalline lattice of the common silicate minerals, trace amounts of most of the geochemically less abundant elements are found. Their presence in the common rocks is dependent on becoming trapped by isomorphous substitution where they replace physically similar atoms of the more abundant elements. For example, lead is found in most common rocks as a substitute for potassium in feldspars and mica, and zinc substitutes for iron and magnesium, reaching concentrations of a few hundred parts per million. Similar replacement can also occur in the common ore minerals such as metal oxides and sulfides; rarely do a number of the substituting elements form discrete minerals. For example, rubidium does not form minerals of its own in nature but is dispersed in potassium minerals, where it substitutes for the more abundant and chemically similar potassium.

Currently, most metals are produced from oxide and sulfide minerals, and to a lesser extent from carbonates, phosphates, and native metal. A few exceptions include such alkali metals as lithium, rubidium, and cesium, and other metals such as beryllium, scandium, zirconium, and hafnium, which are produced in part from silicates. Some nickel is also produced from hydrous silicates. Other exceptions are sodium and magnesium, which are produced in part from seawater.

Elements that have a geochemical affinity for sulfur tend to form separate sulfide phases during magmatic differentiation. Generally, these sulfide phases form when geological circumstances raise the local concentrations of the metals above some threshold level. Below that level the metals are found only in isomorphous substitution in silicates. This threshold level has been referred to as a "geochemical barrier," which for copper may be a concentration on the order of 0.1 percent.[6] With few exceptions, such as gold, uranium, and gallium, this barrier may be in the range of 0.1 to 0.01 percent for all geochemically scarce metals.[7] Gold and uranium are exceptions on the low side in that they are known to form separate minerals at grades well below 0.01 percent. Gallium is an exception in the other direction, rarely forming ore deposits even though it is twice as abundant as lead in the earth's crust.

There are a number of reasons why most metals are not produced from silicate minerals. Silicate bonds are very stable and, consequently, a greater amount of energy is required to break them than to extract metals from oxides, sulfides, or other ores. Also, because most metals have a chemical affinity for oxygen or sulfur, they tend to form distinct mineral species that contain higher percentages of the metals than found in silicates. In addition, the physical and chemical properties of the metallic nonsilicate minerals differ sufficiently from those of the silicates to facilitate separation and concentration of the mineral grains from a host silicate rock. An appreciation of the differences between silicates and oxides, sulfides, and other currently mined ore minerals is important to an assessment of the future availability of resources in the earth's crust.

Overview of the World's Mineral Resources, Reserves, and Production

Estimates of world mineral reserves and resources are difficult to evaluate. As pointed out in Chapter 1, definitions are somewhat subjective and vary among users. Furthermore, reliable resource and reserve data are unavailable on a global basis. Therefore, resource and reserve estimates have little numerical validity and are used in this chapter primarily for comparative purposes. Although considered somewhat conservative, U.S. Bureau of Mines data are generally well regarded and for that reason are used throughout this book to maintain consistency.

Five countries dominate world mineral reserves and production: the United States, the USSR, the Republic of South Africa, Canada, and Australia. The dominance of these five countries is highlighted in Tables 2.1 and 2.2. Their abundant mineral wealth is well illustrated by the fact that for twenty of the twenty-five nonfuel minerals considered, the five countries hold 30 percent or more of the world's reserve base. Furthermore, they hold 50 percent or more of the world's reserve base for fifteen of these mineral commodities. The prominent position of the USSR is also readily apparent in that it has reserves of all twenty-five minerals, for only five of which the reserve base is less than 5 percent of the world's total. Of the other countries, the Republic of South Africa is in an especially fortunate position, having more than 40 percent of the world's reserve base of four mineral commodities: chromium, manganese, platinum, and vanadium.

As others have noted, a surprisingly small number of Asian, African, and Latin American countries account for most of the rest of the world's reserves.[8] Counted as countries that have more than 5 percent of the reserve base of any one of the twenty-five minerals examined, the number of these countries is fewer than thirty. For many of those countries, only one mineral commodity is found at that level of significance. Clearly, the larger and more geologically diversified a country is, the greater its mineral endowment is likely to be. What is also clear is that the world's mineral resources are not uniformly distributed by regions and certainly not by political boundaries.

Calculations based on reserve base estimates necessarily represent a greater amount of known information than if the same calculations were attempted using hypothetical or speculative resources. Consequently, there is some weighting in Table 2.1 toward the better explored regions of the world.

Table 2.1   Percentage Share of the World's Reserve Base for Twenty-
Five Minerals Among the Five Major Mineral-Producing Countries

Material	United States	Canada	Australia	Rep. of South Africa	USSR	Five-Nation Total
Platinum gp.	1	1	--	81	17	100
Manganese	--	--	5	71	21	97
Asbestos	4	36	--	21	27	88
Chromium	--	--	--	84	2	86
Vanadium	13	--	1	47	25	86
Potash	2	57	--	--	22	81
Lead	20	13	21	4	15	73
Molybdenum	45	8	--	--	20	73
Iron ore	6	10	21	7	25	69
Diamond	--	--	51	7	8	66
Sulfur	6	11	--	--	43	60
Zinc	18	19	13	5	5	60
Cadmium	16	18	14	--	7	55
Silver	17	13	9	--	15	54
Tantalum	--	7	26	--	20	53
Tungsten	8	19	4	--	14	45
Fluorspar	9	--	--	17	16	42
Copper	18	6	3	--	7	34
Nickel	3	13	5	3	7	31
Columbium	--	8	--	--	22	30
Phosphate	15	--	--	7	4	26
Bauxite	0	--	21	--	1	22
Cobalt	10	3	1	1	3	18
Antimony	2	2	3	5	6	18
Tin	1	--	6	--	3	10

Source: Data from U.S. Bureau of Mines, Mineral Commodity Profiles
(selected commodities) and Mineral Commodity Summaries 1985 (Washington,
D.C.: U.S. Department of the Interior, 1985), 185 pp.

Large mineral resources may yet be found in the world's less explored
regions. Over the past twenty years, new mineral discoveries have substantially
increased the reserve base for most minerals, as illustrated in Figure 2.2.
Most of these discoveries have been made in previously unexplored areas
outside the United States.

Turning to production, its concentration in the five countries is equally
pronounced, as might be expected. Half or more of the world's production
of ten of these minerals comes from the five countries with the major
deposits. For twenty of the mineral commodities, 30 percent or more of
the world's production is concentrated in these countries. Brief profiles of
the current mineral positions, production, and policies of these five countries
follow.

The Soviet Union

The Soviet Union is the leading world producer of iron ore, manganese,
asbestos, platinum-group metals, and steel, and it is the second-largest

Table 2.2 Percentage Share of the World's Production for Twenty-Five
Minerals Among the Five Major Mineral-Producing Countries

Material	United States	Canada	Australia	Rep. of South Africa	USSR	Five-Nation Total
Platinum gp.	0	3	0	42	54	99
Asbestos	1	23	1	5	49	79
Vanadium	9	--	0	30	33	72
Molybdenum	49	9	--	--	11	69
Manganese	0	0	7	11	47	65
Potash	6	24	--	--	34	64
Nickel	1	19	14	3	25	62
Chromium	--	--	--	27	29	56
Iron ore	6	5	11	3	31	56
Phosphate	34	--	--	2	19	55
Lead	10	9	13	2	13	47
Diamond	--	--	11	16	20	46
Sulfur	20	12	--	--	11	43
Silver	11	10	7	--	12	41
Antimony	2	3	2	15	17	39
Bauxite	1	--	32	--	6	39
Zinc	4	19	10	--	13	39
Cadmium	9	6	6	--	17	38
Copper	13	8	3	--	12	36
Tungsten	3	7	5	--	21	36
Tantalum	--	--	27	--	--	27
Cobalt	--	7	7	--	9	23
Tin	--	0	4	1	17	22
Columbium	--	20	0	--	--	20
Fluorspar	1	--	--	7	12	20

Source: Data from U.S. Bureau of Mines, Mineral Commodity Profiles
(selected commodities) and Mineral Commodity Summaries 1985 (Washington,
D.C.: U.S. Department of the Interior, 1985), 185 pp. Due to fluctuations in metals markets, these one-year production estimates may not
represent each country's typical market share.

producer of chromium, lead, nickel, aluminum, and gold. In world markets, the USSR occupies key positions for the platinum group metals, chromium, nickel, asbestos, and manganese. Although a large mineral exporter, the Soviet Union is import dependent for some commodities such as tin, bauxite, fluorite, and high-quality steel products.

Through the Soviet Union's completely nationalized economy, production schedules and targets are predetermined in principle by the current Five-Year Plan for economic development. Although the USSR's mineral industry has been a major factor in the country's development, production has frequently fallen below the goals planned. However, the country has large reserves and resources of many minerals and is a significant force in the world economy.

To achieve its world position as a leading mineral producer with a high degree of self-sufficiency, the Soviet Union has followed a resource policy

Figure 2.2 Increase in world reserves of eight metals from 1960 to 1980

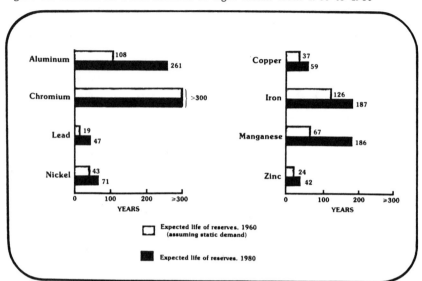

Source: U.S. Bureau of Mines, *The Domestic Supply of Critical Minerals* (Washington, D.C.: U.S. Department of the Interior, 1983), p. 21.

characterized by a willingness to incur substantial costs to promote exploration and production. The emphasis placed on these activities suggests that new reserves will continue to be found, but they are likely to be in more inhospitable frontier regions. Although the costs of Soviet minerals development are rising, decisions regarding production are based primarily on whether they promote or enhance Soviet programs rather than on economic principles.[9] The rising costs, however, are a constraint on inputs available to other sectors of the Soviet economy.

The Soviet Union is also active in assisting in geological exploration and mineral development in a number of developing countries. For example, the Soviet Union claims to be assisting in the development of oil and gas in Afghanistan; tin in Laos; tin, coal, and oil in Vietnam; coal, copper, molybdenum, fluorspar, gold, and phosphates in Mongolia; iron and steel in North Korea; and iron, steel, and alumina in India.[10] Other countries in which the USSR states that it is assisting in minerals development include Algeria, Angola, Ethiopia, Guinea, Iraq, Syria, Ghana, Mali, Mozambique, Nigeria, Cuba, and Turkey. The Soviets claim to have about 2,000 engineers and technicians in countries of tropical Africa alone.

Canada

Canada is the world's largest producer of nickel, zinc, potash, and asbestos, and the second-largest producer of molybdenum and uranium. The country is also an important world source of precious metals (gold, silver, and platinum group), copper, lead, and iron ores. In value, Canada exports around two-thirds of its mineral industry's output (ore, concentrates, smelter and refinery products, and semimanufactured goods) to more than 100 countries, making mineral exports a major contributor to Canada's trade surplus. Nearly 70 percent of Canada's mineral exports are to the United States, which relies on Canada for more than 90 percent of its annual imports of asbestos and potash; 50 to 90 percent of its imports of gypsum, iron ore, nickel, silver, sulfur, and zinc; and 30 to 40 percent of its imports of copper and lead.[11]

Canada remains a land of mineral opportunities. Although slowed by the recent recession, its prospecting, exploration, and mining activities are continuing. Development of a major tin discovery recently made in Nova Scotia may turn Canada from a consuming nation into an exporting nation for that commodity.[12] In annual value and diversity of mineral output, Canada ranks third after the United States and the USSR. Canada produces more than sixty mineral commodities. However, for a number of mineral commodities, such as bauxite, chromium, diamond, manganese, mercury, phosphate rock, tungsten, and vanadium, Canada is resource deficient.

Mineral resources in Canada are under provincial jurisdiction except in the Yukon and Northwest territories, which are under federal jurisdiction. Canada's broad mineral policy objectives include maximizing economic benefits through growth and diversification of the mineral industry, more domestic processing, and export of more advanced or more highly processed mineral and metal products. Mineral exploration and development, mining, and processing are traditionally carried out in the private sector although a number of federal and provincial Crown mineral corporations have existed for many years.

Australia

Australia is rich in mineral resources, producing more than seventy metals and minerals. Australia is the world's leading producer of alumina, bauxite, rutile and ilmenite concentrates, monazite, and zircon concentrates, and it ranks second in iron ore production. Mineral exports account for over one-third of Australia's exports, and the country's importance as a source of mineral commodities is likely to grow in the coming years. Australia is the leading world exporter of alumina, iron ore, lead, ilmenite, monazite, rutile, and zircon; second in zinc; third in bauxite, coal, nickel, and tungsten; and also a major supplier of copper, manganese, tin, and silver. Japan is Australia's single most important export market, taking close to 50 percent by value of Australian mineral exports. Despite its self-sufficiency in most mineral commodities, Australia is deficient in phosphate rock, sulfur, crude oil, asbestos, diamond, and potash.

In Australia almost all mineral rights are the property of the Crown, and the right to exploit them is vested in the various state governments except for the Northern Territory, where they are under the jurisdiction of the Commonwealth government. Mineral rights in certain aboriginal landholdings are privately held.[13] The Commonwealth government is also able to influence overall development and production activities in the minerals industry by use of its statutory powers to regulate international trade, customs, excise taxes, and other taxes. To encourage growth of the Australian mining and materials-producing industries, the Australian government provides accelerated write-offs of capital expenditures to promote increased after-tax cash flows early in the life of materials development projects. Strong emphasis is placed upon the opening of new mines, the construction of new processing facilities, and the development of improved transportation systems. The actual development of the country's mineral resources is based on a system of free enterprise with private companies involved in most of the mining, exploration, development, and mineral-processing operations.

South Africa

Over 50 percent of South Africa's foreign exchange earnings are from minerals. Despite South Africa's otherwise troubled economy, the mineral industry has generally remained relatively strong, although experiencing the belt-tightening common to the minerals industries worldwide. The Republic of South Africa is the world's largest producer of gold and vanadium; second-largest producer of chromium, manganese, and platinum-group metals; and third-largest producer of industrial diamonds. In general, South Africa has provided 5 percent or more of the United States' domestic consumption of nine mineral commodities, seven of which appear on the national stockpile list of strategic and critical materials.

The mining industry in South Africa is largely privately held although the state participates through lease arrangements or royalties. The state can also develop mineral deposits, but generally encourages private development. The state has entered into large-scale mining and processing of ferrous minerals, coal, and phosphate rock. Of all the major developed mineral producers, South Africa is the most laissez-faire in welcoming foreign investment and has allowed business to determine its own markets without political interference from Pretoria.[14] In the long run, South Africa's reserve position assures it continued prominence as a major world mineral exporter, provided political stability can be maintained

The United States

The United States enjoys a rather rare system regarding minerals development, wherein mineral ownership on private lands resides with the landowner rather than the provincial or national government. In the case of public lands, the federal government serves as the agent of the owner. (This particular point will be the subject of a later section.) It is largely as a result of this mineral ownership arrangement, operating through a profit-oriented private enterprise system, that the mineral potential of the United States developed early and grew rapidly.

Of the ninety-odd metals and nonmetals the United States produces, the twenty highest valued minerals generally account for well over 90 percent

Figure 2.3 Ratios of eight mineral resources to forecasts of demand up to the year 2000

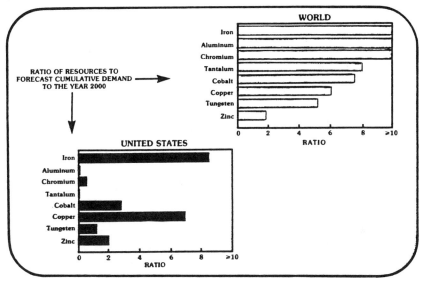

Source: U.S. Bureau of Mines, *The Domestic Supply of Critical Minerals* (Washington, D.C.: U.S. Department of the Interior, 1983), p. 20.

of the total production value.[15] Among the metals having the highest values are iron ore, copper, and molybdenum; among the nonmetallics with large production values are cement, stone, sand and gravel, and phosphate rock. On a mine basis in 1984, the United States produced 49 percent of the world's molybdenum, 13 percent of its copper, and 10 percent of its mercury and lead.

U.S. resources of some minerals such as copper and iron are large, but domestic resources are relatively small for other minerals such as bauxite and tantalum. This situation is illustrated in Figure 2.3, which shows the ratio of U.S. resources to cumulative demand forecasts for eight metals up to the year 2000. For comparison, the same ratio is also shown for world resources.

Adequacy of U.S. and World Resources and Reserves Through 2000

One question of concern to policy planners is the adequacy of future minerals supplies. This question can be divided into two parts: the near term, which for the purposes of this discussion will be through the year 2000; and the long term, which extends beyond 2000. Because numerical estimates of minerals needs and production in relation to reserve base data lose validity rapidly with increasing projection into the future, this section will use numerical data to focus only on the near term. The long term will be examined in a more conceptual manner in the following section.

For the United States the question of adequate mineral supplies is generally couched in terms of import dependency for the materials needed to sustain the economy in the near or very near term. In the absence of a shift in national commitments or significant new technological developments, what projections might be made of future import dependency? An attempt has been made to address this question. Using U.S. Bureau of Mines data for projected domestic primary production in the year 2000 and the estimated annual consumption in that year, net import reliance as a percentage of apparent consumption has been calculated for each mineral commodity listed in Table 2.3.

Table 2.3 indicates that we now obtain substantial quantities of some essential minerals from foreign sources. There would also appear to be little doubt that, barring dramatic changes, this situation will continue in the foreseeable future. The uncertainty, however, is in interpreting its significance.

With regard to the world picture, Table 2.4 lists projections of world cumulative demand through the year 2000 and reserve base estimates (insofar as they are adequately defined) for each of the minerals considered strategic and critical for the United States. Whereas the United States is limited in its ability to provide its own mineral needs, the world as a whole is in a much better position. Worldwide there are huge quantities of identified mineral resources contained in deposits whose development depends not only on an adequate economic return, but also on the availability of risk capital and security of the investment. As Table 2.4 indicates, for the world as a whole the current reserve base estimates are more than adequate through the year 2000 in most cases. Three problem areas might appear: industrial diamonds, asbestos, and tin. In the case of industrial diamonds, technological advancements for producing larger sizes of synthetic diamonds are likely well before 2000. Asbestos consumption has been declining and large subeconomic deposits are available and likely to be developed if prices increase sufficiently. Likewise, sufficient tin resources are available to sustain present production rates well into the next century.

The remainder of this section summarizes the current U.S. and world posture for those mineral materials considered sufficiently strategic and critical to warrant their being included in the National Defense Stockpile. Mine production and reserve base data included in this section are taken from *Mineral Commodity Summaries 1985* of the Bureau of Mines and represent estimates for the year 1984.

Ferroalloy Metals

Chromium. Although the United States is a major consumer of chromium, it lacks reserves and primary production (Table 2.3). Secondary production such as the recycling of stainless steel scrap satisfies from 10 to 20 percent of domestic demand. Domestic resources are estimated at about 13 million tons of chromium ore. These resources are of low grade and are not well

Table 2.3 U.S. Net Import Reliance Through 2000 for Selected Mineral
Commodities

Material	Percentage of Total 1984	2000	Percent Increase in Demand Expected Annually Through 1990
Antimony	54	94	1.1
Asbestos	75	90	static
Bauxite/alumina	96	93	6.3
Cadmium	56	69	1.8
Cesium	100	100	3.2
Chromium	82	100	6.5
Cobalt	95	71	3
Columbium	100	100	5
Copper	21	11	1.8
Corundum	100	100	decline 1.4
Gold	16	56	2
Gypsum	38	31	1.9
Iron ore	19	17	decline 2
Lead	18	20	1.3
Lithium	E[a]	E	5.6
Magnesium	E	18	5
Manganese	99	100	3
Mercury	60	100	decline less than 1
Sheet mica	100	100	decline 3
Molybdenum	E	E	0.8
Nickel	74	66	2.5
Phosphate rock	E	E	1.8
Platinum gp.	91	100	2.5
Potash	74	67	1.8
Salt	10	11	1.5
Selenium	51	35	2
Silver	61	64	2.2
Strontium	100	100	1.6
Sulfur	17	12	3.2
Talc	E	0	3
Tantalum	94	35	3
Tin	79	99	1
Tungsten	71	82	15.9
Vanadium	41	47	3
Zinc	67	58	2.2

a. E = net exports.

Source: Data from U.S. Department of the Interior, Bureau of Mines,
Mineral Commodity Summaries 1985, and *Mineral Facts and Problems*, 1980
edition.

located relative to the points of consumption. The major U.S. chromite
deposit is in the Stillwater Complex in Montana. This deposit, containing
about 80 percent of the domestic resource, extends over thirty miles in
length. Other relatively small deposits are found along the Pacific rim in
California, Oregon, Washington, and Alaska. Most of these resources are
in beach sands found in Oregon.

Table 2.4 Forecasts of World Mineral Demand Through 2000

Mineral (Units)	Current Reserve Base	Projected Cumulative Demand	Ratio of Reserve Base to Cumulative Demand
Antimony (short tons - s.t.)	5,175,000	2,114,000	2.4
Asbestos (1,000 s.t.)	104,000	205,000	0.5
Bauxite (million s.t.)	22,300	2,560	8.7
Beryllium (s.t.)	-	9,030	-
Bismuth (s.t.)	204	131	1.6
Cadmium (s.t.)	840,000	518,000	1.6
Chromite (1,000 s.t.)	7,540,000	182,000	41
Cobalt (1,000 s.t.)	9,200	665	14
Columbium (1,000 s.t.)	4,550	457	10
Copper (1,000 s.t.)	562,000	215,000	2.6
Diamond (million carats)	990	3,992	0.2
Fluorspar (1,000 s.t.)	645,000	136,000	4.7
Graphite (1,000 s.t.)	170,000	15,000	11
Iodine (1,000 s.t.)	2,000	420	4.8
Lead (1,000 s.t.)	149,000	85,000	1.8
Manganese ore (million s.t.)	12,000	510	24
Mercury (76 lb. flasks)	7,200,000	4,742,000	1.5
Mica, sheet (s.t.)	-	156,650	-
Nickel (1,000 s.t.)	111,000	21,000	5.3
Platinum gp. (million troy oz.)	1,200	150	8
Quartz crystal	-	-	-
Talc (1,000 s.t.)	330,000	242,000	1.4
Tantalum (s.t.)	38,000	28,000	1.4
Thorium (1,000 s.t. ThO_2)	1,280	14	90
Tin (1,000 s.t.)	3,300	6,760	0.5
Titanium (1,000 s.t.)	220,000	45,200	4.9
Tungsten (1,000 s.t.)	3,800	1,450	2.6
Vanadium (1,000 s.t.)	18,250	1,100	17
Zinc (1,000 s.t.)	320,000	158,000	2

Source: Data from U.S. Bureau of Mines, Mineral Commodity Summaries 1985, Mineral Facts and Problems, 1980 edition, and various Mineral Commodity Profiles.

World chromite mine production in 1984 was 9.2 million short tons from a reserve base of over 7.5 billion short tons (Table 2.4). By far the largest known reserves are in the Bushveld Complex in the Republic of South Africa. These reserves are estimated to total over 900 million tons of chromite that, together with the 830 million tons of reserves in the neighboring Great Dyke region of Zimbabwe, make this area the world's primary long-term source of chromium. World resource estimates total about 36 billion tons, of which over 99 percent is also in southern Africa. World chromium resources are sufficient to meet conceivable demand for centuries.

Cobalt. The United States has no mine production or reserves of cobalt. Domestic cobalt resources are estimated at around 1.4 million tons, of which the largest identified resource is in the Ely area of Minnesota. Other important resources are located in Maine, Missouri, Idaho, Montana, California, Oregon, and Alaska. Most U.S. cobalt resources, even where large, would not be economically producible in the foreseeable future.

World mine production of cobalt in 1984 was 29,100 short tons. The world reserve base is estimated at 8 million tons of cobalt, of which nearly 30 percent is in Zaire. In addition there are another 12 million tons of identified cobalt resources worldwide, of which about 75 percent is in nickel laterite deposits in tropical regions such as the Philippines, Indonesia, and New Caledonia, or in Australia. In addition, large amounts of cobalt are known to exist in nodules and crusts on the ocean floor. At present rates of production, total world reserves would last close to 100 years. Growth in demand could easily be accommodated by current resources or future development of seabed deposits. Consequently, world cobalt supplies appear adequate for the foreseeable future.

Columbium (Niobium). There is no significant domestic columbium production, and U.S. reserves are negligible. The United States has about 800 million pounds of columbium resources, all of which are low grade. The largest deposit, containing about 75 percent of the domestic resources, is in Gunnison County, Colorado. Development of this deposit would probably depend on other factors such as coproduction of thorium and rare-earth minerals. Other known deposits are located in Idaho, Arkansas, and Oklahoma.

World mine production of columbium in 1984 totaled 23 million pounds. Reserve base estimates are 9.2 billion pounds of contained columbium. World resources total about 38 billion pounds of contained columbium, of which the largest amount by far is located in Brazil. World resources are considered more than adequate to supply projected needs.

Manganese. For statistical purposes, the U.S. Bureau of Mines defines manganese ore as containing 35 percent or more manganese; it uses the general term manganiferous ore for grades lower than 35 percent, but not less than 5 percent. According to these terms there is no domestic production of manganese ore and the United States has no reserves of ore containing 35 percent or more manganese. A small amount of manganiferous ore (approximately 2 percent of annual consumption) is produced, but this production is generally regarded as part of the iron ore industry, which both mines and consumes it.

The United States has several large low-grade deposits that could be mined for manganese, but at significantly higher prices than those currently prevailing. Although some of these deposits are in need of further evaluation of their potential, identified domestic resources of manganese are estimated to be about 74 million tons of contained manganese located in the following areas: Artillery Mountains, Arizona; Batesville, Arkansas; San Juan Mountains, Colorado; Aroostook County, Maine; and the Cuyuna Range, Minnesota. In addition, a very large deposit of very low-grade manganese has been identified in South Dakota, consisting of manganiferous nodules and shale.

This deposit has been investigated and would be of greater resource potential if the nodules could be separated readily from the shale, but at present this is not technically feasible. A lead time of at least three years would be needed before any of these deposits could make a noticeable contribution to supply.

World mine production of manganese in 1984 totaled about 24.9 million tons. The world reserve base of manganese ore is about 12 billion tons, with 11 billion tons of this located in the Republic of South Africa and in the Soviet Union. Australia, Brazil, and Gabon have the largest share of the remainder. World reserves are considered more than adequate to meet world demand for the next twenty years. Identified world resources are estimated to contain an additional 1.6 billion tons of contained manganese, of which the greater part is also in the Republic of South Africa and in the USSR. Manganese in deep seabed nodules and crusts also represents a large potential resource, but at present should not be added into resource estimates until the data are more firm.

Nickel. Domestic mine production plus nickel produced as a byproduct of refining domestic copper ore satisfied less than 5 percent of the apparent U.S. consumption. The United States generally recovers more than 40,000 tons of nickel annually from recycling. The U.S. reserve base is estimated at 2.9 million tons, primarily located in Oregon and in similar nickeliferous laterite deposits in California and Washington. Low-grade domestic nickel resources are large. These include sulfide deposits, which contain 140 million tons of nickel in rock averaging 0.2 percent nickel. One of the major deposits of this nature is in the Duluth gabbro of northwestern Minnesota.

World mine production of nickel in 1984 was 768,000 tons (nickel content). The world's reserve base is estimated at 111 million tons of contained nickel. Identified world resources contain 143 million tons of nickel in rock averaging 1 percent or more nickel. In addition, significant amounts of nickel from deep seabed nodules could also be considered to have potential for future development. World nickel resources appear adequate to meet projected demand through the end of the twentieth century.

Tungsten. Domestic production of tungsten ranges from one-third to one-half of U.S. demand. Most of the tungsten mined in the United States comes from California, Colorado, and Nevada. In addition, recycling yields about 2,800 tons. The United States has a reserve base of around 172,000 tons of tungsten. Other domestic resources in lower grade deposits contain two to three times as much tungsten.

World mine production of tungsten in 1984 was estimated at 43,200 short tons. Nearly 55 percent of the world's tungsten resources of 36 million tons are located in China, whereas the United States has less than 10 percent. Other countries with significant resource potential include Australia, Austria, Bolivia, Brazil, Burma, Canada, Malaysia, Mexico, North Korea, Portugal, the Republic of Korea, Thailand, Turkey, and the USSR. World tungsten resources could supply sufficient tungsten to meet projected world demand through the year 2000, but their adequacy much beyond that time would depend on future developments.

Vanadium. Vanadium is generally produced as a by-product and is rarely found in sufficient concentrations to be mined for vanadium alone. One domestic mine located near Hot Springs, Arkansas, does produce vanadium ore. Other domestic firms produce vanadium from uranium ores mined on the Colorado Plateau and from ferrophosphorus slags, a by-product of phosphate mining in Idaho. The United States satisfied from one-half to three-fourths of its apparent consumption of vanadium from domestic mine production. The U.S. reserve base is estimated at 2.4 million tons of recoverable vanadium. Identified resources total nearly 10 million tons.

The world reserve base for vanadium is estimated at over 18 million tons, nearly half of which is located in the Republic of South Africa. World mine production was about 64,000 tons of vanadium in 1984. World resources of vanadium are estimated in excess of 70 million tons. World resources include vanadium found in titaniferous magnetite, phosphate rock, uranium-bearing sandstones, and in carboniferous deposits such as oil shale, crude oil, coal, and tar sands. At present rates of consumption, world vanadium supplies should last far beyond the year 2000.

Other Metals

Aluminum. Bauxite is the major ore of aluminum. It is also used to produce alumina, which is used independently or processed further into aluminum. In the United States in 1983, bauxite was mined by five companies at six open-pit operations in Arkansas, Alabama, and Georgia, with more than 70 percent of the output from Arkansas. Reserves in Arkansas total about 42 million tons of ore containing about 10 million short tons of aluminum. Additional reserves of 2 to 3 million tons of bauxite in Alabama and Georgia are mined for refractory and chemical uses. Other domestic resources include low-grade, deeply buried, and thin deposits in current mining areas, ferruginous bauxite in Oregon and Washington, and low-grade ferruginous bauxite in soils and weathered basalts in Hawaii. The overall total of these low-grade resources is 300 to 325 million tons of deposits. The domestic resource base, including low-grade deposits, would produce an equivalent of about 50 million tons of aluminum.[16]

Although historically the commercial production of aluminum has been based entirely on bauxite, deposits containing aluminum in other forms are abundant. In the United States, additional potentially economic sources of aluminum include kaolinite and other clay minerals, anorthosite feldspar, and some aluminum-rich rock types such as schists and nephaline syenite. In addition, waste or by-products such as coal ash, copper leach solutions, and dawsonite associated with oil shale could become domestic sources of aluminum.

The current estimate of the world's bauxite reserve base is 22.3 billion tons, of which nearly two-thirds is located in Guinea, Australia, Brazil, Jamaica, and India. Mine production totaled over 78 million tons in 1984. Information on world bauxite reserves and resources is of variable quality. World bauxite resources are estimated at 40 to 50 billion tons including subeconomic and speculative resources. Known world reserves are adequate to meet cumulative world demand beyond 2000. U.S. reserves are equivalent to only the expected consumption for a period of two to three years, and low-grade domestic bauxite resources are also insufficient to meet long-term demand. However, the United States and most other major aluminum-producing countries have virtually inexhaustible subeconomic resources of aluminum in materials other than bauxite.

Antimony. With the exception of one mine in Montana, virtually all domestic antimony production is as a by-product of the refining of base metals (lead, copper, zinc, etc.) and silver ores. Domestic production from primary plants in 1984 totaled 18,000 tons, which includes antimony recovered as antimonal lead from the smelting of lead ores. In addition, over 50 percent of the domestic supply of antimony is now derived from old scrap.

Domestic reserves of antimony total about 100,000 tons, about half of which is associated with other metals and would be recovered at lead smelters. Of the remainder, half is located in the Yellow Pine district of Idaho and the rest scattered in small deposits in Alaska, California, Montana, Nevada, New Mexico, and Washington. The ore grade ranges from 60 percent antimony in hand-sorted ore to parts per million in base metal ores. The reserves in the Yellow Pine district average about 1 percent antimony content. Additional domestic antimony resources may occur in lead deposits in the eastern United States.

World reserves of antimony total approximately 5 million tons, of which nearly half is located in China. World mine production for antimony was 53,500 tons in 1984. The world reserve base of 5 million tons should be adequate to meet the estimated cumulative world demand of 2.1 million tons through the year 2000.

Beryllium. Only one company located in Utah mines beryllium ore in the United States. One other company imports ore. The domestic reserve base of beryllium ore in the Spor Mountain area of Utah is regarded as large. Other known domestic resources of beryllium ore (bertrandite) are in the Gold Hill area of Utah and the Seward Peninsula of Alaska. In addition, small amounts of beryl can be hand sorted from pegmatites in New England, South Dakota, and Colorado. Domestic deposits of bertrandite ores contain about 78,000 tons of beryllium. Identified domestic beryllium resources are estimated to contain 80,000 tons of beryllium. The United States has the potential to become self-sufficient in beryllium.

World reserve base data are poorly defined. World beryllium resources consist entirely of beryl, of which Brazil has the largest known resources. However, quantitative information on the resources is lacking.

Bismuth. All domestic production of bismuth comes from one plant, which recovers bismuth as a by-product of refining lead ores containing bismuth as a minor constituent. Domestic reserves of bismuth are estimated at 30 million pounds in deposits located in Colorado, New Mexico, Arizona, Utah, Montana, Nevada, and California. Other potential sources include by-product recovery from tungsten and molybdenum ores and from coal ash.

Estimated reserves outside the United States are about 200 million pounds. World mine production was close to 8,000 pounds (bismuth content) in 1984. Large unmeasured bismuth resources are known to be present in Mexico, Bolivia, Peru, Australia, China, North Korea, and the Republic of Korea. The current total world reserve base of bismuth is slightly less than the cumulative world demand projected to the year 2000.

Cadmium. The United States produces cadmium as a by-product of refining domestic and imported zinc concentrates. In times of low demand the smelter residuals from which the cadmium is extracted are often stockpiled so that there is not always a direct linkage to the amount of zinc produced. Domestic cadmium-refining production has declined but is still in excess of 1,000 tons anually, enough to meet about one-third of the apparent U.S. consumption. The estimated U.S. reserve base is 176,000 short tons. In addition, large potential resources of cadmium are contained in coal deposits in the mid-continent region, where the cadmium may be recovered from the coal for environmental and other reasons prior to combustion.

The estimated world reserve base is 925,000 tons of contained cadmium, and 1984 world refinery production was 19,400 tons. World resources of cadmium are based primarily on zinc production data and are estimated at about 10 million tons. Current domestic reserve estimates would not be adequate to supply completely the U.S. demand through the remainder of the twentieth century. However, if the current ratio of domestic to imported sources continues, U.S. reserves would last well into the twenty-first century. World reserves are considered adequate for the foreseeable future.[17]

Copper. The United States is the world's second-largest copper producer, having dropped to second place in 1982 when domestic operating costs were exceeding depressed revenues. U.S. copper production is around 1.2 million short tons, with reserves estimated at close to 100 million tons. Recovery and recycling of scrap is also significant, with about one-quarter of the demand for refined copper being satisfied from recycled scrap. More than 90 percent of the domestic copper reserves are found in five states— Arizona, Utah, New Mexico, Montana, and Michigan. Additional domestic resources are on the order of 320 million tons.

The United States and Chile have the largest production and the largest reserve bases, followed by the Soviet Union. World mine production in 1984 was 8.95 million tons, and the world reserve base is currently estimated at 562 million tons. Over 1.6 billion tons of additional copper are contained in other land-based resources. Seabed nodules represent another potential resource of possible significance. Demand for copper, when projected into the twenty-first century, could strain known reserves if new sources or reduced needs are not forthcoming.

Lead. The United States produces about 15 percent of the world's lead with domestic mine production on the order of 375,000 tons. In addition, recycled lead satisfies approximately half the domestic consumption. The domestic reserve base is nearly 30 million tons, of which about three-fourths is found in Missouri. Most of the remaining reserves are located in

Washington, Idaho, Montana, Colorado, Utah, Arizona, and California. Additional resources total 52 million tons.

World mine production was estimated at almost 3.2 million tons in 1984 from a reserve base of 150 million tons. The United States has the largest lead reserves in the world, followed closely by Australia and Canada. World lead resources are large and are estimated to be around 1.4 billion tons including subeconomic resources. Reserves are more than adequate to meet the probable cumulative demand beyond the year 2000.

Mercury. The United States currently produces around 19,000 flasks of mercury annually. Each flask contains 76 pounds of mercury. The bulk of the production is from one mine at McDermitt, Nevada, with the rest recovered as a by-product of gold refining. The domestic reserve base of 200,000 flasks is found primarily in Nevada. Most of the additional domestic resources of about 450,000 flasks are located in California and Nevada.

World mine production in 1984 was estimated at 187,000 flasks. Spain holds the largest reserve base, amounting to about one-third of the 7.2 million flask world total. World mercury resources are estimated at 17 million flasks, primarily in Spain, the USSR, Yugoslavia, and Italy. Present world resources should be more than adequate to meet projected demand well into the twenty-first century.

Platinum-Group Metals. Platinum, palladium, rhodium, ruthenium, iridium, and osmium are closely related and commonly occur together. They are among the rarest of the metallic elements. Primary domestic production of the platinum-group metals is entirely as a by-product of copper production. U.S. primary production totals less than 10,000 troy ounces, and secondary production from scrap over 300,000 troy ounces, against an apparent consumption of around 2 million ounces. The domestic reserve base is 16 million troy ounces. Estimated U.S. resources are 300 million troy ounces, mostly located in the Stillwater Complex in Montana, the Duluth gabbro in Minnesota, and placer deposits in Alaska.

Nearly all the world's production (6.7 million troy ounces in 1984) is mined in three countries—the USSR, the Republic of South Africa, and Canada, of which the first two account for 95 percent. The world reserve base totals 1.2 billion troy ounces. World resources of platinum-group metals are estimated at 3.3 billion ounces, or several times the currently projected demand through the year 2000.

Tantalum. The United States produces a small, essentially insignificant amount of tantalum. Over 7 percent of the domestic demand for tantalum is met from recycled material. There are no tantalum reserves in the United States, but about 3.4 million pounds of tantalum resources. Tantalum resources that have received some interest include small placer deposits in Dismal Swamp and Bear Valley, both in Idaho. Other low-grade tantalum resources have been identified in Arizona, California, Maine, North Carolina, South Carolina, South Dakota, Utah, New Mexico, and Alaska.

World mine production was estimated at 740,000 pounds for 1984. Australia, Brazil, and Canada have been the leading producers (although there was no production from Canada's major producer in 1984). The world reserve base is estimated at 68 million pounds. World resources are mainly located in Australia, Brazil, Canada, Egypt, Malaysia, Nigeria, Thailand, and Zaire. World reserves are considered adequate to meet projected demand to the year 2000.

Thorium. Thorium is produced from monazite, a mineral that is a by-product of mining beach sands for titanium and zirconium minerals. Monazite in turn is processed primarily for the rare-earth oxides it contains, leaving thorium as a by-product. One firm has produced thorium from domestic deposits in Florida. Based on the thorium content of monazite production and capacity, the United States has the capacity to produce 600 tons of thorium annually. However, much of this capacity is not developed or utilized. The domestic thorium reserve base is estimated at 220,000 short tons of thorium oxide. Domestic thorium resources are more than an order of magnitude larger. These resources include more than 500,000 tons of thorium oxide contained in placers, veins, and carbonatites plus more than 2 million tons in disseminated deposits in other alkaline igneous rocks.

Recent data on world thorium production are not available but were in excess of 1,250 tons in 1978. The world reserve base is estimated at 1.28 million tons of thorium dioxide. U.S. and world reserves are extensive and pose no supply problems in the foreseeable future.

Tin. U.S. mine production of tin is negligible. Domestic firms produced small quantities of tin as a by-product of molybdenum mining in Colorado and from placer deposits in Alaska. Secondary production yielded about 16,000 short tons, of which 12,000 tons were from old scrap and 4,000 tons from new scrap. Domestic reserves are small and occur mostly in lode deposits on the Seward Peninsula of Alaska. Estimates of additional resources total about 150,000 tons.

Tin is produced in a number of countries, with world mine production estimated at 230,000 short tons in 1984. The world reserve base is around 3.3 million tons. Additional world resources are found in Southeast Asia, Australia, Bolivia, Brazil, China, and the USSR. World reserves appear to be adequate to meet the cumulative projected demand through the year 2000.

Titanium. Titanium is produced from the minerals rutile and ilmenite. Rutile is far less common than ilmenite but is the primary feedstock for titanium metal production. All domestic titanium metal is produced from rutile, whereas rutile, ilmenite, and titaniferous slag are used to produce titanium dioxide pigment. Rutile is produced from one placer mine in Florida, and ilmenite from four operations in New York and Florida. Ilmenite has also been produced from sand deposits in New Jersey. A titaniferous iron ore deposit is mined at Tahawus, New York, to produce ilmenite, but all other domestic titanium mining operations occur in placer deposits.

World mine production estimates for ilmenite and rutile in 1984 were 4.3 million and 395,000 short tons of concentrates respectively. The world reserve base is estimated at 905 million tons of ilmenite concentrates and

135 million tons of rutile concentrates. World ilmenite resources are estimated at about 1 billion tons of titanium equivalent and occur primarily in Australia, Canada, China, India, Norway, the Republic of South Africa, the United States, and the USSR. World reserves appear more than adequate to meet projected demand through the year 2000.

Zinc. Annual U.S. mine production of zinc totals nearly 300,000 short tons. In addition more than 80,000 tons of secondary zinc slab and 75,000 tons of zinc dust and oxide are produced from scrap. The U.S. zinc reserve base is estimated at 59 million tons. Zinc reserves include both zinc ore and zinc that would be a coproduct of lead production. The domestic zinc resource potential could be augmented by many millions of tons through by-product recovery from zinc-bearing coal deposits in the mid-continent region.

The world zinc reserve base is around 320 million tons of zinc content, with 1984 mine production estimated at 7 million tons. World zinc resources are estimated at 2 billion tons. Undiscovered and speculative zinc resources are estimated to total an additional 2.5 to 3 billion tons. World zinc reserves are likely to meet projected demand through the year 2000, but supply in the years beyond would depend on additional discoveries and conversion of resources to reserves.

Chemical and Fertilizer Minerals

Fluorine. Domestic fluorspar production has declined due to decreases in fluorspar consumption in steel output and increased recycling of fluorine in aluminum smelters. Domestic fluorspar production has dropped below 75,000 short tons, with an additional 115,000 tons of fluorspar equivalent being produced from phosphate rock. The U.S. reserve base is estimated to total about 55 million tons of fluorspar containing 25 million tons of fluorine. About half of the mineable ore is found in Illinois and Kentucky, with the rest located in Colorado, Idaho, Montana, Nevada, New Mexico, Texas, and Utah. About 180 million tons of subeconomic resources, mostly located in Alaska, Illinois, and Tennessee, are also available. An additional 16 million tons of fluorine resources are available in phosphate rocks.

Mexico and Mongolia are the world's leading fluorspar producers. Together they accounted for nearly one-third of the 5 million tons produced worldwide in 1984. The world reserve base is estimated at 645 million tons. Identified world fluorspar resources total approximately 290 million tons of contained fluorine. The world resources of fluorine contained in phosphate rocks are estimated at 160 million tons. At current rates of extraction, world reserves of fluorspar will extend beyond the year 2000. Further, additional reserves and increased production of fluorine from phosphate rock are likely to occur.

Iodine. U.S. producers satisfy less than 50 percent of the domestic demand for iodine, producing about 2 million pounds from subterranean brines. The domestic reserve base is about 550 million pounds of contained iodine in brines in Michigan, Oklahoma, California, and Louisiana. U.S. resources in oilfield and other brines are large but poorly quantified.

Half of the world reserve base of 2 million tons of iodine is located in Japan in brines associated with natural gas. World production in 1984 was over 13 thousand tons. Certain seaweeds concentrate iodine up to 0.45 percent on a dry weight basis and could be considered future sources of iodine as they were in the past. Estimated world reserves are more than adequate to meet projected demand in the foreseeable future.

Abrasives and Miscellaneous Minerals

Asbestos. At the present time only three firms located in California and Vermont are still producing asbestos in the United States. Domestic mine production has declined since 1978 due to health and environmental concerns, both of which have increased production costs and resulted in permanent losses of U.S. market segments. Primary or mine production of asbestos in the United States amounts to less than 80,000 short tons. There is essentially no secondary or recycled asbestos. Currently U.S. reserves total about 4 million tons and additional resources are large but primarily short-fiber asbestos. The distinction between domestic reserves and resources is difficult to draw at present, due to changing projections of demand (hence cost).

The world asbestos reserve base is estimated to be around 115 million tons, with 1984 mine production at 5.1 million tons. Overall there are about 200 million tons of identified resources in the world, with an additional 45 million tons classified as hypothetical resources. Presently those world resources classified as "reserves" will not be adequate to meet the cumulative demand projected to the year 2000.

Diamond (Industrial). There are no known reserves of industrial diamonds in the United States. All industrial diamond production in the United States is synthetic grit, which now totals over 70 million carats. There also are no domestic resources of industrial diamonds in the United States; however, diamonds were recently discovered near the Colorado-Wyoming border and may have some potential as industrial stones.

World resource estimates for industrial diamonds are poor and based in many cases on indirect information. World mine production in 1984 was 36 million carats. Reserve base estimates show Australia to have over 50 percent of the world reserve base of 990 million carats. Future supplies of smaller sizes, such as diamond grit and powder, are virtually assured because these sizes can be produced synthetically. The ability to produce larger sizes is improving and may well be competitive before the end of the century.

Graphite. Until 1982 graphite had not been produced in the United States since 1979, when the sole producer closed its mine in Texas. Currently one deposit is being mined in Montana. The domestic reserve base is estimated at 1.1 million short tons. Domestic graphite resources exceed 10 million tons, with the largest deposits located in Texas, Alaska, New York, and Alabama. Natural graphite is also found in Montana, Idaho, and Pennsylvania.

The world reserve base is estimated to be around 170 million tons, with 1984 mine production around 640,000 tons. Additional resource estimates for the rest of the world exceed 1.5 billion tons. World resources are large and adequate to meet projected demand well into the future.

Mica (Sheet). Domestic sheet mica production has declined to almost zero. Currently the United States has no economically recoverable reserves of sheet mica due to the high cost of hand labor to mine and process the mica. Small sheet mica resources occur in New England, the southeastern Piedmont from Virginia to Alabama, the Blue Ridge Mountains in North Carolina, the Black Hills of South Dakota, and northern New Mexico. Other sheet mica resources are found in Colorado, Wyoming, Idaho, Montana, and California.

World resources of sheet mica have not been quantified. The most productive areas are in India, which has been the major world producer for many years. Large reserves are also found in Brazil, Madagascar, and the USSR. The use of sheet mica is expected to decline as newly developed substitutes continue to make inroads on traditional uses.

Quartz Crystal. There is no domestic production of natural quartz suitable for electronic or optical uses. Lascas, a natural material from which cultured quartz crystals can be grown, is produced near Hot Springs, Arkansas. Mine production of lascas has increased to around 2.5 million pounds annually. The reserve base, however, is small.

The bulk of the world production comes from Brazil, which has the largest known deposits of electronic grade quartz. Brazil is also a major producer of lascas. World reserves and resources of electronic grade quartz have not been estimated. Future demand for electronic grade quartz will decline as the use of cultured quartz increases. However, this will mean increased demand for lascas.

Talc. U.S. mine production of talc totals more than 1 million tons produced by twenty-one companies in eleven states. Most of the production comes from Vermont, Montana, Texas, and New York. Reserve base estimates total 150 million tons and domestic resources add another 600 million tons. The United States is self-sufficient in most grades of talc and a net exporter of talc overall.

Almost half the world reserve base of 330 million tons is found in the United States. World mine production in 1984 was in the vicinity of 8.1 million tons. World resources are estimated at approximately 1.6 billion tons. Known reserves can adequately support increased demand through the year 2000 and into the twenty-first century.

Prospects for Long-Term Future Discovery and Development

The long-term future availability of raw materials has been a concern that has periodically surfaced over much of the past century. This concern reached new heights of popular awareness in the 1970s with the sudden price increases in oil and other commodities. The realization that certain essential materials may be in finite supply and hence would become more costly and difficult to obtain displaced some of the complacency that had previously existed. In the past decade a number of geologists, economists, and others have examined the questions of future mineral availability.

Future Availability of Mineral Resources

One approach to the question of long-term minerals supply has been to divide the concern into separate aspects depending on the geochemical abundance of the elements needed. For the abundant rock-forming elements such as titanium, iron, and aluminum, there would appear to be general agreement that as the more concentrated forms of these elements such as oxides are mined and depleted, a gradual shift will occur toward mining silicate minerals that hold concentrates of these metals. This shift has already occurred in the case of iron, and research and technology for producing aluminum from silicates that are high in aluminum content (such as the clay minerals) is well developed if the economics should become favorable. In this case a plot of grade or metal content versus the amount of metal at that grade would produce a lognormal distribution curve as in Figure 2.4. This figure illustrates that as the grade of ore that is mined declines arithmetically, the amount of metal available increases geometrically. The relationship holds until grades lower than those found in common rocks are reached, at which point the top of the hump is reached and the curve declines.

Mining and extracting metals from rock requires energy, a requirement that increases as the grade of the ore decreases. For example, a decrease in ore grade from 1 percent to 0.5 percent requires the mining, crushing, and processing of more than twice as much rock to gain the same amount of metal. More than twice as much raw material is required because it is not possible to extract a metal without some loss. The small percentage of metal that is not recoverable becomes more and more significant as the concentrations of the metal in the rock approach the limits of extractive capability.

In addition, another energy-consuming factor becomes more significant with poorer ores. Lower grade ores often contain the metal in finer grains, which consequently require finer grinding to release the minerals. Both of the cited factors combine to produce energy consumption curves such as those represented in Figure 2.5.

For the geochemically scarce metals, some investigators have suggested that the distribution pattern may be bimodal or possibly multimodal as shown in Figure 2.6.[18] The reasoning is that these metals are both concentrated in deposits of ore minerals (small hump in figure) and found in trace amounts in common rocks (large hump in figure). Current mining could be thought of as extracting metal from the smaller hump, which, when exhausted, would be separated by a large gap from the next material containing these metals. This gap would represent a significant increase in energy needed to mine and process the lower grade material and could well be too large a penalty ever to bridge economically.

Although this bimodal distribution hypothesis has a certain intuitive appeal, many geologists are not in complete agreement with it.[19] Objections

Figure 2.4 Theoretical unimodal frequency distribution curves for metals

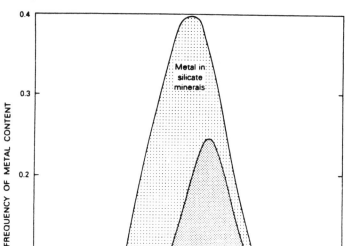

Source: John H. DeYoung, Jr., and Donald A. Singer, "Physical Factors that Could Restrict Mineral Supply." *Economic Geology,* 75th Anniversary volume, 1981, p. 941.

to the bimodal distribution of tonnage and grade are generally based on lack of unambiguous evidence for such distribution curves. In some instances evidence suggesting bimodal distribution of certain elements has been found,[20] whereas in other cases unimodal distributions would seem the better fit.[21] At present there is insufficient information available to determine whether or not the distribution of metal is bimodal.

The attractiveness of the bimodal distribution concept lies in the common perception that ore deposits are formed by relatively unusual combinations of natural processes that are not repeated or preserved. These processes can be described as falling into three general classes. The most important processes are magmatic differentiation and hydrothermal alteration. Supergene enrichment is the third. Magmatic differentiation is the process whereby solids, liquids, and gases separate during the cooling and crystallization of a magma to produce locally concentrated deposits of certain minerals. Hydrothermal alteration is the process whereby hot saline fluids pass through

Figure 2.5 Energy requirements for metals recovery from ores of various grades

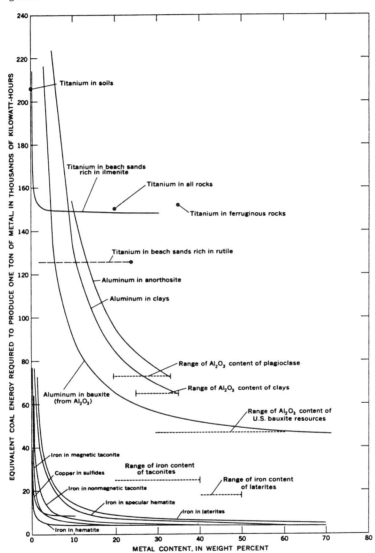

Source: Norman J. Page and S. C. Creasey, "Ore Grade, Metal Production, and Energy." *Journal of Research,* U.S. Geological Survey, January-February 1975, p. 12.

Figure 2.6 Theoretical bimodal frequency distribution of metals in minerals

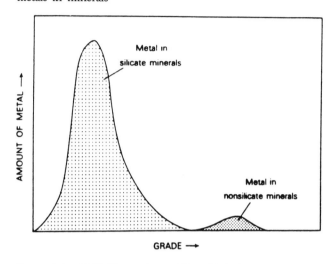

Source: John H. DeYoung, Jr., and Donald A. Singer, "Physical Factors that Could Restrict Mineral Supply." *Economic Geology*, 75th Anniversary volume, 1981, p. 942.

fractures in rock, dissolving or dislodging metals that are subsequently redeposited as sulfides or oxides, even native metal, as the fluids cool. Supergene enrichment is simply the further concentration of metals by weathering or leaching under atmospheric conditions. The combinations of processes needed to produce ore grade deposits of scarce metals are relatively rare and, consequently, such deposits are not common in the crust.

Factors Affecting Future Mineral Supplies

Not only does each ore deposit represent some geologic improbability in the remote past, but the utilization of that deposit depends on a number of other factors that, if not favorable, preclude the deposit from being developed.[22] The first factor affecting the long-term availability of mineral resources is the discovery of new deposits. Without exploration, the supply of metals would gradually diminish through depletion of known deposits. Yet even as the result of a vigorous exploration program, the discovery of a new mineral deposit rich enough to mine is not an automatic consequence. The point has been well expressed: "It is difficult to convey to someone who is not a geologist the magnitude of the problem of finding a mineral deposit, even in a favorable region. To find near-surface deposits beneath the cover of glacial debris and the endless coniferous forests of Canada or beneath twenty meters of lateritic soil in tropical Africa is an awe-inspiring task."[23]

Finding an ore deposit of sufficiently high grade is not enough. Accessibility is also very important. Deposits found near existing infrastructure will be mined before more remote deposits, other considerations being equal. Many deposits that may be found will be in locations that will be extremely difficult or impossible to mine.

A third factor controlling the future availability of mineral resources is the size of the deposit once it has been found. Not only must the deposit be rich enough, but it must also be large enough to warrant the investment needed to develop it. In general, as the remoteness of the location increases, so must the size of the deposit necessary to offset the costs of the new infrastructure that will be required to develop it.

Another consideration is that for each type of ore deposit recognized, the largest deposits are the easiest to find and tend to be discovered first. For any deposit type, the few largest-tonnage deposits contain the majority of the total metal available. For example, as shown in a study of 165 porphyry copper deposits, the largest 10 percent of the deposits contained 64 percent of the metal content (past production plus resources), and the largest 50 percent of the deposits contained 94 percent of the metal.[24] For nickel, only seven deposits were found to account for more than 50 percent of the metal in a total of 156 nickel deposits; for tungsten, three deposits among thirty-two accounted for 59 percent of the tungsten; and for molybdenum, three of thirty-four porphyry molybdenum deposits accounted for 65 percent of the metal. Consequently, in regions where many deposits have been found, the remaining discoveries are likely to be smaller and smaller and will contribute less and less to overall supply.

Whether for each small decrease in grade there is progressively a large increase in tonnage of ore available (Figure 2.4) or whether there is a bimodal or discontinuous grade-tonnage relationship (Figure 2.6) is not certain. What is certain is that mining lower grade material will tend to increase metal prices because of increased energy consumption per unit of metal produced. Mining progressively lower grade ore in the past has been subsidized in a sense by low energy prices. More recently this trend has been reversed, and mining lower grade ores will certainly increase the price of metals. In the long term, effects of such development will not be physical shortages, but persistent and perhaps at times rapid increases in real prices of metals.

Prospects for Increasing Domestic Raw Materials Supplies

A number of measures have been proposed and a few have been instituted to reduce import dependency by effectively increasing the nation's domestic supply posture. At the front end of the supply picture is the exploration and development necessary to locate and bring into production new ore bodies. This process has accelerated considerably as the country's consumption of raw materials has grown. In the last few decades, technology has aided increasingly in exploration for and location of new mineral deposits.

Further down the supply chain, other technological aspects include measures to allow economic utilization of lower grade ores, such as improvements in mining technology and in extraction and processing technology. Finally, a completely new technology is being developed that, if successful and in the right market conditions, could bring forth a new supply of cobalt, manganese, copper, nickel, and other metals from deep seabed nodules.

Aside from technological developments and increasing exploration activity, institutional programs and policies have served both to limit and to expand the domestic minerals resources potential. Major expansions of domestic minerals production have occurred under the provisions of the Defense Production Act. Primary among the institutional limitations are tax policy and concerns over the use of public lands for minerals exploration and development. These topics as well as those on technology and exploration will be addressed in the following sections.

Increased Exploration and Development

Conventional prospecting, which until recently was the source of almost all mineral discoveries, is no longer a significant factor in the United States with the possible exception of Alaska, because in more than one hundred years of intensive prospecting, nearly all visible indications of mineralization have already been identified. Found by explorers, prospectors, and geologists at little or no cost of discovery, many of these deposits still provide a significant portion of the country's output. Mineral exploration today relies primarily on geologic inference, based on substantial geologic knowledge and creativity, with special input from geophysics and geochemistry. Geophysical and geochemical surveys are part of most exploration projects today, and they are the principal methods used to locate target areas in a large number of exploration projects. The source of almost all new mineral discoveries over the past thirty years has been modern exploration groups employed by medium-to-large companies; such exploration groups have replaced the individual prospector of the past.

Advancing technology, greatly increased costs, and the low grade or hidden character of most of the remaining undiscovered deposits in the coterminous United States have contributed to the declining role of the individual prospector and the small miner in recent years. The high cost of modern mineral activity and the low probability of success carry obvious implications for the smaller or undercapitalized participants in mineral activities in the United States. One example of the dramatic escalation in exploration costs is found in data from Canada. During the period from 1951 to 1969 exploration costs increased fourfold while the probability of finding a new ore body decreased ten times.[25] During this period discovery costs rose from 0.6 percent to 2 percent of the value of the minerals discovered in Canada. The corresponding figure for the western United States rose from 1 percent to 2.2 percent between 1955 and 1969. Others have estimated that, at a minimum, tenfold increases in exploration costs are to be expected as exploration progresses to higher levels of sophistication.[26]

The authors of a recent study in which a number of mining firms were surveyed for information on exploration success rates and expenditure levels found that each economically successful exploration project must pay for ten to one hundred failures. Given such a ratio, an exploration company should expect to spend 80 to 90 percent of its budget on failures.[27]

Some insight into the probability of finding a new ore body might be gained by considering the likelihood that an exploration firm must suffer a string of failures that may be longer than that for the average success/failure ratio. This problem has been expressed as "the law of gambler's ruin" as follows:

> This rule expresses the rather serious chance of going broke when the odds for success are small, merely by a normal run of bad luck regardless of the long-run expectations of gain. The only sure way of avoiding this special risk of gambler's ruin is to have enough capital, and the will, to continue the play many times and thus ride out the inevitable runs of bad luck. For example, if the probability of success is one in ten for each venture, there is a 35 percent chance that ten successive ventures will fail in a row. But if one has the capital to continue the play through a run of 100 failures, then the chance of gambler's ruin is only three in 100,000.[28]

However, the division of projects into successes and failures, where success is defined as the discovery of a mineral deposit that can be economically developed at current prices, is somewhat artificial and misleading. As pointed out in one study:

> Many exploration projects result in the discovery of mineral deposits that, although not currently commercial because of low ore grade or lack of infrastructure, may be commercially developable in ten to fifty years as a result of advances in technology, development of infrastructure, or simply higher prices for the minerals. Such discoveries, which are sometimes referred to as "technical successes" or "on-the-shelf" deposits, are clearly not total failures. Furthermore, even when no significant concentration of mineralization is discovered, the information developed on the surface and subsurface geology and on trace mineralization is almost always valuable to future exploration activity. In fact, mines have been "discovered" in company files that contain such information formerly not thought to be worth following up, but subsequently found to be extremely significant in light of new technology or new theories of ore formation.[29]

The United States is still a mineral-rich country. At least thirty-five proven ore deposits were discovered in the United States in the last ten years, with a total gross in-place value of over $100 billion.[30] New discoveries will continue to be made, primarily as the result of sophisticated exploration techniques, new geologic concepts, and refinements in geochemistry and geophysics. Large amounts of capital will be needed for minerals exploration and development. Thus, the picture suggests a need to assess the desirability of, and mechanisms for providing financial incentives and assistance for, domestic minerals exploration and development.

Research and Technology Development

As mineral deposits are mined and depleted, new deposits must be found or new technology developed to utilize resources not previously considered. In this context, mining has been referred to as an entropic process that transforms the potential energy of mineral resources into useful work. As written elsewhere:

> We can therefore regard the present period as a unique opportunity in the history of this particular planet whereby the geological capital which has been accumulated over hundreds of millions of years in the form of ores and fuels can be spent to produce enough knowledge to enable man to do without the geological capital which he exhausts.[31]

Several prominent examples of the value of past technological advances in the area of mineral mining and processing can be cited. Historically, in the area of minerals development, one of the more impressive technological advances was the development of taconite processing in the 1950s. It not only created significantly expanded domestic iron ore reserves from known low-grade resources at a time when domestic reserves were becoming depleted, but also created potential reserves out of similar low-grade resources elsewhere in the world.

Significant advances are being made in exploration technology. Remote sensing from satellites has become a major factor in preliminary investigations of remote or densely vegetated areas of the earth's surface. Another major development in mineral exploration over the last few years has been in the use of mathematical approaches to the prediction of ore location, grade, and tonnage.

It is beyond the scope of this book to examine all the highly technical areas of the minerals industry where research and development might improve exploration and discovery, mine productivity, minerals recovery, cost reduction, and environmental controls. Although significant advances have been made in geochemical and geophysical exploration and remote sensing, additional concepts and methods need to be tested, and existing ones retested.

In a recent study of research and development funding for nonfuel minerals and materials in the United States, the investigators found that R&D in minerals supply and recycling constituted only 10 percent of the federal funding and 12 percent of industry funding as contrasted with the 90 percent and 88 percent remainder, respectively, which was all spent on utilization.[32] These data would suggest that research and development in minerals supply, a vital base of the minerals industry, is not receiving great emphasis.

An example of the research and development contribution to the creation of domestic supplies of a critical and strategic nonmineral material is the guayule development program. Guayule is a plant that is native to arid regions of the southwestern United States, and during the first half of the century it was a major source of natural rubber. During and following World War II, however, successful government-financed efforts to develop synthetic rubber and excess postwar stocks of natural rubber from heava trees in southeast Asia contributed to the demise of the domestic guayule industry. With increased concern over the U.S. supply of natural heava rubber (for which synthetic rubber is not a good substitute in some applications) and the U.S. supply of petroleum (the raw material for synthetic rubber), there is renewed interest in commercializing guayule. Successful commercialization of guayule for production of natural rubber in the United States would reduce import dependency and would decrease substantially stockpile requirements for rubber.

In 1978 the U.S. Congress passed the Native Latex Commercialization and Economic Development Act (P.L. 95-592). Under the act a Joint Commission on Guayule Research and Commercialization was established, with chairmanship alternating between the Department of Agriculture and the Department of Commerce. Research efforts are directed toward obtaining higher yields per acre and getting commercially valuable products from the by-product resin. Cost estimates for guayule rubber-processing facilities are being made. It is hoped that, compared to the 900 pound-per-acre yields that were common during World War II, it may be possible today to get 2,000 to 2,500 pounds of rubber from an acre of guayule.

The Defense Production Act

In addition to the traditional marketplace economic incentives for minerals development in the United States, financial incentives have also been provided. One of the most successful of these measures was the Defense Production Act of 1950, which helped meet the nation's need for increased raw materials supplies during the Korean War. Several projects involving strategic and critical mineral commodities were brought into production through a system of price guarantees, purchase commitments, direct loans, loan guarantees, and certificates of necessity for tax benefits. During the Korean War period the Defense Production Act supply expansion programs reached a total of over $8.4 billion in gross transactions with an ultimate cost of approximately $0.9 billion.[33] These programs were instrumental in increasing U.S. aluminum capacity by 613,000 tons, which resulted in the doubling of production; in increasing copper mine capacity by one-quarter or 300,000 tons; in initiating nickel mining in the United States; in creating the domestic titanium industry; in quadrupling U.S. tungsten mining; in expanding the world columbium and tantalum mining and processing industries; and in expanding supplies of many other strategic and critical materials. In the case of some of these projects, such as manganese and chromite development, domestic mining ceased once the government purchase contracts were terminated.

Certificates of necessity, allowing rapid tax amortization of facilities used for defense purposes, were also issued under the Defense Production Act during the Korean War period. The total amounts certified in mineral-related industries were as follows: mining, $2.2 billion; primary metal industries, $5.7 billion; chemical and allied products, $2.9 billion; products of petroleum and coal, $3.0 billion; and pipeline transportation, $1.4 billion. Subsequent to the Korean War period the only use of the Defense Production Act to support domestic production of nonfuel minerals was an $83 million loan in 1967 to help develop a new copper mine.[34]

Federal Lands Policy

Another current issue with regard to increasing domestic minerals production is the restriction on mineral exploration and development activities on public lands. During the nineteenth century, the attention given to management of public lands was primarily toward settlement and development. This attitude is evident in the Mining Act of 1872, which authorizes free exploration and occupation of mineral lands and conveys ownership of the minerals found, except coal, by filing a mining claim. Rights of surface ownership can also be obtained for modest fees by applying for a title document or "patent."

The Mineral Leasing Act of 1920 provided some limitations by removing fossil fuel and both fertilizer and chemical minerals from conveyance of ownership under the Mining Act and reserving them for leasing at the discretion of the Secretary of the Interior. The Mineral Leasing Act provided for the establishment of prospecting permits; leases for exploration, development, and production of minerals; and royalties and rents. This act has been subsequently amended to remove more lands from disposal (i.e., more minerals from conveyance of ownership) under the Mining Act. Other acts and secretarial orders have withdrawn lands for National Parks and other purposes and have designated National Forests and Wilderness Areas. At issue is the conflict between those who perceive responsible mineral development activities to be a high priority use of public lands and those who regard preservation of the natural and esthetic values of public lands to be a higher goal.

The total amount of land directly affected by mining and mineral development in the United States over the past two hundred years is about 4 million acres, which is less than 0.2 percent of the total land area of the country. Although it is argued that this figure may be misleading because it does not include tailings ponds and ore processing,[35] these additions would not change greatly the magnitude of the figure. Roughly one-third, or 743.2 million acres, of the land in the United States is owned by the public. Some recent studies have indicated that from 40 to 70 percent of all public lands may now be entirely or partly closed to mineral exploration and development. Tables 2.5 and 2.6 show one inventory of available federal lands for mineral development.

Faced with conflicting land uses, managers want precise estimates of an area's mineral resources in order to evaluate alternatives. However, the type of detailed information needed to support most planning or withdrawal

Table 2.5 Availability of Federal Onshore Land for Development of Fossil Fuel and Fertilizer Minerals - The Status in 1975[a] (Millions of Acres)

Designated Use	Formally Closed		Highly Restricted		Moderate or Slight Restriction	
Military	22.9	(2.8%)	–	–	–	–
Indian (nonreservation)	0.9	(0.1%)	–	–	–	–
National parks, recreation areas, historic sites	26.0	(3.2%)	0.2	(0.0%)	0.4	(0.0%)
Wildlife protection	1.9	(0.2%)	29.4	(3.6%)	–	–
Wild and natural areas	0.2	(0.0%)	29.7	(3.5%)	65.3	(8.0%)
Agricultural, stockraising, water supply, flood control	7.8	(0.9%)	9.1[b]	(1.1%)	65.8	(8.0%)
Energy development	7.4	(0.9%)	16.1[b]	(1.9%)	–	–
Mineral conservation	23.9	(2.9%)	4.8	(0.6%)	0.1	(0.0%)
Spatial surface occupancy	5.4	(0.7%)	0.5	(0.1%)	–	–
Other or none	–	–	0.6	(0.1%)	242.5	(29.4%)
Subtotal non-ANSCA[c]	96.4	(11.7%)	81.4	(9.9%)	374.1	(45.4%)
Alaska Native selections	49.2	(6.0%)	–	–	30.8	(3.7%)
Alaska States selections	39.1	(4.7%)	–	–	16.4	(2.0%)
ANSCA d-1	71.4	(8.7%)	–	–	–	–
ANSCA d-2	65.0	(7.9%)	–	–	–	–
Subtotal ANSCA	224.7	(27.3%)	–	–	47.2	(5.7%)
Total	321.1	(39.0%)	81.4	(9.9%)	421.3	(51.1%)

a. The Alaska situation was changed in late 1978 by major new executive withdrawals that resulted in no increase (over prior ANSCA withdrawals noted in this table) in the land formally closed to development of the fossil fuel and fertilizer minerals.
b. 9.0 overlaps stricter ANSCA withdrawals and is not included in totals.
c. ANSCA: Alaska Native Claims Settlement Act.

Source: U.S. Congress, Office of Technology Assessment, Management of Fuel and Nonfuel Minerals in Federal Land: Current Status and Issues (Washington, D.C.: U.S. Government Printing Office, 1979), p. 216.

decisions is relatively expensive to obtain—and even then obtainable for less than 10 percent of federal lands.[36] Unless extensive predevelopment work has been done by industry and the information has been made available to the government, potential mineral resources generally are not quantified.

By comparison, range-carrying capacity and forest production are relatively simple to determine and quantify. Without a similarly unequivocal statement of an area's mineral resources, it is possible for managers unfamiliar with mineral resource occurrence to assume that valuable deposits may not be present. Consequently, decisions on land-use allocations then are made that adversely affect the availability of the lands for future exploration. Further, it is argued that because mineral exploration and development activities are

Table 2.6 Availability of Federal Onshore Land for Development of Hardrock Minerals - The Status in 1975[a] (Millions of Acres)

Designated Use	Formally Closed	Highly Restricted	Moderate or Slight Restriction
Military	22.9 (2.8%)	– –	– –
Indian (nonreservation)	0.9 (0.1%)	– –	– –
National parks, recreation areas, historic sites	18.9 (2.4%)	7.3[b] (0.9%)	0.4[b] (0.0%)
Wildlife protection	30.0 (3.7%)	1.3 (0.2%)	– –
Wild and natural areas	1.0 (0.1%)	28.9[b] (3.6%)	65.3[b] (8.2%)
Agricultural, stockraising, water supply, flood control	12.7 (1.6%)	4.2[b] (0.5%)	41.9 (5.2%)
Energy development	5.9 (0.7%)	15.2[c] (1.9%)	2.4 (0.3%)
Mineral conservation	28.5 (3.6%)	– –	0.3 (0.0%)
Spatial surface occupancy	5.4 (0.7%)	0.5 (0.1%)	– –
Other or none	1.0 (0.1%)	– –	242.1[b] (30.3%)
Subtotal non-ANSCA[d]	127.2 (15.9%)	48.4[b] (6.1%)	352.4[b] (44.0%)
Alaska Native selections	49.2 (6.2%)	– –	30.8[b] (3.9%)
Alaska State selections	– –	– –	55.5[b] (6.9%)
ANSCA d-1	30.0 (3.7%)	– –	41.4 (5.2%)
ANSCA d-2	65.0 (8.1%)	– –	– –
Subtotal ANSCA	144.2 (18.0%)	– –	127.7[b] (16.0%)
Total	271.4 (33.9%)	48.4[b] (6.1%)	480.1[b] (60.0%)

a. The Alaska situation was changed in late 1978 by major new executive withdrawals that, according to rough estimates provided to OTA by the Bureau of Land Management's Alaska Native Claims Office, resulted in a net increase (over prior ANSCA withdrawals noted in this table) of approximately 13 million acres (1.6%) in the land formally closed to hardrock mineral development.

b. 3.6 (0.5%) of the total highly restricted acreage (0.4 in national parks, etc., 0.1 in wild and natural, 2.7 in agricultural, etc.), and 114.1 (14.3%) of the total moderate or slight restriction acreage (0.4 in national parks, etc., 0.1 in wild and natural, 27.3 in other or none, 30.8 in Alaska Native, and 55.5 in Alaska State) were formally closed to the Mining Law but available through Federal lease, Native lease, or State location or lease.

c. 9.0 overlaps stricter ANSCA withdrawals and is not included in totals.

d. ANSCA: Alaska Native Claims Settlement Act.

Source: U.S. Congress, Office of Technology Assessment, Management of Fuel and Nonfuel Minerals in Federal Land: Current Status and Issues (Washington, D.C.: U.S. Government Printing Office, 1979), p. 217.

commonly seen as disruptive of renewable resource activities, decision makers are often strongly persuaded to prevent mineral-related activities in favor of other, less disruptive uses.

Other issues related to the question of access to public lands revolve around management concepts such as multiple use; repeal or amendment of the mining laws to improve coordination in land management; bringing all public land under a leasing system; and improving coordination of federal, state, and local controls and tax requirements.

Tax Policy

Government tax laws and other policies also play an important part in investment in the domestic minerals industries. Because of the cyclical nature of the mining industry, high profits earned during periods of great demand may be offset by losses during periods when the economy slows or demand changes. Efforts to moderate high prices and profits through taxes or price controls would reduce the peaks but not fill the valleys, thus reducing the industry's ability to accumulate capital over the entire business cycle.

On the other hand, certain federal income tax provisions are intended to encourage investment in mining. The percentage depletion allowance permits mineral producers to deduct a certain percentage (between 5 and 22 percent, depending on the mineral and whether the operation is domestic or foreign) of the value of the mineral produced in computing taxable income. This provision has been an issue of controversy since it was first introduced in 1926 and extended to other minerals than oil and gas in 1932. Supporters claim that the percentage depletion allowance is a proven incentive for investment in the minerals industries and that its contribution to cash flow has allowed production from properties that otherwise would not attract investment. They maintain further that special tax provisions are necessary to compensate for the greater risk inherent in the minerals industry. Critics claim that the percentage depletion allowance is an inefficient subsidy, and that it is hidden from view because it is acounted for as a reduction in revenues rather than an increase in budget expenditures. They also contend that it understates the magnitude of government intervention because it is conveyed in after-tax dollars.[37]

Ocean Resources

Thus far the discussion of resource availability has been focused entirely on conventional land-based mining. The oceans, too, offer a limited promise of mineral potential. The waters of the world's oceans and the seabeds that underlie them contain vast quantities of minerals. Ocean mineral resources can be divided into three basic categories: dissolved solids that can be recovered directly from seawater, near-shore placer and other surficial deposits that can be recovered by dredging, and deep seabed resources requiring sophisticated and expensive technology. Ocean minerals have been recovered from the first two of these categories for several years. More recently an interest has developed in recovering deep seabed resources.

Perhaps ultimately the most significant of the ocean mineral resources will be those of the deep seabed. These resources consist of three types: nodular surface concretions of manganese, iron, copper, nickel, and cobalt that form in geologically stable areas of the ocean floor; manganese and cobalt crusts that are found in many areas, often on submarine ridges and seamounts; and polymetallic sulfide deposits that have recently been observed forming in ocean-spreading centers where crustal plates are slowly moving apart.

To date, most commercial interest in deep seabed resources has been focused on mining nodules. U.S. firms have played a prominent role in exploring, sampling, and analyzing these deposits for commercial viability, and in developing the sophisticated technology for their recovery and for the metals extraction. One area of primary interest to commercial mining firms is located between the Clarion and Clipperton fracture zones in the northeastern equatorial Pacific. Based on a mining operation requiring 3 million tons of nodules per year, the Clarion-Clipperton zone could support twenty-five to fifty mining projects over a fifty-year period. Thus far no commercial recovery has taken place, largely because recent economic analysis indicates that the expected profitability of the first generation of participants in deep sea mining will probably be in the lower range acceptable for commercial ventures—i.e., that it will require large amounts of investment capital.[38] Further, there are uncertainties related to national and international legal and regulatory actions, particularly in how the actions may affect the investment climate.

Antarctic Mineral Resources

There are no *known* petroleum or mineral resources in Antarctica.[39] However, as a result of technological innovation, continuing scientific research in Antarctica, and the currently recognized need to seek additional sources of mineral supply, the resource potential of Antarctica is today receiving new attention. Further driving this interest is the desire to establish on a firm basis an international accord under which any mineral deposits could be developed if and when discovered and shown to be economic. The consultative parties to the Antarctic Treaty, of which the United States is a member, have initiated this effort.[40] Yet because of the numerous physical constraints and engineering difficulties to discovery and development of mineral deposits in Antarctica, it is unlikely that any such deposits will be economically developed for many years if at all. Despite this conclusion, adequate knowledge of the mineral resource potential of Antarctica must be actively sought so that proper decisions can be made about the possible presence, distribution, and future use of these resources.

One of the most promising lines of inference about the possibility of rich mineral deposits in Antarctica is the fact that it was once contiguous with both South Africa and Australia before the dynamics of plate tectonics and continental drift moved the three land masses apart. Why (or so geologists ask) should two of these three land areas be rich in minerals, as both South Africa and Australia are known to be, but not the third? Clearly only climatic and international constraints have prevented greater efforts at finding out.

The possibilities raised by deep seabed and Antarctic deposits are not intended to signal an end to discussions of the further development of known domestic and world mineral resources. Thus far the current status and the prospects for near- and long-term minerals development have been reviewed in relation to projected U.S. and overall world needs. The problems attendant upon the continued discovery of high-grade deposits and the production of metals from progressively lower grade ores have also been raised. However, the issues so far discussed in relation to increasing minerals supply within the United States or in those areas worldwide that are not subject to national jurisdiction are but part of the picture. Another key part involves the other developed and the developing countries and their respective roles in present and future minerals production and trade. This subject will be addressed in the following chapter.

Notes

1. K. K. Turekian, "The Composition of the Crust." In *Origin and Distribution of the Elements*, ed. L. H. Ahrens (Oxford, U.K.: Pergamon Press, 1968), pp. 549–557.

2. Ralph L. Erickson, "Crustal Abundance of Elements and Mineral Reserves and Resources." In *United States Mineral Resources*, ed. Donald A. Brobst and Walden P. Pratt, U.S. Geological Survey Professional Paper 820 (Washington, D.C.: U.S. Government Printing Office, 1973), pp. 21–25.

3. For a discussion of crustal abundance of minerals and geochemical considerations, see Deverle P. Harris and Brian J. Skinner, "The Assessment of Long-Term Supplies of Minerals," in *Explorations in Natural Resource Economics*, ed. V. Kerry Smith and John V. Krutilla (Baltimore: Johns Hopkins University Press, 1982), pp. 247–326, and F. M. Vokes, "The Abundance and Availability of Mineral Resources," in *World Mineral Supplies, Assessment and Perspective*, ed. G.J.S. Govett and M. H. Govett (Amsterdam: Elsevier, 1976), pp. 65–97.

4. V. E. McKelvey, "Relation of Reserves of the Elements to Their Crustal Abundance." *American Journal of Science*, vol. 258-A (1960), pp. 234–241.

5. Erickson, pp. 21–25.

6. Committee on Resources and the Environment, *Mineral Resources and the Environment* (Washington, D.C.: National Academy of Sciences, 1975), pp. 128–142.

7. Brian J. Skinner, "A Second Iron Age Ahead." *American Scientist*, May-June 1976, pp. 258–269.

8. M. H. Govett, "Geographic Concentration of World Mineral Supplies, Production, and Consumption." In Govett and Govett, pp. 99–145.

9. James S. Grichar, Richard Levine, and Lotfollah Nahai, *The Nonfuel Mineral Outlook for the U.S.S.R. Through 1990*, Bureau of Mines, U.S. Department of the Interior (Washington, D.C.: U.S. Government Printing Office, December 1981), 17 pp.

10. Richard M. Levine, "The Soviet Union." In *Mining Annual Review 1983* (London: Mining Journal Ltd., 1983), pp. 447–463.

11. Walter C. Woodmansee and Charlie Wyche, *Mineral Industries of Canada, Australia, and Oceania*, Bureau of Mines, U.S. Department of the Interior (Washington, D.C.: U.S. Government Printing Office, July 1979), pp. 28-57.

12. *Metals Week*, 7 November 1983, p. 3.

13. *International Minerals/Metals Review 1982* (New York: McGraw-Hill, 1982), pp. Australia 1-31.

14. Domestic Policy Review of Nonfuel Minerals, *Background Papers: Report on the Issues Identified in the Policy Review* (Washington, D.C.:18 July 1979), p. II-14.

15. Bureau of Industrial Economics, *1984 U.S. Industrial Outlook* (Washington, D.C.: U.S. Department of Commerce, 1984), p. 16-1.

16. U.S. Bureau of Mines, *Mineral Facts and Problems* (Washington, D.C.: U.S. Government Printing Office, 1980), pp. 9-33.

17. U.S. Bureau of Mines, *Mineral Facts and Problems*, pp. 131-142.

18. Skinner, pp. 258-269.

19. See, for example, D. A. Singer, "Long-Term Adequacy of Metal Resources." *Resources Policy*, June 1977, pp. 127-133. See also John H. DeYoung, Jr., and Donald A. Singer, "Physical Factors that Could Restrict Mineral Supply." *Economic Geology*, 75th Anniversary volume, 1981, pp. 939-954.

20. D. P. Cox, "The Distribution of Copper in Common Rocks and Ore Deposits." In *Copper in the Environment*, ed. J. O. Nriagu, Part 2 (New York: John Wiley and Sons, 1979), pp. 19-42.

21. Kenneth Deffeyes and Ian MacGregor, *Uranium Distribution in Mineral Deposits and in the Earth's Crust*, U.S. Department of Energy, Grand Junction Office (Colorado), Report GSBX-1479, 1978, 508 pp.

22. See, for example, F. E. Trainer, "Potentially Recoverable Resources—How Recoverable?" *Resources Policy*, March 1982, pp. 41-52.

23. Govett and Govett, p. 4.

24. DeYoung and Singer, pp. 942-943.

25. G.J.S. Govett, "The Development of Geochemical Exploration Methods and Techniques." In Govett and Govett, pp. 343-376.

26. Committee on Resources and the Environment, *Mineral Resources and the Environment*, pp. 147-148.

27. U.S. Congress, Office of Technology Assessment, *Management of Fuel and Nonfuel Minerals in Federal Land: Current Status and Issues* (Washington, D.C.: U.S. Government Printing Office, 1979), p. 67.

28. Louis B. Slichter, "The Need of a New Philosophy of Prospecting." *Mining Engineering*, June 1960, pp. 570-577.

29. U.S. Congress, *Management of Fuel and Nonfuel Minerals in Federal Land*, p. 62.

30. U.S. Congress, House Committee on Interior and Insular Affairs, Subcommittee on Mines and Mining, *U.S. Minerals Vulnerability: National Policy Implications* (Washington, D.C.: Government Printing Office, 1980), p. 72.

31. Kenneth E. Boulding, *The Meaning of the Twentieth Century* (New York: Harper and Row, 1964), p. 143.

32. Battelle-Columbus Laboratory, *The Problem Analysis Phase: Task 8—Assessing the Adequacy of R&D*, Report to the National Science Foundation, 23 February 1979, 315 pp.

33. U.S. Congress, Senate Committee on Banking, Housing, and Urban Affairs, *Defense Production Act Extension of 1981*, Report No. 97-93 to accompany S. 1135 (Washington, D.C.: U.S. Government Printing Office, 1981), p. 3.

34. U.S. Congress, Congressional Budget Office, *Strategic and Critical Nonfuel Minerals: Problems and Policy Alternatives* (Washington, D.C.: U.S. Government Printing Office, August 1983), 85 pp.

35. Council on Environmental Quality, *Hard Rock Mining on the Public Land* (Washington, D.C.: U.S. Government Printing Office, 1977), p. 12.

36. Domestic Policy Review of Nonfuel Minerals, *Background Papers*, pp. III-17 to III-20.

37. Ibid., pp. I-30 to I-32.

38. Lance N. Antrim and James K. Sebenius, "Incentives for Ocean Mining under the Convention." In *Law of the Sea*, ed. Bernard H. Oxman, David D. Caron, and Charles L. O. Buderi (San Francisco: ICS Press, 1983), pp. 79–99.

39. John C. Behrendt, ed., *Petroleum and Mineral Resources in Antarctica*, U.S. Geological Survey Circular 909 (Washington, D.C.: U.S. Government Printing Office, 1983), 75 pp.

40. Other countries include Argentina, Australia, Chile, France, the Federal Republic of Germany, Japan, New Zealand, Norway, Poland, the Republic of South Africa, the Soviet Union, the United Kingdom, Brazil, and India.

3

The International Flow
of Materials

Current Trading Patterns

The Global Picture

The geologic parameters by which mineral resources are distributed bear little or no relationship to the demographic, climatic, and other factors that have influenced industrial development and created increasing demand for raw materials. As summarized in hearings before the Senate Committee on Energy and Natural Resources:

> Minerals are unequally distributed and generally occur in small areas relative to land mass, in distinct pockets throughout the earth's crust. Therefore, the location of these deposits is determined by geologic and not by geographic or political considerations. . . . An equally important international problem is the growing trend among world governments to intervene in markets, in the free marketplace, to achieve political and economic and, in some cases, strategic objectives.[1]

Although as shown in the preceding chapter, geologic parameters determine the locations of mineral deposits, they are not the sole criteria in determining where mineral production will take place. As others have pointed out, "While the pattern of world mineral production is determined in part by geological factors, it is primarily the result of historical, political, and economic factors."[2]

The problem of minerals supply is fundamental to a modern industrial economy. No industrially developed country is entirely self-sufficient in raw materials. Some countries, particularly those with large land areas, geological diversity, and relatively low population density, are more nearly self-sufficient than others. Such countries include Canada, Australia, the USSR, and the Republic of South Africa. The United States, although dependent on imports, is more self-sufficient than many smaller developed countries such as Japan and the countries of Western Europe. Indeed, the United States is a major minerals-producing country. For comparison, the relative import positions in nonfuel minerals of the United States, the European Economic Community (EEC), Japan, and the Eastern Europe Council for Mutual

Figure 3.1 The contribution of imports to minerals consumption in developed countries

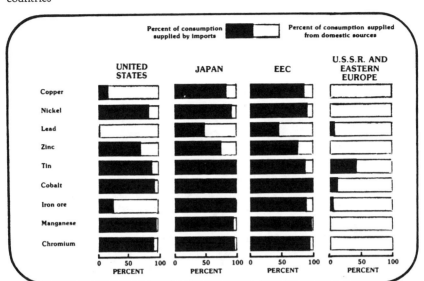

Source: U.S. Bureau of Mines, *The Domestic Supply of Critical Minerals* (Washington, D.C.: U.S. Department of the Interior, 1983), p. 31.

Economic Assistance (COMECON) are illustrated in Figure 3.1.[3] The EEC and Japan are 75 and 90 percent dependent on imports, respectively, and there is mounting evidence that the Soviets are finding it more difficult to meet their own and other Eastern bloc requirements.

Although the EEC and Japan are largely dependent on raw minerals imports, they also are major exporters of minerals in processed form, in competition with U.S. producers. The United States, the EEC, and Japan depend on the same sources of supply for certain minerals such as cobalt, chromium, and platinum. These suppliers include Zaire, Zambia, the Republic of South Africa, and the Soviet Union. Although it will remain a net exporter, the Soviet Union may become more import dependent in the next decade for some minerals such as bauxite, chromium, copper, lead, titanium, and zinc.[4]

Contrary to the common perception that the world's mineral trade flows primarily between developing and developed countries, only about half the industrialized countries' imports originate in the Third World. Currently, the United States obtains about 67 percent of its iron ore and 54 percent of its raw zinc imports (accounting for about 40 percent of all its industrial raw materials imports) from mines in other developed nations. On the other hand, developing countries' shares of total U.S. imports of bauxite, lead, and copper in 1984 were 100 percent, 93 percent, and 76 percent respectively.[5]

Three developed countries dominate the world export trade of nonfuel minerals. These countries are Australia, Canada, and the Republic of South Africa. The importance of these countries in the world market is not related as much to the absolute magnitude of their minerals industries as to the high ratio of production to internal demand. (Both the Soviet Union and the United States are larger minerals producers but consume much of what they produce.) For example, Australia, Canada, and the Republic of South Africa together have been supplying over 35 percent of the world's iron ore exports in recent years. Australia alone accounts for about 40 percent of all bauxite/alumina exports.

Trade is critical for developing countries, many of which are highly dependent on export earnings. Moreover, a number of developing countries depend largely on exports of only a single commodity for income. The existence of strong minerals trade among the developed countries does not imply that trade with the Third World is of lesser importance. Fifty percent of the world exports of manganese come from the developing world. Zaire and Zambia, contiguous states in central Africa, annually produce about 60 percent of the world's cobalt, and in South America a single nation, Brazil, produces over 85 percent of the world's columbium. These countries, like the major exporters among developed countries, have relatively small domestic markets for these commodities, leaving them with a large surplus for export.

The centrally planned economies (principally the COMECON nations and China) are a relatively minor source of minerals moving in international trade, producing about 11 percent of the world's mineral exports. The bulk of the trade of the centrally planned economies is committed to intra-bloc flow. However, the USSR has been an important supplier of certain raw materials to the West. For example, over the period 1979 to 1982, 16 percent of the U.S. platinum-group metals and 17 percent of the U.S. chromite imports originated in the USSR.[6]

Through the financing of minerals development, bilateral trade patterns between certain developing and developed countries have sometimes formed, making individual minerals suppliers more important to certain importers than would be indicated by the former's share of world production or exports. Indonesia, for example, supplies 22 percent of Japan's bauxite requirements, although it produces only 3 percent of the world's exports of bauxite.[7]

In the aggregate, however, world exports in most commodity markets have tended to be less concentrated than world imports of mineral raw materials. For example, 65 percent of world imports are concentrated by member countries of the Organization for Economic Cooperation and Development (OECD), whereas world exports are more widely distributed among many producers in the developed, developing, and common market countries. This imbalance has given bargaining strength to the importers, who frequently have more potential sources of supply than the exporters have outlets. As a result, the local dominance of individual exporters may often be more a matter of convenience than of necessity. This situation may also have bearing on the slim prospects for the formation of successful commodity cartels, as will be examined in a later chapter.

The U.S. Scene

The recent decline in economic activity has increased the attention given to questions of national economic, trade, industrial, and materials and minerals policies. In his economic report to Congress on 2 February 1983, President Reagan stated, "I am committed to a policy of preventing the enactment of protectionist measures in the United States, and I will continue working to persuade other nations of the world to eliminate trade-distorting practices that threaten the viability of the international trading system upon which world prosperity depends." The U.S. trade deficit reached a new high of $42.7 billion, much of that due to imports of crude oil and petroleum products. Clearly oil is in a class by itself as the largest value commodity in world trade, and care should be taken not to use its cost as a measure of the importance of nonfuel minerals. The trade deficit in nonfuel minerals was $19 billion in 1984, compared to $12 billion in 1983. No single commodity in the U.S. nonfuels minerals trade is overwhelmingly large in value, although most of the $19 billion deficit could be attributed to net imports of six commodities (iron and steel, gold, platinum, aluminum and bauxite, gem stones, and silver).

Western Europe, Canada, and Japan are the principle trading partners of the United States for raw and processed minerals. In 1981 these geographical areas accounted for approximately two-thirds of the U.S. raw and processed minerals trade. For processed minerals, Western Europe and Japan supply most of our imports—largely steel and other materials processed from imported materials. For raw minerals or materials, more than two-thirds of our industrial imports come from Canada, South Africa, Mexico, and Australia. Developing countries such as Jamaica and Malaysia, however, are significant suppliers of some critical minerals such as bauxite and tin. The major source countries for several mineral commodities are illustrated in Figure 3.2.

The nature of U.S. minerals trade has gradually shifted over the past eighty years from imports of relatively few minerals that could not be produced in the United States to greater overall reliance on imports. Currently, in cases where the United States has a choice between producing or importing certain minerals, price usually determines the mix, and the economic benefits of minerals trade accrue to the consumers. This shift in minerals imports since 1900 is illustrated in Figure 3.3. If the percentage of most imports has not increased significantly, nevertheless the trend is upward. Recently the greatest change has been in increased reliance on imports of processed and refined minerals, and the subsequent loss of domestic processing capacity.

In 1981 U.S. import dependence on raw minerals was about 25 percent of consumption. However, the import picture is more pronounced for metallic minerals. Foreign sources supply 40 percent of our needs for

Figure 3.2 Major sources of U.S. mineral imports

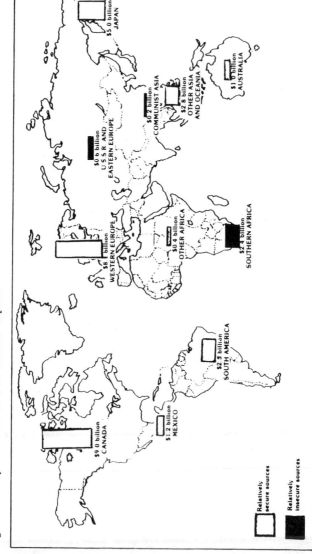

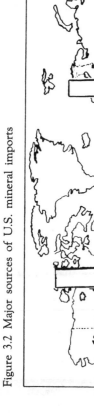

Source: U.S. Bureau of Mines, *The Domestic Supply of Critical Minerals* (Washington, D.C.: U.S. Department of the Interior, 1983), p. 32.

Figure 3.3 Trends in U.S. mineral imports since 1900

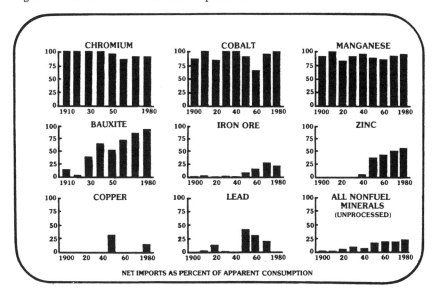

Source: U.S. Bureau of Mines, *The Domestic Supply of Critical Minerals* (Washington, D.C.: U.S. Department of the Interior, 1983), p. 26.

unprocessed metallic minerals, primarily iron ores and ores of other ferrous metals (used in steel) such as chromium, manganese, nickel, and columbium. In combined total value, more than one-third of U.S. needs for nonferrous metals such as copper, aluminum, and zinc are supplied by imports (Figure 3.4).

Although the overall U.S. mineral import reliance is close to 25 percent, the country is more than 50 percent dependent on imports of twenty-five critical minerals. To highlight the situation further, the U.S. Bureau of Mines has distinguished between relatively secure and relatively insecure foreign sources of supply. Relatively insecure sources (they are potentially subject to supply disruptions) include Communist-bloc countries and countries in southern Africa.[8] Overall only 10 percent of our mineral imports are from insecure sources, but these countries supply over half our requirements for a few critical minerals such as cobalt, chromium, and platinum. Other minerals that may be vulnerable to supply disruptions include manganese, columbium, rutile (titanium ore), bauxite, tin, and tungsten. Furthermore, some of the processed minerals imported from Europe and Japan originate from insecure sources. Whether from secure or insecure sources, most materials are shipped into the United States by water. The security of maritime trade routes over which commodities are transported to the United States is of concern, especially in times of national emergency. However, this topic is too broad to be developed adequately here.

Figure 3.4 U.S. import dependency for various classes of minerals

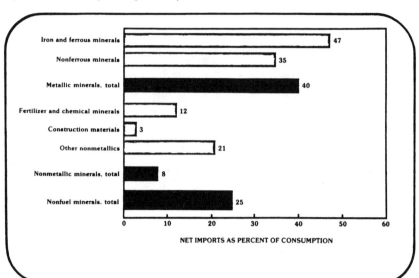

Source: U.S. Bureau of Mines, *The Domestic Supply of Critical Minerals* (Washington, D.C.: U.S. Department of the Interior, 1983), p. 27.

Trends in Future Supply

Projections of future markets are rarely accurate, particularly if they are extended ten years or more into the future. The entry of minerals from a new mineral development project into the market often requires five to ten years from the time investment decisions are first made. This long lead time and the uncertain projections of future market developments have often resulted in cyclic imbalances in metals markets.

Recently, nearly all the major international minerals markets have experienced a state of oversupply. Depressed minerals demand resulting from global economic recession was met by unwillingness on the part of many developing country producers to reduce their exports, thus aggravating this situation. The minerals industries in general, not only those of Third World countries, have been noted for their unwillingness or inability to restrict output quickly in the face of depressed demand; in this respect it may not be justified to attribute this phenomenon only to the Third World. Relatively high fixed costs and large shutdown and start-up costs restrict flexibility in both private and government-controlled mining operations.[9] It should also be noted that some low-cost national producers in the Third World (e.g., Chile's Codelco and Papua New Guinea's Bougainville Copper Ltd.) maintained their profitability in 1982 despite the low prices and depressed demand that forced the entire U.S. copper industry into the red.[10]

Because the minerals industry is at the front end of the economy, industrial expansion or contraction has a magnifying effect on it. That is, as consumers reduce expenditures, not only is a lesser amount of raw materials consumed in the form of final goods, but a lesser amount is consumed in producing the equipment that manufactures those goods. Thus, in the early 1980s the U.S. minerals industry felt the effects of industrial contraction much more greatly than did the economy in general. For example, in 1982 the real GNP fell 1.6 percent while the consumption of iron ore, copper, zinc, and bauxite declined more than 30 percent on the average.

Adding to the problem for the minerals industry, as already noted, many minerals-exporting countries strive to maintain export earnings through high levels of minerals production, even at depressed prices. For many developing countries, their export earnings are needed to help maintain economic stability and meet the interest payments on international debts they incurred to finance development during past decades. Indeed, the cumulative impact of depressed demand and high levels of minerals production is to create large producer stocks and curtail investment in discovering and developing new minerals sources. Thus, it is likely that the cycle will eventually shift again to one of undersupply as demand slowly increases against a mineral production capacity that will remain fairly static until new lead times for new minerals finds and their development can be met. The increasing cost and shifting arrangement of financing future minerals development will gain new significance as decisions can no longer be postponed; thus, the next section will examine practices and policies affecting where and how new minerals supplies and productive capacity may be developed.

Investment in Developing Countries

Despite expectations of increasing demand for strategic and critical materials, projections indicate sufficient reserves of most minerals to last at least through the end of this century and in some cases well beyond.[11] However, the comfort of these reserves alone will not assure the future availability of reasonably priced supplies. In the long run, sufficient investment also is necessary to insure that the exploration needed to replace depleted deposits will occur, and that the capacity to provide needed supplies will be developed. During the 1970s about $12 million was spent for each major mine discovery in Australia and $30 million in Canada;[12] average exploration costs in the United States were even higher.

Over the past two decades mining investment in developing countries has steadily declined. The distribution of exploration budgets of the multinational corporations (MNCs) dropped from 60 percent devoted to developing countries in 1960 to 12 or 13 percent in 1973, and mine construction expenditures in the developing countries also decreased.[13] By the early 1970s, when approximately $300 million to $350 million were spent annually on nonfuel mineral exploration activity worldwide, approximately 80 percent of this amount was concentrated in the United States, Canada, Australia, and the Republic of South Africa.[14]

U.S. mining investment patterns have paralleled this worldwide trend. In the 1950s about 60 percent of U.S. direct capital investment in foreign mining ventures was channeled into developing countries.[15] By 1965 the proportion had declined to 30 percent, and it dropped to 21 percent by 1982. Both in the United States and worldwide, a reversal had occurred in the earlier trend to look toward the less developed countries for investments in new minerals deposits. This reversal was driven by several factors. Chief among them were fears—and examples—of nationalization of foreign industries by many of these countries, accompanied by defaults on interest payments for debts already incurred. The latter problem has reached crisis proportions that today threaten both the political stability of some of these countries and the fiscal solvency of many banking institutions that are holding the notes for the debts.

Constraints on Minerals Investments. The threat of political risk still seriously impairs the attractiveness of developing countries for new mining investment. Even where expropriation has not occurred, developing countries have come to regard development of their natural resources as a sovereign right, and many have severely limited the conditions under which foreign investors can develop them. Although expropriation is still a concern, foreign investors are now more likely to find the economies of their operating agreement with the host country suddenly eroded by the imposition of new taxes or restrictions on dividend transfers.[16] Even countries such as Canada and Australia have occasionally sought by such means to increase their share and control of profits from the development of their mineral resources.[17] With regard to developing countries, investors are considerably less trustful of political and economic stability.

Compounding the problems of investor confidence in the host country are the constraints on venture capital created by inflationary pressures on project costs. Financing these costs has not only reduced profits for the mining industry in general, but, concomitantly, has reduced the availability of capital for new mining ventures.

Project Costs and Projections. The major difficulty in increasing materials production lies in raising the necessary capital. It is not uncommon today for the construction of a new mining and processing operation to cost more than a billion dollars; many such projects cost more than $350 million, and those costing less than $100 million have become rare. Costs per annual ton of gross ore produced have increased sharply over the past decade and, for some basic industrial metals, now range from $100 up to $20,000 per annual ton of production capacity, as illustrated below.[18]

Material	Cost per Annual Ton in 1977 Dollars
Alumina	600
Aluminum metal	2,400
Bauxite	100
Copper	7,000
Iron ore	225

Lead	1,400
Nickel	20,000
Zinc	17,500

A recent study has indicated that an overall investment level of about $278 billion will be needed by the global minerals industry to keep mine production equal to expected demand through the year 2000.[19] Allowing for lower demand growth forecasts that have materialized since the late 1970s, it would still seem likely that difficulties may arise in financing that level of investment. According to recent surveys, currently planned worldwide mining investment amounts to around $86 billion.[20] These mine and plant construction projects range from those now under construction to projects in the initial proposal stage, and some even suspended or deferred; hence, these investment plans would be spread over a five-to-ten-year period. Even if all these projects were to be completed, they still represent only about half the investment level likely to be needed by the year 2000.

Considering the current relatively depressed state of mining investment, it would appear likely that a period of supply shortages for some essential mineral commodities could occur before the turn of the century. Combining this likelihood with the trend of investment preference (for the security of higher cost resource opportunities in the developed world rather than less secure, lower cost opportunities in developing countries), another likelihood is an escalation in prices. Significant price and supply fluctuations could threaten the ability of consumers and producers alike to plan efficiently for the future.

U.S. Policies and Programs Affecting Foreign Minerals Development

There is no coordinated national policy regarding minerals production or enhancement of minerals investment in foreign nations. The spectrum of interests is wide. Domestic mining companies compete for market position with producers who rely on imported ore. Consumer interests in lower cost raw materials can compete with national security interests. Reducing budget deficits, promoting human rights in foreign relations, and restoring the competitiveness of U.S. industry are other related concerns. Consequently, it is no wonder that government responses to these diverse considerations have been piecemeal at best and primarily initiated on an ad hoc basis. Essentially no effort has been made to achieve internal consistency among programs affecting the minerals industry. Agencies often find themselves working at cross-purposes in pursuing their individual policy objectives. Authority for minerals programs is widely dispersed and the occasional presidential commission or coordinating committee given the task of establishing some focus upon this situation generally lacks either the political will or the institutional authority to do so. The federal policies and programs related to the foreign minerals development and trade that are briefly reviewed in the following sections illustrate the complexity of these policy conflicts, as well as the desirability for seeking their resolution.

The Agency for International Development. The Agency for International Development (AID) was created in 1961 within the Department of State to administer the U.S. bilateral development assistance program. Since its formation, AID has been the principal government source of grants and concessionary loans for U.S. development projects abroad. With the establishment of the International Development Cooperation Agency (IDCA) under Reorganization Plan No. 2 of 1979, AID became a component of IDCA. In 1981 the Bureau for Private Enterprise was established within AID to strengthen private-sector participation in providing development assistance to underdeveloped countries. The new bureau assists interested U.S. firms in putting together investment packages in developing countries and advises host governments on matters of streamlining investment laws and regulations. Such assistance is open to all sectors provided that the projects are oriented toward development. However, the extent to which this bureau will encourage and support mining projects in particular is not certain. In the past decade the emphasis of government agencies has been on creating jobs and meeting basic human needs rather than on such capital-intensive projects as mining. Whether this trend will continue or be reversed is uncertain.

The Trade and Development Program. The International Development Cooperation Agency's Trade and Development Program (TDP) was established in 1980. The TDP is the only government agency with a specific congressional mandate to encourage the development of overseas mineral supplies. Section 661 of the Foreign Assistance Act authorizes the president to use funds presently allocated to TDP to facilitate "open and fair access to natural resources of interest to the United States." The TDP provides grants for planning and feasibility studies and coordinates government-to-government technical assistance training by other federal agencies. Among the program priorities are the requirements that the projects be central to the host country's mineral development and that they involve procurement of U.S. goods and services. The relatively small funding capability (around $10 million annually) may limit the impact of the program. Among the initial projects funded are development feasibility studies of cobalt resources in Morocco, chromium in the Philippines, and manganese in Gabon.

The International Program of the U.S. Geological Survey. For more than forty years the U.S. Geological Survey has been providing technical assistance to foreign countries through its International Program. More than seventy countries have received assistance in geological surveys and mineral exploration over the years. These projects have not only contributed to U.S. foreign policy interests, but some are credited with the discovery of major mineral resources. Among the discoveries cited are manganese in Brazil, copper in Pakistan, potash in Thailand, and lithium in Bolivia. In recent years, assistance through the International Program has declined sharply. For example, in 1969 and 1970 the Geological Survey had approximately twenty-five projects in nineteen countries involving more than one hundred specialists. Most of the projects were funded by AID. At the end of 1979 AID funded only two such projects.

Although considerable potential remains, this program is unlikely to match its past achievements without revitalization through executive or legislative mandate. The participation of consumer government geological teams in surveying and prospecting with developing countries' resource agencies not only can increase the consumer's knowledge about world resources availability, but also frequently can result in investment opportunities for its own mining industry. This last point has been noted by developing country officials with regard to the absence of the U.S. Geological Survey and growing presence of competitors' survey agencies in countries such as Argentina, Peru, and Zimbabwe.[21]

Bilateral Investment Treaties. Another means of encouraging private-sector investment in developing countries might be the conclusion of bilateral investment treaties with potential mineral suppliers. The Department of State has recently negotiated a model investment treaty with Egypt that establishes a common understanding and legal base for initiating investment, arbitrating and settling disputes, repatriating capital, and providing compensation in the event of expropriation. Other developing countries are reportedly interested in similar arrangements. However, because the prospects of successfully negotiating a bilateral investment treaty are much greater with countries where our current relations are already fairly conducive to investment, it seems likely that the overall impact of bilateral investment treaties may be slight. Moreover, the existence of a treaty may not by itself be sufficient to persuade a mining firm to invest in another country. To some extent this is borne out by the West German experience with bilateral investment treaties (forty such agreements with developing countries in effect at the end of 1980), as described in one study:

> Investment, however, has not routinely followed signing of a treaty. An official in the Ministry of Economics pointed out that there are countries with which there is very little private investment. On the other hand, German companies are clamoring to invest in Brazil although there is no agreement in force. Brazil's investment climate has been considered excellent, thus making deposits there economically attractive.[22]

The U.S. Export-Import Bank. The Eximbank was created in 1934 to provide financial support for U.S. export sales. Its financing programs include direct loans, financial guarantees to private lenders, and commercial and political risk insurance. During World War II and the Korean War eras, these and other programs empowered to the Eximbank were used to advantage in developing minerals deposits in foreign countries and securing new sources of strategic and critical materials for the U.S. National Defense Stockpile. In recent years the Eximbank's support for mining, including feasibility studies and first-stage processing, has been declining as a percentage of its total direct loans and financial guarantees.

In principle, the Eximbank is available to improve the competitive position of U.S. firms operating in the international market. Often U.S. firms find themselves at a disadvantage in bidding for minerals projects against consortia sponsored by the governments of other importing countries. The Eximbank can address this disadvantage by offering loan guarantees and risk insurance to U.S. firms and by providing low interest loans to foreign purchasers of U.S. goods and services. About one hundred U.S. mining and processing operations in foreign countries are being supported by one or more of these programs.

Although the Eximbank has been authorized to increase its credit support of U.S. firms by providing below-market loans and other subsidies to companies competing with government-supported foreign enterprises, the prevailing philosophy is to avoid subsidies and other financial involvement in export competition. In this vein the current federal administration has stressed the urgency of strengthening the 1976 Arrangement on Guidelines for Officially Supported Export Credits, which is the international agreement setting minimum permissible export credit interest rates.

Conflicting interests can also arise when the Eximbank extends credit to buy U.S. equipment that will be used by a foreign producer who is competing in international markets with U.S. firms. Recently two such cases became issues, one with regard to a $75.7 million capital equipment loan from the Eximbank (the World Bank was also involved for an additional amount) to expand a Mexican copper mining and smelting operation, and the other for $35 million in credit for equipment to expand the Moroccan phosphate industry.[23] Both caused consternation for U.S. mining firms. Thus, a dichotomy of interests exists in the orientation of export policy.

The Overseas Private Investment Corporation. The Overseas Private Investment Corporation (OPIC) is a government corporation created by Congress in 1969 to facilitate the flow of U.S. private capital and technical services to developing countries by providing political risk insurance and finance programs. Its insurance program provides protection against losses due to war or insurrection, expropriation, and an investor's inability to repatriate profits because of the host government's breech of specified contractual obligations or change of law. Recently OPIC has been given the statutory authority to issue civil strife insurance as well. The finance programs provide direct or guaranteed loans to U.S. firms investing in developing countries.

A number of requirements are placed on OPIC that may tend to limit support for mining projects in developing countries. First, before OPIC can approve any project in a country, that country must have a "suitable arrangement" with the United States in order to protect OPIC's rights as an insurer and creditor. Although nearly one hundred developing countries have entered into agreements that would permit OPIC operations, some Latin American countries in particular have not.[24] The extent to which the latter situation inhibits investment is uncertain, as it would appear that with promising geological quality, good economics, and manageable political risks, firms will invest without the involvement of OPIC.

OPIC is also required to consider the record of human rights in developing countries before approving projects in these countries. Again it is uncertain whether this requirement has inhibited private investment. Few proposals have been denied (only 1 out of 528 over a three-year period from 1978 to 1981). Yet because this policy is widely known, investors may not submit project proposals at all if the proposals appear likely to be rejected on such a basis.

Another requirement incorporated into the Overseas Private Investment Corporation Act amendments of 1978 made direct loan and feasibility study funds available to the minerals sector, but only for small projects. The legislation states that the projects must be sponsored by or significantly involve U.S. small businesses and that expenditures cannot exceed $4 million per year. Because most mining firms interested in foreign investment are relatively large, it is doubtful that this assistance would be particularly useful to the industry. Again a conflict of laudable goals and purposes may negate much of the effectiveness of a program.

The Export Trading Company Act. In an effort to gain a more competitive position for U.S. firms vis-à-vis foreign government–sponsored consortia, the 97th Congress passed the Export Trading Company Act. Under this act, U.S. companies that wish to participate in projects with foreign consortia could obtain certification from the Department of Commerce to prevent possible antitrust suits from arising with regard to their projects. The act also authorizes commercial banks to participate in export trading companies to strengthen these companies' financial posture.

The Changing Nature of Competitive Minerals Trade

International trade in minerals at market-established prices is becoming eroded through policies that tie specific producers to specific importers.[25] Many mineral-exporting countries over the past decade have sought to guarantee markets for their production via bilateral export agreements. Correspondingly, some minerals-deficient countries have sought to assure stable and adequate levels of supply through negotiated import agreements. Respectively, these agreements have been termed export performance requirements and develop-for-import projects. In a sense, both types of agreements are export requirements; the difference is in who solicits or imposes the requirement. Both processes intrude on the minerals supply available to free trade and thus diminish the competitive market. These types of arrangements are described in the following sections.

Export Performance Requirements. Export performance requirements are transactions imposed by the host country in exchange for purchase of production machinery or plants. Two types of arrangements are commonly used to satisfy these requirements, production sharing and buyback agreements.

Production sharing is a type of joint venture whereby the suppliers of equity capital agree to take a portion of the future annual production in return for their investment. These commitments generally extend over a twelve-to-fifteen–year period and are fairly recent to the metal mining and processing sector.

In buyback arrangements, credits toward purchase of future output are extended to a foreign buyer who has provided mining and processing machinery. Buyback arrangements usually have commitments extending over a period of five to eight years.

Develop-for-Import Projects. Develop-for-import projects are agreements whereby a developed importing country agrees to finance a minerals development project in exchange for a long-term commitment from the host country for a specified quantity of the resultant exports. Typically the developed country provides technical assistance in construction as well as financing for the project. The credit and development loans that support export of machinery and assistance are at below-market rates to ensure fulfillment of the future export obligations.

Develop-for-import mechanisms include the same buyback and production-sharing agreements described above. In addition, they also involve import compensation or service contract arrangements for such aid as management, exploration, or production expertise. Service contracts are often for an eight-to-ten–year time frame. Develop-for-import and export performance requirements can be mutually satisfied in the same transaction. For example, in 1981 France's Export-Import Bank extended $435 million in subsidized credits to finance export of an alumina-aluminum complex to India. In exchange, India agreed to ship 400,000 tons of alumina per year to France. This satisfied the develop-for-import interests of France. At the same time, India's export performance requirements were met when, in addition, France agreed to purchase other aluminum in excess of India's needs from the aluminum smelter.

The major difference between develop-for-import projects and more conventional production-sharing joint ventures is that conventional production-sharing joint ventures are financed on the expectation of a reasonable return on the investment. On the other hand, the emphasis in a develop-for-import agreement is on a stable source of supply through subsidized credits. Consequently, develop-for-import projects will be less sensitive to market prices in that the output of the projects is committed.

Implications for the Future. Develop-for-import trade agreements may lead to development of additional world mineral supplies, but an attendant reduction of market flexibility will result. Because less capacity will be available to respond to changes in demand, price fluctuations in the remaining free market will tend to be amplified.

The present amount of minerals trade committed to develop-for-import projects is still very small, but it has grown significantly in the past five years. The develop-for-import mineral quantities (production capacity) completed by the end of 1984 include 69.1 million tons of iron ore, 3.1 million tons of nickel ore, 2.4 million tons of manganese ore, and nearly 2 million tons each of alumina and bauxite.[26] Although these quantities are a relatively minor portion of world minerals trade, they nevertheless represent a growing concern.

Trends in Future Consumption

As mentioned earlier, the minerals industries have long been beset with cyclic activity and profitability dependent on the state of the world economy. The depressed economic swing of the early 1980s proved no exception. The only certainty is change. Change in minerals consumption will not only be brought about by economic activity, but also, in the longer term, by technology. Substitution driven by cost, weight reduction, environmental concerns, or a host of other factors can significantly alter future minerals demand. This section will explore some of the causes and directions of future consumption patterns.

Developed Countries

The effects of economic and technological change on minerals demand are likely to be felt most strongly in developed countries where the bulk of industrial production takes place and research in materials utilization is conducted. Changes in consumption can be measured by unit of input relative to the output of the general economy. For example, in 1972 the U.S. economy consumed an average of 0.0016 ton of primary copper for each million dollars of GNP that was created. By 1984, only 0.0006 ton of copper was needed as input to produce a million dollars of the U.S. GNP. Using the implicit price deflator for the gross national product to adjust for constant dollars (1972 base), the 1984 copper consumption becomes 0.0014 ton per million dollars of GNP. The change in production mix was brought about by cost competition, technological development, substitution in raw materials, conservation, shifts in types of final goods and services desired by consumers, and other related factors. The difference amounts to a reduction of 12.5 percent in the amount of copper that would otherwise have been consumed. Supporting this example of one metal in one country, other examples worldwide have shown a general trend toward a reduction in the intensity of use of most materials, which if continued could lead to reductions of 10 to 20 percent below recent levels by the year 2000, with the possible exception of the use of aluminum.[27]

The evolution of industries to satisfy societal goals also affects the consumption of materials. Current trends to build smaller automobiles and improve fuel economy may have significant impacts on materials needs. What is described as a materials revolution is going on in the automobile industry, featuring such materials as new high-strength steels, fiber-reinforced composites and structural plastics, and high technology ceramics. Currently the U.S. automobile industry accounts for about 20 percent of the nation's consumption of iron and steel, 15 percent of its aluminum, 12 percent of its copper, 70 percent of its lead, 35 percent of its zinc, and 40 percent of its platinum. By the mid-1980s the average automobile will weigh under 3,000 pounds. Although it will still be 50 percent steel by weight, some 150 pounds of aluminum, 350 to 400 pounds of new grades of high-strength steels, and around 250 pounds of plastics will be used in the car. The use of gray cast iron will be decreased by about 40 to 50 percent by comparison with a car of the late 1970s.[28] Clearly changes and trends such as these will have far-reaching effects on materials consumption patterns as society enters the twenty-first century.

Overall, changes in world demand for mineral raw materials will be an evolutionary process determined largely by the level of economic growth and technological development in industrialized countries. In particular, changes in the developed market economies—which currently account for over 65 percent of world mineral demand—will be of some interest. Together, the centrally planned economies, the developed industrialized nations of the West, and Japan currently consume nearly 95 percent of the world's supply of raw materials. However, because the instruments of change vary greatly over regions of the globe, the prospects for various segments of the world economy must be evaluated independently to assess the aggregate future course of minerals consumption.

Developing Countries

If the developed countries have, as many analysts believe, entered the postindustrial age, a decline in the intensity of raw materials consumption should be expected to occur. Conversely, developing countries that are struggling toward industrialization will be increasing their intensity of use. Slower growth rates of materials demand in developed countries will tend to affect the relative growth rate of foreign trade in these materials. In the long run, export markets for raw materials produced in developing countries will tend to grow more rapidly with other developing countries than with the developed countries.[29]

Compared to past decades, the economic growth of developing countries has slowed in the current decade. It seems unlikely that developing countries can regain the average annual growth rate of 5.7 percent that they achieved in the 1970s. Forecasters now suggest that over the coming decade developing countries may look toward a more modest 3.9 percent annual growth rate.[30] Nevertheless, this rate would still be 15 to 20 percent higher than the rate forecast for developed countries. The general decline in rate of economic growth can be attributed to a number of factors, not the least of which is the high rate of inflation in countries where the value of exports has been declining relative to the cost of imports (boosted mainly by the increased cost of petroleum). Related concerns include the significant increase in the indebtedness of developing countries to international lending institutions, aggravated where the restructuring of that debt has been necessary.

When the average annual growth rate of developing countries in the 1970s was 5.7 percent, their average annual increase in consumption of raw materials was 10.6 percent. Even with a downturn in economic growth as forecast, the developing countries' percentage share of world mineral consumption is likely to increase by the year 2000. Although this increase may not be great in percentage, the implications for world minerals trade and availability of supply could be significant.

Centrally Planned Economies

The Soviet economy is going through one of its worst periods since World War II. The economy grew at an annual rate of 6 percent in the 1950s, 5 percent in the 1960s, 3.5 percent in the mid-1970s, and it probably will grow by only 2 to 2.5 percent annually in the 1980s.[31] Despite this slowdown in economic growth, the USSR has been able to maintain its position as the world's second-largest producer of industrial products. Although it is generally acknowledged that Soviet productivity is relatively inefficient in the utilization of raw materials, the resource base of the Soviet Union is one of the greatest in the world. Minerals development in the Soviet Union continues to remain an important aspect of Soviet economic growth, and minerals exports generated by such development may play a growing role in the world minerals trade.[32]

The People's Republic of China is also well endowed with mineral resources. However, several problems combine to make China's future position in world minerals trade somewhat speculative. Currently, China is following much the same course as other countries striving to further their industrial development. This course will undoubtedly lead to increased minerals consumption. China's lack of mineral-processing capabilities tends to make it an exporter of raw materials and an importer of value-added products.[33] In addition, the lack of adequate transportation infrastructure currently inhibits expansion of minerals development. Finally, China's inefficient and inadequate energy generation could become a limiting factor to industrial development. Consequently, the future role of China in international minerals trade is still uncertain.

The global course of future mineral development and consumption is changing, but the outlook is mixed. Slowing of economic growth combined with decreasing intensity of use of raw materials in industrialized nations will help mitigate the continuing need for new supplies. However, the overall growth in demand will continue, probably at annual rates of 1 to 3 percent. In several developing countries, minerals needs are likely to increase at a slightly greater rate than economic growth, probably at rates of 3 to 4 percent. To meet this growth in needs, more than half again as much mineral production capacity as now exists will be required by the end of the century. The location and financing of this development will largely determine the future flow of materials in international trade.

Notes

1. See the testimony of David Swan, vice-president of Kennecott Corporation, in Senate Committee on Energy and Natural Resources, Subcommittee on Energy Resources and Materials Production, *Materials Policy, Research, and Development Act. Hearing on H.R. 2743*, 29 and 31 July 1980, 96th Congress, 2nd Session. Publication No. 96–142 (Washington, D.C.: U.S. Government Printing Office, 1980), pp. 215–216.

2. M. H. Govett and G.J.S. Govett, "The New Economic Order and World Mineral Production and Trade." *Resources Policy*, December 1978, pp. 230–241.

3. The EEC countries are Belgium, Denmark, France, Greece, Ireland, Italy, Luxembourg, The Netherlands, the United Kingdom, and West Germany. The COMECON countries are Bulgaria, Cuba, Czechoslovakia, East Germany, Hungary, Mongolia, Poland, Romania, the Soviet Union, and Vietnam.

4. U.S. Bureau of Mines, *The Domestic Supply of Critical Minerals* (Washington, D.C.: U.S. Department of the Interior, 1983), p. 31. See also Daniel S. Papp, "Soviet Non-Fuel Mineral Resources: Surplus or Scarcity?" *Resources Policy*, September 1982, pp. 155–176.

5. U.S. Bureau of Mines, *Minerals Yearbook: Volume 1, Metals and Minerals* (Washington, D.C.: U.S. Department of the Interior, 1981).

6. U.S. Bureau of Mines, *Mineral Commodity Summaries 1984* (Washington, D.C.: U.S. Department of the Interior, 1984), pp. 32 and 116.

7. Leonard L. Fischman, *World Mineral Trends and U.S. Supply Problems*, Resources for the Future Research Paper R–20 (Baltimore: Johns Hopkins University Press, 1980), p. 224.

8. U.S. Bureau of Mines, *The Domestic Supply of Critical Minerals*, p. 30.

9. John J. Schanz, Jr., "Mineral Economics—Perspectives of the Past, Present, and Future." In *Economics of the Mineral Industries* (New York: American Institute of Mining, Metallurgical and Petroleum Engineers, 1976), p. 814.

10. See, for example, "High Grade Codelco Shows the Way in 1982 and Keeps Up the Pressure." *Mining Journal*, 1 April 1983, pp. 215–216.

11. See, for example, *The Global 2000 Report to the President: Volume II, The Technical Report* (Washington, D.C.: U.S. Government Printing Office, 1980), p. 224.

12. R. Bosson and B. Varon, *The Mining Industry and the Developing Countries.* World Bank Research Paper (Oxford, U.K.: Oxford University Press, 1977), p. 32.

13. N. A. Butt and T. J. Atkinson, "Shortfalls in Minerals Investment." *Resources Policy*, December 1982, pp. 261–276.

14. Bosson and Varon, p. 31.

15. Butt and Atkinson, p. 265.

16. U.S. General Accounting Office, *Federal Encouragement of Mining Investment in Developing Countries For Strategic and Critical Minerals Has Been Only Marginally Effective*, GAO/ID-82-38 (Washington, D.C.: U.S. General Accounting Office, 3 September 1982), p. 5.

17. Butt and Atkinson, p. 270.

18. Ibid., p. 265.

19. Raymond F. Mikesell, *Political and Economic Factors Shaping the Investment Climate For Exploration and Development of Nonfuel Minerals* (Washington, D.C.: U.S. State Department, October 1978), p. 80.

20. "Mining Investment 1984." *Engineering and Mining Journal*, January 1984, pp. 33–47.

21. U.S. General Accounting Office, *Federal Encouragement of Mining Investment in Developing Countries For Strategic and Critical Minerals Has Been Only Marginally Effective*, p. 37.

22. Ibid., p. 36.

23. See "Congressmen Protest Loan to Mexican Copper Projects," *American Mining Congress Journal*, 13 April 1983, p. 16, and "Fuss Over Morocco's Phosphate Threat," *Chemical Week*, 28 September 1983, pp. 58–60.

24. U.S. General Accounting Office, *Federal Encouragement of Mining Investment in Developing Countries For Strategic and Critical Minerals Has Been Only Marginally Effective*, p. 26.

25. The discussion of international trade agreements draws heavily upon James I. Walsh, "The Growth of Develop-for-Import Projects," *Resources Policy*, December 1982, pp. 277–284; James I. Walsh, "Is Free Trade in Minerals a Myth?" *Materials and Society* 7:1 (1983), pp. 13–18; and P.C.F. Crowson, "The National Mineral Policies of Germany, France, and Japan," *Mining Magazine*, June 1980, pp. 537–549.

26. Walsh, p. 281.

27. Wilfred Malenbaum, *World Demand for Raw Materials in 1985 and 2000* (New York: McGraw-Hill, 1978), p. 2.

28. U.S. Congress, House Committee on Science and Technology, *Seventh Biennial Conference on National Materials Policy* (Washington, D.C.: U.S. Government Printing Office, March 1983), p. 43.

29. Malenbaum, p. 4.

30. *World Development Report, 1980* (Washington, D.C.: World Bank, 1980), p. 6.

31. *International Minerals/Metals Review—1982* (New York: McGraw-Hill, 1982), p. Soviet Union 2.

32. Theodore Shabad, "The Soviet Minerals Potential and Environmental Constraints." *Materials and Society* 7:1 (1983), pp. 21–25.

33. E. Sabina Brady, "Problems and Issues Involved in the Exploitation of China's Material Resources." *Materials and Society* 7:1 (1983), pp. 39–43.

4
Strategic and Critical Minerals and Materials in the United States

Early U.S. Attempts to Define Strategic and Critical Materials

Origins of the concept of strategic and critical materials can be traced back to World War I. The all-out wartime economy disclosed for the first time the nature and extent of the nation's deficiencies in raw materials. Due to the relatively short duration of U.S. involvement in the war, the raw materials situation was appreciated primarily by only the few specialists acquainted with the problem. Congress, however, was also not inattentive and in amending the National Defense Act in 1920 directed the assistant secretary of the navy and the assistant secretary of war to make plans for industrial mobilization and for procurement of essential raw materials. In response to this mandate, the secretaries of navy and war late in 1922 created the Army and Navy Munitions Board (ANMB) as the agency for coordinating army and navy interests in mobilization and in procuring strategic raw materials. The ANMB undertook a number of studies including a review of a report of the War Industries Board, which had observed that during the war the country was constantly threatened with a shortage in available supply of several essential materials and had recommended that the government devise some system for protecting and stimulating the internal production of these materials.[1]

At that time a "strategic" material denoted a material essential to the conduct of a program of modern warfare. Inasmuch as this definition included virtually every material used in wartime, it came to designate a material whose domestic supply would not be sufficient to meet wartime needs. In attempting to seek a more precise definition, the Army and Navy Munitions Board formulated two different classifications to indicate the seriousness of specific shortages:

Strategic materials are those essential to national defense, for the supply of which in war dependence must be placed in whole, or in substantial part, on sources outside the continental limits of the United States; and for which strict conservation and distribution control measures will be necessary.

Critical materials are those essential to national defense, the procurement problems of which in war would be less difficult than those of strategic materials either because they have a lesser degree of essentiality or are obtainable in more adequate quantities from domestic sources; and for which some degree of conservation and distribution control will be necessary.[2]

Except for a brief period during 1939–1940 when the classification "essential materials" was added, these definitions remained in effect until 1944. The "essential" classification included those materials essential to the national defense for which no procurement problems were anticipated, but that would require surveillance for possible reclassification as events might necessitate.

By 1944 it had become apparent that it was no longer practical to distinguish between the preexisting classifications of strategic and critical materials. Consequently a new definition was approved that combined them. This definition of strategic and critical materials emphasized their essential uses in a war emergency, which would require their "prior provision."

After adopting this one broad definition with emphasis on the relative importance of "prior provision," the ANMB then proceeded to define three major subdivisions, labeled Groups A, B, and C, based on the need for, or feasibility of, stockpiling versus other alternatives. Group A comprised those strategic and critical materials for which stockpiling was deemed the only satisfactory means of insuring an adequate supply for a future emergency. Examples included bauxite, cobalt, industrial diamonds, mercury, nickel, and zinc. Group B contained additional strategic and critical materials for which stockpiling was considered practicable to a limited extent, because adequacy of supply could otherwise be insured either by stimulation of North American production or by partial or complete use of available substitutes. Examples included fluorspar, magnesium, molybdenum, and wool. Group C consisted of strategic and critical materials not then recommended for stockpiling because of difficulties of storage. Examples included cork, iron ore, leather, petroleum, and petroleum products.[3] The listing of materials by groups was not intended to imply that materials in one group were more important to national security than those of another group. The division was entirely on the basis of the need for physical stockpiling or other "prior provision."

Current Ideas and Definitions

The terms "strategic" and "critical" have been defined in various ways since they were linked in 1944. A number of lists of strategic and/or critical materials have been generated at various times, but there is still no formally accepted list, nor is there a single, formally accepted definition in the literature for what constitutes a strategic or critical material.

One difficulty in establishing such a definition is related to the variety of applications a material may have. Even when a particular mineral is critical to one industry, it may not be of importance to another unless its output depends on the other industry, or its use depends on the output of the other industry. As a result, the definition of a truly strategic and critical material will vary not only among industries, but also among enterprises within an industry. From an industrial or individual company's viewpoint, the "degree of criticality" would be gauged in terms of the company's product with respect to the performance of required functions and market role. At this level, the criticality of materials could involve a different set of priorities and policy-influencing factors, such as functionality, product design, product performance, and cost, which appear to assume more immediate and important roles than availability or foreign-source dependency.

At the national level, the current definition incorporated into Public Law 96–41, the Strategic and Critical Materials Stock Piling Act of 1979, reads as follows:

> The term "strategic and critical materials" means materials that (A) would be needed to supply the military, industrial, and essential civilian needs of the United States during a national emergency, and (B) are not found or produced in the United States in sufficient quantities to meet such need.

However, this definition is sufficiently general to leave much to interpretation. The Federal Emergency Management Agency (FEMA) has clarified these terms in its operational definition used to formulate national stockpile policy and planning guidance. It defines strategic as the relative "availability" of a material and critical as its "essentiality."[4]

A frequently used indicator of potential availability is the estimated percentage of U.S. consumption that is satisfied by imported supplies. However, one study found that such an indicator is simplistic and often misleading in that it fails to take into account the relative importance of the mineral to the U.S. economy and the relative uncertainty in the future supply.[5] Another study suggests that continuing long-term analysis and planning to assure the future availability of minerals and materials should begin with a clear definition of the terms "strategic" and "critical." In this regard the report states:

> "Strategic" should relate to the probability of a supply disruption or sharp price increase in a given nonfuel mineral or material market and its expected duration, while "critical" should relate to the adverse impact that would occur if supplies are disrupted or prices are sharply increased. Clarifying these terms would reduce the number of markets deemed strategic and critical, thereby focusing attention on those where the United States is most vulnerable.[6]

Still another study has suggested a somewhat broader definition to encompass short-term disruptions in price and availability:

> Critical materials were once characterized by the level of U.S. dependence on imports, the importance of the commodities to the U.S. economy, and the likelihood that supplies might be interrupted. It now seems more appropriate to identify critical materials by the volatility of international markets, the effects of price and supply variations on other sectors of the economy, and the likelihood that uncontrollable events (war, drought, embargo, etc.) could

seriously disrupt markets. Practically, this requires the addition of many agricultural commodities to the list of critical raw materials, as well as some domestically produced minerals such as copper.[7]

The multitude of views on what constitutes a strategic and/or critical material suggests that not only are the definitions unclear in general, but that the distinction between the terms is also unclear. Much as some distinctions between peace and limited war have become blurred, the roles of strategic and critical materials in industrial uses and in national defense now appear to overlap. Extended international contests among competing political and economic philosophies are characterized by varying degrees of economic warfare and cold war, as well as by occasional limited hostilities of shorter term. In the view of one expert:

> The security of industrialized democratic societies depends in large measure not only upon military strength in being but also upon strong economies that provide maximum employment, production, and purchasing power. Such economies facilitate development of sophisticated military material and provide a mobilization base with substantial elements capable of being rapidly converted to defense-supporting production. Viewed in this context, *adequate supplies of virtually every known material are a strategic necessity.*[8]

In this view, strategic and critical materials would be defined in the very broadest sense. In the absence of a single accepted definition, other approaches to identifying the strategic and critical nature of materials have developed. The vulnerability index concept is one such method.

The Vulnerability Index Concept

Attempts to determine the criticality of materials to the U.S. economy have included assessments based on methods of ranking or indexing. The purpose of indexing is to target those materials of greatest concern and provide a focus for policy considerations. Generally, indexing models are set up so that those minerals that rank highest on the index have the greatest expected cost of disruption and thus are most deserving of policy attention.

One pilot study that attempted to determine the feasibility of developing a Critical Minerals Index (CMI) for the United States began by dividing the proposed CMI into two components, which were evaluated separately and then combined in a composite index.[9] The first component of the CMI was termed the Mineral Disruption Index, which measures the likelihood that a mineral market will be in a state of disruption during each year of a specified future time period. A number of political and economic factors determine the likelihood of a market disruption. Examples of market-disrupting events and their causative factors include:

- *Collusive price agreements* caused by producers exercising supply restriction through either a formal or informal cartel. These disruptions can be of relatively long duration.

- *Shift in demand* due to changes in life-styles and standards of living, income increases, a shift from a substitute, or inventory accumulation. The shift in demand could cause spot or cyclical shortages if the reaction in prices and supply does not occur with adequate speed.

- *Embargoes* undertaken for political reasons and resulting in the total or partial cessation of imports of nonfuel mineral supplies to the United States or its allies.

- *Labor strife* involving internal union conflicts, strikes, lockouts, labor-government relations, or labor–foreign investor relations, and varying in duration.

- *Transportation bottlenecks* occurring as a result of conflict along transportation routes, poor transportation networks, system overload, restriction of access routes, and other factors.

- *Violent conflict* occurring within producer countries or between producers and consumers, competitive producing countries, or producers and any other countries. It can take the form of local rebellion, regional war, riots, border skirmishes, and sabotage.[10]

Although a future market-disrupting event cannot be predicted with certainty, experts in the field were asked to make judgments on a mineral-by-mineral basis which were then quantified into an index number. The disruption index, if assessed correctly, should yield indications of when future supply problems might occur.

The second component of the CMI was the Mineral Cost Index. To establish priorities for policy attention, it is important to predict the cost that might be imposed upon the economy if a disruption should occur. At least eight factors were identified that influence the magnitude of the cost likely to result for the United States from a disruption in the import market. These factors are listed in Table 4.1. After each of the eight factors has been evaluated, a supply demand model can be used to estimate the range of costs likely to arise.

Combining the disruption and cost indexes produces the Critical Minerals Index. The CMI value of each mineral represents the expected cost to the economy, reflecting both cost and probability that a disruption will occur. However, in exercises such as this, a single numerical best estimate is but one point in an entire range of possibilities. In a worst case situation, maximum costs could range from ten to one hundred times the expected costs.[11] Obviously, caution must be exercised in attempting to implement policies and programs based on a CMI indication of costs. An incomplete or incorrect weighting of possible future disruptive events could lead to a waste of resources if policies and programs are implemented that represent

Table 4.1 Factors Influencing the Magnitude of Cost of a Market
Disruption for Imported Supplies

Factor	Influence
1. Magnitude and duration of disruption	The greater the portion of an imported supply lost and the longer it is lost, the greater the cost to the U.S. economy.
2. Total annual U.S. demand for the mineral	Loss of some portion of the supply will cause the price of the remaining supply to rise. The more units consumed at the higher price, the greater the cost to the economy.
3. Availability of alternative sources of supply of the disrupted mineral; e.g., additional sources of foreign production, private inventories, and government stockpiles	Alternate sources, even when more costly than sources prior to the disruption, may significantly reduce the amount by which prices rise during the disruption and, thus, may reduce the total cost to the economy.
4. Time required to produce and/or deliver additional supply from alternative sources	The longer the delivery time for a new supply, the more slowly disrupted prices can be reduced, and the higher the cost to the economy.
5. Availability of other minerals that can be used by consumers as substitutes for the disrupted mineral	Same type of influence as in No. 3 above, except that this influence works through the demand side of the market.
6. Time required to adapt consuming technologies to use of substitute materials	Same type of influence as in No. 4 above, working through the demand side of the market.
7. Expectations about the future by decision makers who control potential alternative sources of supply	If decision makers face a significant risk that future prices may not cover the cost of developing new sources, a supply from the alternative sources will not be forthcoming and the cost to the economy may be greater (e.g., the existence of a suppliers' cartel).
8. Expectations about the future by decision makers responsible for investments to adapt consuming technologies for substitute minerals	Same type of influence as in No. 7 above, except that this influence works through the demand side of the market.

Source: Office of Minerals Policy and Research Analysis, Department of
the Interior, Developing a Critical Minerals Index: A Pilot Study
(Washington, D.C.: U.S. Department of the Interior, July 1979), p. 12.

Table 4.2 U.S. Army War College Determination of the Most Strategic
Materials for the United States

Material	Vulnerability Index[a]	Major Supplier Countries
Chromium	34	USSR, Rep. of South Africa
Platinum metals	32	USSR, Rep. of South Africa
Tungsten	27	Canada, Peru
Manganese	23	Brazil, Gabon
Aluminum	22	Jamaica, Canada
Titanium	20	Australia, Canada
Cobalt	20	Zaire, Canada
Tantalum	16	Zaire, Brazil, Canada
Nickel	14	Canada, Norway
Mercury	11	Canada, Mexico, Spain
Tin	6	Malaysia, Thailand

a. Higher number indicates greater vulnerability.

Source: U.S. Army War College, Strategic Studies Group. In Bohdan O.
Szuprowicz, How to Avoid Strategic Materials Shortages (New York: John
Wiley and Sons, 1981), p. 21.

"overkill" in solution. On the other hand, lesser programs and policies
pursued with a false sense of security could provide too little protection
in the event of a significant market disruption.

Another process to determine the vulnerability index of imported materials
was explored by the U.S. Army War College. The War College Strategic
Studies Group used a method of "critical danger point indicators," from
which the group found eleven minerals to be highly important for defense
and industry (Table 4.2). A list of critical danger point indicators might
include lack of domestic reserves and resources, lack of substitutes, little
opportunity for recycling, too small a number of foreign suppliers, vulnerable
transport network, insecure or hostile foreign suppliers, and intensive use
in critical applications, among others.

Inevitably there are some who have suggested a refinement to this
process.[12] Once the critical factors have been identified, a number of events
and conditions could trigger a supply disruption. Examples of such events
and conditions conducive to a crisis would include wars, revolutions, civil
unrest, cartels, strikes, labor supply and cost, terrorism, new regulations,
nationalism, etc. The occurrence of such events would modify the weighting
of the critical factors and consequently indicate an improvement or worsening
of supply vulnerability. The vulnerability index would then reflect the
weighting of the critical danger points according to the conditions conducive
to crisis.

West Germany has also attempted to develop a "political risk factor
index." The German approach has been to develop a risk factor ranging
from a low risk of 100 to a high risk of 500 for a number of critical
materials. The German study found that the following materials were
significant in their political risk index:[13]

Material	Index
Chromium	370
Manganese	300
Asbestos	295
Tungsten	290
Cobalt	280
Vanadium	280
Titanium	270
Platinum	270
Aluminum	230
Nickel	225
Molybdenum	225
Copper	220
Tin	215
Lead	190
Zinc	180

The most difficult task in developing a vulnerability index is the assignment of meaningful numerical values to the various critical factors affecting supply. Some are fairly easy to quantify, such as import dependence, but others such as the ideology of foreign suppliers are not. The weight given various factors also depends on the time frame of the index—whether it is intended for long-range or short-range predictions and concerns. For example, long-range evaluations would consider resource potential and future trends, whereas short-term projections would consider only reserves and events likely to occur as an immediate result of existing conditions. Obviously shorter term projections are likely to be of greater accuracy than longer range ones, but are of more limited use in formulating long-term policy.

The vulnerability index concept can find application other than at the national level. Industries or individual corporations can construct such indexes for strategic planning purposes. With the availability of computers today, data bases can be stored electronically and easily updated. Complex risk assessment models with many variables can be readily calculated. A system of this nature, however, is only as good as the information it contains. For this reason a numerical index may appear to convey more precise information than it is based upon. Decision makers are still left with evaluating criteria for establishing the criticality and strategic nature of materials.

Criteria for Establishing Criticality and Strategic Nature

As pointed out in one study, "The first step in measuring the magnitude of potential U.S. vulnerability in a given market is to establish definitive strategic and critical criteria."[14] In a December 1980 report on a workshop on U.S. vulnerability to disruption of imported materials, experts on potential availability problems identified sixteen criteria that could be quantified to some degree:[15]

1. Number of sources of supply and their location.
2. Total U.S. consumption from overseas sources of supply.
3. Degree of importance to the U.S. economy.
4. Ease with which industry can substitute for the material or service.
5. Ease with which the material can be recovered and recycled.
6. Rate of increase in consumption.
7. Need for the material by the military for national defense.
8. Dollar amount used by the United States.
9. Importance to the economies of the nation's allies.
10. Extent of worldwide competition for dwindling supplies.
11. Length of time required to expand sources of supply.
12. Sudden shock impact of interruption of supply.
13. Time required for substitution.
14. Probability of an interruption, and the length of time likely to be involved.
15. Extent to which the material is used as a catalyst in a chemical process, i.e., the leverage factor.
16. Political and economic aspects of supply.

Some of the listed criteria concern the criticality of the material. Among the criteria of this nature are the degree of importance to the U.S. economy, the ease with which industry can substitute or recycle, military need, and time requirements for substitution. Other criteria are primarily of strategic concern, such as the number of sources of supply and their location, the amount of U.S. consumption from overseas sources, the extent of worldwide competition for supplies, and the political and economic aspects of supply.

A critical need must, at the very least, reflect that prolonged supply interruption would significantly compromise the nation's capacity to defend itself from enemy attack. A critical need also implies that beyond this primary military consideration, continued lack of the material would soon exert a paralyzing effect upon basic industries essential to the nation's economic well-being, as well as essential to the maintenance of a high level of back-up defense capability. These two criteria typically imply catastrophic consequences to the nation if the material were to become unavailable. Examples of heavily imported materials frequently cited as meeting these criteria are chromium and manganese, essential to the production of stainless steel, and cobalt, essential to the production of aerospace hardware.

Beyond the essential need in both defense and basic industry, limited potential for substitution is a third criterion of criticality. Potential substitutes are available for many materials. Not infrequently, a material of choice has become the preferred material for relatively minor reasons, for example, a temporary price advantage or marginal consumer appeal. In such instances, a substitute material could, if necessary, be used with minimum technological disruption and without undue economic hardship. In most cases, however, the current material of choice has been selected on the basis of long-term availability, price, and desired chemical or physical properties. This is particularly true for critical military and aerospace applications. Only rarely can a substitute material be found that is not significantly inferior in one or more respects. Typically, employment of the substitute may involve considerably increased expense and some degree of degradation of properties or performance, or of both. An example of such a substitution is the use of nickel instead of cobalt in superalloys.

Some applications exist that virtually cannot be met by any material except the current material of choice. Although such applications are relatively rare, the materials for them can legitimately be considered indispensable. Examples of such materials include chromium in high-strength steels and high-temperature, corrosion-resistant superalloys; manganese in stainless steel; and tantalum for capacitors in jet-engine control systems, or in carbides for metal-working machinery and tools.

Finally, the time needed to develop, test, and implement the use of a substitute is an important consideration. In a national emergency, efforts directed toward developing substitutes would take resources away from other important needs and could only pay off if the emergency were of sufficient duration to allow adequate development time.

Strategic factors such as (1) the political and economic stability of major foreign suppliers, (2) concentration of production and/or processing capacity in one or several foreign countries, (3) the geographic proximity of foreign suppliers to the United States, and (4) the feasibility of developing significant domestic production must be considered in estimating the probability of a supply disruption or sharp price increase of a particular mineral.

The potential for unexpected government changes in supplier countries must be understood and monitored on a continuing basis. State monopolies are now in operation in many developing countries and are controlling the production and distribution of raw materials. Often a sudden change in government is accompanied by the formation of a new ministry or state agency responsible for the production of all minerals in a country. New trading relations may suddenly be preferred. Such changes can significantly affect the supply of raw materials.

It is almost axiomatic that the fewer the existing sources of supply for a needed industrial material, the greater the concern expressed over its potential unavailability. As is frequently the case, if these few sources also represent relatively new nations currently exploring ways to establish their political, economic, and military security, then these expressions of concern often approach alarm.

Recent history has shown that such concerns are not without foundation. For example, difficulties experienced in cobalt production from Zaire, which alone possesses almost 30 percent of the world's known reserves, contributed to supply and demand imbalances in the late 1970s, as well as to a dramatic increase in price. The quadrupling of cobalt prices after the 1977 invasion of Zaire's Shaba province demonstrates that importers' perceptions of vulnerability can have a substantial impact on the conditions of international trade. It is now known that despite expectations that supply shortages would develop as a result of the invasion, Zaire actually increased its production of cobalt in 1977. Other supply factors included the upward revision of U.S. stockpile goals, which temporarily led to a cessation of stockpile sales of cobalt. Thus, consumers' perceptions rather than actual production supply problems were the principal factors in bidding up prices. Further, when a major fraction of the world's known reserves of any important industrial material is controlled or held by relatively few nations, the current global climate of resources competition almost necessarily raises the question of feasibility of formation of an OPEC-like cartel for that material. Again consumer perceptions may be more critical than actual market control that such organizations may gain.

Although lack of multiplicity of supplier nations is most often the object of primary concern to those who are worried about continuity of supply, it should by no means be the only—nor necessarily the major—cause for concern. For example, legitimate concern also can be expressed over the need to transport large tonnages of certain materials from distant supplier nations by sea. Two obvious examples are manganese ore, more than 90 percent of which is imported from Gabon, Australia, the Republic of South Africa, and Brazil; and ferromanganese, of which 69 percent is imported from the Republic of South Africa and France (for the latter, from ore originating elsewhere). More than 1.1 million short tons of these two materials combined were used in the United States in 1983; essentially all would have been imported had it not been for material released from the National Defense Stockpile (approximately 90,000 short tons of manganese ore).[16] Clearly, great difficulty would be experienced in any attempt to transport such huge quantities of material by air, if sea lanes should become blocked during a wartime emergency.

Considerations such as the above often promote interest in shifting to imports from nations geographically closer to the United States, particularly Canada and Mexico. For example, the import level of another high-volume material, fluorspar, now amounts to almost 760,000 short tons per year, of which Mexico currently provides about 58 percent.[17] Imports of fluorspar from such distant nations as China, Italy, and the Republic of South Africa could be reduced or possibly eliminated by increasing imports from Mexico and promoting increased domestic production of phosphate rock, which contains fluorine that could be recovered as a by-product.

The lack of adequate domestic resources is an obvious strategic criterion. Within the context of the availability of domestic materials resources, "lack" appears to be a highly relative term. Generally it has been taken to mean that no significant domestic resources of a material are known to exist, and little or no geological evidence suggests that such domestic resources are likely to be found. Even so, vast areas of the United States—and especially areas of certain western states and Alaska—remain insufficiently explored to determine definitely the presence or absence of minerals resources. Until an adequate minerals assessment of these lands has been made, the question of presence or absence of domestic resources necessarily must remain open.

"Lack" also has been taken to mean that although significant domestic deposits of the material may be known to exist, they are not believed to be sufficiently extensive in quantity or quality to warrant development. Further, they may exist in such remote, inaccessible locations as to preclude their economic extraction under foreseeable circumstances. Again, neither quantity nor concentration can be determined definitively without resorting to such advanced stages of exploration as the taking of drill core samples. Additionally, new developments in minerals extraction and processing technology always leave open the possibility of economic utilization of ores having progressively lower concentrations; indeed, such new developments have been the traditional experience of the U.S. mining industry. Likewise, inaccessibility is also relative and subject to reassessment as conditions change. During a long-term emergency, for example, economic considerations could become secondary in importance in assessing the development of these kinds of domestic resources.

In another sense, "lack of availability" places primary emphasis upon the word "availability"; that is, resources of a material may exist but may not be available for exploitation. This situation may occur when the area in which the resources are located has been set aside for some other purpose, for example, a national forest, park, or wilderness area. Such considerations are, of course, always subject to change depending upon congressional response to changes in the public's outlook and priorities.

Finally, "lack" may be used simply to denote "not enough"; that is, although significant domestic resources of the material may exist and be under development, the output, for whatever reasons, still remains—and will remain after further development—inadequate to satisfy U.S. demand.

Thus, depending upon the personal outlook of the expert, the three "critical" and four "strategic" criteria discussed in this section can be used to measure the degree of strategic and critical nature, or import vulnerability, of each material. To qualify as a material for which an import vulnerability exists, the material should satisfy several if not all of these criteria. Those materials that appear to satisfy the criteria certainly include bauxite (aluminum), chromium, cobalt, columbium, manganese, the platinum-group metals, and tantalum. These materials will be discussed in the context of the criteria in the following section.

Materials of Particular Concern

Keeping in mind the view that "adequate supplies of virtually every known material are a strategic necessity"[18] but that concern centers on those materials deemed strategic and critical for National Defense Stockpile purposes, one can now consider only those seven materials listed above for which the industrial health and defense of the United States are most vulnerable to potential supply disruptions. In this context, all seven materials appear to meet to a significant degree all of the seven criteria discussed previously as a test of criticality and strategic nature, and of U.S. import vulnerability. That is, they are all essential to the military and industrial economy, and they lack substitutes, domestic supply, and multiple and stable sources; they also involve vulnerable transportation. Although a case could be made for adding other materials to this restricted list or for deleting some of these seven, they appear to be the ones attracting the greatest amount of concerned attention.

Bauxite/Aluminum

Aluminum is continuously essential to the nation's economy. The output of primary aluminum metal in the United States in 1983 was valued at over $5.7 billion. About 25,000 firms in the United States engage in processing and fabricating aluminum products. From a 1981 base, a year of low apparent metal consumption, domestic consumption of aluminum is expected to increase by 6.7 percent annually through 1990. Aluminum's high strength-to-weight ratio makes it extremely important to the transportation industry, in particular to aircraft production, which accounts for about 10 percent of the transportation market.

The production of aluminum metal is the third step in a process that begins with bauxite or other ore, continues with the smelting of bauxite into alumina (doubling the aluminum content), and ends with refining the alumina into metal. Increasingly, bauxite-producing countries are moving to the second stage of the process and are exporting larger amounts of alumina. This shift shows up in U.S. imports as increased alumina imports, with bauxite imports remaining fairly level.

The United States imports over 90 percent of the raw materials needed to make aluminum. The principal exporting countries to the United States are Guinea, Australia, Jamaica, and Surinam. Recently, exports from Guinea and Australia have been increasing while those from Jamaica and Surinam have declined. Most of the bauxite exported to the United States is from Jamaica, Guinea, and Surinam, and most of the alumina from Australia and Jamaica. Brazil, with a large bauxite reserve base, is also likely to become a major exporter to the United States.

Exporting countries tend to maintain established trade patterns with importing countries over long periods of time, due largely to their ties with the major aluminum firms that developed the deposits as a source of their raw materials. Domestic bauxite resources, as an alternative, are small relative to U.S. consumption, and the domestic ore is high in silica, making it difficult to process. The principal U.S. bauxite deposits are in central Arkansas, with total resources estimated at 40 million long tons. However, a large portion of these resources may be highly or prohibitively costly to mine because of location, field size, stripping ratio, etc.[19] Another 2 or 3 million tons of bauxite suitable for refractory and chemical uses are present in Alabama and Georgia. More than 90 percent of the bauxite mined in the United States is by open pit, and in the event of a national emergency, a three- or fourfold increase in domestic production might be achieved through further shifts and the addition of surface mining equipment. Yet this step could only reduce import dependency from over 90 percent to around 70 percent.

Although bauxite is currently the principal ore of aluminum, other and lower grade domestic sources of aluminum could be mined, for example, clays, anorthosite, and alunite. The United States has large resources of such materials and could meet its aluminum needs from them if the technology were developed and the higher cost were acceptable. However, some four to seven years would be required to select a process and design, build, and test the facilities to produce alumina from such materials on an industrial scale.[20]

An additional concern is related to the energy-intensive nature of aluminum production and the competing needs for electric power in the United States. This problem has caused the domestic aluminum industry to look toward smelter construction on foreign soil, where raw materials and energy are available and less expensive. On the one hand, this move is a solution; on the other, it exacerbates the import and industrial problem.

Substitutes for aluminum in some of its applications include copper, steel, wood, zinc, magnesium, titanium, and plastics. However, substitutes generally involve major modifications in equipment or processes that require time to develop and must offer significant economic or performance advantages if they are to be undertaken in the absence of a national emergency. One study has suggested that unless all materials concurrently become in short supply, aluminum supply shortages would not be critical.[21] Yet a national emergency could meet that otherwise unlikely condition.

Chromium

Chromium is one of the elements most essential to modern industrial needs. It is used as an alloy to increase hardness and impact strength in steel, and to provide resistance to oxidation, corrosion, wear, and galling. The combination of mechanical and chemical properties enhanced by chromium makes these steels highly versatile in a wide range of products, including stainless steel, tool and alloy steels, and special-purpose alloys.

There is no known substitute for chromium in stainless steel. A wide variety of industrial materials can substitute for stainless steel, but at a sacrifice in price and performance. In special alloys, nickel, columbium, vanadium, cobalt, or molybdenum can be substituted for chromium in certain applications, but most of these materials are also strategic and critical.

Domestic mine production ceased in 1961, except for 1976 when a previously closed mine was temporarily rehabilitated and operated. Domestic chromite resources are limited and of low grade. Most of these are located in the Stillwater Complex of Montana, with additional but smaller deposits in Oregon and northern California. There has been some interest in trying to develop a chromite deposit in Grant County, Oregon, but the economics of the prospect have been considered doubtful.[22] Even under conditions of a national emergency, domestic production of chromium could supply only a small fraction of U.S. requirements. In addition, the cost of developing and producing for most of these deposits would be three to five times as great as the economic cost under normal conditions.

The greatest concern over the vulnerability of chromium supplies lies in the fact that the world's major chromium deposits are concentrated in southern Africa—primarily in the Republic of South Africa and Zimbabwe—and in the USSR. The Bushveld Complex of South Africa contains the largest known chromium deposit in the world. However, the security of supply lines from southern Africa has traditionally been a subject of concern, recently aggravated by concern over Soviet intervention in the struggles for majority rule and Soviet support for political factions in the region. One study concluded that the United States is strategically more vulnerable to a long-term chromium embargo than to an embargo of any other natural resource including petroleum.[23]

Cobalt

Cobalt is considered critical to the United States because of its many military and essential industrial uses. Cobalt alloys are used in jet engines to withstand high temperatures, as a binder in cemented carbides for metal cutting, in the hard facing of mining and drilling tools, in forming dies and rolls in the steel industry, and as a desulfurizing catalyst in refining petroleum.

The basic problem regarding cobalt is an essentially complete U.S. dependence on foreign supply—and that largely from one country, Zaire. Although attempts are being made to diversify supply sources, higher grade deposits are concentrated in only a few areas of the world. Complicating the matter is the fact that cobalt is produced primarily as a by-product of the mining of other metals, primarily copper and nickel; thus its production is tied to that of those primary metals.

There is no cobalt mining in the United States today. A small amount of cobalt had been recovered from domestic ores prior to the 1970s. The largest cobalt-mining district in the United States has been the Blackbird district of Lehmi County, Idaho. The Blackbird mine was relatively rare in that cobalt was mined as the principal metal. Recent plans to reopen the mine have been shelved as a result of the return of cobalt prices to mid-1970s levels. Further, unless a cobalt-processing facility were built the ore would have to be shipped overseas for processing. Cobalt has also been produced as a by-product from copper-nickel ores near Fredericktown, Missouri (closed in 1961), and from iron ore near Cornwall, Pennsylvania (closed in 1971). A firm planned to reopen the Missouri mine but it, too, canceled those plans with the recent drop in cobalt prices. Even if these deposits were reopened, the United States would still be largely import-dependent for cobalt, as production rates would not be sufficient to satisfy the annual domestic consumption.

Nickel can be substituted for cobalt in some uses, with little deterioration in performance. However, in many critical applications, performance might suffer without cobalt alloys. Efforts are underway to develop nickel and ceramic substitutes for cobalt in such critical applications, but several years may be required to successfully produce the substitutes—if at all—and carry out tests for critical military applications. There has also been some success in lowering the cobalt content of some alloys without apparent degradation in performance.

A high degree of concern over the vulnerability of the United States in cobalt supply arises over the stability of the primary cobalt-producing region in southern Africa. Unrest that contributed to sharp price increases in recent years has been attributed in part to Soviet influences. Whether the current moderation in the price of cobalt will be maintained over the longer term is yet to be seen.

Columbium (Niobium)

Columbium is an essential element in superalloys used in jet and turbine engines. It also has broad application as an alloying element in specialty steels in such uses as girders, beams, pipelines, industrial machinery, ship's plate, railroad equipment, and automobiles. Columbium carbide has important uses in machine-cutting tools. Other potential uses include cryogenic applications.

The United States has no columbium reserves and relies essentially on imports. Given a lead time of several years, in a national emergency the United States could develop adequate low-grade resources in Colorado and Idaho to become self-sufficient in columbium for a limited period of time, but these resources would soon become exhausted.[24] Moreover, these deposits would be substantially more expensive to produce than the cost of imports from foreign sources.

Recycling currently is insignificant. Recovery of columbium from secondary sources presents technological and logistical problems that will increase as uses diversify and new alloys are developed.

The United States consumes about one-fourth of the world's columbium production. Nearly three-fourths of the U.S. imports are from Brazil, primarily in the form of concentrates, ferrocolumbium, and other columbium-bearing materials. The company exploiting this source in Brazil is integrating more production into ferrocolumbium and pure columbium oxide, which will strengthen its near-monopoly position in the world market.[25] Canada and Thailand are also important suppliers. Other foreign sources include Nigeria, Malaysia, and Zaire. Excluding Eastern Europe and the USSR, Brazil possesses over 90 percent of the rest of the world's reserve base of columbium, with 8 billion pounds of contained columbium. The USSR has resources estimated (with questionable certainty) at 7 billion pounds, much of which is probably of lower grade than would be economically recoverable in a free market. Thus, Brazil is the long-term supplier of strategic importance to the United States for columbium.

Manganese

Manganese is a critical raw material for the steel industry, which is the base upon which a substantial portion of the U.S. economy depends. The importance of manganese in steel making derives primarily from its deoxidizing, desulfurizing, and conditioning properties. In alloys it imparts strength, toughness, hardness, and hardenability to steel, and it is also alloyed with aluminum, magnesium, and copper for various special parts or structures such as ship propellers.

The United States has no manganese reserve base today and is dependent almost entirely on imports. Recycling is insignificant. Identified domestic manganese resouces are estimated to contain about 74 million tons of manganese, located in the Artillery Mountains, Arizona; San Juan Mountains, Colorado; Aroostook County, Maine; and near Batesville, Arkansas. Metallurgical and/or mining problems are inherent in recovering manganese from all these low-grade deposits, but for most of them research has indicated that the problems are surmountable, although at varying degrees of increased cost depending on the deposit.[26] A lead time of at least three years, probably more, would be necessary to develop any significant production from these domestic resources.[27] Based on current and projected prices and on the low quality of the domestic resources, the United States will continue to be import-dependent for manganese in the foreseeable future.

Imports include both manganese ore (typically 35 to 54 percent manganese) and ferromanganese (74 to 95 percent manganese) produced in either blast or electric furnaces. Most of these U.S. imports originate in Gabon, Brazil, the Republic of South Africa, and Australia. The Republic of South Africa and the USSR together have more than 80 percent of the world's manganese resources.

Of strategic concern is the fact that the United States depends on only a few nations for most of its manganese. These same nations are increasing their ferromanganese production, so that the United States is importing increasing amounts of processed manganese while its domestic ferromanganese industry declines. In the event of a supply disruption, mainly manganese ore, if any, would be available from other suppliers. Consequently, with a declining ferromanganese industry, the United States would be hard pressed to utilize the ore.[28] Of critical concern is the fact that there is no practical substitute for manganese in steel making.

The Platinum-Group Metals

Platinum and five other closely related metals constitute the platinum group; the other five are palladium, rhodium, iridium, ruthenium, and osmium. They are among the scarcest of metallic elements but have become nearly indispensable to modern industry because of their unusual physical and chemical properties. Platinum-group metals are used primarily in two types of applications: first, as catalysts in the automotive industry, chemical industry, and petroleum refining; and second, as corrosion-resistant materials in a wide variety of industries including the medical, electronic, chemical, and glass-making industries.

Nearly 90 percent of the platinum consumed in the United States is from newly mined and imported material; most of the rest is from recycled metal. Thus, the United States is virtually 100 percent import-dependent for new supplies of platinum-group metals. Domestic mining provides less than 1 percent of the nation's demand for platinum metals. Domestic reserves are small, although there are fairly large resources, primarily in the Stillwater Complex of Montana. Several domestic firms have conducted exploration and evaluation of platinum-group metals in this area.

Domestic mine production could not be increased quickly if foreign supplies were cut off. Before such new U.S. sources of platinum metals could be brought to the point of producing precious-metal concentrates, an entire mining and smelting operation would have to be built, a complex undertaking that could not be achieved under normal circumstances in less than several years.[29] Furthermore, in the case of the Stillwater Complex, difficult decisions would have to be made concerning the effects of such an operation on an unspoiled wilderness area. Even if domestic production could be developed, it would not be likely to satisfy domestic demand. Refinery capacity would also have to be increased, because most platinum-group imports are refined metal in unwrought or semifabricated form.

Of strategic concern is the large concentration of the world's platinum reserves in two countries, the USSR and the Republic of South Africa. The only other major platinum-group producing country is Canada, but its output is considerably less, amounting only to about 6 percent of world mine production.

In the event of a national emergency, part of the domestic consumption could be redirected into essential needs, and recycling could help extend supplies because most uses of platinum-group metals are nondissipative. Substitutes could entail replacement by other materials for platinum-group products or replacement by other elements in alloys. In general it is easier to substitute metals of the platinum group for one another than to use alternative materials. Alternative materials can include tungsten, gold, nickel, silver, and silicon carbide in electrical uses, and rare-earth elements, nickel, molybdenum, tungsten, chromium, cobalt, vanadium, and silver in catalysts. In certain uses where corrosion resistance is crucial, stainless steel or ceramics can be substituted, but generally at the cost of shorter useful life or some contamination of the product. Furthermore, stainless steel requires chromium, which comes from source areas subject to the same geopolitical disruptions as the platinum-group metals.

Tantalum

Tantalum has unique electrical, chemical, and physical properties that are of great importance in electronic components, metal-working machinery, nuclear reactor components, and aerospace applications. The tantalum capacitor has become the standard for reliable performance in electronic systems.

The United States is almost completely import-dependent for tantalum, as recycling is difficult and provides only 3 percent of the supply. Import sources include Thailand, Canada, Malaysia, Brazil, Zaire, and Australia. The materials imported are primarily tantalum concentrates and tantalum-containing tin slags. Although the world reserve base for tantalum is large relative to current consumption, political and social unrest in certain source countries could cause supply interruptions. Currently the United States consumes about 60 percent of the world's annual tantalum production. Military and aerospace uses account for about 25 percent of the nation's tantalum consumption, and this figure would increase to 50 percent in a national emergency.[30]

Domestic production of tantalum raw materials ceased in 1959. Domestic resources of tantalum occur in placer deposits in Bear Valley and Dismal Swamp, Idaho. The tantalum content of these deposits is low, and it is not likely to be recovered commercially. However, in an emergency these sources could supply national needs, given sufficient time.[31] Other states with known low-grade deposits of tantalum-containing minerals are Arizona, Colorado, Maine, North and South Carolina, South Dakota, Utah, New Mexico, and Alaska.

In most cases substitutions for tantalum can be made only at substantial sacrifice in performance or cost. Aluminum and ceramic capacitors are competitive in less demanding applications. Tungsten, titanium, and columbium carbides can substitute for tantalum carbide in cutting tools. However, in an emergency, maintaining adequate supplies of these strategic and critical materials would also be likely to present problems. Substitutes in other applications include tungsten and rhenium in high-temperature uses, and glass, titanium, zirconium, columbium, and platinum in corrosion-resistant equipment.

Summary of Supply Vulnerability

The seven strategic and critical metals discussed above clearly have differing degrees of supply vulnerability. In a national emergency, it would appear that supplies of chromium, manganese, cobalt, and the platinum-group metals would be most vulnerable. Bauxite is of slightly less concern depending on the circumstances, because it comes from a number of producing countries closer to home and because much of the bauxite production and processing has been financially tied to U.S. firms.

Given sufficient time, which an adequate stockpile could offer, the United States could possibly supply its own needs for tantalum. In the case of columbium, domestic needs could possibly be met from domestic production for a limited period of time. However, in each of these cases, somewhat draconian measures would be involved in the rapid start-up and increase in domestic production, which would occur at the expense of other sectors of the economy. A stockpile adequate to cover the needed lead times would also be required. These lead times probably would exceed three years—the current assumed minimum duration of a national emergency for stockpile planning purposes.

An additional factor is the possibility of increasing supplies of some of these materials from nations contiguous to the United States—e.g., Canada and Mexico. Although this possibility would not reduce import dependency, it would reduce transport vulnerability in the event of an emergency. However, it would also entail the development of additional capacity in those nations, which would necessitate political decisions as well as assurances of a continued export market.

Notes

1. Report of the War Industries Board, in Department of Social Sciences, *Raw Materials in War and Peace* (West Point, N.Y.: United States Military Academy, 1947), 221 pp.
2. Ibid., p. 87.
3. Army and Navy Munitions Board, *Circular 4* (Washington, D.C.: 14 January 1946).
4. U.S. General Accounting Office, *Actions Needed to Promote A Stable Supply of Strategic and Critical Minerals and Materials*, GAO/EMD-82-69 (Washington, D.C.: U.S. General Accounting Office, 3 June 1982), p. 6.
5. Office of Minerals Policy and Research Analysis, Department of the Interior, *Developing a Critical Minerals Index: A Pilot Study* (Washington, D.C.: U.S. Department of the Interior, July 1979), pp. 1–2.
6. U.S. General Accounting Office, *Actions Needed to Promote A Stable Supply of Strategic and Critical Minerals and Materials*, p. 6.
7. U.S. Congress, Congressional Budget Office, *U.S. Raw Materials Policy: Problems and Possible Solutions* (Washington, D.C.: U.S. Government Printing Office, December 1976), p. 17.
8. John D. Morgan, Jr., "Strategic Materials Overview." In *A Congressional Handbook on U.S. Materials Import Dependency/Vulnerability*, House Committee on Banking, Finance and Urban Affairs, Subcommittee on Economic Stabilization (Washington, D.C.: U.S. Government Printing Office, September 1981), p. 29. The italics are the original author's.
9. Office of Minerals Policy and Research Analysis, *Developing a Critical Minerals Index*.
10. Ibid., pp. 7–8.
11. Ibid., p. 18.
12. Bohdan O. Szuprowicz, *How to Avoid Strategic Materials Shortages* (New York: John Wiley and Sons, 1981), pp. 273–295.
13. Ibid., p. 286.
14. U.S. General Accounting Office, *Actions Needed to Promote A Stable Supply of Strategic and Critical Minerals and Materials*, p. 7.
15. U.S. Congress, House Committee on Science and Technology, *Emerging Issues in Science and Technology: A Compilation of Reports on CRS Workshops* (Washington, D.C.: U.S. Government Printing Office, December 1980), pp. 17–18.
16. U.S. Bureau of Mines, *Mineral Commodity Summaries 1984* (Washington, D.C.: U.S. Department of the Interior, 1984), p. 96.
17. Ibid., p. 50.
18. Morgan, p. 29.
19. Charles River Associates, Inc., *Policy Implications of Producer Country Supply Restrictions: The World Aluminum/Bauxite Market*, a commodity supply restriction

study prepared for the National Bureau of Standards (Washington, D.C.: U.S. Government Printing Office, March 1977), p. 45.

20. U.S. Bureau of Mines, *Mineral Facts and Problems* (Washington, D.C.: U.S. Department of the Interior, 1981), p. 25.

21. Leonard L. Fischman (project director), *World Mineral Trends and U.S. Supply Problems,* Resources for the Future Research Paper R-20 (Baltimore: Johns Hopkins University Press, 1980), p. 459.

22. *American Metal Market,* chromium section, 19 December 1980 (New York: Fairchild Publications).

23. National Materials Advisory Board, *Contingency Plans for Chromium Utilization,* NMAB-335 (Washington, D.C.: National Academy Press, 1978), 373 pp.

24. U.S. Bureau of Mines, *Mineral Facts and Problems,* p. 222.

25. National Materials Advisory Board, *Tantalum and Columbium Supply and Demand Outlook,* NMAB-391 (Washington, D.C.: National Academy Press, 1982), p. 5.

26. G. L. DeHuff and T. S. Jones, U.S. Bureau of Mines, *Manganese,* Mineral Commodity Profiles (Washington, D.C.: U.S. Department of the Interior, 1979), p. 7.

27. U.S. Bureau of Mines, *Mineral Facts and Problems,* p. 553.

28. National Materials Advisory Board, *Manganese Reserves and Resources of the World and Their Industrial Implications,* NMAB-374 (Washington, D.C.: National Academy Press, 1981), p. 71.

29. National Materials Advisory Board, *Supply and Use Patterns for the Platinum-Group Metals,* NMAB-359 (Washington, D.C.: National Academy Press, 1980), p. 6.

30. National Materials Advisory Board, *Tantalum and Columbium Supply and Demand Outlook,* p. 1.

31. U.S. Bureau of Mines, *Mineral Facts and Problems,* p. 918.

5
U.S. Materials Import
Dependency and Vulnerability

Current Status of U.S. Materials Imports

Much confusion continues to exist over what is meant by U.S. materials "import dependency" and "import vulnerability." Despite the fact that the two terms are significantly different, they frequently are used almost synonymously. Before discussing the differences, it is useful to consider how the U.S. materials import posture has changed over time, and what that posture is today.

Changes in the U.S. Import Posture

The eighteenth-century economy of the American colonies, as noted earlier, was based almost wholly upon renewable domestic resources, with wood the major fuel. Indeed, from the late eighteenth through the nineteenth century, the United States exhibited a fairly high degree of materials self-sufficiency. This picture began to change significantly, however, with the onset of the twentieth century and the eruption of World War I. Even so, domestic materials resources still provided a large share of U.S. industrial manufacturing requirements.

Materials import dependency began to take on more serious consequences following World War II, as the nation began to shift from a manufacturing to a predominantly services economy. Furthermore, import dependency was accelerated by a decline in domestic materials production caused largely by two factors: first, the exhaustion of the richest domestic ore deposits, those that could be mined most efficiently and economically, and second, the emergence of foreign competition that could mine and ship materials ores over great distances more cheaply than domestic producers could mine similar ores locally. Equally significant was a third factor: the emergence of high-technology industries that required new, high-performance materials using minerals that were not available domestically. These three factors— exhaustion of primary ore deposits, foreign competition, and the need for high-technology materials—have largely been responsible for the fact that U.S. materials import dependency is still increasing and is likely to continue to do so.

Figure 5.1 Net U.S. imports of selected materials as percentages of domestic consumption

MAJOR SOURCES

Material	Percentage	Major Sources
COLUMBIUM	100	Brazil, Canada, Thailand
MICA (sheet)	100	India, Belgium, France
STRONTIUM	100	Mexico, Spain
MANGANESE	99	So. Africa, France, Gabon, Brazil
BAUXITE & ALUMINA	96	Australia, Jamaica, Guinea, Surinam
COBALT	95	Zaire, Zambia, Canada, Japan
TANTALUM	94	Thailand, Malaysia, Brazil, Canada
FLUORSPAR	91	Mexico, So. Africa, China, Italy
PLATINUM GROUP	91	So. Africa, UK, USSR
CHROMIUM	82	So. Africa, Zimbabwe, USSR, Philippines
TIN	79	Thailand, Malaysia, Indonesia, Bolivia
ASBESTOS	75	Canada, So. Africa
NICKEL	74	Canada, Australia, Norway, Botswana
POTASH	74	Canada, Israel
TUNGSTEN	71	Canada, China, Bolivia
ZINC	67	Canada, Peru, Mexico, Australia
BARITE	64	China, Morocco, Chile, Peru
SILVER	61	Canada, Mexico, Peru, UK
MERCURY	60	Spain, Japan, Mexico, Turkey
CADMIUM	56	Canada, Australia, Mexico, Peru
SELENIUM	51	Canada, UK, Japan, Belg.-Lux.
VANADIUM	41	So. Africa, Canada, Finland
GYPSUM	38	Canada, Mexico, Spain
IRON & STEEL	23	Japan, EEC, Canada
COPPER	21	Chile, Canada, Mexico, Peru
SILICON	21	Canada, Brazil, Norway, Venezuela
IRON ORE	19	Canada, Venezuela, Liberia, Brazil
LEAD	18	Canada, Mexico, Australia, Peru
SULFUR	17	Canada, Mexico
GOLD	16	Canada, Switzerland, Uruguay
NITROGEN (fixed)	14	USSR, Canada, Mexico, Trinidad & Tobago
ALUMINUM	9	Canada, Ghana, Japan, Venezuela

Source: U.S. Bureau of Mines (1984).

Extent of Current Materials Imports

How extensive is the import dependency for materials, which so far has been discussed mainly piecemeal? A good indication of import levels for some major industrial raw materials is given in Figure 5.1. More comprehensive data, including those on which the figure is based, are given in Table 5.1, but are not as readily visualized as in the figure. However, the foreign source list in the table is of importance, and the percentage data for the eighty-eight nonfuel materials listed are rearranged in Table 5.2 to highlight clearly those materials that are imported to the greatest extent.

As can be seen from column A of Table 5.2, net imports of eighteen of the materials are less than zero; that is, net exports of these materials are made. Thus, only the remaining seventy need be considered further. Of these, the U.S. Bureau of Mines currently lacks sufficient information concerning five materials, as shown in the next-to-last column of Table 5.2, thus reducing the number for consideration to sixty-five. A further reduction

Table 5.1 Net U.S. Imports of Major Industrial Raw Materials As
Percentages of Domestic Consumption

Material	Estimated 1984	Major Foreign Sources (1980-1983)
Aluminum (metal)	9	Canada, Ghana, Japan, Venezuela
Antimony	W	Metal: Bolivia, China, Bel.-Lux., Mexico Ore: Bolivia, Mexico, Canada, Rep. of South Africa Oxide: Rep. of South Africa, Bolivia, China, France
Arsenic	W	Sweden, Canada, Mexico, France
Asbestos	75	Canada, Rep. of South Africa
Barite	64	China, Morocco, Chile, Peru
Bauxite/alumina	96	Bauxite: Jamaica, Guinea, Surinam Alumina: Australia, Jamaica, Surinam
Beryllium	W	China, Brazil, Rep. of South Africa, Switzerland
Bismuth	W	Peru, Mexico, United Kingdom, Fed. Rep. of Germany
Boron	E	Colemanite: Turkey, Yugoslavia Boric acid: Turkey, France, Argentina, Mexico Ulexite: Turkey
Bromine	E	Israel, United Kingdom, France
Cadmium	56	Canada, Australia, Mexico, Peru
Cement	9	Canada, Spain, Mexico, Japan
Cesium (compounds)	100	Fed. Rep. of Germany
Chromium	82	Rep. of South Africa, Zimbabwe, USSR, Philippines
Clays	E	United Kingdom, Canada, Fed. Rep. of Germany, Mexico
Cobalt	95	Zaire, Zambia, Canada, Japan
Columbium	100	Brazil, Canada, Thailand
Copper	21	Chile, Canada, Mexico, Peru
Corundum	100	Drawdown of stocks of material imported from the Rep. of South Africa
Diamond (industrial stone)	100	Rep. of South Africa, Zaire, United Kingdom, Bel.-Lux.
Diamond (bort, powder, dust)	E	Ireland, Rep. of South Africa, Japan, United Kingdom
Diatomite	E	Mexico
Feldspar	E	Canada, Sweden, Norway
Fluorspar	91	Mexico, Rep. of South Africa, China, Italy
Gallium	NA	Switzerland, Fed. Rep. of Germany, Canada
Garnet	E	None
Gem stones	100	Bel.-Lux., Israel, Rep. of South Africa, India
Germanium	NA	Bel.-Lux., United Kingdom, Fed. Rep. of Germany, China
Gold	16	Canada, Switzerland (mostly Rep. of South Africa origin), Uruguay
Graphite (natural)	W	Mexico, China, Brazil, Madagascar
Gypsum	38	Canada, Mexico, Spain

Table 5.1 (cont)

Material	Estimated 1984	Major Foreign Sources (1980-1983)
Hafnium	W	France, Fed. Rep. of Germany, United Kingdom
Helium	E	None
Ilmenite	W	Australia, Canada, Rep. of South Africa
Indium	NA	Bel.-Lux., France, Italy, United Kingdom
Iodine	W	Japan, Chile
Iron ore	19	Canada, Venezuela, Liberia, Brazil
Iron and steel	23	Japan, Europe, Canada
Iron and steel scrap	E	Canada
Iron and steel slag	NA	Not available
Kyanite/minerals	E	Not available
Lead (metal)	18	Canada, Mexico, Australia, Peru
Lime	1	Canada, Mexico
Lithium	E	China, Fed. Rep. of Germany, France
Magnesium	E	Canada, Norway, France, Italy
Magnesium compounds	6	Ireland, Greece, Canada, Japan
Manganese	99	Ore: Rep. of South Africa, Gabon, Australia, Brazil Ferromanganese: Rep. of South Africa, France
Mercury	60	Spain, Japan, Mexico, Turkey
Mica (natural) scrap and flake	3	Canada, India
Mica (natural) sheet	100	India, Belgium, France
Molybdenum	E	Canada, Mexico
Nickel	74	Canada, Australia, Norway, Botswana
Nitrogen (fixed)	14	USSR, Canada, Mexico, Trinidad, Tobago
Peat	38	Canada, Fed. Rep. of Germany
Perlite	4	Greece
Phosphate rock	E	Morocco, Mexico, Netherlands Antilles
Platinum-group metals	91	Rep. of South Africa, United Kingdom, USSR
Potash	74	Canada, Israel
Pumice and pumicite	29	Greece
Quartz crystal (industrial)	E	Brazil
Rare-earth metals	16	Monazite: Australia, Malaysia
Rhenium	W	Chile, Fed. Rep. of Germany
Rubidium	NA	Canada
Rutile	W	Australia, Sierra Leone, Rep. of South Africa
Salt	10	Canada, Mexico, Bahamas, Chile
Sand and gravel (construction)	E	Canada
Selenium	51	Canada, United Kingdom, Japan, Bel.-Lux.
Silicon	21	Canada, Brazil, Norway, Venezuela
Silver	61	Canada, Mexico, Peru, United Kingdom
Sodium carbonate	E	Canada
Sodium sulfate	4	Canada, Belgium, Mexico
Stone (crushed)	-	Canada, Bahamas
Stone (dimension)	57	Italy, Canada, Mexico, Portugal

Table 5.1   (cont.)

Material	Estimated 1984	Major Foreign Sources (1980-1983)
Strontium	100	Mexico, Spain
Sulfur	17	Canada, Mexico
Talc and pyro-phyllite	E	Canada, Italy, Australia, France
Tantalum	94	Thailand, Malaysia, Brazil, Canada
Tellurium	W	Canada, Hong Kong, United Kingdom
Thallium	100	Bel.-Lux., Fed. Rep. of Germany, Norway, Japan
Thorium	100	France, Netherlands, Canada, Malta
Tin	79	Thailand, Malaysia, Indonesia, Bolivia
Titanium (metal)	9	Japan, China, USSR
Tungsten	71	Canada, China, Bolivia
Vanadium	41	Rep. of South Africa, Canada, Finland
Vermiculite	2	Rep. of South Africa, Brazil
Yttrium	100	Monazite: Australia, Malaysia
Zinc	67	Ore and concentrates: Canada, Peru, Mexico Metal: Canada, Peru, Mexico, Australia
Zirconium	W	Zirconium: France, Japan, Canada Zircon: Australia, Rep. of South Africa

Note: Net import reliance is imports less exports and adjustments for government and industry stock changes.   Apparent consumption is U.S. primary and secondary production of each material plus net imports.

W = data withheld
- = none
E = net exports
NA= data not available

Source: U.S. Bureau of Mines, Mineral Commodity Summaries 1985 (Washington, D.C.: U.S. Department of the Interior, 1985), pp. 4-5.

is necessary because information concerning nine materials, as shown in the last column, is withheld from publication by the bureau.[1] Finally, given the deletions already necessary, a defensible step could be to emphasize those materials for which imports currently amount to more than 50 percent, thus removing from immediate consideration the twenty-three materials shown in column B. Thirty-three materials are left for consideration.

Some analysts make an exception for the titanium in column B because of its critical importance to the aerospace industry and the lack of a suitable substitute for such use. However, U.S. producers maintain a significant domestic capacity for both titanium sponge and ingot; furthermore, large quantities of scrap titanium that are now exported could be used domestically in an emergency. Therefore no exception is made here. Nor is an exception made for aluminum metal, since it is essentially included under bauxite/alumina in column G. Hence, of the eighty-eight materials listed in the tables, only thirty-three will be given consideration in further detail, namely those materials listed in columns C through H of Table 5.2, for which net imports currently amount to 50 percent or more.

Table 5.2 Net U.S. Materials Imports As Percentages of Domestic
Consumption (Rearranged from Table 5.1)

A (Export)	B (0-49)	C (50-59)	D (60-69)	E (70-79)
Boron	Aluminum (9)	Antimony (52)[a]	Barite (64)	Asbestos (75)
Bromine	Cement (9)	Cadmium (56)	Gallium (61)[b]	Ilmenite (75)[b]
Clays	Copper (21)	Selenium (51)	Mercury (60)	Nickel (74)
Diamond	Gold (16)	Stone, dimen-	Silver (61)	Potash (74)
(bort,	Gypsum (38)	sion (57)	Zinc (67)	Tin (79)
powder,	Iron ore (19)			Tungsten (71)
dust)	Iron and			
Diatomite	steel (23)			
Feldspar	Lead			
Garnet	(metal) (18)			
Helium	Lime (1)			
Iron and	Magnesium			
steel	com-			
scrap	pounds (6)			
Kyanite/	Mica			
minerals	(natural)			
Lithium	scrap and			
Magnesium	flake (3)			
Molybdenum	Nitrogen			
Phosphate	fixed (14)			
rock	Peat (38)			
Quartz	Perlite (4)			
crystal	Pumice and			
(industrial)	pumi-			
Sand and	cite (29)			
gravel (con-	Rare-earth			
struction)	metals (16)			
Sodium	Salt (10)			
carbonate	Silicon (21)			
Talc and	Sodium			
pyro-	sulfate (4)			
phyllite	Sulfur (17)			
	Titanium			
	metal (9)			
	Vanadium (41)			
	Vermiculite (2)			

a. Data for antimony taken from Mineral Commodity Summaries 1984.
b. Data for gallium, graphite, and illmenite taken from Mineral Commodity
   Summaries 1983.

Reducing the eighty-eight materials to thirty-three by the reasoning given
above is not intended to imply that the fifty-five materials thus eliminated
are not of industrial significance. Indeed they are, and many are absolutely
essential for major industrial processes. Rather, the defense is that despite
the industrial importance of some of these materials, they are of relatively
minor concern with regard to import dependency and vulnerability as
determined from the criteria discussed in Chapter 4.

Seven of the remaining thirty-three materials were selected in Chapter
4 as being particularly vital with regard to current import levels: aluminum/

Table 5.2 (cont.)

F (80-89)	G (90-99)	H (100)	Data Unavailable	Data Withheld
Chromium (82)	Bauxite/ alumina (96)	Cesium compounds	Germanium	Arsenic
	Cobalt (95)	Columbium	Indium	Beryllium
	Fluorspar (91)	Corundum	Iron and	Bismuth
	Manganese (99)	Diamond,	steel slag	Hafnium
	Platinum-	industrial	Rubidium	Iodine
	group	stone	Stone,	Rhenium
	metals (91)	Gem stones	crushed	Rutile
	Tantalum (94)	Graphite (natural)[b]		Tellurium
		Mica (natural)		Zirconium
		sheet		
		Strontium		
		Thallium		
		Thorium		
		Yttrium		

Source: Table derived from U.S. Bureau of Mines, Mineral Commodity Summaries 1985 (Washington, D.C.: U.S. Department of the Interior, 1985), pp. 4-5.

alumina/bauxite, chromium, cobalt, columbium, manganese, the platinum-group metals, and tantalum. In fact, these materials number more than seven, but as noted earlier for convenience of discussion, aluminum, alumina, and bauxite are considered as one material, as are the platinum-group metals.

The current import levels for these seven materials, ranging from 82 percent for chromium to 100 percent for columbium, are reviewed in Table 5.3. If one considers only virgin materials and omits the contribution of recycled scrap, import levels for these materials would be greater than

Table 5.3 Net U.S. Imports of Seven Strategic and Critical Materials, with Major Foreign Sources

Material	Net Import Level	Current Recycling Level	Total Including Recycling	Major Foreign Sources (Percentage of U.S. Imports Provided)
Bauxite/alumina	96	0	96	Ore: Jamaica (37), Guinea (36), Surinam (8), other (19) Alumina: Australia (79), Jamaica (11), Surinam (7), other (3)
Chromium	82	18	100	Chromite contained in chromite and ferro-chromium: Rep. of South Africa (55), Zimbabwe (8), USSR (7), Philippines (6), other (24)
Cobalt	95	5	100	Zaire (37), Zambia (12), Canada (10), Japan (7), other (34)
Columbium	100	0	100	Brazil (75), Canada (7), Thailand (6), other (12)
Manganese	99	0	99	Ore: Rep. of South Africa (31), Gabon (29), Australia (17), Brazil (12), other (11)
Platinum-group metals	91	6	97	Rep. of South Africa (49), Great Britain (15), USSR (13), other (23)
Tantalum	94	6	100	Thailand (38), Malaysia (10), Brazil (10), Canada (8), other (34)

Source: U.S. Bureau of Mines, Mineral Commodity Summaries 1985 (Washington, D.C.: U.S. Department of the Interior, 1985).

indicated in the table. This observation reflects the fact that the Bureau of Mines, in calculating import dependency levels, reduces these levels to account for resource recovery and recycling. For some of the materials in the table—especially bauxite/alumina, columbium, and manganese—this distinction is of relatively small consequence because little of these materials is yet recovered for recycling (although increasing amounts of aluminum metal are now recovered). For others the distinction is quite significant, as shown in the third column of the table. If import levels are calculated based wholly upon virgin materials consumption, then one obtains the figures given in the fourth column of the table, most of which under this condition approach 100 percent.

Whether or not the recycling component should be included when calculating import dependency figures remains a matter of debate. Some analysts prefer to include it, arguing quite correctly that used material that is reclaimed and recycled, even if originally imported, reduces the amount of new materials that must be imported. Other analysts contend that use of recycled material in such calculations tends to deemphasize what ought to be the primary concern regarding current high levels of materials imports, namely, that virtually all strategic and critical materials now entering the nation's industrial pipeline are imported from abroad and that, consequently, the nation does in fact import almost 100 percent of this material. In practice, it makes little difference which approach is taken if the data are clear in indicating whether recycled material is being included. One advantage of including it—and highlighting the contribution that recycling already makes to materials supplies—is the encouragement of additional recycling.

Finally, it should be noted that the data provided in Table 5.1 and extracted in Table 5.2 are by no means precise. Tracking materials imports and exports is a complex endeavor, and aggregated data are therefore subject to significant uncertainty. Furthermore, not all forms of materials are included in the tracking process. Materials imported as finished or semi-finished assemblies or subassemblies may not be included; e.g., automobile parts or electronic components. As such imports assume an increasingly larger proportion of domestic consumption, the recorded import levels will increase accordingly. Hence the figures now in the tables can be considered conservative; that is, they most probably reflect minimum estimates of the current level of U.S. materials imports.

The Question of Possible Self-Sufficiency

In view of the large (and increasing) levels of materials imports discussed above, it is not uncommon to hear calls for steps to reduce such imports drastically, or even eliminate them entirely—that is, to make the nation essentially self-sufficient in basic industrial raw materials. Similar calls for national self-sufficiency have been made in the past for petroleum, without success. The calls for self-sufficiency in nonfuel materials are also unlikely to be realized, for both technological and economic reasons.

Technological Considerations. The primary reason why materials self-sufficiency is realistically impossible to achieve has already been discussed in Chapter 3, namely, that materials are not distributed geographically according to how and where they are needed. The need for materials is determined largely by such factors as the extent of industrialization of a particular area of the world, its technological sophistication, its population density, and the consumption habits of the resident population. It is probable that earlier in human history the availability of materials coincided with some of these other factors, because people tended to settle near ready sources of food, materials, and natural transportation. But with the phenomenal growth of populations and the unprecedented explosion of technology, such population centers have long outgrown the local resources that may initially have made them seem so attractive. Consequently, major population centers today are no more self-sufficient than nations are, and for all practical purposes, like nations are incapable of becoming self-sufficient.

Economic Considerations. In some respects, economic factors may be even more influential and more complex than the technological factors. The United States possesses at least some domestic resources of almost all the materials listed in Table 5.2, including those that are now imported at levels approaching or equal to 100 percent. But it would cost more to produce materials from these low-grade resources than it now costs to import the materials from abroad. Thus, a considerable proportion of current imports of materials arises for purely economic reasons: if the nation were willing to underwrite the cost of exploiting these low-grade or marginal resources, import levels could be reduced.

Realistically there is a limit to the extent to which import levels could be reduced by ignoring strictly economic considerations. For example, in 1979 the United States consumed 1.2 million short tons of chromite and 528,000 short tons of chromium ferroalloys, for an apparent consumption of chromium metal of 610,000 short tons.[2] Thus, even if the current estimated domestic chromium reserve base of about 13 million short tons of chromite ore could be developed regardless of cost, it would not long supply a major fraction of projected demand.

A second economic option is to develop substitutes for materials that are now imported. Such development would be very costly, and no private company can justify the costs when suitable materials at lower cost are readily available. Instead, it is almost a truism that the materials currently in use invariably are the materials of "first choice" based upon both economic and technological suitability for the purposes for which they are used. Hence, substitute materials may not only be more expensive for a given application but may not perform as well. Despite these drawbacks, however, import levels could be reduced through the development of substitute materials, provided the federal government would underwrite much of the cost.

The impracticality of total materials self-sufficiency has been aptly illustrated by the parable of "lifeboat ethics":

How many people would a group of three lifeboats support if we were to assume that one has the only containers of food, a second has the only containers of water, and the third has the only instrument that will open the containers? To require self-sufficiency would preclude the cooperation without which all would perish and the provisions go unused.[3]

Clearly, if the developed, industrialized nations were required to rely solely on their own natural resources, most would have to make major adjustments in their current consumption practices, and much of the Third World would be in deep economic depression.

Increasing U.S. Import Levels

It should be clear that although technological and economic factors may be predominantly responsible for the current import level for a given material, in general these factors represent a complex mix and cannot easily be separated into one kind of factor or another. Perhaps what is most important, however, is the recognition that—given sufficient time—almost any material can be done without, at a price. Thus far, few instances exist where any nation has been willing to pay that price. Notable exceptions—aimed at reducing petroleum imports—include Brazil, which has invested heavily in facilities to produce methanol from biomass materials, and the Republic of South Africa, which has developed a substantial capacity to produce synthetic fuels from coal. However, unwillingness to pay the price of second-choice technologies has long been an accepted aspect of U.S. national policy, as recognized by the National Commission on Materials Policy in its recommendation that "traditional U.S. economic policy be maintained by relying upon market forces as a prime determinant of the mix of imports and domestic production."[4] It is this policy that has caused U.S. materials imports to increase over the past several decades, thereby leading to the problems to be discussed later, in Chapter 7. The commission did qualify its recommendation by noting that such considerations as national security, the health and viability of domestic materials industries, and fair competition should influence public economic policy. Indeed, a major conclusion of the commission was that "Where dangerous and costly reliance upon imports appears to be the result of existing trends, the Government must intervene."[5] Despite these words written in June 1973, the government has done little, if anything, to stem the increasing flow of imported materials. Only relatively recently has this lack of government activity drawn much criticism that the nation's national security might be endangered by excessive reliance on imports of strategic and critical materials.

Imports of Advanced Manufactured Materials

The major concern over materials imports has long focused upon imports of raw materials as classified in Tables 5.1, 5.2, and 5.3. However, equally disturbing is a growing trend toward increased U.S. imports of a variety of advanced manufactured materials,[6] including rapidly solidified metals, structural and electronic ceramics, polymer blends and electronic and optical polymers, and composite materials in general. These materials can no longer be considered optional: modern weapons systems are becoming increasingly dependent upon them, and modern consumer products increasingly require them to remain competitive with foreign products.

Ironically, although the United States pioneered many of these new technologies, it appears to be rapidly losing its lead. For example, substantial efforts in the field of rapid solidification technology are currently being undertaken in Belgium, France, Italy, Japan, the Soviet Union, Sweden, Switzerland, the United Kingdom, and West Germany. In the field of organic matrix composites technology, which has become essential to the aircraft industry, Japan and the United Kingdom are heavily involved. Metal matrix composites are being pursued by a number of European countries as well as by the Soviet Union. In the newer field of ceramic/ceramic composites France, Japan, West Germany, and the Soviet Union are substantially involved.

At present, the United States continues to maintain a substantial commitment to these technologies, but that commitment increasingly is becoming eroded by the economic pressures of international competition. As foreign manufacturers become more dominant in the U.S. market, domestic suppliers and manufacturers inevitably will suffer production capacity losses as well as a much-reduced ability to maintain their technological edge. In many respects the situation bears a striking resemblance to that now existing for ferroalloys, to be discussed later in this chapter. In both situations during peacetime, supplies are plentiful and are cheaper when imported from abroad. Most supplier nations are politically and economically stable and are friendly to U.S. interests. In an emergency, however, freedom from import disruptions could not be guaranteed. Furthermore, the demand for these materials could be expected to increase substantially during the emergency, precisely when supplies are most likely to be interrupted. U.S. manufacturers typically carry relatively low inventories of such materials to minimize overhead costs, and thus are particularly vulnerable to potential supply disruptions. For example, U.S. computer manufacturers may carry only a few days' inventory of the substrates used as chip carriers for large computers, approximately 70 percent of which are manufactured by a single Japanese firm, Kyocera. Such highly concentrated foreign sources clearly increase potential U.S. vulnerability to supply interruptions.

Thus, the United States is becoming increasingly dependent upon imports of advanced, sophisticated manufactured materials upon which vital components of its military and civilian technologies depend. Continued unchecked growth of such imports can only serve to exacerbate further the nation's current vulnerability to supply interruptions of strategic and critical raw materials.

Some General Aspects of Materials Imports

Clearly, the importation of materials involves both benefits and liabilities. The major economic benefit is that materials can be obtained from the least costly source, wherever that may be, and the costs of finished products are kept correspondingly low in comparison with what they otherwise would be. Ideally, free international trade thus represents the most rational use of the world's materials resources. Promoting self-sufficiency through the subsidized development of marginal domestic resources runs counter to economic efficiency worldwide.

Moreover, the importing of materials by developed nations is critical to the economies of many developing nations that have only one or two major resource assets upon which they rely for the foreign exchange they need to purchase needed supplies of food, energy materials, and finished products. For example, the mineral industry of the Republic of Zambia provides about 90 percent of that country's foreign exchange credit, of which copper forms a major component. Bauxite and alumina alone account for about one-fourth of Guinea's gross domestic product (GDP) and almost 95 percent of its export revenue. Other examples include the importance of bauxite exports to Guyana, Jamaica, and Surinam; manganese exports to Ghana; tin exports to Bolivia and Thailand; and copper and cobalt exports to Chile and Zaire. If these nations should lose their primary markets for the materials they now export, their economies would soon collapse, with an attendant increase in international economic and political tensions.

Importation of materials also increases international trade, which, on balance, helps promote good international relations. Trading, whatever the problems involved, at least helps to keep open lines of communication that may also prove useful in promoting discussion and settlement of nontrade problems. Totally self-sufficient nations would be much more likely to become isolated, a condition that ultimately could endanger world peace.

Still another benefit of import dependency should be noted, not because it is a worldwide benefit but more because it is frequently described as a regional benefit, namely, the "export" of environmental pollution abroad. Mining and mineral-processing operations are notoriously damaging to air and water quality, and often to the landscape itself. To the extent that ores and processed materials are imported from abroad, the environmental pollution resulting from such operations occurs in the country of origin rather than in the consuming nation. Thus it can be said that such pollution has essentially been exported to the source country. However, environmental pollution, wherever it occurs in the world, ultimately may affect all citizens of all nations. Certainly such phenomena as acid rain know no international boundaries. Thus, it makes considerable sense to eliminate this apparent benefit through the imposition of similar environmental controls on all production of materials, wherever such production may take place. Although much progress is being made in this direction by many developing nations, it remains true that other such nations still find it necessary to accommodate a certain level of pollution because they cannot afford environmental protection through the diversion of funds so badly needed for the basic necessities of food, more pressing health problems than pollution, and shelter.

Among the major economic disadvantages of high levels of materials imports is the "export" of jobs overseas to those nations from which materials are now imported. Although the mining and ore-processing industries are not unusually labor intensive, substantial numbers of jobs are nevertheless lost when domestic operations are closed down and replaced by imports. The domestic smelting industry has been hit particularly hard and may soon cease to exist, as will be discussed later in Chapter 7. As the trend continues toward importing greater proportions of refined and processed materials, even more domestic jobs will be lost, possibly forever. Conditions are further exacerbated by the fact that domestic production and processing costs are typically greater than are those for underdeveloped countries. Under such conditions it is inevitable that U.S. production will decrease while imports increase.

Probably the major drawback of high levels of materials imports is the strategic one, which is the central issue of this book. As domestic industries become weaker or close down because their outputs have been replaced by imports, the United States loses the industrial capability to produce these materials domestically. Although this loss may be quite bearable during peacetime, it could become intolerable in time of war, when supplies from abroad are interrupted. The war could be between other nations, with the United States suffering some of the international consequences. It is this strategic aspect of materials imports that has given rise to calls for reduction of the imports to less critical levels and the achievement of a greater level of materials self-sufficiency.

Clearly U.S. materials imports must be considered in perspective. On the one hand, a certain level of importation appears both beneficial and unavoidable. As noted elsewhere, "[T]he uneven geographical distribution of physical resources over the earth, and the slowly alterable distribution of technical skills, enterprise, and capital necessary for working these resources, and . . . the existing pattern of national political boundaries" assures that there is no escape from international raw materials interdependence.[7] On the other hand, high import levels for certain key materials carry grave implications for national security policy. The gravity of these implications largely depends upon an assessment of the extent to which such imports represent either a "dependency" or a "vulnerability," particularly during a period of international hostilities or outright war, as discussed below.

Import Dependency and Vulnerability

The word "import" is unambiguous applied to international trade. Hence, reasonably accurate data can be kept by federal agencies to relate annual materials consumption to domestic materials production and quantities of materials imported. From these data, the level of importation for any given material can readily be calculated as a percentage of domestic consumption. It is these calculated averages that are given in Figure 5.1 and Table 5.1.

The term "import dependency" is not similarly unambiguous; the word "dependency" involves a value judgment, whereas "import" does not. The fact that a large percentage of domestic consumption of a particular material is imported from abroad does not in itself constitute a dependency upon the imports. Dependency implies existence by virtue of necessity, and necessity implies unavoidability or indispensability. As noted earlier in this chapter, a large proportion of U.S. materials imports are neither unavoidable nor indispensable; rather, these materials are imported by choice because it is cheaper or more convenient to do so. Thus, in a strict sense, it is inaccurate to say that the United States is "dependent" upon imports of those materials for which it possesses adequate domestic resources, if it chooses for economic or other reasons not to exploit those resources. For example, the current U.S. reserve base of strontium is about 1.5 million short tons of contained strontium, or about 11 percent of the entire world reserve base. Yet no domestic strontium has been produced since 1959, and the nation's "import dependency" for strontium is 100 percent.[8] A similar situation exists for many other materials listed in Tables 5.1, 5.2, and 5.3, for which domestic resources or alternative ores are available but currently remain unexploited for various reasons. However, for certain other materials such as industrial diamonds and manganese, there is virtually no domestic reserve base, and hence an "import dependency" for them can truly be said to exist. The value judgment referred to above concerns whether or not these different categories of materials should be lumped together from the viewpoint of "import dependency." Because that is now almost universally the practice, prudence would dictate that the same practice be followed here to avoid confusion. Hence, it will be assumed that the United States is indeed "dependent" upon the levels of materials imports that now exist, even though that "dependency" is in fact somewhat artificial.

The term "import vulnerability" is still more ambiguous, involving value judgments regarding both what "vulnerability" means and under what precise conditions it is considered to exist. Consequently, any determination of import vulnerability depends strongly upon the specific criteria selected to define it. Because such criteria differ for different experts, it is hardly surprising that their expert views on vulnerability vary enormously, although they use the same import dependency data.

In view of this broad range of expert opinion, it is useful to summarize the current attitudes toward materials import dependency, review the specific vulnerability criteria from Chapter 4 that led to the listing of materials in Table 5.3, and consider the concept of materials import vulnerability in some detail.

Current Attitudes Toward Import Dependency

In view of differences over whether a market economy or a goal of greater national self-sufficiency should carry the greater weight in determining the extent of materials imports, it is hardly surprising that opinions differ over the consequences of loss or change in such imports. Some observers point out that materials per se represent only a small fraction of the nation's gross national product and that a slowdown or a cessation of materials imports would not be disastrous to the economy. According to this view,

> [A]ny modern industrial economy and particularly the United States is incredibly quick to adapt to shortages of particular materials. Substitutes are quickly discovered, synthetics developed, and ways found to minimize the use of short-supply items. . . . If all imports to the United States were cut off and every one of our overseas investments expropriated, the U.S. economy would not collapse. Our living standards would suffer, but not by a large amount.[9]

On the other hand, many other observers take the opposite view, contending that a cessation of critical nonfuel materials imports could create economic disruptions potentially more devastating than any that might occur from a cutoff of petroleum. Indeed, some maintain that the nation's essential industries might be shut down within six months, and that continued lack of such supplies could cause a reversion of forty or fifty years in the nation's current standard of living and technology.[10]

These two views represent the opposite ends of a wide spectrum of beliefs that are conditioned by each observer's concept of the role of materials in the economy, and the flexibility of the economy in adapting to changes in materials availability. Probably closer to the truth than either of these extreme views is the median view, also held by many, that the U.S. economy could indeed eventually adapt to almost any materials supply disruption but that, depending upon the particular materials involved, the time required could be lengthy and subject to painful economic disruptions.

Criteria for Determining Import Vulnerability

For reasons already noted, it is intellectually inconsistent to assume automatically that import dependency for a given material is equivalent to a vulnerability or a threat. Yet such an assumption is frequently made.[11] Thus, it is important when using such value concepts as "vulnerability" and "threats" to assess exactly what it is that appears to be vulnerable or threatened. To some, the vulnerability or threat may be largely economic: excessive imports ultimately may be seen as adversely affecting the economic growth rate of the Western nations, thereby restricting employment potentials, endangering societal stability, and ultimately reducing the material standard of living. To others, the vulnerability or threat may be seen in strategic or military terms: for example, in reducing the defense capabilities of the North Atlantic Treaty Organization vis-à-vis the Warsaw Pact nations, or in making difficult the prosecution of a limited war, or even in increasing the risk, if one exists, of an attack by a nation that might perceive itself as stronger. Clearly, then, unless the type of vulnerability or threat is explicitly specified, all statements in which these two value concepts appear become nearly useless.

Perhaps the most defensible way to assess vulnerability is in terms of measurable criteria that yield indexes of vulnerability as discussed at length in Chapter 4. There the necessity was also pointed out of applying the criteria on a commodity-by-commodity basis, because the validity of a particular criterion may vary greatly for different commodities.

In assessing materials import vulnerability, some analysts attempt to distinguish between factors that are primarily "strategic" and factors that are primarily "critical." In general, strategic factors are those that affect the continued availability of materials, especially those that must be imported from abroad. Thus, major strategic factors include the status of domestic resources, the diversity of foreign sources, the relative stability of supplier nations, and the safety of materials supply lines. By contrast, critical factors are those having to do with the relative importance of specific materials to the economy and to national defense. Thus, major critical factors include how essential a material is to major industrial processes, its importance to advanced weapons systems, and the extent to which substitute materials could be found in an emergency.

Whether or not any useful purpose is served by attempting to distinguish between strategic and critical factors is open to debate. Thus defined, many materials are critical but not strategic. For example, such materials as antimony, copper, iron ore, lead, magnesium, mercury, molybdenum, silicon, tungsten, and vanadium can all be considered as critical because of their industrial and defense-related applications and because, at least for some uses, no cost-effective substitutes are known. Yet they are hardly strategic inasmuch as domestic supplies would undoubtedly suffice in an emergency. Hence, as defined above, critical materials essentially have little or no effect upon import vulnerability.

The distinction becomes even less useful in practice because most materials that qualify as being strategic also qualify as being critical. The four materials most frequently cited as of major concern—chromium, cobalt, manganese, and the platinum-group metals—easily meet the requirements for both. Not only are domestic supplies of these materials inadequate or almost nonexistent, but supplier nations are few in number, are either politically unstable or unfriendly to U.S. interests, and are located far from the United States. All four materials are essential to both civilian and defense-related industries, and no suitable substitutes are known for some important defense-related applications. For many other materials, varying degrees of distinction between their strategic and critical designations are usually of value in discussing import vulnerability *if* there are first some strategic concerns.

The Question of U.S. Import Vulnerability

Several factors have served to increase perceptions of U.S. materials import vulnerability over the past several decades. First, as the nation has become dependent upon larger quantities and varieties of goods and services, its dependence upon the outcomes of foreign economic, political, and military events has increased accordingly and, consequently, its potential vulnerability to future such events.

Second, as the frontiers of technology have been pushed forward, the need for specialized materials has grown dramatically: the arms race, the development of missiles and space satellites, the advent of nuclear technology, and the continuing revolution in electronics all have resulted in increased demands for new or improved materials. As these demands go on increasing, and as materials-fed technology becomes ever more pervasive, vulnerability to supply disruptions will also become more serious.

Third, many of these new or improved materials are derived from foreign sources originally under the control of U.S. corporations or U.S. allies that invested in mineral-rich countries and operated mines and processing facilities largely for the benefit of Western markets. At the time, little demand for such materials would have existed without these markets. However, circumstances have changed and the United States and its allies no longer exercise the dominant control over these foreign materials supplies that they previously enjoyed. Increased Third World nationalization, expropriation, forced changes of agreements, increased taxation, and limits on the percentage of foreign ownership in new mines and facilities all have greatly limited U.S. influence upon these foreign sources of materials. This loss of control reduces the reliability of the sources as stable suppliers of materials to the United States.

Not all analysts are convinced that a materials import vulnerability of any kind actually exists, although their view clearly appears to be a minority view at present. They maintain that aggregate import dependency statistics actually provide an inaccurate assessment of U.S. materials import dependency so that, by neglecting the effects of such factors as recycling and metal scrap exports, import dependency is made to appear much greater than it really is. Although valid, this argument leads in turn to a misleading view of virgin materials dependency, as discussed earlier.

Another argument rejecting import vulnerability is that although U.S. resources and reserves of some materials may indeed be low or nonexistent, major resources and reserves of such materials do exist in regions elsewhere in the world and are constantly in changing but adequate supply under the influences of geographical knowledge, demand, price, and technological innovation. Such resources, it is argued, are available to the United States despite ideological or other differences that producer nations may have with the United States, and the availability of these resources mitigates against import vulnerability. However, this argument ignores the statistical fact of import dependency and provides small comfort if such resources and reserves are denied to the United States during an emergency.

A further argument rejecting import vulnerability is that materials import dependency for many materials could be reduced dramatically, if necessary, by development of known domestic resources and exploration to reveal hitherto unknown resources. It has been suggested, for example, that future exploration may very likely reveal domestic resources of chromium, cobalt, and platinum that could meet 20 to 25 percent of U.S. consumption of these materials, and that development of the mineral resources of Stillwater, Montana, alone could yield up to 25 percent of U.S. platinum needs, as well as significant amounts of chromium. Likewise, it is noted that production of even modest amounts of deep-seabed manganese nodules, on the order of 4 to 5 million tons per year, could provide up to one-third of U.S.

manganese requirements and more than 90 percent of its cobalt needs.[12] The difficulty with this reasoning, as noted earlier, is that such domestic ore deposits may not materialize and, even if they should, will be expensive to exploit. Further, the large-scale commercial exploitation of deep-seabed resources is not yet a near-term feasibility.

Other analysts point out that import vulnerability may not exist despite high levels of import dependency provided that adequate quantities of materials are available when needed. This argument relies chiefly upon maintaining large stockpiles of materials that are now heavily imported. Clearly, if such stockpiles could be large enough to meet all essential needs in any conceivable emergency, vulnerability would indeed be eliminated, despite continued dependency. This argument, of course, is the underlying concept of the Strategic Petroleum Reserve and the National Defense Stockpile, neither of which as yet has received adequate federal financial support. Consequently, neither represents at present an adequate protection against potential supply disruptions.

Arguments like those given above are useful in that they tend to dramatize the fact that materials import dependency does not necessarily translate into vulnerability as many analysts assume. On the other hand, it would be a serious mistake to allow such arguments to undermine the need to consider and attempt to resolve the very real problems resulting from high levels of materials import dependency.

Considerations Involving the Department of Defense

Unquestionably much of the current concern over U.S. materials import vulnerability has to do with perceptions that an interruption of supplies of some imported material, particularly those listed in Table 5.3, would compromise severely the nation's ability to defend itself or its allies from enemy attack. The extent to which these perceptions are valid is difficult to determine.

It is clear from Chapter 4 that the nation's military complex, and especially the aerospace industry, cannot at present function without substantial quantities of strategic and critical materials. Although during peacetime the Department of Defense consumes only about 5 to 10 percent of total U.S. consumption of most of these materials, it is an extremely vital 5 to 10 percent.[13] During a period of limited war, as in a nonnuclear confrontation, this percentage could be expected to double.[14]

The aerospace industry, which accounts for about 36 percent of total defense procurement, consumes the following approximate percentages of total domestic consumption of chromium, cobalt, tantalum, and titanium: chromium, 6 percent; cobalt, 30 percent; tantalum, 8 percent; and titanium, 2 percent. However, it consumes about 65 percent of all titanium metal and sponge. Although the aerospace requirements for some strategic and critical materials—especially chromium and tantalum—are small relative to total annual domestic consumption, the need is especially critical.[15]

Consequently, the Department of Defense has examined closely its materials requirements in terms of supply and demand, major defense supply sources, and U.S. industrial capacity. Defense requirements have changed as military needs shift more to problems involving processed and manufactured materials, rather than raw materials. However, current government attention, according to a Defense Department source, remains dominated by concern over raw materials and the desirability of subsidizing domestic mining, which is likely to be both ineffective and wasteful. Among the suggestions made regarding effective steps that could be taken to promote defense-related materials needs are taking a fresh approach to both the gathering of statistics and their analysis, improving interagency materials coordination, maintaining an effective National Defense Stockpile, and strengthening the materials industries where possible within the general framework of an improved U.S. industrial climate.[16]

The "Resource War"

Few issues related to minerals and materials appear to have elicited as much public interest and concern as the resource "war" that some experts now claim is being waged by the Soviet Union against the United States and its allies. Although this term has been used rather loosely in much of the discussion of the subject, several conditions appear to be commonly accepted, as follows:

- The Soviet Union is losing its position of relative materials self-sufficiency and hence is becoming increasingly dependent upon materials resources located outside its area of military and political control.

- Because of this dependency, the Soviets are starting to consider materials availability not merely as an economic issue but also as a strategic one.

- In strategic terms, the Soviets are attempting to acquire or control materials assets in sufficient quantities to deny to the United States and its allies the quantities of materials their economies now require.

- Such materials denial is being pursued in Soviet attempts to subvert, destabilize, win over, or even physically take over governments of nations now supplying the Western powers. These activities are being conducted through a strategy of confrontation extending beyond normal economic competition but falling just short of conventional military conflict.

As identified by these elements, the resource war—that is, if it indeed exists—may be defined as a deliberate Soviet policy to supply its own materials needs while denying materials to the West, to the extent that such denial is possible short of outright war. This charge is serious and, if true, could pose fundamental materials resource problems for the United States if the Soviets should win the "war." Hence, it is essential to consider the charge in some detail.

Concerns Over Materials Geopolitics

As defined, the resource war can be considered an advanced exercise in materials geopolitics rather than war, in that the prospect of actual military conflict over materials appears remote at present. Thus limited, the subject is by no means new, inasmuch as materials have long been the focus of international conflict, intrigue, and controversy. Past world materials political-economic relationships have been rife with pressure politics, cartels, nationalizations, embargoes, taxes, trade agreements, foreign assistance programs, and in some cases outright military adventures. Materials geopolitics may thus be defined as "the politicization of economic relationships and rapidly evolving changes in the use of force and economic power to maintain, gain, or deny access to relatively localized and exploitable resources."[17]

Geopolitical factors relative to materials are in a state of constant flux because of the fluidity of market supply and demand, the rise and fall of mineral commodity prices, new and developing technologies, and the relative accessibility of materials resources. Such factors grow in importance as the world's richest and most readily accessible materials deposits become depleted, as populations grow and drift in location, and as the Third World nations seek to use their growing political power to institute a "New International Order."

In the United States, concerns over materials geopolitics have been heightened by several developments over the past few years. First, longstanding efforts to promote a unified national policy for materials finally culminated in passage of the National Materials and Minerals Policy, Research and Development Act of 1980 and the National Critical Materials Act of 1984.[18] The legislative activity leading to these acts not only promoted widespread interest in this subject throughout Congress and the technical, academic, and industrial communities, but also elicited considerable exposure in popular newspapers, magazines, and on television. Thus this legislation, and other legislation that is expected to follow in future years, is likely to assure continued high visibility for minerals geopolitics.

Second, new initiatives by the Reagan administration to improve the nation's defense posture vis-à-vis that of the Soviet Union have shifted U.S.-Soviet relations toward a return to the cold war. Indeed, Soviet leader Mikhail Gorbachev recently stated that "a kind of ice age is being observed in relations between the USSR and the United States."[19] These initiatives have created much controversy concerning the extent to which expenditures for defense can be increased to the perceived detriment of social spending. With the continued availability of strategic and critical materials vitally necessary to this defense buildup, minerals geopolitics necessarily becomes a dominant feature of the controversy.

Third, the current reassessment of the U.S. defense posture, combined with perceptions of Soviet activity in southern Africa, the Middle East, and elsewhere in the Third World as threatening the resource base of the West, heighten concern that the current level of U.S. materials import dependency cannot be tolerated indefinitely from a strategic point of view. And fourth, increased concern over materials import dependency naturally has become a rallying point for those who have long criticized the gradual deterioration of U.S. mining capabilities and the alleged excessive growth of political power and influence on the part of environmental interests. This fourth concern is largely about whether the materials potentially available on public lands could and should be exploited to reduce import dependency. Thus, the impetus provided by new legislation, by heightened concerns over the adequacy of U.S. military strength, by perceptions of a possible resource war developing, and by increased development of domestic materials resources to reduce current levels of materials import dependency all have helped to promote a revival of concern over materials geopolitics.

Beyond the above factors, however, lies the enormous popular appeal of such a term as the "resource war." War is easily understood, whether hot or cold. Further, experiences gained in gasoline lines in 1974, along with the sharp increases in gasoline prices, have made people much more aware of how a dependency upon foreign supplies of needed materials can influence—and indeed seriously disrupt—their lives. In effect, materials geopolitics has come down from purely academic heights to assume a place in America's sitting rooms.

The Current Soviet Resource Posture

Although materials geopolitics broadly concerns all materials-related activities that take place among nations, those of major concern are the recent activities of the Soviet Union that may be considered as having somewhat sinister overtones. It is thus of some importance to examine these activities, as well as the current resource posture of the Soviet Union and recent events bearing upon that posture.

It is not easy to obtain a clear picture of Soviet resources and reserves because the USSR does not exchange such information to the extent that many other nations do, nor does it reveal with much accuracy any information on its exports and imports—especially to and from satellite countries. Much of what is known concerning Soviet resources has already been summarized in Chapter 2. A useful assessment of the current Soviet import position can be obtained to the degree possible by combining what information is available with some well-educated guesses. The best source of aggregated information of this kind is the U.S. Bureau of Mines, which provides an annual assessment of Soviet minerals dependency, as shown in Figure 5.2. A comparison of this figure with Figure 5.1 reveals that the Soviet Union is relatively materials self-sufficient as compared with the United States. The Soviets import appreciable percentages (given in parentheses) of only nine industrial raw materials—barite (49), bauxite/alumina (48), cobalt (47), fluorspar (53), mica sheet (13), molybdenum (15), silver (10), tin (33), and tungsten (43)—and relatively small percentages of two others—iron and steel (3) and zinc (2). Of these, only four—barite, bauxite/alumina, cobalt, and fluorspar—approach 50 percent of consumption. Significantly, the Soviets are completely self-sufficient for the strategic and critical materials listed for

Figure 5.2 Net Soviet imports of selected materials as percentages of consumption

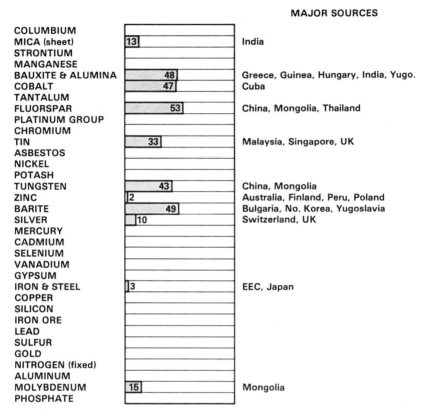

MAJOR SOURCES

COLUMBIUM		
MICA (sheet)	13	India
STRONTIUM		
MANGANESE		
BAUXITE & ALUMINA	48	Greece, Guinea, Hungary, India, Yugo.
COBALT	47	Cuba
TANTALUM		
FLUORSPAR	53	China, Mongolia, Thailand
PLATINUM GROUP		
CHROMIUM		
TIN	33	Malaysia, Singapore, UK
ASBESTOS		
NICKEL		
POTASH		
TUNGSTEN	43	China, Mongolia
ZINC	2	Australia, Finland, Peru, Poland
BARITE	49	Bulgaria, No. Korea, Yugoslavia
SILVER	10	Switzerland, UK
MERCURY		
CADMIUM		
SELENIUM		
VANADIUM		
GYPSUM		
IRON & STEEL	3	EEC, Japan
COPPER		
SILICON		
IRON ORE		
LEAD		
SULFUR		
GOLD		
NITROGEN (fixed)		
ALUMINUM		
MOLYBDENUM	15	Mongolia
PHOSPHATE		

Source: U.S. Bureau of Mines (1984).

the United States in Table 5.3 except for bauxite/alumina and cobalt. This relative materials self-sufficiency, as contrasted with the heavy dependence upon imports by the United States and its allies, continues to give military planners much cause for concern.

Much evidence points to the fact that the Soviets, at least since the early 1970s, have at enormous cost exerted every effort to achieve the highest possible level of materials self-sufficiency. Economic costs, at least until recently, have appeared secondary to the expansion of production, and consumption has been limited to available or anticipated supplies. As a result of this costly effort, observers have estimated that the only truly strategic material the Soviets are heavily dependent upon is natural rubber.[20]

As for the possibility of a resource war, in recent years the Soviet import/ export situation has undergone significant change. Starting in the late 1970s, Soviet exports of some materials suddenly ceased, and at about the same time the USSR began purchasing some of these and other materials on world markets. At one time, for example, the Soviets were significant exporters of chromium, the platinum-group metals, and manganese—all of which are included in Table 5.3. Recently, however, the country has imported high-grade chrome ore from Iran and has become a buyer of cobalt as well as lead, copper, zinc, aluminum, and molybdenum—materials for which the Soviets still are considered to be relatively self-sufficient.

Although U.S. government officials who monitor Soviet trade are reluctant to discuss publicly the possible explanations for these changes in Soviet import/export policy, other analysts have been less reluctant to do so. They have suggested that the Soviets may have instituted a policy of effectively stopping all exports of strategic materials to the West, and of competing aggressively with the West for supplies available from Third World nations. Such a policy, if true, implies a concerted effort on the part of the Soviets to make it difficult for the Western nations to acquire such materials for themselves. Conversely, others suggest that the Soviets are already so heavily dependent upon the foreign exchange earned from materials exports that they can hardly afford to engage in preemptive buying in an effort to reduce the supply available to the West. They note instead that it is not uncommon for the USSR and other Eastern European countries to barter for material resources from Third World countries in exchange for Soviet machinery and military equipment ordered by those countries, thus avoiding the need for hard currency transactions usually required of Third World countries by Western nations.

It is entirely possible that because free-market prices for some of these materials had begun to increase rapidly, the Soviet purchases may merely have been a hedge against inflation. It is also possible that despite generally rising materials prices, Soviet costs have been rising even more, thus forcing at least a temporary abandonment of the Soviet policy to retain its past level of materials self-sufficiency. The latter possibility may be a very real one due to the large scale on which the Soviets have exploited their materials resources, thereby depleting their higher grade, most accessible deposits and necessitating the development of more costly and less accessible deposits, as has been true of the United States for many years. Another explanation may be that the Soviets, also like the United States, are building up stockpiles of strategic and critical materials for military purposes. Whatever the reason for this recent change in Soviet materials policy, it is conceivable that it may be more than a temporary phenomenon and hence may spell additional trouble for the West for the foreseeable future.

As noted in a recent survey of Soviet nonfuel materials, it is likely that the Soviets will continue to maintain a strong commitment to develop and exploit their domestic materials resources despite difficulties arising from shortages of both capital and labor. Throughout the 1980s, they are most likely to remain relatively self-sufficient with respect to their requirements for nonfuel materials, including improvements in their supply position for aluminum, cobalt, chromium, copper, gold, nickel, the platinum-group metals, and titanium. On the other hand, they will probably have to import a relatively small percentage of their requirements for lead, molybdenum, tin, tungsten, and zinc as they attempt to expand domestic production of these materials.[21] Whether these efforts will result in a significant change in the current Soviet import/export posture remains to be seen.

Past Soviet Actions

Indications of Soviet intent to promote difficulties for the West have been heightened in the past by the somewhat intemperate remarks made from time to time by various Soviet leaders. For example, in 1960 Nikita Krushchev advocated that the Soviet Union increase its influence upon the mineral-rich Third World nations in order to hold the West hostage to Moscow.[22] However, perhaps the most memorable statement was that made by Leonid Brezhnev in 1973: "Our aim is to gain control of the two great treasure houses on which the West depends: the energy treasure house of the Persian Gulf and the mineral treasure house of central and southern Africa."[23] The reference to the "energy treasure house of the Persian Gulf" requires no further elaboration. The reference to the "mineral treasure house of central and southern Africa" emphasizes the importance of such minerals-rich nations as Angola, Botswana, Gabon, Mozambique, Namibia, Zaire, Zambia, Zimbabwe, and—perhaps the most important of all—the Republic of South Africa. The combined resources of strategic and critical materials possessed by African nations, and their large fraction of total annual world production of these materials, make them a formidable force in materials geopolitics. As shown in Table 5.4, African nations currently supply major percentages of world production of bauxite/alumina (15), chromium (33), cobalt (60), manganese (21), and the platinum-group metals (40). Moreover, they possess major percentages of the known world reserve base of bauxite (27), chromium (95), cobalt (32), manganese (75), the platinum-group metals (81), and tantalum (26).[24] The danger seen in Brezhnev's remark is that the Soviets may attempt to exert political pressures upon these nations in order to influence materials policies unfavorable to the West. Such pressures might be quite effective in view of the fact that many of these nations have only recently emerged from colonialism, are now undergoing rapid economic development, and are prone to political instability.

Considerable evidence suggests that the Soviets have indeed attempted to influence the materials policies of many Third World nations, and not only by political means. They have demonstrably encouraged such nations to dissociate themselves from the capitalist nations that formerly held them under colonial practices of racist oppression and exploitation; the Soviets clearly recognize that the major, and often only, means available to these nations for such dissociation is the pursuit of adverse materials policies. When such encouragement has proved insufficient, the Soviets have been known to resort to more forceful methods, reflecting a widely held view among many analysts that, at least for the past decade, the Soviets have employed a global strategy increasingly oriented at depriving Western nations of vital raw materials, through support of Marxist liberation movements

Table 5.4 Annual Production and Reserve Base of Seven African Nations for Selected Strategic and Critical Materials[a]

Country	Bauxite/Alumina	Chromium	Cobalt	Columbium	Manganese	Platinum	Tantalum
Gabon					8.3/3.7		
Guinea	14.6/26.5						
Nigeria				0.6/2.2			2.4/13.2
Republic of South Africa		27.6/83.6				40.0/80.8	
Zaire			46.9/25.0	0.3/2.2	12.9/70.8		4.2/8.8
Zambia			13.5/ 6.5				
Zimbabwe		5.3/11.0					
TOTALS	14.6/26.5	32.9/94.6	60.4/31.5	0.9/4.4	21.2/74.5	40.0/80.8	9.8/26.4

a: in percentages of world totals (annual production/reserve base).

Source: U.S. Bureau of Mines, Mineral Commodity Summaries 1985 (Washington, D.C.: U.S. Department of the Interior, 1985).

and the overthrow of any pro-Western governments of materials-rich nations. Examples of such Soviet activity include the following:

- Presence of Cuban troops, as well as East German and Soviet advisors, in southern Africa.
- Direct military interventions in Angola, Ethiopia, Mozambique, and Zaire, and installation of a Marxist-oriented government in Zimbabwe.
- Presence of Cuban soldiers, advisors, or technicians in other African states, for a total of seventeen states.
- Reported covert or subversive Soviet operations in Namibia, the Republic of South Africa, Zaire's Shaba province, and neighboring areas.[25]

Less recent Soviet activities along these same lines, but perhaps more speculative, include the war with Finland, in which the settlement of 1940 transferred to the Soviet Union the Pechenga nickel mines formerly in northern Finland, and the takeover of Hungary, in which some of the most brutal fighting in putting down the Hungarian revolt occurred in the bauxite-mining and aluminum-refining areas, where Soviet troop divisions were most heavily concentrated.[26] It is quite likely that most of the materials produced in the latter area still move to the Soviet Union. Also, it is conceivable that the Soviet invasion of Afghanistan may have been at least partly motivated by Soviet aggressive resource policy, in that Afghanistan possesses significant, although undeveloped, deposits of chromite and uranium ores and currently exports substantial quantities of natural gas and gemstones to the Soviet Union. In sum, it is hardly necessary for all these Soviet activities to represent pursuit of an anti-West resource policy to establish the strong likelihood that such a policy may indeed exist.

Current Status of the Resource War

From the evidence in Soviet words and deeds it is legitimate to ask whether a resource war really is in progress between the United States and the Soviet Union. If not, then the time is at hand to reduce greatly the current level of rhetoric on the subject. However, if a warlike situation does exist, then steps should be taken by the U.S. government to meet the challenge.

As stated elsewhere:

In recent years older distinctions between "peace" and "war" have become blurred. Instead, we see extended contests among competing political and economic philosophies characterized by varying degrees of "economic warfare" and "cold war," as well as sporadic, but thus far limited, actual hostilities. In these times the security of industrialized democratic societies depends in large measure not only upon military strength in being but also upon having virile economies that provide maximum employment, production, and purchasing power. Such economies facilitate development of sophisticated military materiel and provide a mobilization base with substantial elements capable of being rapidly converted to defense and defense-supporting production.[27]

Thus it is difficult within this modern context to define what a war actually is. However, in terms of resources, an offensive war has been defined as the effort "to gain control over the source of the other superpower's main imports of strategic materials in order to acquire the potential to deny the other such resources when deemed to be advantageous to do so."[28] In this context, an offensive resource war represents a strategy of confrontation that extends beyond normal economic competition but falls short of conventional military conflict. A corresponding "defensive" resource war could be defined as an effort to safeguard one's own sources of strategic raw materials from potential threats of denial by an aggressor. Those analysts who are convinced that Soviet tactics represent an offensive war quite naturally exhort the federal government to initiate a defensive resource war in return.

Historical Resource War Activities. In considering whether or not a resource war is now being waged, it should be remembered that international disagreements over materials, and even outright conflicts, have occurred not infrequently in the past. Ancient Rome depended upon the grain extracted as tribute from much of its empire, including Sicily, Spain, North Africa, and Gaval. The Phoenicians, and then the Romans, fought wars over the tin mines of Cornwall. And much of modern European development resulted from the "shiploads of gold and silver bullion extracted from the mines of the New World; the slaves, diamonds, copper, and vegetable oils of Africa; and the cotton, rubber, and spices of India and Malaysia—all taken at gunpoint."[29] Soviet designs upon Poland are said to have included Polish lead and zinc deposits, and France and Germany for many years fought over the iron deposits of Alsace-Lorraine. Rivalries among the great powers during the eighteenth and nineteenth centuries were fueled by competition for resources, and more recently, Roosevelt and Churchill made "equal access" to the world's mineral resources one of the key points of the Atlantic Charter of 1941.[30]

Certainly materials geopolitics has featured prominently in the thinking of military strategists for centuries and has continued to do so during the coldwar period of Soviet-U.S. relations. However, as the cold war waned in the 1960s and the spirit of détente became more firmly established, resources-related questions increasingly turned to issues of international commodity trade policy. Such policy, for example, underlay much of the Nixon administration's view that Soviet exports of raw materials to the West in exchange for technology, food, and capital would promote a climate of growing interdependence that would help maintain world peace. Later, with the spirit of détente more firmly established, the Carter administration's comprehensive Domestic Policy Review of Nonfuel Minerals not surprisingly was dominated by considerations of international commodity trade policy, rather than by considerations of the geopolitics of strategic and critical materials. As noted earlier, the Reagan administration has revived the cold war and both U.S. and Soviet activities may have increased the dangers of a materials "flashpoint."

Current Views. Those experts who maintain that the United States is already engaged in a resource war with the Soviet Union base their views largely upon recent Soviet materials activities and their perceptions of the significance of these activities. A major theme is that the Soviets are following a master plan involving a deliberate effort to undermine the materials position of the United States and its allies, and that this effort, combined with the potential unreliability of some major Third World materials suppliers, poses a real threat to Western powers. The Soviet Union is thus perceived as a hostile state bent upon inflicting as much damage as possible upon the United States and its allies through an aggressive materials policy.

Advocates of this view cite what they view as the aggressively relentless expansion of Soviet influence in all the ways already noted. They even point out the suspicious coincidence that the Soviets reportedly bought a two-year supply of cobalt just before the Katangan rebel invasion of Zaire that cut off cobalt production from that country's mines, and they note that the Soviets continue to be directly involved in political unrest in that area.[31] Soviet military support of Iraq and Syria is also noted, with regard to fuel interests.

Other experts see no sinister motive behind recent Soviet initiatives in world resources supply and demand but, rather, consider the activities simply the logical result of economic changes now taking place in the Soviet domestic resource posture. Sooner or later, they note, a shift in the position of the Soviet Union from that of a supplier nation for many materials to that of an importer nation must take place. They emphasize that this is an economic situation associated with the growth of industrialization, not a military situation.

The concept of a resource war appears to have little credibility among U.S. allies, especially some European nations and Japan. This lack of concern, it has been suggested, may derive from the fact that these nations are more experienced trading partners of the Soviet Union and hence may be more skeptical of Soviet ability to wage such an offensive. Others see the specter of a resource war being much overblown, especially by the Reagan administration. Still another view is that although the Soviets may indeed seize every opportunity possible to promote economic mischief, such activities hardly qualify as long-range, well-thought-out strategies that call for costly countermeasures by the United States. And to some analysts the Soviet interest in south African countries arises primarily because the area represents a fertile breeding ground for political and military disturbances that may adversely affect the West; the presence of strategic materials important to the West is merely an additional factor the Soviets can exploit.

Some experts, indulging in a bit of cynicism, have expressed the view that the presumption of a resource war may serve the best interests of the Reagan administration in its current effort to build up national defense. Still others, noting the strong support of the concept by the nation's mining interests, suggest that the concept is being exploited to promote a crash program of exploration for strategic minerals on federal lands, or to obtain more favorable tax treatment for the mining industries. It has also been suggested that the resource war is really a "media event" to draw attention to minerals issues and problems and, within this context, may already have accomplished its purpose.[32]

Thus far, little support for the concept of a resource war has been pronounced *officially* by the federal government. For example, minerals experts in the Central Intelligence Agency and the National Security Council profess to have found no real evidence of a concerted Soviet strategy to cut off the West from its critical materials supplies.[33] Likewise, State Department officials have expressed little support for the concept, stressing instead the need for preserving political continuity in international relations.[34]

A General Assessment. In view of the strong arguments that can be made on either side of the resource war issue, it is not easy to determine the extent to which the conditions given earlier for the existence of a resource war have indeed been met. The point is not entirely academic inasmuch as major materials policy responses by the U.S. government must necessarily be influenced strongly by perceptions of Soviet intent in this important area. U.S.-Soviet rivalry for world influence has now dominated world politics for three decades and is likely to continue doing so for at least another. Quite possibly, resource problems will contribute to existing conflicts or even become the primary cause of conflict. In the extreme, as noted elsewhere, "cases show well that nations do indeed resort to violence when their sources of vital minerals are endangered."[35]

Yet it seems highly doubtful that such a negative outlook is warranted, at least at present. Insufficient evidence exists to warrant the conclusion that the Soviets have some grand design on the world's supply of strategic and critical materials, or are prepared to promote actual warfare between themselves and the Third World or the Western powers over the disposition of such materials. Much evidence does exist, however, to suggest that the Soviets are indeed making "economic capital out of political trouble and political capital out of economic trouble."[36] Consequently, U.S. materials import dependency, with its problem of maintaining uninterrupted access to foreign sources of strategic and critical materials, will undoubtedly continue to pose a real challenge to Western policymakers.

Certainly much of this challenge will be economic in nature. It is no secret that the Soviet Union and its Eastern-bloc allies lack the foreign exchange necessary to compete successfully in world markets for all the imports they now require. Further, with the partial exception of the USSR itself, they also lack the project capital necessary to develop fully their domestic resources of such materials. Consequently, it is possible that in order to establish an adequate world resource share, the Soviets may require entry into the market by different rules than those customarily followed by the West, adding intimidation and subversion to purely economic considerations.

The recent Soviet behavior is not new. In fact, the Soviets are playing an old game with many of the same rules, augmented by a few recently developed twists. The USSR, and Czarist Russia before it, have actively pursued a calculated policy of expansionism, economic or military, from the time of Peter the Great; hence there should be little surprise over recent Soviet initiatives to obtain materials. The new twists are that, first, the Soviet Union has emerged as a major world economic and military power, thereby dramatically increasing its capacity to subvert the vital interests of other nations, and second, it has an increasing willingness to use both its economic and its military power to accomplish such subversion. Thus, current Soviet moves in the raw materials area may simply represent an extension and expansion of past Soviet behavior in other areas.

A recent factor that bears consideration is the Soviet willingness to use energy-resource policy as a tool of international diplomacy, an effort that appears likely to intensify through exploitation of the Yamburg natural gas pipeline to Western Europe. This project was opposed by the Reagan administration precisely because of the strategic considerations implicit in such energy-resource diplomacy.[37] There appears to be no reason, other than lack of sufficient export potential, for the Soviets not to attempt the same effort in materials-resource diplomacy wherever they can. Development of their Siberian and other materials resources could increase markedly their potential for such diplomatic maneuvering.

A question naturally arises over what approach the United States should take in response to these Soviet initiatives. In general, all of the approaches to be discussed in Chapter 6 represent potentially effective responses that would help moderate the effects of any Soviet successes in "locking up" specific materials resources. Beyond these, it is frequently suggested that U.S. foreign policy toward materials-rich developing nations should be reassessed to encourage the development of more friendly and cooperative relations, notwithstanding the internal politics and policies of such nations; thereby, some of the Soviet geopolitical initiatives could be countered. As recent history reveals, the Soviet Union has not been particularly successful in its "global outreach" program, as a part of which its military power "was to be felt in the conduct of international relations at any place, at any time throughout the world." Indeed,

> As impressive as its military power and formidable as its geo-strategic position have been, the Soviet Union has not always reaped the political success it expected from this outreach policy. Headed by the People's Republic of China, Egypt, and Iraq, but including nations in all areas of the world, the list of Soviet foreign policy failures during the post-Stalin period is long and impressive.[38]

Thus it is possible that an appropriate U.S. foreign policy toward these nations might go a long way toward helping neutralize current Soviet materials policy initiatives detrimental to U.S. interests.

Underlying much of the foregoing discussion is the presumption of continued Soviet aggressive initiatives aimed at controlling world materials supplies and denying them to the Western powers. However, it has also been suggested that, from the Soviet perspective, it is the West that traditionally has aggressively controlled the bulk of the world's materials output, whether it was Spanish shipments of silver and gold from early Mexico or the vast quantities of materials that England, France, and other European colonial powers took from their colonies in Africa and elsewhere throughout the world. According to this view, Soviet intentions may not be sinister but instead may represent an attempt to neutralize what they regard as excessive Western control of, and access to, strategic raw materials.

Whatever intentions may in fact underlie current Soviet materials activities, it seems clear that the United States must seek to develop an effective response to protect its vital materials interests, and that, at the same time, it must take whatever steps appear necessary to reduce its current level of materials import dependency. Also vital to any such effort must be similar attempts to reduce the materials import dependency of U.S. allies, most of whom—as discussed later in this chapter—are far more import dependent, and with less potential for domestic resource development, than the United States. Only to the extent that the United States and its allies can reduce their dependencies upon strategic supplies vulnerable to Soviet manipulation can the West increase the prospect of failure of an attempt by the Soviets to wage a resource war or to utilize strategic and critical materials effectively as a tool of Soviet international diplomacy.

Some Major Issues of Concern

Decline of the Defense Industrial Base

The discussion in this chapter of materials import vulnerability has focused thus far upon the lack of domestic resources of certain strategic and critical materials and, consequently, the need to import such materials from abroad. However, once these materials have been imported, the need still exists to process and refine them, and to fabricate them into the desired shapes and forms in which they can be used by industry. The processing, refining, and fabricating industries that accomplish these important tasks are a vital part of the nation's defense industrial base, which can be defined as that industrial infrastructure upon which the nation's strategic defense depends. Broadly, the defense industrial base thus includes all of the mines, smelters, factories, production and fabrication facilities, transportation and distribution networks, and other key industrial elements required to produce hardware and software, both military and defense-related, to maintain an adequate level of defense. That portion of the defense industrial base of primary importance to this discussion includes the mining, minerals, and basic metals industries that produce and process materials, and the steel, aerospace, and related basic industries that use these materials for defense-related purposes.

From its height in World War II, the nation's defense industrial base had begun to decline in only the few years before the onset of the Korean

War. Some years later, a report prepared in 1976 by the Defense Science Board's task force on industrial readiness verified that serious deficiencies existed in the ability of the defense industrial base to respond to a wide range of potential contingencies. Following issuance of the Science Board's report, these deficiencies became even more pronounced as the defense-industrial base continued its decline. In an attempt to reverse this decline and strengthen industries essential to defense, the Reagan administration increased defense-related spending dramatically. Indeed, this defense build-up has taken place so quickly that serious questions have been raised as to whether these industries can efficiently and effectively absorb the huge public funds suddenly made available to them.

Factors Contributing to the Decline. The condition of many basic industries in the United States has deteriorated so greatly that some, as earlier noted, are not far from actual extinction. Many reasons underlie this deterioration, some of which have been discussed. Others will be discussed at greater length in Chapters 7 and 8. The two major reasons most often cited are federal regulatory, chiefly environmental, policies that critically affect such industries and the growing expectations of materials-producing nations to become more highly industrialized themselves.

As noted earlier in this chapter, these industries are inherently rather messy and untidy, and they generate as by-products a relatively large quantity of waste materials offensive both to human beings and to the environment. Additionally, the working conditions under which these operations take place tend to be rather noisy, hot, and dirty or dusty, making for relatively unwholesome places to work. Not surprisingly, therefore, these industries have been primary targets of the nation's effort to preserve and restore the environment and to maintain more healthful working conditions. Many of the target plants, unable to afford the high costs of meeting new federal environmental and worker health and safety regulations, have closed down. The building of new plant capacity has been similarly handicapped.

At the same time, new and at times formidable competition in these industries has arisen from developing producer nations. Many such nations, including some of the primary raw materials producers, have been constructing facilities to process and fabricate their raw materials locally so they may ship the more refined products to overseas users. In this context, "processing" means the conversion of basic raw materials into more refined mineral, metal, or other materials products for industrial use. This procedure is economically feasible for the developing nations because the raw materials are close at hand, labor costs are lower than in the industrialized user nations, production facilities are relatively modern, energy often is cheap, and shipping costs for finished products are much lower than are those for bulk raw materials. Consequently, these nations can mine and process materials, then ship the processed materials to foreign users around the world, more cheaply than the foreign users can import and process the raw materials themselves.

The result of this activity has been a "migration" of many basic industries from user nations to supplier nations. In the United States, for example, the steel industry is declining, ferromanganese and ferrochromium processing capacity is sharply reduced, and the domestic processing of a number of industrially important metals—including aluminum, copper, lead, and zinc— is declining rapidly. Indeed, it has been suggested that the United States now qualifies as a "developing nation" because copper, lead, and zinc ores of its own are now exported for processing overseas, then imported again as processed materials.

The Ferroalloys Industry. Ferroalloys are processed from chromium, manganese, and silicon ores. In the form of ferrochromium, ferromanganese, ferrosilicon, and other ferroalloy products, they are indispensable in the manufacture of aluminum, iron, steel, stainless steel, and various kinds of superalloys. Consequently, they contribute importantly to the nation's communications, transportation, and national defense systems. The present U.S. ferroalloys industry consists of seventeen companies operating twenty-nine plants of various capacities. Four other manufacturers produce ferroalloys for their own internal use, not for sale on the open market.

Although a decade ago eleven of these plants produced ferrochromium products, the last operating ferrochromium furnace ceased operations in May 1983. Likewise, only one of the twelve remaining furnaces producing high-carbon ferromanganese is still in production, imports having captured more than 95 percent of the domestic market. Even domestic ferrosilicon producers, who do not depend upon imports of raw materials, have lost more than one-fourth of the domestic market to overseas producers.[39] For example, the Soviet Union has begun to ship ferrosilicon of a type made specifically for U.S. industry to the United States at a price approximately half that of domestically produced ferrosilicon, thereby further weakening the domestic industry.[40]

The shift in U.S. dependency from imports of raw materials to imported processed materials is particularly disturbing because a nation lacking furnace capacity to produce ferroalloys reduces its supply options from the relatively large number of countries able to supply raw ores to the smaller number that are able to supply the processed materials. Significantly, the shift also makes irrelevant the search for domestic resources or the current stockpiling of ores. Despite these concerns, a recent study by the Department of Commerce failed to recommend any significant long-term relief for the domestic ferroalloys industry. The study recommended that currently stockpiled chromium and manganese ores be converted to ferroalloy forms, which would provide some temporary relief to the domestic industry. However, although the study noted that the use of tariffs or import quotas to reduce ferroalloy imports—as requested by the industry—would provide some protection and would help to maintain the capability to process stockpiled ores, it pointed out that such an approach would entail large resource costs for the steel industry and would adversely affect U.S. international trade policy. Furthermore, the study suggested that any gains achieved by the industry would undoubtedly be lost as soon as such benefits were removed. Hence, the study concluded, "Overall, it appears that the use of tariffs, quotas, or other trade measures to assure ferroalloys supply by encouraging domestic producers is not a cost-effective means of reducing supply risks."[41] These conclusions contrast sharply with those of European nations and Japan, which have taken steps to protect their own ferroalloy industries.

In accordance with the Department of Commerce's recommendations, the General Services Administration announced a ten-year plan to upgrade significant quantities of stockpiled chromite and manganese ores into more readily usable forms at an annual cost of more than $40 million.[42] Industry participants are required to pick up the ore from selected storage sites, transport and process the ore, and deliver the high carbon ferroalloys to designated GSA storage depots.

In responding to the Department of Commerce study, the Ferroalloys Association agreed that the stockpile upgrading program would indeed improve the readiness of the stockpile for emergency use, but maintained that the program still fell far short of meeting the nation's security needs. For example, it noted that the stockpile program does not provide the balanced inventory of chromium and manganese ferroalloys and metals needed for modern steel production. Additionally, it pointed out the continued need for domestic ferroalloy furnace and processing capacity sufficient to make up shortfalls in stockpile supplies and to provide processed ferroalloys if imports were disrupted in an emergency.[43] The association concluded that the stockpile upgrading program "fails to address the problem of imports and, at best, will only prolong the death throes of the domestic producers."[44]

The Basic Metals Industries. Various studies of the health of the basic metals industries have concluded that such industries are exposed to a formidable array of difficulties. At least in part because they developed early and led the way in promoting economies of scale, these industries are especially prone today to technological rigidity—resistance to the acceptance of new technology. Further, they are characterized by narrow profit margins, shortage of investment capital, raw materials uncertainty, and general reluctance to invest in research and development of new processes, products, or facilities.

Among the major basic metals industries that have declined substantially in recent years are the aluminum, copper, lead, and zinc industries. Although the United States produces about one-third of the annual world production of aluminum, it must import virtually all of the raw materials—primarily bauxite and alumina—required for new production. Increasingly, the foreign bauxite producers are insisting that alumina and aluminum-producing plants be built in their own countries so that they can export intermediate or end products of higher value than bauxite itself. This trend toward overseas construction of alumina- and aluminum-processing facilities is being encouraged by U.S. aluminum producers, who find substantial advantages in siting new refining and smelting plants in countries like Australia, where ample bauxite resources exist and where energy costs are more favorable than they are in the United States. Although such new facilities are owned by U.S. producers, who thus derive substantial economic benefits not realized through operation of domestic plants, the question arises of whether the shift of such processing capacity abroad increases U.S. vulnerability to potential supply interruptions of aluminum.

Although copper, lead, and zinc are not among the handful of materials considered in Table 5.3 as most strategic and critical, they are of major industrial importance and represent a significant element of the defense industrial base. Yet all three industries have suffered major declines in production, smelting, and/or refining capacities. For most copper-producing nations, smelter output roughly corresponds to the respective share of world mine production.[45] However, the U.S. share of both mining and refining has dropped significantly over the past decade, and U.S. imports of refined copper have increased from 6 to almost 20 percent of U.S. consumption. Lead production also has declined, and a number of smelter-refineries have had to curtail operations or close down completely. It is conceivable that none of the primary lead smelters now operating in the United States could meet current federal lead standards if such standards were vigorously enforced. Similarly, zinc production has declined more than 50 percent in the past fifteen years. As recently as 1969, fourteen zinc smelters were in operation in the United States; nine have now closed. Over the past decade, zinc smelter production has declined from about 1 million tons (1969) to 300,000 tons (1982), and mine production has declined from 534,000 tons (1970) to 280,000 tons (1983). The decline of these industries, and indeed of the U.S. mining and minerals industry as a whole, has caused many analysts to express grave concern over the effects of the decline upon U.S. defense capability.

The Steel Industry. Steel is the most basic industrial metal, accounting for more than three-fourths of all metal used each year in the United States. It plays an essential role in many sectors of the economy, including construction, consumer durables, industrial machinery, and transportation. It also plays a major role in helping to meet defense requirements for combat vehicles, shipbuilding, weapons, and a wide variety of ordnance hardware. However, some 200 domestic steel facilities have been closed permanently since 1974, shrinking U.S. capacity by more than 13 million tons. Current domestic raw steel productive capacity amounts to about 154 million tons, about three-fourths of it accounted for by the eight largest integrated steel producers. Major factors for the industry's decline are sharply increased foreign imports, huge expenditures for pollution control, rapidly increasing energy costs, noncompetitive labor rates, and tax laws biased against capital formation.

Even in the face of these problems, however, considerable modernization has taken place in the industry. New construction has emphasized both basic oxygen and electric furnace capacity, and it also has utilized new technologies to improve the efficiency of existing blast furnace operations. Recently, new "mini-mills" that utilize efficient electric furnaces and continuous casters to produce steel from scrap have flourished. Because such mini-mills are more modern, efficient, and have lower nonlabor costs than other mills, they are expected to steadily increase their market share. Although they accounted for less than 3 percent of domestic steel output in 1960, they produce approximately 18 percent today. Meanwhile, analysts predict that the capacity of big integrated producers will shrink by 45 percent by the year 2000.[46] However, a need will continue to exist for more continuous annealing lines and for additional capacity for producing bake-hardenable steels, dual phase steels, high-quality/high-formability steels, and improved galvanized steels. Yet the general lack of health of the U.S. steel industry—apart from its mini-mills—and the prospects for further decline in the future are a constant source of debate among industry specialists.

Although the United States imports only a relatively small percentage of its iron for steelmaking and exports substantial quantities of coking coal and ferrous scrap, it relies almost completely upon foreign sources for many of the alloying materials used to produce various kinds of high-performance steels. These additive elements include the following, with current import percentages given in parentheses:

Chromium (100)	Hardenability, high-temperature strength, and corrosion resistance.
Cobalt (99)	High-temperature hardness.
Columbium (100)	As-rolled strength.
Lead (Export)	Machinability.
Manganese (99)	Deoxidation, sulfur control, and hardenability.
Molybdenum (E)	Hardenability, high-temperature hardness, and brittleness control.
Nickel (75)	Hardenability and low-temperature toughness.
Silicon (20)	Deoxidation and electrical properties.
Tungsten (48)	High-temperature hardness and hardenability.
Vanadium (14)	Grain size and hardenability.[47]

Defense requirements for steel during peacetime typically amount to only about 5 percent of domestic consumption. Although such requirements would increase substantially during wartime, necessary capacity could be "borrowed" from various consumer uses including automobiles, home appliances, and containers, which typically consume about 30 percent of annual production. Hence, although industry capacity itself lacks any appreciable degree of vulnerability, the ability of the industry to utilize that capacity for vital defense purposes is dependent upon continuing supplies of the alloying materials given above.

In this regard, the Department of Commerce study concluded that, at least with regard to chromium and manganese, the steel industry's import dependency represents a high risk due to the potentially unstable sources of supply, the questionable value of the National Defense Stockpile as currently constituted, and the lack of cost-effective substitutes.[48] Concern was expressed as well over the concentration of supply sources for columbium and vanadium. No industry vulnerability was found with respect to the remaining steel alloying materials—molybdenum, nickel, silicon, and tungsten— because of some combination of adequate domestic supply capacity, reliable import sources, adequate stockpile status, and availability of reasonable substitutes.

Importance to National Defense. It would be difficult to overemphasize the importance of all the foregoing industries to U.S. national defense. Without them, almost the entire defense-related infrastructure would collapse. Virtually no prospect of such a traumatic event exists, because the federal government would be forced to take action to prevent it. Yet some parts of this infrastructure do appear threatened with collapse, and the government has done little about it.

A major difficulty for the government admittedly lies in trying to determine to what extent an industry, or a portion of an industry, can be permitted to decline without endangering the nation's capacity to defend itself. Different experts and analysts will set the limit for this decline at various levels depending upon their individual assessments of the demands that would be made upon these industries during conflicts of varying magnitude, scope, and duration. Thus, as often happens, it becomes almost impossible to form a consensus among responsible policymakers as to what should be done. Hence, these industries continue for the present to erode.

There is little question that a healthy domestic materials industry cannot be sustained without domestic smelters and metallurgical plants, and yet these are among the industries that have suffered the most serious declines. At present, it is probable that the federal government lacks sufficient information to even identify industry problems or to determine the underlying reasons for the decline. Consequently, as these industries become less healthy and less capable of meeting domestic needs, difficulties arise in maintaining an adequate defense posture during peacetime, let alone during a wartime emergency.

The alternative to relying upon domestic capacity is to increase the current level of imports of major industrial processed materials and components, thus displacing further offshore the nation's defense industrial base. The consequences should be clear:

> It will make those parts of our Strategic Stockpile which are in the form of unprocessed or semi-processed materials even more obsolete than they are today, since there will be neither the lead time nor the domestic capacity to convert these raw or semi-processed materials into the necessary defense production forms; and it will place more economic leveraging into the hands of the supplier countries; hence, prices of such materials will continue to seek new levels as dictated by supply control, speculation, and preemptive market maneuvers.[49]

The basic question, therefore, is whether maintaining these industries as strong, effective components of the defense industrial base is essential to national security and, if so, what steps should be taken to arrest their decline and restore their vigor. Potential steps are now being debated under the general rubric of a "new industrial policy" that would seek to assure the competitiveness of U.S. industry in both domestic and international markets, thereby helping to maintain the economic health and strength of these and other essential industries.

Potential Supply Disruptions

As long as the United States perceives economic benefits in a high level of materials import dependency as outweighing strategic considerations, and as long as the National Defense Stockpile remains well below specified levels, the vulnerability of the nation to potential materials supply disruptions will persist. In view of the current level of world economic, political, and military unrest and instability, the possibility of such supply disruptions actually occurring is not at all remote. Indeed, the plurality of factors that may lead to such disruptions—including deliberate actions of foreign governments, civil or military disturbances, and various kinds of natural and human-caused disasters—lead inescapably to the conclusion that we should expect such disruptions from time to time and therefore should be adequately prepared to deal with them.

Foreign Government Actions. The possibility always exists that foreign governments may take deliberate actions to disrupt or restrict the normal flow of a particular strategic or critical material to the United States or its allies. Such actions could be taken to raise prices of the material by creating an artificial shortage, or—as in the case of the OPEC oil embargo in 1973—to express displeasure over U.S. foreign policy and to attempt to influence its future course. Although little evidence exists that any significant interruption for these reasons has occurred in the past for nonfuel materials, tensions arising from a variety of international developments—including the New International Economic Order involving many Third World suppliers, various United Nations' resolutions, nationalizations, unilateral expropriation acts, increased levies upon foreign materials investments, and unilateral price actions—all suggest that the potential for supply interruptions due to actions of foreign governments may be increasing.

Perhaps the most likely supply interruption of this nature is an embargo, in view of its long-established acceptance as an international political weapon, and despite its history of relative ineffectiveness in achieving its desired goals. For example, the effort by the League of Nations in October 1935 to establish an effective raw materials embargo against Italy to protest the Italian invasion of Ethiopia failed when many member nations maintained or even increased shipments to Italy of such critical materials as coal, iron, and oil. Also relatively ineffective were various embargoes against Rhodesia during the 1970s, including participation by the United States with respect to chromite ore. At the opposite end of the scale, the de facto embargo occasioned by the freezing of all Japanese assets in the United States following the Japanese invasion of southern Indochina in 1941 was so effective that it is believed to have helped determine the Japanese decision to bomb Pearl Harbor.[50]

In addition to embargoes, expropriation of foreign-owned enterprises ranks high on the list of probable interruptive actions, especially by Third World nations. For example,

> During 1968–1976, in only 50 of the less developed states, 64 foreign-owned mining and smelting firms and 95 foreign-owned petroleum subsidiaries were expropriated. Nationalized mineral industries in Third World states include bauxite in Jamaica and Guyana, diamonds in Sierra Leone, iron ore in Liberia and Venezuela, copper in Peru, Chile, Zaire, and Zambia, and tin in Bolivia, to name only a few.[51]

Much of the rationale for such action is that it is justified by the fact that many of these nations were plundered for decades, and some perhaps for centuries, when they existed as colonies of the developed nations. However legitimate the rationale, the point at issue is that such unilateral actions significantly increase the possibility of supply disruptions.

Civil or Military Disturbances. Materials supply disruptions may also occur as an unintended side effect of civil or military disturbances, including labor unrest. Such disruptions differ from those described above in that the governments, rather than being the instigators of the disturbance, usually exert their best efforts to halt the disruption and resume the normal flow of materials as soon as possible. However, with the emergence of international terrorism as a political tool, and the increase in nationalist fervor throughout much of the developing world, materials interruptions may at times become the intended effect rather than an unintended side effect. But whether or not directed explicitly at raw materials supplies, acts of sabotage such as the blowing up of bridges and tunnels or the destruction or blockading of major highways serve to interrupt raw materials supplies that are dependent upon public transportation systems. For example, the guerrilla activity that cut the Benguela Railroad during the Angola crisis in 1975 contributed to a shortage of copper and cobalt,[52] and the 1979 destruction of a key bridge linking the mining regions of Zambia with the Indian Ocean port of Dar es Salaam in Tanzania created materials supply disruptions for producers using that route for shipment.[53] Thus, acts of terrorism or political violence, whether directed against mining or processing facilities or against highly exposed transportation routes, can severely disrupt the normal flow of materials from producing nations.

Natural and Human-Caused Disasters. It is not unusual for mines or processing facilities to be temporarily incapacitated by such disasters as internally generated explosions, fires, and other accidents, or by hurricanes or typhoons causing flooding or destruction of processing facilities located near deepwater ports, if not destruction of the port loading facilities themselves. Such disasters can disrupt materials production for many months or even years.

Areas of Greatest Concern. Materials supply disruptions resulting from actions of foreign governments, or from civil or military disturbances, are most likely to occur in nations suffering from endemic political and economic instability. For the most part, such nations exist in Latin America, Southeast Asia, and central and southern Africa, areas that by a coincidence of geology and geography contain a large proportion of the world's resources of chromium, cobalt, manganese, the platinum-group metals, and other important industrial raw materials. The chronic instability of these nations is now considered "the most probable threat to the supply of strategic minerals: unplanned, unpredictable, chaotic interruptions of production and supply."[54]

Unfortunately, with the exception of a few nations that represent major military clients, the United States in its foreign policy has largely neglected these Third World supplier countries. Indeed, as noted in the literature,

> The United States is the least responsive to Third World needs of any industrialized country at this time. U.S. help is small in quantity, and getting smaller. Its quality is declining. It often runs directly counter to the central objectives of the LDC's. . . . It lags far behind the policies of Europe and Japan. The administration and Congress must share in the indictment. The United States regards developing countries both large and small . . . solely as pawns on the chessboard of global power politics. Rewards go only to the shrinking list of explicit collaborators.[55]

It seems only prudent that the United States consider adopting much more cooperative and responsive policies toward these materials-rich developing nations.

Allied Import Dependency and Vulnerability

Past discussions of materials import dependency and vulnerability have focused largely upon the U.S. import posture. This is easy to understand in the light of the widespread acceptance of the United States as the leader of the industrialized democratic powers. Because of this leadership role, U.S. import dependency and vulnerability clearly is of particular significance, and actions taken in this area by the United States obviously have important implications for its allies. On the other hand, it should also be clear that the position of U.S. allies—especially nations of Western Europe along with Japan—is also of great importance regarding the collective security of the North Atlantic Treaty Organization powers. Hence, it is logical to base analyses of requirements for strategic and critical materials upon the combined needs of all the industrialized democracies rather than upon U.S. needs alone—for however strong a position the United States may seek to establish for itself, it is unlikely to prevail in a world in which its allies succumb to hostile forces.

It is somewhat surprising that relatively little alarm has been expressed over the fact that major U.S. allies typically are much more dependent than the United States itself upon materials imports. Materials import dependency for the European Economic Community (EEC) and Japan is shown in Figure 5.3, which may be compared with corresponding data for the United States and the Soviet Union given in Figures 5.1 and 5.2, respectively. For ease of comparison, data for major materials for all four are summarized in Table

Figure 5.3 Net import reliance of the European Economic Community and Japan upon selected nonfuel materials, expressed as percentages of consumption

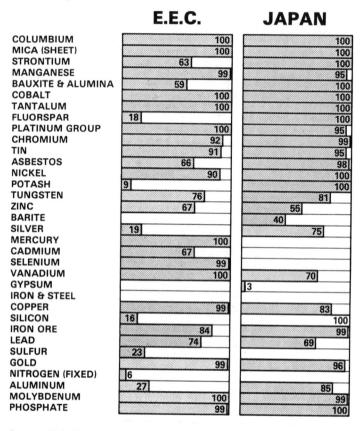

Source: U.S. Bureau of Mines (1983).

5.5. The table shows that the United States and its major allies share a high level of import dependency for many materials, and in particular those listed in Table 5.3 with the exception of bauxite/alumina, for which the EEC exhibits a much lower figure. Both the EEC and Japan exhibit much larger input dependencies than the United States for antimony, copper, gold, iron ore, lead, molybdenum, phosphate, and vanadium.

A recent study undertaken to determine the materials of greatest strategic importance to Great Britain showed that highest priority should be given to chromium, cobalt, tungsten, manganese, vanadium, molybdenum, and the platinum-group metals, for all of which current import dependency levels for that nation equal or approach 100 percent.[56] These materials are considered as the most strategic and critical not only in terms of military

Table 5.5 Materials Import Dependencies for Some Major Consuming Nations, Expressed as Percentages of Consumption

Material	United States	Soviet Union	European Economic Community	Japan
Aluminum	9		27	85
Antimony	54		93	100
Asbestos	75		66	98
Barite	64	49		40
Bauxite/alumina	96	48	59	100
Cadmium	56		67	
Chromium	82		92	99
Cobalt	95	47	100	100
Columbium	100		100	100
Copper	21		99	83
Fluorspar	91	53	18	100
Gold	16		99	97
Gypsum	38			3
Iron and steel	23	3		
Iron ore	19		84	99
Lead	18		74	69
Manganese	99		99	95
Mercury	60		100	
Mica (sheet)	100		100	100
Molybdenum	E	15	100	99
Nickel	74		90	100
Nitrogen (fixed)	14		6	
Platinum-group metals	91		100	95
Potash	74		9	100
Phosphate	E		99	100
Selenium	51		99	
Silicon	21		16	100
Silver	61	10	19	75
Strontium	100		63	100
Sulfur	17		23	
Tantalum	94		100	100
Tin	79	33	91	95
Tungsten	71	43	76	81
Vanadium	41		100	70
Zinc	67	2	67	55

E = net export condition.

Source: U.S. Bureau of Mines (1983-1984 data).

significance and importance to national defense, but also in terms of importance to the nation's economy as a whole. Substitution for these materials is considered to present serious problems, and supplies are considered to be especially vulnerable to interruption.

A broader study of strategic and critical materials requirements of the European Economic Community was conducted by the British House of Lords' Select Committee on the European Communities.[57] The committee solicited information from each member nation on materials considered to be of primary strategic importance in the sense that major economic disruptions would occur if the normal sources of supply of the materials were interrupted. The committee defined "strategic" in terms of "criticality," which was taken as a measure of the contribution made by a material to the nation's economy, and it defined "vulnerability" in terms of the import dependency of each country on the particular material. The study showed that member nations considered the eleven most critical materials to be asbestos, chromium, copper, fluorspar, iron ore, lead, manganese, phosphate rock, the platinum-group metals, sulfur, and tungsten. Import dependency and vulnerability for nine of these materials was found to be uniformly high; the exceptions were fluorspar and sulfur, for which import dependency was 15 and 60 percent, respectively. A condition of "most critical and vulnerable" was found for four materials—chromium, manganese, phosphate rock, and the platinum-group metals—in terms of their strategic, critical, and vulnerability factors.

Some caution should be exercised in drawing conclusions from the data in Table 5.5 because of the relatively different domestic materials postures of the respective nations. For example, whereas the United States exports such materials as molybdenum and phosphate rock, the EEC and Japan are virtually 100 percent import dependent for them. Consequently, in assessing vulnerability to potential supply disruptions, these two materials are of little concern to the United States but of primary concern to its allies. Although neither of these materials is on the list of most critical and strategic materials of Table 5.3, both are of major industrial importance and contribute significantly to national defense. Indeed, if ample domestic resources of these two materials were not available to the United States, both might be high on the strategic and critical list.

Additionally, materials trade patterns are quite different for the United States, the EEC, and Japan, as discussed in Chapter 3. The United States relies much more heavily than either Western Europe or Japan upon sources in the Western hemisphere, and especially upon Canadian and Latin American sources. Western Europe tends to import more from Africa than either Japan or the United States does, and Japan is dependent primarily upon producer nations in southern Asia and Southeast Asia, and upon Australia. These preferences are not surprising, in that both economic and strategic considerations may favor importing materials from those suppliers closest to home. For example, the primary sources of bauxite for the United States are Jamaica and Surinam, whereas for Western Europe they are nations in Africa, and for Japan they are Australia and Indonesia.

Because U.S. allies are so much more dependent than the United States itself upon materials imports, it seems reasonable that such imports should be of major concern in helping shape U.S. economic and foreign policy. Japan and West Germany, for example, are probably the world's two advanced nations that are most import dependent, with France, Great Britain, Italy, and several smaller Western European countries not far behind. Indeed, to some analysts this vulnerability of Western Europe and Japan is considered the single greatest strategic materials threat facing the United States and its allies today.

A major question that would arise in an emergency is whether the United States would find it necessary to share its strategic and critical materials stockpile with its allies, thereby depleting the stockpile more quickly. The question of strategic materials stockpiles, both U.S. and foreign, will be discussed at greater length in Chapter 7. In brief, some of the allied nations, in addition to taking efforts to acquire strategic materials stockpiles, are also taking steps to reduce their import vulnerability by attempting to minimize the prospect of supply interruptions in an emergency. These steps include the aggressive promotion and development of materials sources in friendly nations; long-term trade agreements that would give these nations first call upon available materials; the bartering of goods and services for essential raw materials; and various economic and political initiatives— relating to materials supply and demand—that also affect the United States.

The Prospect of Materials Cartels

Much discussion recently has concerned the possibility that producer nations might consider forming materials cartels to control the production and marketing of certain strategic and critical materials. Such discussion has been stimulated by the past success of the cartel formed by the Organization of Petroleum Exporting Countries (OPEC).

The formation of materials cartels for economic purposes is not new, and the potential economic consequences of such cartels have generally received little attention outside economic and trade circles.[58] What is new concerning the current interest in cartels is the strong focus upon the prospect that materials cartels might be formed not for economic purposes, as in the past, but rather for use as weapons in support of political or military adventures on the part of materials producers. Within this context, serious questions have been raised regarding the possible effects that such cartels might have upon U.S. materials import vulnerability.[59]

The two major questions are, first, whether a small number of supplier nations, if united in action, do indeed possess a sufficiently large fraction of the world's production and reserve base of any material to make cartel formation feasible and, second, whether technology, economics, and the ability of the nations to overcome their differences and take concerted action could make a proposed cartel successful. Table 5.6 makes clear that the first question can be answered affirmatively; strong concentrations of the production and/or reserve bases do indeed exist for all seven of the materials listed in the table. Together, four nations—Australia, Guinea, Brazil, and Jamaica—possess almost two-thirds of the world's known bauxite reserve base and currently account for almost two-thirds of the world's annual production. World production of chromite ore is concentrated in just three other nations—the Soviet Union, the Republic of South Africa, and Albania,

Table 5.6 Major Producer Nations of Selected Strategic and Critical Materials and Their Reserve Bases, Expressed As Percentages of World Totals

Country	Production	Reserve Base
A. Bauxite/alumina		
Australia	31.7	20.6
Guinea	15.2	26.5
Brazil	9.5	10.3
Jamaica	8.8	9.0
Soviet Union	5.8	1.4
Other market economy nations	5.7	13.0
Yugoslavia	4.6	1.8
Greece	4.1	2.9
Hungary	3.7	1.4
India	2.4	5.4
Guyana	2.4	4.0
Surinam	2.2	2.7
	96.1	99.0
B. Chromium		
Soviet Union	29.3	1.9
Republic of South Africa	27.1	83.6
Albania	10.9	0.3
Zimbabwe	5.4	11.0
Turkey	4.9	1.1
India	4.9	0.9
Finland	4.3	0.4
Philippines	4.3	0.4
Other market economy nations	4.3	0.3
Brazil	3.8	0.1
	99.2	100.0
C. Cobalt		
Zaire	48.1	25.0
Zambia	13.8	6.4
Soviet Union	9.3	2.8
Cuba	7.6	21.8
Australia	6.9	1.1
Canada	6.9	3.1
Finland	4.1	0.4
New Caledonia	1.0	10.3
Philippines	0.7	4.7
Other market economy nations	0.7	14.1
United States	0.0	10.3
	99.1	100.0
D. Columbium		
Brazil	78.1	87.9
Canada	20.2	7.7
Other market economy nations	1.3	0.2
Nigeria	0.3	2.1
Zaire	0.1	2.1
	100.0	100.0

Table 5.6   (cont.)

Country	Production	Reserve Base
E. Manganese		
Soviet Union	46.6	20.0
Republic of South Africa	10.8	68.0
Gabon	9.2	3.5
Brazil	9.2	1.4
China	7.2	0.9
Australia	7.2	4.3
India	5.6	1.0
Other market economy nations	3.5	0.6
	99.3	99.7
F. Platinum-group metals		
Soviet Union	53.7	16.7
Republic of South Africa	41.8	80.8
Canada	3.0	0.8
Other market economy nations	1.5	--
	100.0	98.3
G. Tantalum		
Thailand	33.8	26.2
Australia	27.0	26.2
Brazil	13.5	4.0
Other market economy nations	13.5	5.3
Zaire	6.8	13.2
Malaysia	2.7	5.3
Nigeria	2.7	13.1
	100.0	100.0

Source: Calculations based upon data (1984 estimates) given in U.S. Bureau of Mines, Mineral Commodity Summaries 1985 (Washington, D.C.: U.S. Department of the Interior, 1985).

which together currently account for more than two-thirds of the world's annual production. More than three-quarters of the world's annual production of cobalt is accounted for by Zaire, Zambia, the Soviet Union, and Cuba. Brazil and Canada together currently account for about 98 percent of the world's production of columbium, and they possess about 96 percent of the world's reserve base. The Soviet Union and the Republic of South Africa together possess almost 90 percent of the world's reserve base of manganese and account for almost 60 percent of world production. Likewise, these two nations dominate world production of the platinum-group metals, accounting for almost 96 percent of current world production and almost 98 percent of the world's reserve base. Finally, almost two-thirds of the world's current tantalum production is accounted for by only two nations— Thailand and Australia—that together possess more than one-third to almost one-half of the world's reserve base.

Despite the above, the answer to the second question still appears negative. If a materials cartel is to have any real chance of success, it must satisfy most of the following criteria:

- *Stability.* The market for the commodity, despite typical ups and downs, must remain reasonably stable in the sense that demand will continue despite the cartel. In other words, users must not be able to boycott the cartel successfully.

- *New entrants.* The possibility must be remote that nonmembers (if any) can greatly increase production; furthermore, huge capital needs or other requirements must make new entry into the business difficult, time-consuming, and costly.

- *Substitution.* The development and use of substitute materials must be unlikely or extremely costly. In other words, substitute materials either must be unavailable or, if available, must be uneconomic or unsatisfactory.

- *Inelasticity of demand.* World demand for the commodity must be relatively price inelastic; that is, increases in price should not directly and immediately cause reductions in demand.

- *Financial health.* Cartel members—or at least some of them—should have sufficient financial surpluses or resources to enable the entire cartel to sit out any temporary consumer reaction to cartel policies, including during the period required to draw down existing inventories of the commodity.

- *Cohesion.* Members must share goals and objectives sufficiently to enable them to exhibit a cohesive and united front in dealing with consumers of the commodity.

- *Limited membership.* The fewer the members, the more likely that the necessary discipline within the membership can be achieved.

These criteria are rarely met, and certainly have yet to coalesce for any of the materials listed in Table 5.6. It is no easy matter to organize a cartel and, even if organized successfully, to make it work. Typically a brief organizational flurry occurs, but enthusiasm dissipates when it becomes evident that what can be agreed upon fails to address the most difficult issues dividing the membership. Almost any group of major mineral-exporting nations shows highly divergent economic, political, historical, and cultural backgrounds that make for dramatically different philosophies and ideologies. Consequently, despite the fact that current world production and reserve bases for most of these strategic and critical materials are concentrated in just a few countries, the existence of deep political, ideological, and economic disparities makes the likelihood of cartel formation for any of these materials extremely remote.

Notes

1. Typically, data are withheld by the Bureau of Mines when the material is produced by only one company (or a small number of companies), to protect the confidentiality of individual companies within the industry.

2. Ibid., p. 32.

3. Marvin S. Soross, "Lifeboat Ethics versus One-Worldism in International Food and Resource Policy." In *The Global Predicament*, by David W. Orr and Marvin S. Soross (Chapel Hill, N.C.: University of North Carolina Press, 1979), pp. 142-143.

4. National Commission on Materials Policy, *Materials Needs and the Environment Today and Tomorrow* (Washington, D.C.: U.S. Government Printing Office, 1973), p. 1-6.

5. Ibid., p. 9-9.

6. The discussion of imports of advanced manufactured materials is derived from an unpublished paper by John B. Wachtman, Jr., director, Center for Ceramics Research, Rutgers University.

7. Eugene Staley, *Raw Materials in Peace and War* (New York: Council on Foreign Relations, 1937), p. 3.

8. U.S. Bureau of Mines, *Mineral Commodity Summaries 1985* (Washington, D.C.: U.S. Department of the Interior, 1984), pp. 150-151.

9. See the remarks of Charles L. Schultz, former director of the Bureau of the Budget and senior fellow of the Brookings Institution, in House Committee on Foreign Affairs, Subcommittee on National Security Policy and Scientific Developments, *Hearing Symposium*, 92d Congress, 2d session (Washington, D.C.: U.S. Government Printing Office, 1973), p. 150.

10. U.S. Congress, Senate Committee on Foreign Relations, Subcommittee on African Affairs, *Imports of Minerals from South Africa by the United States and OECD Countries* (Washington, D.C.: U.S. Government Printing Office, 1980), pp. ix–xii.

11. This discussion of the concept of vulnerability follows closely that suggested by G. Adler-Karlsson in "The Necessity to Make A Distinction Between Import Dependency, Vulnerability, and Threat." In *Will the Wells Run Dry?* by the Royal United Services Institute (Whitstable, Kent, U.K.: Whitstable Litho, Ltd., 1979), p. 46.

12. Michael Shafer, "Mineral Myths." *Foreign Policy* 47 (Summer 1982), pp. 158–159.

13. See, for example, the Council on International Economic Policy, *Special Report: Critical Imported Materials* (Washington, D.C.: U.S. Government Printing Office, December 1974), p. 20, and also the discussion in *Strategic Materials Management* (Washington, D.C.: Nautilus Press, 1 August 1982), p. 20.

14. Council on International Economic Policy, *Special Report: Critical Imported Materials*, p. 20.

15. U.S. Department of Commerce, *Critical Materials Requirements of the U.S. Aerospace Industry* (Washington, D.C.: U.S. Government Printing Office, October 1981), pp. i–ii.

16. Richard E. Donnelly, *Strategic and Critical Materials: DOD Needs and Supply Problems* In *Seventh Biennial Conference on National Materials Policy*, U.S. Congress, House Committee on Science and Technology (Washington, D.C.: U.S. Government Printing Office, March 1983), pp. 67-78. The conclusions, which appear on pages 43-46 of Mr. Donnelly's paper but were not published in the symposium proceedings,

are those of Mr. Donnelly and do not necessarily represent those of the DOD (Department of Defense) itself.

17. Fillmore C. F. Earney, "Geopolitics of Minerals." *Focus*, May-June 1981, p. 1.

18. The *National Materials and Minerals Policy, Research and Development Act of 1980* (Public Law 96–479, enacted 21 October 1980) and the *National Critical Materials Act of 1984* (Title II of Public Law 98–373, enacted 31 July 1984).

19. Celestine Bohlen, "Gorbachev Assails Speed of U.S. Reply to Missile Freeze." *Washington Post*, 11 April 1985, p. A1.

20. For a discussion of Soviet-bloc resource policies, see Richard M. Levine, "The Soviet Union," in *The Mining Annual Review* (London: The Mining Journal Ltd., June 1983), pp. 447–463, and Bohdan O. Szuprowicz, *How to Avoid Strategic Materials Shortages* (New York: John Wiley and Sons, 1981), pp. 69–89.

21. William K. Severin, "Soviet Nonfuel Minerals: Resource War or Business As Usual?" *Materials and Society* 7:1 (1983), pp. 27–34.

22. American Die Casting Institute, *Position Paper on Minerals and Metals* (Des Plaines, Ill.: ADCI, May 1981), p. 8.

23. "National Mineral Policy." *Mining Congress Journal*, June 1981, p. 30.

24. U.S. Bureau of Mines, *Mineral Commodity Summaries 1985*.

25. For additional background on past Soviet activities, see "Strategic Minerals Acquire New Prominence." *Washington Post*, 15 March 1981, pp. H1–H3.

26. Edwin J. Becht and L. D. Belzung, *World Resource Management* (Englewood Cliffs, N.J.: Prentice-Hall, 1975), pp. 306–307.

27. John D. Morgan, Jr., *Strategic and Critical Materials* (Washington, D.C.: U.S. Bureau of Mines, 1982), p. 1.

28. Ruth W. Arad and Uzi B. Arad, "Scarce Natural Resources and Potential Conflict." In *Sharing Global Resources*, by Ruth W. Arad et al. (New York: McGraw-Hill, 1979), p. 62.

29. Richard J. Barnet, *The Lean Years—Politics in the Age of Scarcity* (New York: Simon and Schuster, 1980), p. 113.

30. Amos A. Jordan and Robert A. Kilmarx, *Strategic Mineral Dependence* (Beverly Hills, Calif.: Sage Publications, 1979), p. 11.

31. "Now the Squeeze Is on Metals." *Business Week*, 2 July 1979, p. 49.

32. William A. Vogley, "Resource War?" *Materials and Society* 6:1 (1982), p. 3.

33. Mark Hosenball and Peter Pringle, "Comrade Glagolev's Gap." *New Republic*, 20 December 1980, p. 19.

34. Cindy Skrzycki, "Resource War Talk Shot Down—State Department Torpedoes Talk of Soviet Minerals Blockade." *American Metals Market*, 21 May 1981, p. 11.

35. Becht and Belzung, p. 307.

36. Hans H. Landsberg, *What Next for U.S. Minerals Policy?* Paper No. 71 (Washington, D.C.: Resources for the Future, October 1982), p. 10.

37. For additional discussion of the Soviet policy, see U.S. Congress, Joint Economic Committee, Subcommittee on International Trade, Finance, and Security Economics, *Energy in Soviet Policy* (Washington, D.C.: U.S. Government Printing Office, 11 June 1981), pp. 94–100.

38. John P. Hardt, "Soviet Nonfuel Minerals Policy: The Global Context." *Journal of Resource Management and Technology*, January 1983, p. 58. An excellent assessment of the nonfuel mineral outlook for the Soviet Union through 1990 is given on pp. 27–62.

39. See the testimony of George A. Watson, president of the Ferroalloys Association, in Senate Committee on Energy and Natural Resources, *Geopolitics of Strategic and Critical Materials* (Washington, D.C.: U.S. Government Printing Office, 1983), p. 110.

40. Stuart Auerbach, "Soviets Scored for Inroads on Strategic Items." *Washington Post*, 2 September 1983, pp. D8–D9.

41. *Critical Materials Requirements of the U.S. Steel Industry* (Washington, D.C.: U.S. Department of Commerce, March 1983), p. 252.

42. News release: *GSA to Upgrade Manganese and Chromite Ores in U.S. Stockpile* (Washington, D.C.: General Services Administration, 9 May 1983).

43. George A. Watson, *Remarks Before the American Society for Metals* (Washington, D.C.: Ferroalloys Association, 27 May 1983), p. 2.

44. U.S. Congress, *Geopolitics of Strategic and Critical Materials*, p. 125.

45. A. Dan Rovig and Richard K. Doran, "Copper: A Decade of Change and Its Meaning for the Future." *American Mining Congress Journal*, December 1980, pp. 32–40.

46. Harry Anderson, "Making Industrial Policy." *Newsweek*, 24 October 1983, p. 98.

47. *Critical Materials Requirements of the U.S. Steel Industry*, p. 19. Data are for 1983 from *Mineral Commodity Summaries 1985* and include the effect of recycling.

48. Ibid., p. iii.

49. Remarks of Arden L. Bement, Jr., before the Senate Committee on Commerce, Science and Transportation, Subcommittee on Science, Technology and Space, 22 June 1982, p. 3.

50. Earney, pp. 10–11.

51. Ibid., p. 12.

52. Timothy W. Stanley, *A National Risk Management Approach to American Raw Materials Vulnerabilities* (Washington, D.C.: International Economic Studies Institute, January 1982), p. 11.

53. Resource Conservation Committee, *Choices for Conservation* (Washington, D.C.: U.S. Environmental Protection Agency, July 1979), p. 51.

54. Shafer, p. 161.

55. C. Fred Bergsten, "The Threat from the Third World." *Foreign Policy*, Number 11 (Summer 1973), pp. 104–105.

56. Materials Forum, *Strategic Metals and the United Kingdom* (London: Institution of Mechanical Engineers, July 1981), p. 3. The Materials Forum was created in the autumn of 1979 by six professional bodies to examine the role of strategic and critical materials in the British economy. The six member organizations are: The Institution of Mechanical Engineers, The Metals Society, The Institution of Mining and Metallurgy, The Institution of Metallurgists, The Plastics and Rubber Institute, and The Institute of Ceramics.

57. For a summary of the 328-page report, *Strategic Minerals*, issued in 1982, see Materials Forum, *Third Annual Report* (London: Institution of Mechanical Engineers, November 1982), pp. 37–42.

58. A comprehensive summary of cartel-like activities for thirty-seven materials is given in Staley, pp. 251–318. Additional information specifically relevant to the United States can be found in Daniel W. Bromley and John Strasma, *The Potential for Cartels, Embargoes, and International Agreements on Commodities Important to the United States* (Washington, D.C.: Library of Congress, 1977), 152 pp.

59. U.S. Congress, House Committee on Interior and Insular Affairs, Subcommittee on Mining and Minerals, *U.S. Minerals Vulnerability: National Policy Implications* (Washington, D.C.: U.S. Government Printing Office, 1980), p. 46.

6
Approaches to Reducing U.S. Materials Import Vulnerability

Introduction

For most of the nation's history, the focus upon materials has been on assuring sufficient supply to meet existing demand, rather than upon attempting to influence or minimize demand. This is because readily available materials supplies appeared inexhaustible and, realistically, in today's world it is extremely difficult to do much to affect the demand for materials. As the human population increases and its expectations continue to focus upon a higher standard of living—a standard heavily dependent upon all kinds of materials—the prospects for achieving a decrease in the demand for materials become dimmed. Of the six approaches most commonly suggested for reducing materials import vulnerability—conservation, substitution, recycling, stockpiling, improving foreign sources of supply, and increasing domestic production—only the first approach directly concerns demand, both total and per capita. The second approach—substitution—seeks to reduce demand for specific materials by providing suitable substitutes, but says nothing directly about the overall level of materials demand. The third approach—recycling—also does not directly address demand, but would help only indirectly by seeking to use the same materials more than once. The other three approaches deal strictly with supply: stockpiling to assure continued supplies during an emergency; improvement in the reliability of foreign sources to minimize the probability of any such emergency; and increasing domestic production to replace foreign imports with domestic supplies. Thus, it is easy to understand why most attention continues to be focused upon materials supply rather than upon materials demand.

Fortunately, even though most of these approaches may do little or nothing to reduce import dependency, all six can be used effectively to help reduce import vulnerability. In discussing the first five approaches below, emphasis is placed upon opportunities for reducing materials demand, and hence presumably import dependency, wherever they may exist. However, the primary focus is upon reducing import vulnerability. The sixth approach—increasing domestic production—has already been addressed in Chapter 2 and elsewhere.

Conservation

As noted above, the conservation approach is actually the only one that seeks to reduce materials consumption, either totally or per capita. Unlike substitution, it would not eliminate dependency upon any currently imported material, but would reduce the amount of material that needs to be imported. In so doing, it would reduce the current level of import dependency by increasing the relative proportions of domestically produced or recycled materials. Additionally, it would reduce the amount of material that must be carried in the National Defense Stockpile.

Conservation is defined as efficient use of materials from the initial extraction of mineral deposits, through the processing and manufacturing stages, to ultimate disposal or possible recovery for reuse. By focusing upon the efficient use of materials throughout the entire materials cycle, conservation affords opportunities at all levels of materials usage.

Conservation in Industry

A fundamental problem in attempting to encourage materials conservation in industry is that, with the exception of special cases such as precious metals, there are few natural incentives—other than natural market forces—for materials producers and users to practice conservation. Unfortunately, artificial incentives are difficult to devise. On a wartime basis, of course, a great deal can be accomplished to conserve scarce supplies, as demonstrated during World War II through materials allocation regulations. But such regulations are hardly tenable except in the case of outright emergency. Hence, economic and fiscal incentives must be relied upon if conservation is to be encouraged, and it is difficult to demonstrate that such measures can be made effective.

Lack of Incentives. In the metals industry, a number of points or stages exist—from the extraction of the initial ore to the production of metal stock—where significant losses of material occur. In principle, these losses could be reduced, but in practice it is generally uneconomical to do so. Rather than seek to reduce losses so that scarce domestic mineral deposits will last longer, producers (that is, those who process basic ores) find it economically advantageous to turn to imports or to switch to ores of lower metal concentration. For instance, over the past sixty years or so the copper producers in the United States have had to switch to ores of significantly lower concentration, yet their initial purification and refining processes suffer losses of about 15 percent of the metal content of the material processed.[1] The reason producers generally find it economically advantageous to switch to lower grade ores rather than seek large reductions in waste and losses is that the value of the lost or wasted material is small compared to the cost of more efficient recovery. The major exceptions are the precious metals such as platinum and gold. Producers of these metals insure practically no loss or waste, as might be expected.[2]

Much the same is true of the nonmetals segments of the materials industry, where materials producers respond to immediate economic incentives rather than to the more remote goal of materials conservation. Except where raw or input materials are extremely expensive (extremely scarce), materials producers avoid the added costs of attempting to use as much of the material as technically possible. Rather, they use production processes and methods that optimize profits for all those materials that are currently available in abundance.

In the metals industries the basic metals producers know that when the domestic ores currently in use are depleted, foreign sources of the same ore or a comparable ore will generally be available. If foreign sources fail to materialize or become depleted, then producers will shift to other ores, possibly domestic again, containing the same metal but currently more expensive to process in terms of the cost per unit output. A large part of the added cost of switching ores may result from the need to change capital equipment to handle the new ores. This changeover can be very expensive, because the basic metals industry is highly capital-intensive. For that reason producers generally find it less expensive to import conventional foreign ores than to switch to new types of domestic ores as the conventional domestic resources are depleted. A classic case has been the shift by domestic aluminum producers to imported bauxite in preference to exploiting domestic aluminum-bearing clays.

Because there is such a powerful incentive to continue using the same type of raw materials, materials producers will often develop a heavy dependence upon foreign resources, even though adequate domestic resources of a different type of ore are available. But they will not switch until it becomes economically advantageous to do so, that is, until foreign supplies become sufficiently expensive to warrant the major investments required.

Producers sometimes engage in post facto conservation by reprocessing mine and mill tailings as well as other recoverable waste products before switching to new raw materials. However, most such reprocessing is avoided because it is more expensive per unit amount of production than switching to a new resource supply. Thus, little post facto conservation is practiced.

At present few market incentives—if indeed any—exist to encourage materials conservation by the basic materials-producing industries. Since national strategic considerations are largely unrelated to production economics, it is both unrealistic and unfair to expect these producers to be much affected by purely strategic concerns. Hence materials conservation is not a producer's goal, but a national goal whose primary importance in the short term relates to national security, and in the long term to the assumed, although not assured, need for continued availability of those nonrenewable resources that may, in any practical economic sense, ultimately be exhausted.

At first glance it would seem that national security interests would create incentives for standby regulations to limit production losses of strategic and critical materials, and to limit the use of some materials to essential purposes, so that in the event of an emergency, stockpiles and/or domestic production of ores could be stretched. However, it can be debated whether conservation regulations of any sort are acceptable in the absence of an outright emergency. Such regulations would inevitably increase prices and possibly reduce the quality of certain products, as was demonstrated by the nation's wartime experiences in the 1940s. Yet in the absence of regulations, a market economy makes it unlikely that national incentives for materials conservation can be converted into workable and acceptable policies for materials producers.

Minimizing Losses in Production Processes. Materials differ widely in type and form, but because major attention is typically focused upon strategic and critical metals supplies, the discussion here will be focused upon conservation possibilities in the metals industries, with brief indications of how the losses in a few other industries may differ from metals losses.

The principle losses of basic metals in the metals-producing industries typically occur in the mining, milling, and concentrating stages. Except where the final product is quite valuable, fairly large amounts of theoretically available material are discarded because it is not worth the expense to recover, and it is difficult to process, material that is relatively dispersed. This material is discarded in a variety of forms including mine tailings, low purity or contaminated concentrate, mill tailings, and sometimes as slag. Occasionally, however, changes in economic conditions do justify the effort to reprocess this discarded material. For instance, both the silver and the copper industries have reprocessed the tailings from the extremely high-grade ore deposits that were available about fifty to one hundred years ago. But in general, market competition in the basic materials industries is so strong that producers cannot realistically assume the additional expense of recovering and reprocessing secondary material.

In the iron and steel industry, about 23 percent of the theoretically available material is discarded prior to the production of metallic iron and steel. The comparable figure for the aluminum industry is about 14 percent, and for the copper industry about 18 percent.[3] In contrast to these industries, the platinum industry discards only about 0.5 percent of its incoming material because the high price of platinum justifies an intensive conservation effort.

The situation is quite different in the fabricating industries that transform basic materials into final products. These industries manufacture products such as automobiles, chemicals, plastics, and other types of finished goods. They employ basic materials to make products that are widely marketed. The basic feedstock materials that these industries utilize have considerable value, so that a definite incentive to minimize losses exists. For example, the scrap steel resulting from the manufacture of automobiles can be easily and inexpensively processed into new steel stock; hence it is collected and reprocessed rather than discarded.

Even in the fabricating industries, however, the waste material from production processes cannot always be reprocessed. For example, considerable waste results in making parts out of heat-injected or polymerized plastic because the excess material from the production processes has been physically transformed and cannot be restored to a useful state. Certain liquids and gases used in many production processes become contaminated and cannot be reused because of the high cost of purification.

Barring technological breakthroughs or a massive system of government controls, there appears no simple or general solution to the problem of how to reduce losses in materials production. In the basic materials industries, where production is from basic mineral ores, it is evident that improved techniques for separating ore from rock and other impurities are needed. Included are improved grinding, beneficiation, and concentration techniques. In many cases these techniques would have to be tailored to the specific mineral ores being processed, particularly where chemical treatments are involved.

Matching Materials Capabilities to Uses. It stands to reason that material can be conserved if an effort is made to tailor specific materials properties and capabilities to specific uses. For example, only the stiffest acceptable metal would be used where absolute stiffness is a requirement, or the most acceptable ductile metal where a part must stretch without breaking. Certainly a great deal can be accomplished by seeking such optimization of uses, but the concerns of design engineers are much more complicated than that.

Design engineers must work to satisfy several criteria at the same time. Optimal matching of material properties with uses is always a central consideration. The materials selected for use in production must also be available in sufficient supply, and they must be affordable. It is of no use to select a material that is optimal in terms of its properties but that cannot be produced in sufficient quantities to satisfy production demand. Nor is it reasonable to use expensive titanium in many high-performance airplane wings if aluminum will do almost as well at a fraction of the cost. Beyond these "rational" engineering considerations there are often potent aesthetic or marketing factors at work in materials selection. These are the types of constraints that affect the selection of materials in actual practice. In effect, engineers and designers face many constraints in matching materials properties to specific uses.

Despite such constraints, a great deal could be accomplished to conserve specific materials if the need arose. For example, appreciable amounts of tin could be saved if plastics were used as liners for "tin" (steel) cans. Similarly, a considerable amount of cadmium could be saved if a suitable way were found to coat nonstainless steel screws, bolts, and other parts intended for outdoor use with some other material, possibly a tough plastic. With proper development, applications, and installation, plastics might be the preferable materials for many such applications, or at least provide entirely suitable substitutes for certain applications so that tin and cadmium supplies could be used in applications where no substitutes are available. Similar examples can be found for most other metals, including the strategic and critical materials discussed later in this chapter.

In a great many instances, materials are used for applications in which their properties are not optimally suited. Other, more suitable materials may not be manufactured on a regular basis (if at all) or in large quantities because of lack of demand, or because of the high cost of initiating production of a difficult-to-make material that might be used only in a few specific applications. Thus, designers and engineers are likely to be unaware of the potential availability or existence of materials that could be used to advantage, particularly for specialized applications.

Yet there is always the question of fabrication problems with new materials. From a production standpoint it may be preferable by far to continue with materials that are in common use because so much is known about how to form, join, and machine them, and because production facilities and machinery are available to utilize standard materials. It is for such reasons that new and exotic materials are slow to come into common use, and may first be produced only in connection with specialized defense or space applications in which expense and convenience must be subordinated to functional capabilities.

On a slightly lesser scale, a considerable amount of effort is expended by private industries to optimize the uses of materials in the normal course of events, particularly where worthwhile reductions in weight, size, and overall capability of products can be achieved at reasonable cost. This effort may well have accelerated in response to the escalation in price of those materials whose production is particularly energy-intensive. The improvements that can be made are often dramatic, although at times not fully appreciated by the general public.

Many of the properties being sought for materials today are of interest primarily because of the advance of high technology in other areas. The development of the laser and its tremendous potential as a communications device has prompted the development of new ultra-clear glasses to be employed in fiber optical systems. Fibers of such glasses are in many ways superior to current metallic copper conductors for communications transmission and may well replace a substantial fraction of the demand for copper. However, this "improved function" replacement is occurring only because of the development of laser technology, which permits improved communication through the use of higher (optical) frequencies. The same sort of transmutation has occurred throughout the electronics industry with the replacement of electron tubes by semiconductors. Now silicon and germanium are in demand in place of the tungsten previously used in producing electron tubes.

In brief, although it is evident that significant materials conservation can be accomplished through better matching of materials capabilities to the functions to be served, the process of implementing such matching is tremendously varied and often depends on other technological advances. The incentives for engineers and designers are generally to improve functioning at least cost, but the ability to make the substitutions that are implied depends on the availability of the required replacement materials in the commercial marketplace, on the problems in fabricating the new materials into the desired items, and on a host of other considerations. Given the incentive of possible outright future shortages of critical materials, the economic and technical practicality of optimal matching and substitution can shift enormously. Thus, the long-term impacts of a shortage of a particular material can be much less serious then one might anticipate, despite short-term disruptions that can be very difficult.

Research and Development in Industrial Conservation. Research and development provide the basis for new materials production processes as well as for new materials themselves. Both activities are absolutely essential if materials supplies are to remain adequate in the future. Significant materials research and development activities began about the time of World War II and, accelerating under the strong federal support that began at about that time, blossomed from an empirical, disjointed effort into a quite exact science that now promises the possibility of fabricating materials "to order" with specified properties. Although that prospect is by no means yet at hand, materials scientists and metallurgists are already able to produce a few classes of materials pretty much as desired. Certainly this is true in the field of semiconductors, ferrites (for computers), optical glasses (including those used in lasers), and broad classes of composite materials. The list already is enormous, although the need and potential for the future remain tremendous.

In basic materials production from ores, the promise for the future is also greater than past experience suggests. Improvements in mining technology promise to allow both the mining of deeper ores and of smaller veins of material; many deposits cannot now be economically mined because they are either too deeply buried or are in configurations that are too narrow to be mined profitably. Research into the extraction of ore from rocks and other impurities could cut losses in milling and processing by considerable amounts, as mentioned above. The successful development of such processes could greatly extend the availability of many resources, some of which are currently available only in limited supply.

Research on processing ores into final materials is another area promising rich rewards in the relatively short term. If techniques can be found for economically processing ores that are less rich, or that are relatively rich and abundant but are difficult to process chemically, then the extent of domestic resources could be expanded significantly in some critical cases and the nation's dependence on some foreign sources of supply reduced.

Among the various areas of materials science and engineering that would benefit from greater understanding, metallurgy still presents many of the most formidable problems, even though it is probably among the oldest of the materials sciences, dating back as far as 2,500 years. Although many of the properties of metals have been catalogued exhaustively, they are not yet understood in fundamental respects. Consequently, many central areas of metallurgy have to be approached on an empirical basis. Improved understanding might offer the promise of finding further substitutes for such strategic and critical materials as manganese, chromium, and cobalt.

It is impossible to enumerate here the full importance of research and development for materials conservation, primarily because materials are so varied in form that possibilities exist almost everywhere. Perhaps the areas of greatest potential are composites and nonmetallic materials of all varieties. After thousands of years in which man used mainly stone, wood, metal, and natural fibers as basic materials, research and development has vastly multiplied the classes of materials. Some of these materials are used primarily in highly specialized applications, as in electronics. Others are used in place of, or to augment, traditional construction materials, traditional fabrics, and many other conventional materials. The increased development and use of new materials also offers the prospect of added emphasis upon "design for recycling," in which products and materials are so designed as to make their ultimate recovery and reuse as simple as possible and, hence, more economic. These new materials are not only direct products of research and development, but often the by-products of research into seemingly remote areas of materials science and engineering.

One of the primary attributes of research and development is that it often increases possible options by producing a useful new technology that makes available a broad range of alternatives. In so doing, it may increase productivity, decrease costs, conserve energy and materials, and improve performance. Much modern technology is increasingly being built on advances in materials, from exquisitely crafted semiconductors for microelectronics to highly complex composites with literally astounding performance characteristics. New techniques for processing materials, undreamed of only a few decades ago, have made these new materials and their properties possible, frequently achieving their results with significant savings in the quantity of material used. Among some of the more important resulting techniques are the following:

Rapid solidification technology (RST). This general term covers a number of techniques for cooling metal alloys at such extremely high rates as 1,000 to 1 million degrees Celsius per second. Thus, a metal can be cooled from its melting point to room temperature in a few thousandths of a second. The result of such rapid cooling ranges from freezing an alloy in microcrystalline form to producing a more smoothly glassy state if time is insufficient for even very tiny crystals to form. Because of the absence of grain boundaries and the presence of protective films, strength, toughness, and corrosion resistance are greatly improved. Such rapidly solidified alloys, usually obtained as powders or thin foils, can then be processed by conventional techniques into larger pieces that may retain the initial microstructure or glassy state. This technique offers the potential for producing highly corrosion-resistant alloys without the use of chromium, superalloys without cobalt, and aluminum alloys that could possibly displace titanium and exotic alloy steels in some aircraft structural applications.

Hot isostatic processing (HIP).[4] This processing technique originally was developed as a relatively low-volume process for the cladding of high-cost nuclear fuel elements, but over the past two decades many broad applications have been found for its commercial use as an idealized hot-processing or forging operation, or as a high-pressure heat treatment. Basically, the process involves subjecting the work undergoing processing to isostatic gas pressure at elevated temperature, typically carried out with an inert gas in a pressure vessel containing an internal furnace. Three different kinds of processes are now commonly employed: powder consolidation, diffusion bonding, and the healing of casting defects.

Powder consolidation is commonly called hot isostatic pressing, hot isostatic compaction, or isostatic hot pressing. Powders, which may have been produced by rapid solidification (as described above), are preformed by a variety of techniques (for example, cold isostatic pressing, die pressing, cold press and sinter, or vibratory filling) depending upon the handling characteristics of the particular powder and the shape to be fabricated. After preforming, the powders are consolidated while hermetically sealed in a container impervious to the high pressure/high temperature gas. Containers and other tooling that may have been used to form internal configurations are then removed and the consolidated piece is subjected to whatever additional processing is required.

Diffusion bonding is also known as gas-pressure bonding, isostatic diffusion bonding, or HIP welding. The process is similar to powder consolidation except that the required shapes are built up of structural components fabricated from wrought materials, rather than from powders. As with powder consolidation, the bonding of surfaces takes place within a hermetically sealed container. The third process—healing of casting defects— closely resembles diffusion bonding except that a sealed container is unnecessary, because most casting defects are below the surface being treated, that is, they are within the body of the part undergoing treatment. However, lack of a sealed container necessitates maintaining a relatively high-purity pressurizing gas to prevent contamination.

Near-net-shape technology. As the name implies, this technology involves initiating processing operations with a shape as close as possible to that of the final shape of the part desired, thereby reducing to a minimum the quantity of excess material that must be removed by cutting, machining, grinding, or other processing operations. Consequently, material is conserved both in the initial formation of the near-net shape and in the processing to final shape. A variety of techniques can be used to produce the near-net shape, including powder metallurgy, investment and precision die casting, precision stepped extrusions and forgings, improved welding and joining techniques, superplastic forming, isothermal and near-isothermal forging, and (as discussed above) hot isostatic processing.[5]

Approaches to Materials Conservation

Although many approaches to conserving materials have been suggested from time to time, the discussion here will be limited to those general approaches that seem most likely to offer the best possibilities for success. Two major opportunities for materials conservation—substitution and resource recovery—are discussed separately later in this chapter.

Product Design. Improved product design offers many promising and fruitful avenues to materials conservation. In some cases improved design can serve to reduce actual production losses by minimizing the amount of material that must be discarded as scrap. For instance, the amount of material that becomes scrap from a piece of sheet steel depends in part on the shape and layout of patterns to be cut from the material. Careful design layout of the production processes and sequences can sometimes save a great deal of material. Likewise, the use of computerized methods for product design and for the control of manufacturing processes can help to minimize the excessive use of strategic and critical materials.

Improved design offers even greater benefits, however. Often there is a tendency to "overdesign and overbuild" many of the products produced today. In many cases, more careful engineering can produce items that have improved durability with fully adequate strength but using much less material. The trend toward smaller and lighter automobiles is an excellent example of this kind of materials conservation. As engineers achieve lighter weight in cars by designing for greatest strength per unit of material used, they are also able to reduce the strength requirements for many other components because of the lesser weight that must be carried. Although this trend in producing automobiles was undertaken primarily to conserve fuel rather than nonfuel materials, it has resulted in a substantial reduction in the demand for such metals as chromium. Better design of automobile engines likewise could substantially reduce or even eliminate the need for platinum-group metals for automobile emission-control catalysts.

In some cases, entire product lines can be miniaturized with great savings in materials as a result of technological advances in electronics and other fields. For example, a veritable revolution in the size and weight of many products of office equipment, kitchen appliances, and scientific or technological equipment has taken place over the past few decades.

Current efforts to reduce the amount of materials required for a given application through improved product design reflect a fundamental change in philosophy on the part of design engineers. In the past, most products were designed with the view that materials were both abundant and cheap. During the extractive and manufacturing periods, as discussed in Chapter 1, this was essentially the case. Because the materials were readily available and often represented the least costly factor of manufacture and production, little incentive existed to minimize materials costs either in original product design or in subsequent redesign. Instead, primary emphasis was placed upon savings in labor, often accomplished not only with more and better machinery but also the more extravagant use of material in overdesigned products. Such excesses made economic sense at the time because they helped avoid early breakdown and premature return of products to the factory for reworking and repair.

This picture has now changed as a result of increased concern over diminishing domestic materials supplies, higher levels of materials import dependency, and the increased cost of materials per se. Greater recognition is now being given to the need to conserve materials wherever possible, especially to conservation opportunities available at the product design stage.

Yet it should be recognized that very real limits exist in the extent to which materials usage may be reduced in a particular product. For example, it has been estimated that about 160 of the 180 pounds of metal contained in a modern refrigerator are steel, and that almost 60 pounds of this steel could be saved through redesign and employment of other materials. But doing so would result in "increased manufacturing costs, increased cost of investment in engineering and equipment, decreased durability, and reduced safety . . . a large price to pay for the small savings of metal possible."[6]

Reduction of Waste. Good product design, as discussed above, offers one obvious avenue for reducing waste. However, in considering all ways in which reduction in waste can contribute to the conservation of materials, caution must be exercised in dealing with the value judgments involved. Even product design involves these judgments. For example, is it sufficient that the materials selected for a given purpose just meet in quantity and type the minimum standards of performance? Or would the use of slightly more materials, or the employment of a material having slightly more effective properties, allow exceeding the performance standards and thereby possibly improve both reliability and durability? Design engineers may quite justifiably differ in their answers to such questions, and ultimately may base their final decisions not on materials selection alone, but on such nonmaterials factors as selling price of the product, potential liability in the event of product failure, extent of warranty offered, or reputation of the manufacturer for better-than-average quality.

There is no end to value judgments in discussing waste reduction. Many people label as waste any use of resources not having their approval. Such disapproval typically is directed in two ways. First, it is expressed in the "excess packaging" concept—disapproval of the quantity of material consumed in attempts to protect goods during shipment, storage, and delivery. Excess packaging may indeed at times occur, but packaging—both in materials and in labor—represents a substantial cost to the manufacturer and usually is constrained by economics. And second, the term waste is applied typically to the multitude of products identified as throw-aways: plastic single-use razors with nonrenewable blades, or flashlights with built-in batteries that cannot be recharged. Such products are manufactured largely for convenience and without regard to the materials consumed. Certainly both product packaging and throw-away products consume a substantial quantity of materials as contrasted with more traditional ways of using materials, but whether they constitute waste is open to debate.

Consumer "waste" is important because it is closely related to the conservation of many of the materials that appear on various strategic and critical materials lists. For example, far more chromium is consumed for automobiles, refrigerators, sinks, bright decorative trim, and for other consumer uses than in all defense-related uses combined. A reduction in such consumer uses would most certainly reduce substantially the amount of chromium imported by the United States each year. But are chrome-plated hubcaps and bumbers on automobiles, or stainless steel kitchen sinks, necessarily "wasteful?" Clearly, because of the value judgments involved, little progress can be made toward conserving materials by reducing "waste" in the consumer area, especially in peacetime.

Conservation of materials by industry, unlike conservation by consumers, can be addressed more scientifically. For example, techniques exist for reducing the critical material content of some slags, and for reducing the loss of strategic and critical materials in grinding, pickling, and scaling operations. Machining losses can be reduced by casting or forging to closer tolerances, and losses can be further reduced through new, advanced processes such as those described earlier. Use of continuous-casting technology in steelmaking can improve yields by 10 to 20 percent, but only about 22 percent of U.S. steel is made to date in this way, as contrasted with 45 percent for European-made steel and 70 percent for Japanese-made steel.[7] In the aerospace industry, which accounts for almost 40 percent of total defense procurement, losses can be reduced by improving the "buy/fly" ratio, or the ratio of the weight of material that must be purchased compared with the weight of material in the final product. Because virtually all metal-shaping processes are inherently inefficient, the buy/fly ratio for a typical airframe component made from titanium may be as high as four-to-one.[8] Again, use of advanced shaping technologies can potentially lower such ratios significantly.

Increased Use of Abundant and Renewable Resources. During most of human history, materials that were both abundant and renewable made up the largest portion of the resources needed to sustain life and build civilizations. Clay, straw, and wood were the usual building materials; animal skins and natural fibers typically were used for clothing; wood, peat, and even dried animal feces were burned for energy; and animal power—chiefly horses or mules—served for transportation. As civilizations became more advanced and complex, reliance upon these "natural" resources gave way to the use of less abundant and often nonrenewable resources. Steel and concrete are now the primary building materials; synthetic fibers made from natural gas or petroleum have largely replaced such natural fibers as wool and cotton for clothing and fabrics; first coal, and then natural gas and petroleum, have replaced wood and peat, with a currently reduced reliance upon coal for energy purposes; petroleum-powered vehicles made from steels, plastics, and a variety of generally scarce and nonrenewable resources have replaced animal power for transportation; chemical fertilizers have replaced natural manures; and plastics have replaced wood and rubber in many applications.

These replacements have occurred largely because the new materials offer significant advantages in utility, cost, or quantity over the old materials, and the trend is likely to continue. As noted in the literature,

New technology is being built increasingly on advances in materials. We will eventually shift away from reliance on increasingly scarce natural materials and process common raw materials into exotic new compounds with astounding performance. Tomorrow's marketplace will be infused with those new materials.[9]

The widespread use of these new materials, however, often has resulted in unforeseen social costs—including degradation of environmental quality—that now are raising questions regarding the extent to which this materials revolution may go on. Concern here, however, is primarily with the effect this revolution has had upon reducing or exhausting domestic nonrenewable resources and increasing the nation's materials import dependency and vulnerability, for many of the "common raw materials" that are fashioned into exotic new ones are not common at all and are being depleted.

Certainly it would be exceedingly difficult to slow this shift from one form of resources to another in view of the widespread acceptance and use of so many nonrenewable materials in all forms. However, the possibilities should not be overlooked. Conservation of scarce and nonrenewable resources depends on at least two major efforts: less materials usage overall and—for a given level of usage—a return wherever possible to the use of resources that are renewable and abundant.

Composite Materials. Continuing advances in metallurgy are permitting and encouraging the increased use of specialized steels and of alloys of such other metals as aluminum to achieve major weight reductions in components while maintaining considerable strength. Composite materials are finding a wide range of uses, sometimes totally supplanting metals and at other times incorporating metals to a limited extent to provide better structural properties than metals can provide alone. Composites, as discussed earlier in Chapter 1, comprise several different materials operating in unison, for example, reinforced concrete with metal rods or wire to provide resiliancy and resistance to tension and shear forces, while the concrete itself provides strength against compressional forces. Long carbon fibers or filaments can provide tremendous tensional strength to plastics, and they have come into widespread use in the manufacture of yacht hulls and masts, major aircraft structural components including wings and fuselages, and a host of other important structures. These materials on occasion have replaced another, somewhat more familiar composite, fiberglass-epoxy. Although composites are by no means a panacea for all materials problems, they do offer the potential of engineering properties that are competitive with, and often better than, those of the metals that they are gradually replacing. Clearly, a very large frontier of opportunity exists for the use of composites.

Improved Product Life. Materials can also be conserved by making products to last longer. For example, computers can be enlisted to help in the design, manufacturing, and inspection stages of product development to improve the structural integrity, reliability, and resistance to failure of products using strategic and critical materials. Employment of advanced coatings, high-performance alloys, and microstructures formed through rapid solidification metallurgy can help to prolong product life by minimizing wear, erosion, and corrosion. The useful life of existing structures and components often can be extended through the development of improved techniques for nondestructive evaluation, analytical testing, repair, maintenance, in-service monitoring, and rework procedures. One example of such an approach to materials conservation is the use of advanced coatings for industrial tools, not only to extend tool life, but also to reduce the content of strategic materials used in the tool alloys themselves. Another example is the use of advanced bearing alloys to extend by an order of magnitude the life of bearings operating in adverse and hostile environments. Still other examples include the use of base metals to replace the platinum-group metals in hybrid electronic circuits, advanced coating techniques to minimize the use of the noble metals in electrical connector contacts, and the use of cobalt-free alloy systems for the hard-facing of engine exhaust valves.[10]

Reduced Materials Usage. Perhaps the most direct approach to materials conservation is simply to use less. Although decreased materials usage is widely held to be equivalent to a decreased level of "creature comfort," one may nonetheless question whether the average individual's quality of life has been improved proportionately by the consumption of 22,000 pounds of materials per capita per year today as contrasted with the 1,200 pounds consumed in 1776. Unfortunately, reduced materials usage involves value judgments even more than does the avoidance of waste, as discussed earlier.

All use of materials, as well as their conservation, involves trade-offs that different people react to quite differently. Some people profess the desire to return to a simpler life-style that would reduce or even eliminate our current dependence upon increasingly complex and exotic materials. Others suggest that we do not actually have to do without modern conveniences, as long as we make good use of what we have. However, in general, the simpler a civilization's life-style, the greater the ratio of time required to work for survival to the time available for recreation and higher pursuits:

> The point is not to stress the fact that mankind once existed with a small fraction of our materials supply, so why couldn't we; but rather it is to inquire, knowing what we know now, to what extent, in what direction, and at what cost a greatly restricted materials menu would force us to modify our way of life.[11]

Such modifications can be achieved much more readily during periods of emergency, as demonstrated during World War II. Despite the heavy losses resulting from allied aerial bombardment, Germany—with relatively small supplies of metals and ceramics—nonetheless steadily increased its production of military aircraft, trucks, munitions, and other war materiel from 1939 to 1944. German consumption of key metals during this period was but a fraction of U.S. consumption: copper and manganese, one-tenth; tin, one-twentieth; nickel, one fortieth to one-fiftieth; and other vital metals in proportion. Yet Germany ended the war with larger stocks of these metals than existed at the beginning of the war. This astonishing feat was accomplished by substituting metals that were plentiful for those that were scarce, disregarding as necessary the criteria of cost and performance; by redesigning equipment to eliminate or curtail the requirements for metals that were becoming scarce; by the extensive use of secondary materials; and by drastic curtailment of civilian requirements.[12]

During peacetime, of course, different criteria prevail and the dual requirements of cost and performance typically dominate materials choices and usage. The problem during peacetime is thus largely whether materials supply can continue to keep abreast of accelerating materials demand. It is popular to assume that technology will always make available whatever materials supplies are required, and therefore that no need exists to slow the growth of materials demand. But to place one's future well-being entirely in the hands of the technologists seems unwise in view of the reality of the nation's current materials import dependency.

Thus it is possible that no steps that could be taken today are likely to reduce significantly the status of U.S. import dependency in the near term. Nonetheless, it is important that we begin now to encourage a conservation ethic that includes a respect for materials and the role they play in our lives, so that we can live comfortably with what we need but ultimately learn to live equally comfortably with less than we now think we need.

Substitution

Materials substitution is attractive because it seems to offer a tempting panacea for import vulnerability: one simply stops importing materials from abroad and substitutes those that are available domestically. The simplicity of this view of substitution is rescued at least in part from simplemindedness by the widespread recognition that modern technology constantly fosters shifts in usage from one material to another. For example, nonmetallic materials like plastic and glass have replaced metals in a wide variety of uses. Likewise, technology is constantly developing entirely new materials, for example composites, to provide improved substitutes for traditional materials. Indeed, it has been pointed out that materials substitution has existed for millennia, with the Bronze Age replacing the Stone Age, the Iron Age replacing the Bronze Age, and the emergence today of man-made and reused materials.[13] Thus it is easy to understand the widespread appeal that substitution holds.

Traditionally, a push-pull relationship has always existed between materials (including substitutes) and technology. On the one hand, the development of new or improved materials has provided the push to foster development of new or improved products; and on the other hand, more ambitious engineering and product objectives have provided the pull on the materials sector to develop new or improved materials. This relationship, however, is rarely a completely smooth one, as discussed below.

Some General Considerations

In general, substitution of one material for another for a particular use rarely takes place easily. Some of the major driving forces behind such substitution will be discussed presently, and these driving forces must typically overcome many obstacles. First, as noted earlier, unless a technological breakthrough has occurred through research and development, the materials currently in use invariably represent the materials of "first choice" based upon both economic and technological suitability for the purpose for which they are being used. To replace them, a substitute material ideally must satisfy several conditions:

- *Cost effectiveness.* The substitute material must be no more expensive that the material being replaced.

- *Availability.* The substitute material must be readily available in adequate quantities. Specifically with respect to strategic and critical materials, the substitute should be available domestically, or (less than ideal) should be available from geographically contiguous nations (primarily Canada or Mexico) or from overseas allies.

- *Properties.* The physical and chemical properties, behavior, performance, and longevity of the substitute material should be comparable to those of the material being replaced.

- *Compatibility.* The substitute material should be suitable for processing and fabrication with minimal changes in existing technology, capital plant, and processing and fabricating facilities.

Few substitutes for strategic and critical materials satisfy the above criteria to a significant extent. Either the substitute material proves to be more costly than the original, or some loss in unique characteristics, quality, or performance occurs. For defense purposes, the increase in cost may not be critical, but the loss in performance may be unacceptable.

Second, development and utilization of a substitute material takes a great deal of time. A lengthy period is required to produce initial quantities of the potential substitute material, which must then be subjected to a period of prolonged evaluation and testing, usually for each application envisioned. This effort includes the engineering work necessary to validate not only the suitability of the material from a manufacturing point of view, but also its durability and reliability when used in specific products. It also includes the need to optimize cost, design, and functional features, and to develop specifications. Once this work has been completed successfully, the developers must convince the design engineers that the new material should be used— often a formidable task in that the design engineers may be inherently conservative and strongly inclined to stick with what they know works. Even after the substitute has gained adequate acceptance, time is required to construct adequate facilities to produce it in commercial quantities. And finally, user production facilities must be adapted to permit use of the substitute material.

This sequence of events is both very costly and very time-consuming. For example, it has been estimated that the cost of introducing a plastic tailgate for an automobile would be about $300,000 and require at least ten years from limited production to full production.[14] To replace many uses of chromium, the National Research Council has estimated that five to ten years or more would be required to develop suitable substitutes, depending upon particular uses.[15] Although obviously some reduction in development time and cost may occur when an existing material can be substituted for another existing material—as in substituting aluminum for copper—rather than substituting a newly developed material, many modern plants are so finely tuned to materials currently in use that major alterations of plant and equipment may be necessary to accommodate almost any substitute material.

Third, materials substitution is made difficult by the sheer complexity of highly specialized uses involving a wide variety of materials employed in sophisticated hardware and systems. In substituting one material for another, typically each substitution opportunity is unique and hence must be considered on an item-by-item and application-by-application basis. For example, finding substitutes for chromium involves literally thousands of alloys utilized in millions of engineering applications.

Several other considerations are important in attempting to identify appropriate substitute materials. One is not to replace a critical material by another that may turn out to be equally critical. For example, when cobalt became in short supply and its price escalated dramatically during 1978 and 1979, new magnetic alloys were developed that contained less cobalt but more chromium, itself a highly critical material. Some abundant materials, like aluminum and magnesium, require relatively large amounts of energy for their extraction and processing, typically much more than that required for some of the less abundant materials they might be candidates to displace. In an era of high energy costs and potential energy scarcity, energy intensiveness thus tends to offset the advantage of abundance.

Another consideration, where possible, is to substitute renewable resources—especially forest products, fibers, and natural rubber—for nonrenewable resources, although such possibilities are rather limited. Finally, it is important not to overlook that relatively complex composite materials may offer the best possibility for replacing some strategic and critical materials in many applications. Unfortunately, difficulties in recovering the materials in the composites from waste for recycling and reuse will be significantly increased.

Kinds of Substitution

Although substitution at first glance may seem a simple concept, the replacement of one material by another, it is in fact much more complex and of several types.[16] Descriptions and examples of three forms of substitution will illustrate the point.

Material Substitution. Most popularly viewed, especially in lay terms, materials substitution is the basic concept of replacing one material by another. Examples include the replacement of cobalt in metal alloys by nickel and the replacement of steel by carbon fiber composites. At present, substantial efforts are being made to find suitable replacements for a number of strategic and critical materials and many other imported materials. Of particular interest is the substitution of nonmetallic materials, especially ceramics and polymers, for strategic and critical materials.[17]

Process Substitution. Going beyond the simple concept of substituting one material for another is the broader concept of substituting one process for another, thereby moving substitution one step further from end-item use. Examples include the use of casting rather than forging, or the use of clays as a feedstock for aluminum rather than the traditional bauxite. Where cost is a dominant factor, development of a less costly process might accelerate materials substitution by making the potential substitute material less expensive to use. With respect to the aluminum example, if processing costs for producing aluminum from domestic clays could be only marginally reduced, aluminum produced from such clays would be economically competitive with aluminum produced from imported bauxite.

Function Substitution. Substitution by function is still further removed from end-item use; it involves a fundamental rethinking of each task and how it can be accomplished best. Examples include the substitution of transistors for vacuum tubes and of jet engines for piston/propeller engines. Such substitution is typically far-reaching, ultimately extending into areas that often are unforeseen. For example, the transistor facilitated the development of large-scale computers, complex control systems, and a broad range of industrial, medical, and leisure products. In virtually every case of functional substitution of transistors for vacuum tubes, significant savings were achieved in both the amounts of materials needed and in the level of energy required to carry out the desired task.[18]

It is interesting to note that all three of the above classes of substitution—material, process, and function—can take place "at any of the steps in the resource, processing, and manufacturing cycle, from raw materials through primary products, parts manufacture and components to final design and assembly."[19] Some further examples of these classes of substitution for different categories of materials are given in Table 6.1.

Driving Forces Behind Substitution

Although many forces drive materials substitution, the two major forces are economic and strategic. Economic driving forces for substitution are always at work. Indeed, it is considered a commonplace of economic theory that, design conservatism apart, if the price of a commodity increases by a substantial amount, a substitute for that commodity ultimately will be found. The search for such a cheaper substitute inevitably involves engineering trade-offs between performance and cost in an attempt to strike an acceptable compromise between technical and economic feasibility.[20] Thus, economic substitution, sometimes referred to as "displacement," occurs naturally as economic and technological factors make one material more advantageous to use than another, either because it is cheaper or because it offers the potential of equal or improved performance at equal or lower cost.

In assessing economic feasibility, a point sometimes overlooked is that the principal consideration in selecting a new material is the cost of the

Table 6.1 Examples of Substitution Involving Various Classes of Materials

Category of Material by State of Manufacture	Class of Material by Use		
	Physical/Structural	Reagents and Intermediates	Energy/Fuels
Raw, semifinished, and finished materials	Alunite for bauxite Raw polyester for raw cotton Alcoa's chloride aluminum reduction process for Hall process Basic oxygen furnace for open hearth steelmaking	Recovered sulfur for Frasch sulfur Natural brines for rock salt Mining of natural soda ash for Solvay process soda ash Phosphoric acid from furnace phosphorus for wet process acid	Western coal for Eastern coal Gasified coal for natural gas Fuel oil for natural gas Formed coke for metal-lurgical coke
Components and applications	New copper or aluminum alloys for copper alloys in automobile radiators	Hydrochloric acid for sul-furic acid in pickling Direct application to soil of anhydrous ammonia for liquid application of ammonium salts	Lead-free gasoline for regular gasoline Propane for fuel oil
Systems	Air-cooled for water-cooled engines Mass transit for auto-mobiles Video telephone communi-cations for business transportation	Not applicable	Geothermal for coal-fired steam boiler Solar heating system for natural gas heating system

Source: Derived from H. Dana Moran, "Substitution— Some Practical Considerations." In Engineering Implications of Chronic Materials Scarcity, Office of Technology Assessment (Washington, D.C.: U.S. Government Printing Office, 1977), p. 285.

finished part, and not the cost of the material per se. Thus, a cheaper material that is difficult to fabricate may be more costly to use than a more expensive material that is cheaper to fabricate.

In contrast to economic substitution, strategic substitution (sometimes referred to as "emergency" substitution) occurs primarily because the current material of choice is no longer available in the quantities required. Hence, cost becomes secondary, although not necessarily irrelevant. Strategic substitution may take place even though use of the new material is unfavorable both economically and technologically.

The most interesting examples of strategic substitution under crisis conditions occur during time of war. For example, at the start of World War II, a German submarine contained about fifty-six tons of copper, contrasted to only twenty-six tons toward the end of the war. Alloy steel was virtually eliminated from railroad cars, motor vehicle radiators were made from iron instead of copper, and vanadium was substituted for molybdenum or nickel in gun tubes, depending upon size.[21] In the United States, steels containing boron were used during the war as a substitute for high-strength chromium-nickel alloy steels, but at the cost of many failures because the fatigue properties of such steels were considerably lower than those based on chromium as an alloy metal.[22] These wartime crisis substitutions illustrate the fact that the use of materials during an emergency is not necessarily constrained either by cost or by long-term performance.

To a considerable extent, one major difference between economic and strategic substitution is simply a matter of time. As discussed earlier, several years of research and development may be required to move from laboratory concepts through demonstration and implementation in materials development. Even more time may be required to develop and certify a new high-performance substitute alloy for military use. When sufficient time exists, economic substitution may take place naturally as perceptions dictate the desirability of developing new and advanced materials and processes. Where adequate time is lacking, emergency substitution almost invariably results in additional costs and, possibly, reduced performance.

A primary purpose of maintaining a National Defense Stockpile, as discussed later in this chapter, is to provide a cushion of time during which the material of choice, although no longer available through normal channels, is nonetheless available from the stockpile until a substitute material can be developed to take its place. In a very real sense, therefore, a stockpile of sufficient size eliminates the need for immediate emergency substitution for defense purposes.

Technology "on the Shelf"

In view of the importance of the time factor in materials substitution, it is frequently suggested that a need exists for a "technology stockpile" analogous to a materials stockpile. Such a technology stockpile would serve to reduce the time required to make substitute materials available during an emergency and, therefore, would reduce correspondingly the quantities of materials required in the materials stockpile. The concept of stockpiling technology, sometimes referred to as "substitution preparedness," involves in its broadest sense not only an "information bank" for the stockpiling of information derived from research, development, and testing of potential substitute materials, but also the stockpiling of information on new processes and fabrication techniques that would be required to make practical use of these substitute materials. Such a compilation of information implies that considerable work has been carried out along the entire chain of development from laboratory to factory, including the use of substitute materials in prototype assemblies and the evaluation of their performance. In its broadest terms, substitution perparedness could also conceivably include the stockpiling of the capital equipment that would be required to supply essential defense requirements for the substitute material.

Even minimal levels of technology "on the shelf" obviously would be very expensive. At present, few if any incentives exist to encourage such efforts by private industry, which generally does not conduct research to develop new materials unless forced to do so either by supply disruptions or by excessive increases in materials costs. As long as adequate quantities of preferred materials remain available at reasonable cost, it is unrealistic to expect the private sector to undertake the cost of exploring alternatives that may never be needed. Hence, any significant move toward implementing a substitution preparedness effort would almost necessarily require a major initiative on the part of the federal government.

Several important questions concerning substitution preparedness remain unanswered. First, what would be the role of the federal government? In all likelihood, very strong cooperation would be necessary between the government, private industry, and the materials-oriented professional and technical communities to get such a program underway. Second, exactly what should be included? Several possibilities were mentioned above, but much further thought is required in assessing these possibilities as they apply to specific strategic and critical materials. Third, how long would a substitution information bank remain current? An information stockpile, like a materials stockpile, tends to suffer obsolescence unless it is continuously updated. Performance specifications change, and an acceptable substitute for a given application in 1985 may no longer be acceptable in 1995. Thus, additional costs would be incurred in keeping the substitution information bank up to date. And fourth, since the payoff for substitution preparedness comes only through ultimate production and use of the substitute material, meaningful availability of the substitute material could only be achieved by significant expenditures of capital for plant and production facilities.

Clearly, technology "on the shelf" is potentially a very costly approach to reducing materials import vulnerability. Conceivably, much of the technology thus developed might never be put to use. Hence, investment in such technology must necessarily be weighed against the cost of such competing approaches as increased stockpiling, materials conservation, and resource recovery and recycling. Yet the strategic need for quickly available substitutes for at least some critical materials might justify the cost. Partly offsetting these costs would be the potential that some of this technology might find its way into the economy, given changing conditions. Additionally, the gathering in one place of all scientific, technical, and engineering information and data that would help promote materials substitution would be useful in many ways in both peacetime and war.

Substitution Related to Other Factors

Materials substitution is bound intimately with conservation, processing, fabrication, and design. Conservation, whether achieved by reduced usage, less wastage in materials fabrication and processing, or improved design, clearly reduces the pressure for substitution; hence, for some materials, conservation may represent a more economical and efficient means for reducing the need for imports. Improved processing and fabrication techniques can not only help to conserve materials but may also facilitate the introduction of new materials that, not infrequently, have performance characteristics remarkably superior to those of the materials that will be displaced. Also, specifications for many materials uses are now being reconsidered. For example, superalloys containing such critical materials as chromium and cobalt are being reevaluated to determine to what extent the concentration of these metals can be reduced without significantly affecting the desired properties of the alloys.[23]

For some materials, substitutes of equal or greater performance characteristics have not been found. For example, tantalum is considered by some experts as potentially the most critical of all materials with regard to import dependency. No suitable substitutes yet exist for tantalum capacitors in such critical applications as control systems for jet engines. Furthermore, new single-crystal jet engine blades containing 8 to 12 percent tantalum could, if widely employed, consume approximately half the current world production of tantalum. Nor do suitable substitutes yet exist for tantalum carbide metal-working machinery and tools, or other tantalum uses in aerospace structures and superalloys. For less critical applications, reasonable substitutes for tantalum include columbium in superalloys and carbides; aluminum and ceramics in electronic capacitors; silicon, germanium, and selenium in electrical rectifiers; glass, titanium, zirconium, columbium, and platinum in corrosion-resistant equipment; and tungsten, rhenium, molybdenum, iridium, hafnium, and columbium in high-temperature applications.

Because of the heavy degree of dependence of the aerospace industry upon strategic and critical materials, the National Aeronautics and Space Administration in July 1980 launched a three-pronged approach to reduce aerospace requirements for chromium, columbium, cobalt, and tantalum. The first approach involves basic metallurgical research to discover ways in which the concentrations of these metals in aerospace alloys can be reduced without compromising the performance of the alloys. For example, a promising possibility is the replacement of cobalt, columbium, and tantalum by other metals in nickel-based superalloys. Concurrent with this approach is a second that involves the development of new aerospace technology that will permit the redesign of selected engine components so that only those parts actually undergoing high-stress engine forces need be made of the superalloys. Finally, another concurrent approach is a search for entirely new classes of materials that may be more accessible and less expensive, but that nonetheless will be capable of meeting rigorous aerospace performance standards.[24]

Some Technological Aids to Substitution

The virtual nonexistence of ideal substitute materials has been ameliorated considerably by the development of a wide variety of complex synthetic materials, and also by the development of new techniques and processes that often radically change the behavior and properties of existing materials. Although much of this activity is still experimental, much also has been applied successfully to achieve acceptable substitutes for specific materials for defense applications, as discussed in an earlier chapter and reviewed below.

Composite Materials. Composite materials, although used for many years in a variety of applications, are now receiving additional emphasis in applications where their use can help to replace strategic and critical materials for defense purposes. Of increased interest are composites employing metal or ceramic fibers embedded in metal or ceramic matrices for high-temperature use, and plastics reinforced with graphite, glass, or metallic fibers for replacement of stainless steel and other metals in such applications as aircraft wing structures and components that require light weight and good corrosion resistance. Carbon composite sheets are already being used for airframe parts, and the feasibility of a small, commercially designed airplane made largely of composite materials has already been demonstrated. Prospects for composite materials replacing the high-performance metals appear extremely promising.

Coatings. Various kinds of coatings are also receiving considerable attention, especially with the development of new techniques and processes for their application. Of major interest are coatings containing zirconia to provide thermal barriers to reduce metal operating temperatures, various coatings to increase the corrosion resistance of steels, boron or carbide treatment to produce hard surfacing for extended part life, and special coatings to resist oxidation or sulfidation of materials operating under extreme conditions, such as turbine blades. Included under the general concept of coatings are cladding, hard facing, surface alloying, electron beam and laser glazing, thermal spraying, sputtering, laser alloying, ion implantation, vacuum evaporation, boronizing, and surface diffusion bonding.

Use of such techniques can lead to such functional benefits as corrosion protection and high performance, while conserving strategic and critical materials that would otherwise be required for such purposes. For example, cladding can permit the use of a thin layer of a highly corrosion-resistant material over a lower cost, less corrosion-resistant material; the use of a more noble metal clad to one that is less noble; the insertion of a clad transition material between dissimilar metals; and the tailoring of multilayer systems for various kinds of hostile environments.[25]

New Techniques and Processes. New exotic techniques and processes are providing new opportunities for materials substitution that are only now being widely employed. Rapid solidification techniques are being used to produce metallic powders or particulates with unusual properties. Ion implantation techniques, long used by the semiconductor industry, can produce surface "coatings" of implanted chromium, cobalt, or other metals having properties similar to those of the implanted metals themselves. Additionally, much work continues in the search for substitutes through use of amorphous metals, superconducting alloys, electrically active or high-temperature ceramics, advanced glassy materials, solid state materials, and new and improved superalloys.

Resource Recovery and Recycling

The recovery and recycling of waste materials represents an important potential means for reducing the nation's materials import vulnerability. The potential exists not only for recovery of materials in short supply but for improved utilization of the billions of tons of other mineral, agricultural, municipal, and industrial wastes generated each year in the United States. At present, many major materials are recycled and reused, at least to some extent. The major issue of immediate concern here is to what extent additional recycling may be feasible for strategic and critical materials.

Background

The traditional approach to materials usage has been that of aggressive promotion and satisfaction of consumer markets through the production, use, and disposal of products made largely from virgin materials resources. This approach was encouraged by the vast, seemingly inexhaustible materials resources available domestically, as well as by the need to make these resources available for a rapidly growing population and an expanding economy. Collection and recovery of materials for reuse was economically unattractive, often prohibitively costly, and usually such materials were considered less desirable than were virgin materials. As a result, the nation developed an economy based largely upon consumption and disposal—the "throw-away" lifestyle—rather than upon materials conservation, recycling, and reuse.

Gradually this situation is changing. Ironically, periodic shortages of many materials began to occur at the same time that municipalities across the country were struggling to dispose of vast quantities of solid wastes containing a substantial proportion of these materials. Almost too late it has become clear that, at least for some materials, a need exists to couple the "disposal output" to the "feedstock input" in the materials pipeline, thereby establishing a closed materials cycle that would help meet raw materials needs while simultaneously helping to solve critical problems in the generation of mineral, agricultural, municipal, and industrial wastes.

The term "recycling" is popularly used in several different ways. In the most limited sense it denotes the recovery of a material from waste for use in the subsequent manufacture of the same product, as in the recycling of old newspapers into fresh newsprint. In a slightly broader sense it denotes the use of recovered materials in the manufacture of other products of the same genre, as in the recycling of mixed wastepaper into new paper of any kind. More broadly still, recycling simply denotes "reuse": the reuse may be for the same purpose (for example, empty bottles or other containers returned for refilling; aluminum cans returned for use in making either more cans or other aluminum products) or for purposes other than those originally intended (empty glass or other containers used for flower pots, or crushed and compacted into building blocks; transformation of wastepaper into nutrients and compost; burning of old crankcase oil for heating purposes). Not even the recovery of a particular material from among several used in the manufacture of a product is a new meaning for recycling; precious metals have been recovered in this way for years.

Some Advantages of Materials Recycling

From the point of view of the present discussion, the obvious primary advantage of increased materials recycling is the extent to which it may help reduce import dependency and vulnerability. However, a second major advantage that also has to do with import dependency concerns energy. In general, it takes much less energy to collect and reprocess waste material into usable feedstocks than it does to extract and process virgin materials. Hence, increased materials recycling can reduce the nation's requirements for energy and, therefore, the need to import energy fuels from abroad.

A third advantage of recycling is that it reduces the drain on domestic resources, thus helping to preserve them for future use. Had really significant levels of recycling been achieved early in the nation's development, it is probable that the richest deposits of some materials might not have been exhausted so quickly. Recycling, however, has never been a recognized national goal, nor does it have that status today.

A fourth advantage of recycling is its potential beneficial effect upon the economy. In general, it costs less in capital investment for plant and equipment to handle recycled materials than to handle virgin materials, thereby reducing the need for new capital and stretching available capital further. At the same time, the availability of recycled material can serve to offer at least a partial immunity to market fluctuations resulting from price changes, primary material shortages, or possible actions by cartels.

But perhaps the classic rationale for recycling concerns its impact upon the environment. Even today, despite widespread concern for preserving or improving environmental quality, a major fraction of all waste is disposed of in landfills and open dumps. The cost of this disposal, including collection, hauling, and dumping fees, amounts to a truly staggering amount each year. And despite these costs, much waste still manages to find its way as pollution into the land, water, and air on which we depend. Thus, somewhat ironically, the current impetus for recycling materials has come not from the desire to conserve or make better use of our materials resources, but rather from our belated recognition that pollutants are simply "misplaced" materials that degrade the environment.

Problems in Recycling Waste Materials

In view of the recognized advantages of recycling waste materials, it may seem strange that the recycling levels for most materials remain so low. The reason is that, despite the desirability of recycling, formidable obstacles stand in the way. Most of these obstacles involve economic or institutional factors that are difficult to overcome, as the following examples suggest.

Integrated Producers. Many primary processors of materials are "integrated," that is, they own the sources of the materials they process and fabricate. Thus, a pulp or paper mill may own its own forests and prefer logs of known quality from those forests as its primary feedstock, rather than wastepaper of mixed or unclearly known quality. A metals producer may own its own mines and prefer to extract its own ore rather than use possibly less dependable sources of secondary materials. The situation is complicated by various tax and subsidy issues, too complex to discuss here, but that frequently serve to make it cheaper for the integrated producer to produce and use company-owned virgin material feedstocks than to purchase waste material feedstocks.

Consumer Prejudice. The suspicion continues to exist on the part of many consumers that products made from recycled materials may be inferior to those made with virgin materials, or that somehow products made from recycled materials are unwholesome or unclean. In most cases such fears are groundless, for after the waste materials have been reprocessed into new feedstock material, such material is indistinguishable from virgin feedstock material. Indeed, the two are frequently mixed together in various proportions during use. Only in cases where it proves uneconomic to reprocess waste materials to remove all contaminants may some of them remain, provided their presence does not detract from the usefulness of the final product. For example, inks are sometimes not entirely removed from wastepaper being reprocessed into pulp for new paper, which may then appear somewhat speckled or slightly off-white in color. Such defects are purely cosmetic, however, and do not interfere with the usefulness of the product, which may be less expensive than an identical product made solely from virgin materials.

Collection and Separation. Another and very great obstacle is the twofold problem of collection and of whether mixed wastes should be separated at their source before collection, or collected first and then separated at a central waste separation center. Collection of wastes is expensive, and mixed wastes may contain too much material not intended for recovery. Separation at the source, prior to collection, keeps different kinds of wastes segregated and thereby makes subsequent processing easier and less expensive. On the other hand, source separation is tedious, often unreliable, and complicates the process of collection. Separation of mixed wastes at a central collection point offers the advantage of economy of scale but requires a considerably greater investment in plant and equipment, much of which is subject to malfunction and breakdown in handling a wide range of inputs.

Markets. It is almost an axiom of recycling that unless a market exists for recycled material before it is collected, separated, and sorted for resale, the material may only pile up until it is disposed of in a dump or landfill. Among the contributing reasons is that materials markets decrease during each economic downturn or recession, leaving virgin materials as the feedstocks of primary choice; the markets for secondary materials dry up. Unless a secondary materials dealer can continue to underwrite the cost of collection and storage of waste materials while waiting for the economy to improve and the market to grow again, the materials must be disposed of, usually by dumping.

Jurisdictional Disagreements. Not infrequently, efforts to increase recycling are delayed or frustrated by the failure of local, city, county, regional, or state jurisdictional bodies to agree on what approach to take regarding the recycling or disposal of waste materials. Waste generation is oblivious to political boundaries, with the result that logical geographical collection and separation areas often overlap several different political jurisdictions that have widely differing concepts of how to deal with materials wastes. Often such differences make agreement on a common approach impossible, and little if any recycling results.

Some Approaches to Increased Recycling

The problems encountered in attempting to increase the proportion of waste materials recycled help suggest some possible approaches that might be taken to attain this objective. A few of these approaches are presented here.

Incentives. It is often argued that a major reason for the relatively low rate of recycling at present is that various tax laws and subsidies skew the materials markets toward virgin materials, making secondary materials uneconomical to use. Many such subsidies, it is claimed, date from much earlier times when development of the nation's natural resources base was in the public interest and was supported by the federal government in various ways. Such benefits are now so firmly entrenched in our economic and political system as to preclude their removal, even though they have long outlived their usefulness and indeed may now be counterproductive to the vital interests of the nation. Proponents of the use of secondary materials call for similar benefits that would help to equalize the competition between virgin and secondary materials and would at the same time contribute to environmental quality by promoting increased recovery and reuse of waste materials. Such benefits would include cash subsidies for construction of recycling facilities and equipment, government-backed loans and loan-guarantee programs, and various kinds of tax subsidies, investment tax credits, bonds and bond financing, accelerated depreciation on recycling plants and equipment, and tax credits for the use of recycled materials.[26]

User Education. It is possible that much of the prejudice against the use of recycled materials, and against the use of products containing them, derives from ignorance on the part of users, both industries and final consumers. Hence a number of private organizations now help to disseminate information concerning recycled materials, lobby the government for incentives such as those described above, and generally exert educational efforts in an attempt to overcome the prejudice against recycled materials. Yet the efforts of such groups have been insufficient to promote really significant levels of recycling. Thus, proponents of recycling argue that efforts should be undertaken at all levels of government—local, municipal, state, and federal—to educate both industries and consumers regarding the benefits that can be derived for the entire nation from increased levels of materials recycling.

Markets. Other than for such materials as metallic home and prompt industrial scrap and their equivalents for some other kinds of waste materials (as discussed later in this chapter), secure markets for most waste materials generally do not exist. Some efforts have been made by the federal government to specify a certain level of recycled material content in some of the products purchased by government agencies such as the General Services Administration, but these efforts, however well motivated, have failed to increase significantly the market for recycled materials. Hence, some analysts maintain that the federal government, in addition to undertaking the incentives discussed above, also should undertake a more active role in promoting markets for recycled materials. A step in this direction was taken when legislation was enacted to develop standards for certain waste materials, since such standards would increase the marketability of the recycled materials concerned.

Initial standardization efforts, mandated under the Energy Policy and Conservation Act, directed the National Bureau of Standards to develop test procedures to determine whether recycled oil was substantially equivalent to virgin oil for particular end uses.[27] Much more comprehensive efforts were mandated by the Resource Conservation and Recovery Act,[28] directing the Bureau of Standards to publish guidelines for the development of specifications to classify waste materials in terms of their physical and chemical properties and those other characteristics of significance in promoting their use in lieu of virgin materials. The program specified by this second act included four discrete approaches to encourage increased recycling:

1. The development of accurate specifications for recovered materials.
2. The stimulation of secondary materials markets.
3. The promotion of proven recycling technology.
4. The encouragement of exchanges of technical and economic data relating to resource recovery facilities.

Additionally, the second act called for the stimulation of markets for recycled materials by identifying the geographical locations of existing or potential markets, by identifying the economic and technical barriers to the use of recovered materials, and by encouraging the development of new uses for recycled materials.

In response to the above legislative requirements, the Bureau of Standards established an Office of Recycled Materials that over the period from 1976 through 1982 essentially fulfilled the objectives sought by the legislation. More than 125 publications and reports were issued over this period, and the methods and standards developed by the bureau have been adopted throughout the recycling community.[29]

It has also been suggested that the federal government should encourage the stockpiling of waste materials either by subsidizing such stockpiles in the private sector or by maintaining the stockpiles itself. Materials could be stockpiled during market downturns, then sold during market recoveries. Critics, however, have derided the notion as "the stockpiling of garbage."

Advanced Technology. Much of the difficulty encountered in recycling waste materials arises because the technology for doing so is not sufficiently well developed or reliable. We can speak here of technology on two different levels, the macro and the micro. On the macro level, a need exists to separate waste consisting of various mixed materials—for example, metals, glass, plastics, paper, and various combinations thereof—into their various constituents. Most municipal solid wastes, and some industrial wastes, fit this need. Although much development work has been done on different methods and techniques to achieve the separation, and although much of the required equipment has been developed, is quite sophisticated, and is currently in use, on the whole the equipment has neither lived up to expectations nor has it completely solved the problems of mixed waste separation.

Problems of separation on this macro level would be somewhat alleviated if wastes were separated at the source, rather than mixed with other kinds of waste before collection. For example, it has been suggested that when military and jet engines are periodically stripped down and reassembled with new components, the discarded components could be properly identified according to whether they are nickel- or cobalt-based, and thereupon segregated and saved for recycling. Likewise, it has been pointed out that the producers of cutting tools know the source and chemistry of such tools as well as of the high-speed steels they use; hence, they, too, could identify, segregate, and sell their valuable scrap for recycling.[30]

On the micro level a need also exists to develop procedures and techniques for separating such materials as composites, alloys, and coated and clad materials into their constituent, elemental forms. The technology for this level of separation scarcely exists as yet, and that which does exist is still in its infancy. However, when this technology ultimately is developed, the potential for recycling strategic and critical materials will be vastly improved. And not until the technology on both levels has become considerably more advanced than it now is can we anticipate significantly higher levels of recycling for many materials.

Design for Recycling. Perhaps one of the most promising approaches to increased recycling is that of designing complex materials and products specifically so that, upon disposal, they can be separated more readily into their constituent materials. Such design, if widely practiced, could greatly alleviate some of the problems of waste separation. For example, if aluminum instead of copper were used for the wiring harness in automobiles, the steel scrap in junked automobiles would not only be more valuable but would be easier to recycle, because copper along with other impurities is detrimental to most steels, whereas aluminum can be tolerated better. Unfortunately, such design considerations are rarely practiced as yet.[31]

Recycling of Strategic and Critical Materials

The recycling of strategic and critical materials such as those listed in Table 5.3 is made more difficult by recently evolved, technologically related problems. Ironically, many recycling problems have arisen or have been exacerbated by the development and increased use of the complex and sophisticated artificial materials that may serve as the best substitutes for strategic and critical materials. Some of the major classes of such materials are listed below with comments on difficulties in their recycling.

Composites. Attempting to recycle a complex composite material is incredibly difficult, if not impossible, by current technology. Removal of the fibers from the general matrix material is possible if the latter can be liquified or dissolved away, but this is by no means assured. Such separation is especially unlikely when the matrix material is a high-temperature ceramic or a thermosetting plastic.

Alloys. A good proportion of the strategic and critical materials listed in Table 5.3 is used primarily in industrial alloys. As with composites, separation of these alloys into their constituents is extremely difficult, if at all possible. As such alloys become increasingly more complex and sophisticated, separation becomes more formidable and hence less likely.

Coatings. Increasing use is being made of various coatings, claddings, and platings to provide desirable properties for plastics, ceramics, steels, and other basic industrial materials. Removal of such coatings from the underlying base material is generally much more readily accomplished than the separation of composites or alloys into their components. Often such coatings are relatively thin and can be dissolved away without damage to the base material, or if thicker can be stripped away by suitable procedures. Both coating and base material can then be recycled.

Plastics. Plastics are difficult to recycle partly because an incredibly large number of different plastics is now in use and partly because no really good technique has yet been developed either for separating different kinds of plastics from one another or for separating plastics from other materials. Because of these difficulties, a large percentage of plastics and plastics-containing waste is still dumped or incinerated for energy recovery.

As should be clear from the above, the recycling of strategic and critical materials is made difficult because of the increasingly exotic and complex combinations of materials now used in many high-technology and defense applications. Considerable research is now being directed toward possible separation of specific materials combinations, largely by the Bureau of Mines.[32] For the present, however, success in recycling some of these materials will continue to depend primarily upon applications where a scrap material can be reused directly in its existing alloy form, as when steel scrap is used by the steel industry. Even here, there are distinct limits to the amount of scrap that can be used in a mix with virgin materials without the mix becoming "poisoned" with trace materials alloyed in the scrap. For example, purity requirements currently complicate the use of recycled chromium for jet engines.

Despite difficulties, significant percentages of some strategic and critical materials are being recycled, as shown earlier in the third column of Table 5.3: chromium, 18 percent; platinum-group metals, 6 percent; tantalum, 6 percent; and cobalt, 5 percent. However, these levels of recycling are inadequate to influence substantially the need to import these materials from abroad, and consequently to lessen appreciably U.S. vulnerability to potential supply disruptions for these materials.

Stockpiling

Unlike the three approaches to reducing import vulnerability discussed to this point—conservation, substitution, and recycling—the stockpiling of materials does not help to reduce import *dependency* because by and large the stockpiled materials must be imported from abroad before they are stockpiled. Nonetheless, stockpiling helps to reduce import *vulnerability* because an adequate stockpile, properly maintained, administered, and used, can protect against the adverse effects of a sudden interruption of supplies of any of the stockpiled materials. Indeed, it would be difficult to over-emphasize the fact that stockpiling is the *only* approach that could significantly reduce import vulnerability over the near term. All of the other approaches require much more time to implement because they remain severely constrained by lack of suitable technology. Stockpiling is not subject to such constraints. Its only real constraint is in the time taken to order, pay for, transport, and store the required materials.

In view of all these factors, it is highly regrettable that the federal government has never permitted stockpiling to realize its full potential as a strategic factor in national defense. In the past, no Congress or administration has provided sufficient funds to permit rapid achievement of stockpile goals. Furthermore, barring a dramatic change in political climate, adequate funding for the stockpile is unlikely to be provided in the near future.

Historical Overview

The stockpiling of strategic and critical materials has been under consideration in one sense or another for more than a century. As long ago as 1880 congressional hearings were held on the subject of materials availability.

However, not until real difficulties were experienced in obtaining some critically needed strategic materials during World War I was the concept of a materials stockpile considered seriously. As a result of those wartime experiences, Barnard M. Baruch—former chairman of the War Industries Board—recommended in a report to President Woodrow Wilson in December 1919 that action be initiated to assure that adequate supplies of raw materials would be available in the event of a future emergency. Subsequently, actual planning for a stockpile of strategic materials was initiated by the Army General Staff in 1921 when military leaders became concerned about the possibility of materials shortages in future military conflicts. The War Department in 1922 commissioned a joint committee of the American Institute of Mining and Metallurgical Engineers and of the Mining and Metallurgical Society of America to study the question and, two years later, this joint committee recommended that strategic and critical materials be purchased, imported, and stockpiled.

The stockpile did not materialize, however, although over the next fifteen years new concerns arose from Japanese conquests in Asia during the 1930s that threatened to cut off vital U.S. imports from that area. Also of concern was the growing possibility of war breaking out in Europe. Finally, in 1937 the navy was authorized to purchase $3.5 million worth of materials determined by the secretary of the navy to be necessary in time of war. Among the materials purchased were manganese, manila fiber, optical glass, tin, and tungsten. Although an additional $1 million in materials was added during the next two years, the total outlay for strategic and critical materials at this time was very modest.

The National Stockpile. Stockpiling in the contemporary sense originated as a result of mobilization efforts preceding World War II. The initial national stockpile was authorized by the Strategic and Critical Stock Piling Act of 1939, which served to formalize and institutionalize the concept of strategic materials stockpiling.[33] Stockpiling policy, as stated in this 1939 act, provided not only for the acquisition of basic industrial raw materials necessary for the production of military equipment, but also for materials considered essential to the civilian, defense-supporting industries. Additionally, the act called for the increased development of mines to exploit domestic deposits of strategic and critical materials, thereby trying to lessen what was considered a dangerous and costly dependence upon foreign nations for materials in time of national emergency. An appropriation of $100 million for the period 1939 to 1943 was authorized for the purchase of strategic and critical materials as determined by the secretaries of war, navy, and interior, acting through the Army and Navy Munitions Board. Materials designated as strategic and critical at this time included chromite ore, quartz crystals, rubber, and tin—all of which were purchased from foreign sources.

Ironically, the stockpiling program established by the 1939 act was interrupted by the outbreak of World War II after only $70 million of the authorized $100 million was spent. The need to expand rapidly the nation's defense capabilities resulted in new authority for the Reconstruction Finance

Corporation to produce, acquire, and transfer strategic and critical materials either through existing corporations or through the creation of new corporations. Only the U.S. government, through the RFC, was authorized to import strategic and critical materials. In fact, the RFC, with the help of the federal government, established such operational arms as the Rubber Reserve Company, the Metals Reserve Company, and the Defense Supplies Corporation to acquire and distribute strategic and critical materials and avoid the need for government agencies to carry out such activities. Because of the need during the war to use materials almost as quickly as they could be acquired, the Army and Navy Munitions Board essentially suspended procurement of materials for the national stockpile during the war. When appropriations for the stockpile lapsed in 1943, they were not extended.

Despite all efforts to acquire adequate quantities of strategic and critical materials during the war, serious shortages and disruptions of supplies nonetheless occurred for such materials as copper, natural rubber, tin, and tungsten. The war drew heavily on the nation's reserves of raw materials, leaving them dangerously depleted, and the life of some remaining reserves could be measured in only a few years. It thus became obvious to strategic planners after the war that additional stockpiling initiatives were necessary. The 1939 act was therefore superseded in 1946 by a new act of the same name that provided several new and important authorities.[34] As noted in the policy statement of this new 1946 act, the major purpose and intent was to provide for the acquisition and retention of stocks of strategic and critical materials, and also to encourage simultaneously the development and conservation of domestic sources of such materials. The government was empowered to assume control of all inventories of strategic and critical materials acquired both immediately prior to and during the war, and its authority to promote the development of mines to exploit domestic deposits of such materials was reaffirmed and made more explicit than it had been in the 1939 act. In continuity with the earlier act, the secretaries of war, navy, and interior retained the authority to determine which materials were strategic and critical and the total amounts of each material to be stockpiled. However, the three secretaries were directed to consult with the secretaries of agriculture, commerce, state, and treasury in making these determinations.

In greatly expanding the scope of the 1939 act, the 1946 act in many respects completed or rounded out the first major federal initiative to provide for the strategic and critical materials needs of both industry and the military during a wartime emergency. It was estimated that these needs would require a stockpile of about $2.1 billion worth of materials, only $300 million of which were already on hand; the remaining $1.8 billion was to be purchased at the rate of $360 million a year for a period of five years. Unfortunately, Congress appropriated only $100 million of the first year's $360 million and, although somewhat larger sums were appropriated in succeeding years, by the end of the five-year period in 1950 the stockpile program was only about 40 percent complete. With the onset of hostilities in Korea, appropriations accelerated markedly and, in a period of only six months during late 1950 and early 1951, almost $3 billion was appropriated, which amounted to more than triple the sums that had been provided during the previous four years.

The Defense Production Act Inventory. The sudden acceleration of the national stockpile in late 1950 owed its inception to the fact that as prospects for war in Korea became more imminent, further steps would be required to assure adequate supplies of strategic and critical materials for the United States. These concerns led to passage of the Defense Production Act of 1950, which provided authority for virtually all of the economic measures taken to facilitate mobilization during the Korean War.[35]

Essentially, the act authorized the government to:

1. Divert scarce resources to the production of military weapons and other essential programs.
2. Stockpile strategic and critical materials.
3. Expand production of needed materials, equipment, and components.
4. Minimize the adverse economic impact of the defense buildup.

Under the seven titles of this act, the president was given broad powers to issue priorities, allocate scarce materials, prevent hoarding, control prices, buy and sell materials for current use, and offer incentives to expand production.

After the Korean War was over, the four titles of the act that had provided the president with economic controls were allowed to expire. The remaining three, still in effect today, provide the primary basis for developing and maintaining a continuing state of defense industrial preparedness. Of these, Title III, "Expansion of Productive Capacity and Supply" (discussed previously in Chapter 2), most directly concerns the stockpiling of strategic and critical materials.

Two aspects of Title III are especially relevant to the present discussion. The first aspect is that under the terms of this title, the federal government may undertake a variety of steps to promote increased domestic production of materials considered essential for defense or, in effect, those materials currently being stockpiled. One of the important steps authorized is the guaranteed purchase of materials during periods when market demand is weak, thereby encouraging private industry to develop and maintain productive capacity that may be needed during an emergency. Materials produced and purchased under this provision of the act were initially stored in a second federal stockpile—essentially independent of the national stockpile discussed previously—known as the Defense Production Act Inventory.

In effect, the Defense Production Act provided the government with new and sweeping authority to expand production capacity and supplies, both domestic and foreign. However, in conferring the power to purchase, store, and sell raw materials, the act did not call for the DPA Inventory to supersede the national stockpile, which continued operation under the Munitions Board. In some ways the DPA Inventory differed sharply in purpose and use from the initial stockpile. Whereas the purpose of the national stockpile was to acquire a reserve of strategic and critical materials for use during wartime, the purpose of the new materials inventory was to provide a guaranteed market for the additional materials produced under government-sponsored expansion programs. Expansion of production capacity was the primary aim, and the purchase and stockpiling of the materials thus produced was secondary. In practice, however, materials not sold to private industry were sold to the Munitions Board for the national stockpile. By the end of 1962, acquisitions for the inventory totaled about $3.5 billion as a result of expansion contracts and domestic purchase programs. Of this, about $2 billion in materials had been transferred to the national stockpile.

The Supplemental Stockpile. In addition to the two stockpiles discussed above, a third stockpile—the supplemental stockpile—was established by the Agricultural Trade Development and Assistance Act of 1954. Although the primary purpose of this act was to facilitate the disposal of agricultural surpluses abroad, the stockpiling of strategic and critical materials was to benefit in two ways. First, bulky and perishable agricultural materials that were costly to store could be bartered for strategic materials that were much less bulky or perishable and less costly to store. Second, the agricultural materials could be sold outright and the funds used to purchase strategic materials. Sales of surplus agricultural materials, and purchases of strategic materials with the foreign funds thus obtained, were to be administered by the secretary of agriculture and, once materials were obtained, they were to be subject to the same limitations governing disposal that applied to the other two stockpiles. The 1954 act also expanded and reemphasized the role of the Commodity Credit Corporation, which had been authorized to barter agricultural surpluses for foreign strategic materials under terms of the Commodity Credit Corporation Charter Act, as amended in 1949.[36]

In practice, no strategic materials were ever purchased using foreign currency from agricultural sales as funds; acquisitions were obtained exclusively through bartering. Before 1954, bartering operations conducted under CCC authority were carried out only on a limited scale, but these operations increased substantially with the passage of the 1954 act. Virtually all materials obtained through bartering from 1954 to 1956 were channeled into the national stockpile. During the following six years, however, the larger portions of materials obtained through bartering went into the supplemental stockpile after the needs of the national stockpile had been met.

The National Defense Stockpile

Activities undertaken by the federal government to stockpile strategic and critical materials often have been confused and contradictory. The existence of three separate stockpiles—the national stockpile, the supplemental stockpile, and the Defense Production Act Inventory—has not made matters any easier. Consequently, these three stockpiles were consolidated into a single National Defense Stockpile under the authority of the Strategic and Critical Materials Stock Piling Revision Act of 1979.[37] This new act retained the major provisions of the 1939 and 1946 acts but revised and updated both to conform to current stockpile policy and to strengthen the role of Congress in stockpile policymaking.

The 1979 act also provided specific guidelines to be followed in determining which materials should be included in the National Defense Stockpile, and the quantity of each. Additionally, the act created a National Defense Stockpile Transaction Fund to support acquisition of materials for the stockpile and to receive funds resulting from sales of materials from the stockpile. The act specifically requires that all funds derived from stockpile sales can be used only for the purchase of other materials for the stockpile. Further, the act directs the president to take steps to encourage the development of new domestic supplies of strategic and critical materials, especially from the treatment and utilization of lower grade domestic ores; to encourage the development of substitutes for these materials; and to encourage the use of barter in acquiring and disposing of stockpiled materials.

Other Kinds of Stockpiles

Stockpiles of materials owned and controlled by the federal government are by no means the only kind of stockpiles that currently exist or that have been proposed. Virtually every company that produces or uses industrial materials maintains at least some level of its own stockpile. Foreign governments increasingly are either establishing or considering establishing stockpiles, and many cartel-like organizations maintain buffer stockpiles of the materials of concern to them. Additionally, increased thought is being given to the prospects of establishing a stockpile, either federally or privately managed, that would be used solely for economic purposes.

Private Stockpiles. As mentioned above, most producers and users of industrial materials maintain substantial inventories of essential raw and semi-finished materials primarily to maintain continuity of delivery or production in the event that a disruption should occur in normal operating procedures. To the extent that these inventories include materials that are included in the National Defense Stockpile, the private stockpile goals for such materials are correspondingly reduced. However, it has often been suggested that private companies should be encouraged to carry larger inventories as an alternative to the federal stockpile. Among the advantages cited for such enlarged private inventories are the following:

Private management. The management role of the federal government in acquiring, maintaining, and disbursing strategic and critical materials would be reduced significantly, if not entirely eliminated. Direct federal expenditures for stockpiling would be reduced correspondingly.

Increased efficiency. The range of materials needed by private industrial companies is staggering if one considers the number of materials involved, the various qualities and grades, and the kinds of shapes and forms used in industrial processes. Only a limited number of materials is included in the National Defense Stockpile, and typically in forms—for example, raw ores—that are fairly far removed from the production line.

Improved delivery. Because a private stockpile would be located either at or near the site of the firm that owns it, little or no delay would be experienced in making the materials immediately available for use. By contrast, shipment of materials from a central federal stockpile storage depot to a particular user's plant can take considerable time.

Rapid turnover. As the manufacturing procedures of a private user change over time, corresponding changes take place in the materials inventory or stockpile. This rapid turnover keeps the inventory relatively fresh and current. By contrast, a centralized federal stockpile cannot possibly be responsive to the variety of such changes throughout the U.S. defense industrial establishment.

Despite these advantages, little actually has been done to encourage a buildup of private stockpiles to reduce the demands upon the National Defense Stockpile. One reason is that many private producers and users dislike the idea. Part of this dislike arises from past failure of the government to consult with private industry, and especially with the minerals industry, concerning stockpile policymaking. Most contact with industry has been limited to requests for technical information and to the timing of stockpile sales or to the prices of materials to be disposed of from the stockpile. Part also arises from the mining industry's view that the stockpile has been used in the past to manipulate commodity prices and to intervene in the marketplace for other economic, or even political, purposes. At the same time, the industry has been subjected to a wide variety of regulatory and legal constraints. Suspicion and distrust have therefore developed between industry and government, making industry cautious about any new proposals that would encourage it to increase its inventories beyond estimated corporate needs as an alternative to larger government stockpiles.

But perhaps the primary reason for the lack of increased private stockpiles is economic. The costs of maintaining additional inventories above normal business inventory needs are substantial in terms of acquisition costs, maintenance, and perhaps most important of all, the need to finance inventories at relatively high interest rates. Apart from a relatively small number of financially strong corporations that could afford to increase significantly their materials inventories when business conditions are weak and commodity prices are low, few companies possess the financial capacity to undertake increased inventories and the attendant economic risks. To encourage them to do so, suitable incentives would have to be provided by the federal government, offsetting reduced federal expenditures for stock-piling. Many industry spokesmen doubt that any such incentives would ever be authorized by Congress in view of the widespread belief that tax incentives to private industry represent inequitable loopholes in the nation's tax system. Further, some critics maintain that increased inventories that would benefit private companies should not be financed in part at public expense.

Foreign Stockpiles. An important consideration in setting U.S. stockpile objectives concerns the status of potential U.S. allies in time of emergency, and especially the nation's NATO allies. As discussed earlier, most such nations are even more dependent than the United States itself upon imports of strategic and critical materials. Nonetheless, at the present time, France is the only major U.S. ally having an operational, official stockpiling policy, largely for chromium, copper, lead, and tungsten.[38] The British have yet to initiate formally a stockpile along the lines of that of the United States, and West Germany has considered and largely rejected the establishment of such a stockpile, opting instead to attempt further diversification of supply sources to avoid the prospect of emergency supply interruptions. Japan, although more heavily dependent upon materials imports than any other U.S. ally, does not now maintain a strategic stockpile, opting like West Germany for diversification of supply sources.[39]

Buffer Stockpiles. A number of international groups exist that maintain so-called buffer stocks of various materials. Such buffer stocks, however, are maintained primarily for economic purposes, that is, to maintain price-support floors for these materials and, thereby, help to stabilize international markets. If the price of any of these materials falls on the open market to the floor support price, the material is purchased for the buffer stockpile, thereby helping to stabilize the price. Then, if a shortage occurs, forcing prices inordinately high, material in the buffer stockpile is sold, again helping to stabilize prices. In practice, the only really significant buffer stock is that maintained by the International Tin Council, which has not been particularly successful in using the buffer stock to stabilize world tin prices over an extended time period.[40]

Economic Stockpiles. Economic stockpiling is the maintenance of stockpiles for purely economic rather than strategic purposes. Although space does not permit extended discussion of the concept here, it is of interest because, first, the rationale for a stockpile of strategic and critical materials is irrelevant as long as those materials could be known to be available for use during an emergency. And second, much evidence exists to support the view that the National Defense Stockpile has often been used for economic purposes. Thus, the major difference between an economic and a strategic stockpile may be not much more than the criteria governing the release of materials from the stockpile, that is, the determination of what constitutes a shortage or an emergency. A secondary difference may be in the kinds of materials to be stockpiled: although many materials are major in both economic and strategic terms, conceivably some materials included in an economic stockpile would not be considered either strategic or critical. But the essential consideration is that any economic stockpile would almost certainly include materials that are currently considered strategic and critical, and that these materials would necessarily be made available for any national emergency.[41]

Major Stockpiling Issues

Although stockpiling represents the only really practical short-term solution to the problem of materials import vulnerability, it is by no means an easy or inexpensive solution. It raises many issues concerning administration and policymaking, as well as problems concerning technology and logistics.

Objectives. The most fundamental factor in determining stockpile objectives is the length of time in years that the stockpile must serve as the primary— and possibly the only—source of strategic and critical materials during an emergency-induced shortage. That factor alone determines the quantities of materials that must be stockpiled, whether deficiencies or surpluses exist for each stockpiled material, and the overall cost of creating and sustaining the stockpile.

In 1945 it was simply assumed that the stockpile should contain sufficient materials to cover all possible shortages during a five-year war fought along conventional lines, as in World War II, and that it should be capable of supporting a military force of about 10 million troops. This five-year objective remained in effect until 1958, at which time the potential use of nuclear weapons in a conflict led to a sharp downgrading of the wartime significance of industrial capacity and, hence, the importance of the stockpile. Clearly, in a nuclear conflict much of the industrial capacity of the nation would be destroyed, thereby reducing the need for strategic and critical materials. Consequently, the stockpile objective was set to cover a period of only three years, to include sufficient materials to support a military force of about 5 million troops. The assumption underlying this decision was that a nuclear war would have to be fought primarily with the equipment and manpower already produced or trained, and deployed, at the outbreak of hostilities.

The reduction of the stockpile objective from five to only three years automatically created large surpluses for many stockpiled materials. Additional surpluses were created in 1973 when the Nixon administration reduced the stockpile objective to a one-year emergency on the basis that

- The world outlook appeared to be more peaceful than it had been in the preceding years;

- Improved technology would facilitate the substitution of available materials for those that might become scarce;

- Defense needs potentially could be met through increased civilian austerity;

- For an emergency of longer than one year, the one-year period nonetheless would suffice to permit mobilization that would sustain the nation's defensive effort for as long as necessary.

It was further assumed that foreign imports would be available, except from Communist and combatant nations.

The effect of the 1958 and 1973 changes was to render many materials surplus, thereby making them available for disposal. Little imagination was required to recognize that the revenues obtained from so massive a sale of stockpiled materials would represent a substantial contribution to reducing budget deficits that were becoming a political embarrassment. However, in March 1975 the Subcommittee on Seapower and Strategic and Critical Materials of the House Committee on Armed Services voted to authorize no further disposals of stockpile materials until a new policy study was conducted, and the subcommittee insisted that the stockpile objective again be based on a three-year emergency.

In August 1975 the National Security Council directed that the requested study be undertaken by an interagency committee. Following completion of this study in July 1976, the administration announced a major, long-range program of acquisitions and disposals for the stockpile to be based on planning for the first three years of an emergency of indefinite duration, assuming large-scale mobilization. The three-year objective was reaffirmed in October 1977 and became a statutory requirement with the passage of the 1979 act. The three-year objective remains in effect at the present time.

The determination of what materials should be included in the stockpile is less controversial than the time issue because it is more technological and less political. Although clearly the Department of Defense has an overriding interest in the choice of materials, many other departments also have individual interests. For example, the State Department is concerned with the extent to which the buying and selling of stockpiled materials influences international economic policy in its effects upon foreign producers and consumers of such materials. The Department of the Interior is concerned with the effect stockpiling may have upon domestic resources policy and upon the health and vitality of the U.S. mining industry in connection with the department's own mandate to provide technical information and expertise to federal policymakers. The Department of Commerce is concerned with the domestic users of stockpiled materials and the need to maintain a strong and healthy defense industrial base. And still other agencies, concerned with national security and defense mobilization, have their own specific concerns, all of which must be recognized in determining stockpile goals for specific materials.

The procedure by which all these individual interests are combined to produce official stockpile goals is beyond the scope of this discussion. However, the overall coordination of this effort is achieved by the Federal Emergency Management Agency, which divides the economy into three sectors—defense, essential civilian, and general civilian—and estimates the individual supply requirements for each sector. It then attempts to predict the gross national product during wartime, and adjusts this GNP figure by use of various "planning factors" based upon such conditions and assumptions as conservation or "austerity" measures adopted by the government during wartime; shifts in composition of personal consumption expenditures; investment expenditures; "material consumption ratios" measuring the physical amount of an item consumed for each unit of output; substitution possibilities for each material; potential foreign suppliers of the materials; political and economic reliability of foreign suppliers; and transportation losses. Following such adjustments, the agency can then estimate the material requirements for each of the three economy sectors under the conditions postulated, and thus determine the requirements for the National Defense Stockpile. The current stockpile goals for sixty-one materials or materials groups, as established in 1980, are being revised.[42]

Implementation of stockpile goals is sought through yearly programs, known as the Annual Materials Plan, calling for the sale and purchase of stockpile materials in such a way as to minimize possible disruption of materials markets. The steering committee for the actual plan, chaired by the Federal Emergency Management Agency, includes representatives from the Departments of Agriculture, Commerce, Defense, Energy, Interior, State, and Treasury, as well as from the Central Intelligence Agency, the General Services Administration, and the Office of Management and Budget. This committee reviews prospective actions involving the sale and purchase of stockpile materials, taking into account the impact of such actions upon international and domestic materials markets, upon the prevailing economic and political climates, upon strategic issues related to national defense, and upon the federal budget.

All of the above-described activity is clouded by its complexity, by the thick curtain of security constraints that hangs over it, and by politically motivated attempts to make the process appear more straightforward and scientific than it really is, largely through the efficient and professional use of supporting studies, computer modeling, data gathering, risk analysis, and the weighing of various policy options. In the final analysis, however, the decisions made represent only the best-calculated guesses that can be arrived at by conscientious people working under formidable conditions of uncertainty and political pressure.

Administration. Virtually from the beginning, the policymaking components of administration—governing the choice of what materials were to be stockpiled, and in what quantities, grades, shapes, and forms—was kept separate from the operative component dealing with procurement, storage, inspection, maintenance, security, rotation, processing, market analysis, shipping, and disposal of excess materials. As noted earlier in this chapter, the 1939 Stock Piling Act directed the secretaries of war, navy, and the interior, acting jointly through the Army and Navy Munitions Board, to carry out the policymaking component, whereas the operating component was under the direction of the Procurement Division of the U.S. Treasury. The president was authorized to release materials from the stockpile during a declared state of national emergency, the threat of war, or actual war. This arrangement of responsibilities was essentially retained intact by the 1946 act, except that the secretaries of agriculture, commerce, state, and treasury were directed to assist in the policymaking component.

In 1947, the Army and Navy Munitions Board was reorganized and given statutory authority, retaining its stockpiling policymaking functions. At about the same time, the Treasury Department's Procurement Division was reorganized as the Bureau of Federal Supply, but retained the stockpiling operative component until that function was transferred in 1949 to the

Federal Supply Service of the newly formed General Services Administration. A further transfer took place when the operating component was shifted to the newly formed Emergency Procurement Service of GSA in 1950.

During World War II, first the National Security Resources Board and then the Office of Defense mobilization had essentially assumed the Munitions Board's stockpile policymaking authorities. After the war, both the NSRB and the Munitions Board were abolished, leaving the Office of Defense Mobilization in charge of stockpile policymaking and the GSA in charge of operations. Subsequently, the policymaking component was transferred to the Office of Emergency Planning.

The split between the policymaking and the operating components for managing the strategic stockpile finally was eliminated in 1973 when the Office of Defense Mobilization was abolished and its policymaking functions were transferred to the GSA's Office of Preparedness. The GSA's Federal Supply Service and Office of Stockpile Disposal continued to serve as custodians and managers of the stockpile. Responsibility was again split, however, when in 1979 the policymaking component was transferred to the National Defense Stockpile Policy Division of the Federal Emergency Management Agency and the management of the stockpile remained with the General Services Administration.[43]

Use of Stockpile Materials. From the wording of the first legislation, the 1939 act, and continuing in later legislation, it was clear that Congress intended stockpiled materials to be used only for strategic, not primarily economic, purposes. The major purpose for this long-standing policy was to prevent accumulated stockpiled materials from overshadowing the private materials markets and possibly exerting a downward pressure on the domestic economy. Hence, by law all stockpiled materials could be released only during an emergency or actual wartime, except for disposals necessitated by technological obsolescence, physical deterioration, or excess inventories. Despite this legislative proviso, over the years materials have been released from the stockpile on numerous occasions under questionable circumstances, in most cases to raise federal revenues or to influence market prices, rather than for strategic reasons. Indeed, some past congressional examinations into the stockpile's history have revealed such numerous and erratic changes in stockpile objectives as to suggest that nonsecurity considerations may well have motivated sales and purchases of many stockpile items.

An example of such manipulation occurred in 1965 when President Johnson forced the aluminum industry to rescind a price increase by threatening to release 300,000 tons of stockpiled aluminum. But perhaps the most memorable example occurred in 1973 and 1974 when President Nixon sought to reduce the stockpile by more than 90 percent, primarily to help balance the budget and to improve foreign exchange. During that period, aluminum, copper, and nickel holdings were eliminated and lead, silver, and zinc holdings were reduced significantly. Although there were some mineral shortages at the time, some analysts have suggested that these metals were chosen for reduction or elimination primarily because they were the easiest to liquidate to raise funds for other, nonstrategic purposes. These incidents, and others like them, led to the reiteration in the 1979 act of the overriding importance of the strategic issue, explicitly stating that the purpose of the stockpile was to serve national defense interests exclusively and consequently the stockpile was not to be used for economic or budgetary purposes (50 U.S.C. 98b).

Costs. The major cost of the stockpile is that of original acquisition of materials. These acquisition costs are, of course, substantially recoverable when materials ultimately are sold from the stockpile and, indeed, it is not unusual for materials to be sold for more than their original purchase price. Because a large fraction of the materials currently in the National Defense Stockpile was acquired prior to 1958, increases in materials prices have increased the value of many of these materials significantly. The effect of this inflation on the current inventory has been dramatic: acquisition costs amounted to about $3.5 billion, whereas the market value as of 30 September 1983 was estimated at approximately $11.1 billion,[44] yielding a "paper profit" of about $7.6 billion.

Other major stockpile costs, not recoverable, include maintenance costs for facility construction, storage and handling, and rotation of stocks; costs for general administration; and costs for machining operations. For the period 1948 through 1977, these costs totaled approximately $650 million, at which time the government ceased publication of such figures. However, it is likely that as of today such costs have totaled about $1 billion.

These costs, as well as initial materials acquisition costs, represent essentially an "insurance program" to guard against the possibility of future shortages in the event of war or other national emergency. Critics often point out that the program is very expensive insurance and that the funds tied up in it might better be used in other areas of federal concern. They cite that if the money had been invested at conventional interest rates, the return would more than compensate for the paper profits mentioned above. These arguments are somewhat naive in that the critics fail to recognize that the strategic stockpile is in effect a relatively small portion of a much larger insurance program known as the Department of Defense.

The Role of Congress Three congressional roles relevant to the stockpile are the passage of legislation, the appropriation of funds, and the oversight or overseeing of various executive branch agencies that have responsible stockpiling functions. The legislative role has already been discussed. With regard to funding, Congress has always been slow to appropriate adequate funds for the stockpile except during wartime. Despite the goals determined for the stockpile and requests by various administrations for funds needed to help meet these goals, Congress with rare exceptions has reduced administrative budget requests by substantial percentages. On the other hand, once materials have been acquired for the stockpile, Congress typically has exhibited much greater reluctance to dispose of them than has the executive branch. Although the president has always been authorized to release stockpiled materials for defense purposes, Congress increased its oversight activities with the passage of the 1946 act to require that both the House and the Senate Military Affairs Committees be formally notified of such releases. It further specified that the disposal of materials for any other reason required its specific approval. Over the years these requirements have been strengthened until, at present, all disposals from the consolidated National Defense Stockpile require specific congressional approval.

Forms of Stockpiled Materials. It is obviously impractical to attempt to stockpile materials in every kind of feedstock used or needed by the nation's industrial defense establishment. Consequently, primary importance must be placed upon including materials in the particular shapes and forms that can be either most directly and immediately used or most quickly converted to forms required by the greatest number of users. Considering the difficulties involved, it is not surprising that the procedures followed in these determinations are often criticized. It has been noted that the stockpile system is too cumbersome to cope with the wide variety of ore types and qualities that companies use or with the frequent changes required by developing technology. Consequently, many companies might have to interrupt production to make major adjustments to their operations in order to use stockpile materials. A favorite example of this kind of difficulty is the stockpiling of chromite ore, as discussed in Chapter 5; the administration is attempting to solve this difficulty by conversion of the ore to more immediately usable ferroalloy forms.

The most appropriate form in which to stockpile materials—for example, ores, concentrates, powders, ingots, scrap, etc.—to assure their most expeditious use is a complex issue that must be considered on a case-by-case basis. Examples and a few general considerations have been discussed earlier; to expand upon them is beyond the scope of this chapter. However, based upon the general considerations, the most useful or appropriate form in which to stockpile a given material is determined by a mix of considerations involving flexibility of materials application, various materials needs of users and processors, foreign vis-à-vis domestic processing capacity, current state-of-the-art processing as contrasted with actual process technology, location of stockpiles relative to industrial plants and processing facilities, absolute magnitude of energy required and its local availability, and the projected time rate of energy demand in a national emergency.[45]

Location. Of central importance is the question of where stockpiles of strategic and critical materials should be located, and how quickly such materials can be transported to users during an emergency. Ideally, stockpiles should be located reasonably close to the industrial plants in which they are most likely to be used. Thus, in a very real sense, transportation and time are also being "stockpiled" along with materials. Unfortunately, the steady migration of U.S. industry, typically seeking preferred economic and labor advantages, has resulted in some stockpile storage sites being located adjacent to former factories but not current ones. For example, bauxite and acid-grade fluorspar are still stored at East St. Louis, Illinois, even though both the refinery and the fluoride plant have closed.[46] Thus, despite the fact that materials are now stockpiled in 113 different locations throughout the United States, clearly they cannot be close to every user facility. Indeed, the virtual impossibility of solving the transportation problem provides one of the most powerful arguments in favor of the private stockpiling option discussed earlier in this chapter.

Deterioration and Obsolescence. The potential contamination or deterioration of stockpiled materials during long periods of storage, or the possibility of such materials being rendered obsolescent by industrial technological developments, is obviously of much concern. Clearly, the stockpile is a dynamic entity, not a static one, and thus requires constant maintenance care as well as periodic reappraisal of the goals for it in terms of domestic and international political, economic, and technological developments. Fortunately, most stockpiled materials tend to be relatively physically and chemically stable and hence reasonably immune to such common forms of deterioration as oxidation or decomposition. Furthermore, proper storage conditions can go a long way toward minimizing physical deterioration as well as contamination during storage. On the other hand, no level of care during storage can protect stockpiled materials from technological obsolescence, as with the chromite ore. A different kind of technological obsolescence is illustrated by currently stockpiled cobalt, which may contain trace elements that would render impossible its use in high-performance superalloys for the aerospace industry. In this instance, the technology for measuring the existence of such trace elements did not exist at the time the cobalt was acquired.

A recent study of stockpiled cobalt, conducted by the American Society for Metals at the request of the Federal Emergency Management Agency, suggested that stockpiled cobalt be classified in terms of three categories—most critical, less critical, and least critical—because the same degree of quality is not needed for all applications. The study showed that the 40.8 million pounds of cobalt acquired for the stockpile during the period 1947 to 1961 is suitable essentially only for the least critical category, although some may qualify for less critical uses. However, all 5.2 million pounds acquired during 1981 and 1982 fully meet the requirements for today's most critical defense and industrial applications. A major recommendation of the study was that the government accept an industry offer to conduct pilot tests, at its own expense, to determine the most efficient procedures for utilizing existing chemical and metallurgical processing technology to upgrade the pre-1980 cobalt to satisfy the requirements for the higher usage categories.[47]

Needed Stockpiling Initiatives

The National Defense Stockpile, as currently constituted, unquestionably affords considerable protection against future supply interruptions that might result from a wartime emergency. This degree of protection, however, falls significantly short of the level of protection that most analysts believe is necessary. Indeed, it does not even provide the level of protection determined necessary by the Federal Emergency Management Agency in setting stockpile goals, in that the quantities of thirty-seven of the sixty-one materials stockpiled are below those goals. Of the most strategic and critical materials listed in Table 5.3, only the inventories of chemical and metallurgical manganese meet or exceed established goals. However, recent purchase commitments for bauxite and cobalt should help to lessen the disparity between the goals and inventories for these two materials. Hence, the most immediate stockpiling objective should be the initiation of a serious program designed to dispose of materials currently in excess of goals, and to acquire sufficient quantities of other materials to meet currently established goals.

In effect, the strategic materials stockpile has been a matter of political contention between various administrations and congresses for a long time. Recently the Reagan administration notified Congress that it would "rely primarily on the strategic stockpile as the primary means of providing for national defense objectives," thereby apparently committing itself to improving the status of the stockpile within the framework of its overall buildup of the nation's defense establishment. However, in the same message it also notified Congress that such improvement would be subordinated to "budgetary constraints and other national priorities."[48] That is, the funding level necessary to make good on its commitment would again largely be ignored.

Unquestionably, achieving stockpile goals is an expensive proposition as well as a political liability during a period of huge budget deficits. Meeting the 1980 goals currently in effect would require the purchase of about $9.8 billion worth of materials, of which about $4.2 billion could be raised through the sale of excess materials, provided the materials markets could absorb such disposals. But even if all these excess materials were sold and the funds applied to the purchase of other, more needed materials, an additional $5.6 billion in new funds would still be required to meet current goals.[49] Despite it strong commitment to upgrading the stockpile, the government currently is allocating only about $100 million per year for that purpose. At this rate, the current goals would be achieved in approximately 100 years.

In view of recurring and frequently persisting neglect of the stockpile, some analysts have suggested that major reforms are needed to remove the stockpile from political and economic influence. In a general perspective, they suggest that the policymaking process be carried out more openly and that stockpile goals reflect more realistically the nature of possible future conflicts, including a modern, conventional war that might very well be much shorter than three years, but highly intense and of global scope. Some believe that insufficient attention is being given to the possibilities of conflicts in some areas, for example in southern or South Africa, upon which the United States depends especially heavily for imports of some strategic and critical materials. They also believe that major U.S. allies are not being sufficiently pressured to change their views and develop strategic stockpiles.

Critics also suggest that goals for stockpiled materials should be determined on the basis of degree of import dependency rather than, as at present, the level of current domestic production. They also believe that to help put policymaking above politics, greater input from concerned industrial experts should be required. Prior to 1962, even the stockpile goals for each material were kept secret by the executive branch on the grounds of national security. Although such extreme secrecy no longer prevails, much of the deliberation in setting goals is not made public; political and economic motives can easily intrude into policymaking. Increased use of the opinions of industrial experts and of such techniques as risk assessment and cost-benefit analysis should help lead to better determination of what particular materials best meet current and future needs and, as discussed earlier, what precise specifications regarding quantity, quality, and form contribute most to utilization of stockpiled materials on a timely basis.

Some experts suggest that stockpile policy should be more closely coordinated with other national policies that affect the domestic minerals industries and foreign trade. Such coordination would not only encourage increased levels of self-sufficiency where domestic resources could be exploited, but also would help both to diversify and to increase the number of friendly, secure, stable, and reliable sources of materials. It would also help remove the stockpile from economic manipulation in stabilization of materials prices, and from political manipulation in the reduction of federal budget deficits.

In the absence of reforms, much contentious use of the stockpile can continue to be predicted. The various federal agencies and administrative offices all have their own constituencies that must be served, presumably in the national interest. For example, producers can view the stockpile as a legitimate sponge to soak up surplus production during economic declines, thereby strengthening facilities that may be needed in wartime. Likewise, users can view the stockpile as a legitimate source of materials when scarcities develop and prices rise too high, thereby providing continuity in defense capability. In response to the pushes and pulls of these and other constituencies, stockpile policy inevitably will diverge from the narrow path of strategic emergency use, statutory prohibitions notwithstanding.

Improved Sources of Supply

The fifth approach suggested at the beginning of this chapter for decreasing U.S. vulnerability to potential interruptions of supplies of imported strategic and critical materials is that of improving the reliability of current sources of supply. As previously discussed, this can be done, first, by diversifying to the maximum extent feasible the number of foreign suppliers for each material and, second, by placing emphasis upon those suppliers that have stable governments, that are friendly to U.S. interests, and that are geographically located as close as possible to the United States.

Several European nations as well as Japan are now pursuing diversification of sources of supply as a primary approach to reducing their own materials import vulnerabilities. Yet at best this approach cannot be expected to do more than compliment the approaches previously discussed in this chapter. On the positive side, the approach may serve to discourage the formation of foreign materials cartels, although admittedly little danger exists at present from this possibility. It also may help to prevent catastrophic interruptions in supply caused by accident, political unrest, or adverse government policy when no large fraction of imports is derived from any one country or area, because simultaneous supply interruptions appear unlikely. But it can do nothing to guard against unanticipated increases in materials demand or against unexpected or abrupt changes in the political, economic, or military status of foreign supplier nations. Furthermore, diversification of sources must be considered as a long-term and relatively expensive approach to decreasing materials import vulnerability, involving subsidies for many potential suppliers whose resources are not yet developed. And even when reliable, stable sources of supply have been developed, no guarantee exists that they necessarily will remain so.

Current Status of Major U.S. Suppliers

The United States at present enjoys materials trade relationships with many nations, the extent of trade being largely determined by economic considerations. In a relatively free economy during peacetime, it is typically the overall cost of materials that determines the nature of such trade relationships. However, for some materials, availability is also a consideration because of the limited number of suppliers. In these cases the development of alternative sources would be exceedingly difficult, if not actually impossible.

Those nations that currently provide U.S. imports of materials are listed in Table 5.1, and for the most strategic and critical materials, in Table 5.3. For the latter, an exceptionally large import dependency exists for four of the seven listed materials or materials groups: alumina from Australia, ferrochromium and the platinum-group metals from the Republic of South Africa, and columbium from Brazil. Although all three nations are relatively stable politically and share many U.S. interests, import dependency upon any one foreign source for three-fourths or more of U.S. requirements for any one strategic and critical material causes concern.

The Potential for Diversification of Supply Sources

The conventional wisdom in considering diversification of supply sources for strategic and critical materials is that national security interests should play the dominant role, economic aspects a subordinate role if necessary, and political, ethical, and moral considerations virtually no role at all. From this point of view the United States frequently has been criticized for its failure to "adopt a consistent foreign policy that realistically reflects U.S. mineral import dependence."[50]

Minerals experts consistently urge the federal government to undertake steps that would increase U.S. influence in the developing countries upon which the United States is already import dependent, and especially to adopt policies that would encourage U.S. industries to invest in the development of the minerals industries of these and other developing nations. In particular, Bolivia, Chile, Gabon, Malaysia, Peru, the Philippines, Surinam, Zaire, and Zambia often are considered likely candidates for increased U.S. foreign investment and influence.

Many European nations as well as Japan have pursued much more aggressive materials investment policies in the developing nations than has the United States. European nations have been involved in Africa for a much longer time and, economically, play a much greater role in trade and aid relations with the developing African countries, consistently providing greater levels of per capita aid. They place primary emphasis upon the political support of black African regimes in the belief that patient diplomacy may eventually wean African states away from Soviet influence. By contrast, African issues are given relatively low priority by the United States, although recently the Reagan administration has given increased attention to African issues that involve either competition with the Soviet Union for vital strategic and critical materials or that concern the support of U.S. positions within the United Nations.

Also recently, considerable attention has focused upon Communist China as a foreign source of strategic and critical materials. Although the bulk of Chinese resources has yet to be determined, there appears little doubt that vast quantities of bauxite, tungsten, titanium, tantalum, vanadium, and possibly other materials exist within its borders. China is anxious to increase its materials exports to earn hard-currency foreign exchange, and in 1980 it formed the China National Metallurgical Import and Export Corporation to promote this objective. China already is the world's largest producer of tungsten, and it exports substantial quantities of titanium, germanium, and gallium to the United States. More recently it has joined the ranks of other developing nations engaged in efforts to export processed as well as raw materials, especially titanium sponge, tungsten metal powder, and ferrovanadium. However, an excessive dependence upon imports of strategic and critical materials from Communist China would hardly seem a prudent course for the United States to follow, at least at present.

Of the developed nations, Australia and Canada are perhaps the two of greatest materials significance to the United States. Both nations are politically stable, exhibit democratic governments friendly to the United States, and possess large domestic resources of many vital materials. The major concern regarding Australia as a primary supplier of strategic and critical materials to the United States is the potential vulnerability of the long supply line in the event of an emergency. Canada, on the other hand, offers many of the advantages of Australia plus a virtually guaranteed supply line.

South Africa occupies a special position regarding U.S. imports of strategic and critical materials—a position discussed in earlier chapters for several of these vital materials. Indeed, overall U.S. dependence upon South Africa for key strategic and critical materials is greater than its dependence upon any other nation. Thus, from a purely strategic point of view, the United States should maintain extremely close ties to South Africa, a policy aggressively encourged by the South Africans themselves. Yet the South African pursuit of its apartheid policy continues to be anathema to U.S. policymakers. Advocates of civil rights continue to insist that a moral obligation exists for the United States to take whatever steps may be necessary to help eradicate this South African policy, including if necessary dissociating itself from the South African government and boycotting South African exports. The effectiveness of such demands has varied over time, approaching new highs during the Carter administration but subsiding during the Reagan administration's pursuit of a "constructive engagement" policy aimed at maintaining good relationships while seeking to promote internal political reform. Unfortunately, this U.S. approach has served to further alienate black African nations that also produce strategic and critical materials of importance to the United States.

In all ways, then, the potential materials problems of the United States in an emergency remain unresolved. Not only the status of the stockpile is uncertain, but also the supply lines and sources of further supply.

Notes

1. Office of Technology Assessment, *Technical Options for Conservation of Metals* (Washington, D.C.: U.S. Government Printing Office, September 1979), p. 43.

2. Ibid.

3. Ibid.

4. The discussion of hot isostatic processing is derived from H. D. Hanes, D. A. Seifert, and C. R. Watts, *Hot Isostatic Processing* (Columbus, Ohio: Battelle Press, 1979), 98 pp.

5. Ardent L. Bement, Jr., "Utilization of Science and Technology to Reduce Materials Vulnerability." *Materials and Society* 7:1 (1983), pp. 87–92.

6. Office of Technology Assessment, p. 70.

7. *Critical Materials Requirements of the U.S. Steel Industry* (Washington, D.C.: U.S. Department of Commerce, March 1983), pp. 191–192.

8. *Critical Materials Requirements of the U.S. Aerospace Industry* (Washington, D.C.: U.S. Department of Commerce, October 1981), p. 26.

9. George A. Keyworth, Jr., "Research and Development for Long-Term Economic Well-Being." *American Ceramic Society Bulletin*, June 1983, p. 676.

10. Bement, p. 90.

11. Hans H. Landsberg, "Materials: Some Recent Trends and Issues." *Science*, 20 February 1976, p. 637.

12. Edward S. Mason, "American Security and Access to Raw Materials." *World Politics*, January 1949, p. 148.

13. D. G. Altenpohl, *Materials in World Perspective* (Berlin: Springer-Verlag, 1980), p. 158.

14. Office of Technology Assessment, p. 64.

15. National Materials Advisory Board, *Contingency Plans for Chromium Utilization* (Washington, D.C.: National Academy of Sciences, 1978), p. 257.

16. See, for example, the discussion in H. Dana Moran, "Substitution—Some Practical Considerations." In *Engineering Implications of Chronic Materials Scarcity*, Office of Technology Assessment (Washington, D.C.: U.S. Government Printing Office, April 1977), pp. 281–298.

17. See in particular W. R. Hibbard, Jr., ed., *Substituting Non-metallic Materials for Vulnerable Minerals* (New York: Pergamon Press, 1984), 459 pp.

18. Alan G. Chynoweth, "Electronic Materials: Functional Substitutions." *Science,* 20 February 1976, p. 725.

19. Moran, p. 284.

20. Analyses of the economic factors involved in substitution for even one particular application can become quite complicated. See, for example, an analysis of the economic factors in the substitution of aluminum for copper, in Subodh C. Mathur and Joel P. Clark, "An Econometric Analysis of Substitution Between Copper and Aluminum in the Electrical Conductor Industry." *Materials and Society* 7:1 (1983), pp. 115–124.

21. Edward S. Mason, "Resources in the Past and for the Future." In *Resources for An Uncertain Future,* ed. Charles J. Hitch (Baltimore: Johns Hopkins University Press, 1978), p. 2.

22. Bohdan O. Szuprowicz, *How To Avoid Strategic Materials Shortages* (New York: John Wiley and Sons, 1981), p. 196.

23. Pat Wechsler, "Superalloy Makers Seek to Cut Use of Cobalt, Chromium." *American Metal Market,* 8 October 1980, p. 9.

24. Bruce Vernyi, "NASA Launches Study of Strategic Metals," *American Metal Market,* 1 February 1982, p. 10, and Hans-Juergen Peters, "NASA Seeks Less Dependence on Foreign Metals," *American Metal Market,* 8 February 1982, p. 11.

25. James T. Skelly, "Clad Metals: Design for Corrosion Control." *Metal Progress,* August 1983, p. 35.

26. For an in-depth discussion of various incentives and policies for promoting increased materials recycling, see Resources Conservation Committee, *Choices for Conservation* (Washington, D.C.: U.S. Government Printing Office, July 1979), pp. 60–120.

27. Energy Policy and Conservation Act (Public Law 94–163, enacted 22 December 1975), Section 383(c): *Federal Actions with Respect to Recycled Oil.*

28. The Resource Conservation and Recovery Act (Public Law 94–580, enacted 21 October 1976), Subtitle E: "Duties of the Secretary of Commerce in Resource and Recovery."

29. For a comprehensive review of the bureau's activities, see: National Bureau of Standards, *The National Bureau of Standards Office of Recycled Materials 1976– 1982,* NBS Special Publication 622 (Washington, D.C.: U.S. Department of Commerce, September 1983), 198 pp. plus appendices.

30. Eugene A. March, "Needed: A National Strategic Metals Policy." Address delivered at the annual meeting of the American Iron and Steel Institute, Waldorf Astoria Hotel, New York, 27 May 1981. Excerpts published in "Two-Pronged Policy for Key Minerals Vital," *American Metal Market,* 29 May 1981.

31. For further discussion of materials recycling, see William U. Chandler, *Materials Recycling: The Virtue of Necessity* (Washington, D.C.: Worldwatch Institute, October 1983), 52 pp., and the proceedings of the conference on *Recycling: Opportunities and Constraints* held in Washington, D.C., on 17–19 July 1984 under the cosponsorship of the Federation of Materials Societies and the U.S. Bureau of Mines.

32. U.S. Bureau of Mines, *Fiscal Year 1984 Research Program: Materials and Recycling Technology* (Washington, D.C.: U.S. Department of the Interior, undated), 15 pp.

33. The Strategic and Critical Materials Stock Piling Act of 1939 (Public Law 76–117, enacted 7 June 1939).

34. The Strategic and Critical Materials Stock Piling Act of 1946 (Public Law 79–520, enacted 23 July 1946).

35. The Defense Production Act of 1950 (Public Law 83–480, enacted 8 September 1950).

36. The Commodity Credit Corporation Charter Act of 1949 (Public Law 81–85, enacted 7 June 1949).

37. The Strategic and Critical Materials Stock Piling Revision Act of 1979 (Public Law 96–41, enacted 30 July 1979).

38. Materials Forum, *Third Annual Report* (London: Institution of Mechanical Engineers, November 1982), p. 39.

39. For further information concerning foreign stockpiles, see Szuprowicz, pp. 226–229; Timothy W. Stanley, *A National Risk Management Approach to American Raw Materials Vulnerabilities* (Washington, D.C.: The International Economic Studies Institute, January 1982), p. 15; and *The National Policy Agenda for Strategic Minerals and Materials* (Washington, D.C.: Federation of Materials Societies, 2 February 1982), p. 200.

40. For an excellent description of the operation of buffer stockpiles, see M. K. Bennett and Associates, *International Commodity Stockpiling as an Economic Stabilizer* (New York: Greenwood Press, 1968), 260 pp.

41. For an in-depth discussion of economic stockpiling, see Office of Technology Assessment, *An Assessment of Alternative Economic Stockpiling Policies* (Washington, D.C.: U.S. Government Printing Office, 1976), 327 pp.; National Commission on Supplies and Shortages, *Studies in Economic Stockpiling* (Washington, D.C.: U.S. Government Printing Office, September 1976), 200 pp.; and James L. Holt and Timothy W. Stanley, *Nonfuel Mineral Stockpiling Policies: the Private Stockpiling Alternative* (Washington, D.C.: International Economic Studies Institute, February 1984), 44 pp.

42. For the most recent information concerning stockpile goals, see *Stockpile Report to the Congress* (Washington, D.C.: Federal Emergency Management Agency, April 1984), 29 pp.

43. Executive Order 12155, dated 10 September 1979, gave the director of the Federal Emergency Management Agency overall authority for, and general direction of, all stockpile planning and operations.

44. *Stockpile Report to the Congress*, p. 3.

45. National Materials Advisory Board, *Considerations in Choice of Form for Materials for the National Stockpile* (Washington, D.C.: National Academy of Sciences, 1982), p. 1.

46. *Critical Materials Requirements of the U.S. Aerospace Industry*, p. 224.

47. American Society for Metals, "Quality Assessment of National Defense Stockpile Cobalt Inventory." In *National Defense Stockpile*, U.S. Senate Committee on Armed Services, Subcommittee on Preparedness (Washington, D.C.: U.S. Government Printing Office, 1984), pp. 12–59. See also National Materials Advisory Board, *Priorities for Detailed Quality Assessments of the National Defense Stockpile Nonfuel Materials* (Washington, D.C.: National Academy Press, 1984), 58 pp.

48. *National Materials and Minerals Program Plan and Report to the Congress*, submitted by President Reagan to Congress on 5 April 1982, pp. 33 and 30, respectively.

49. *Stockpile Report to the Congress*, p. 3.

50. Lee Calaway and W.C.J. van Rensburg, "U.S. Strategic Minerals Policy Options." *Resources Policy*, June 1982, p. 104.

7
Problems Associated with Materials Supply and Demand

Background

Many materials-related problems arise simply because of the size and complexity of the U.S. economy and the efforts of the federal government to exert at least some degree of control over it. Most such problems center upon the U.S. domestic mining and materials industries and the related infrastructure, without which the maintenance of supplies of materials essential to U.S. industry would be impossible. Incredible as it may seem, these vital industries and much of this related infrastructure have been allowed to decline for many years despite widespread agreement that one of the nation's most critical needs is a secure supply of industrial raw materials at reasonably stable prices. Although recently some initial steps have been taken to help arrest this decline, much remains to be done.

Institutional Problems

Institutional problems are largely those concerned in one way or another with government. Ideally, the role of government should be to devise policies and regulations that provide encouragement to the private sector to do whatever is necessary to guarantee the continued availability of essential supplies of minerals and materials. The government should undertake for itself only those initiatives that, for whatever reason, private industry cannot or chooses not to undertake. Government laws and regulations should stimulate resource development and conservation with a view toward creating those conditions that ultimately will permit private industry to make the optimum contribution to the nation's economy. The overriding consideration of any greater governmental intrusion into the economy should be that it takes place only when all other possibilities have been exhausted, and when the prospect of harmful or negative results has been determined to be minimal.

Unfortunately, this ideal is seldom realized in practice and, indeed, sometimes is not even remotely approached. As noted elsewhere with reference to the U.S. mining and minerals industries, the principal role of the federal government "has been to encourage, by tax, military and economic aid, pollution regulation, and other policies, the digging of the Third World."[1] Many analysts agree that government policies affecting these industries have created more problems than they have solved. Unquestionably, among the most pressing government-related problems are those having to do with rules and regulations. Others concern the adversarial relationship that has grown up between government and U.S. industry, industry fears of federal actions under the antitrust laws, and government policy concerning the management of public lands. Although the discussion here concerns primarily the federal government, it should be recognized that similar problems often also occur with respect to state and local governments.

Rules and Regulations

It is axiomatic that a complex, industrialized society cannot function without a system of rules and regulations of some kind. In general, most societies have concluded that a need exists to impose some degree of social control over economic activity in order to change the allocation of economic resources from what would occur naturally in a completely free market economy to a distribution believed to be more socially desirable.[2] Thus, the economic regulation of an industry essentially represents a political conclusion that the marketplace, left completely to itself, will fail to work in the public interest.

Growth of Regulation. Because of the widespread belief in regulation for the public interest, the number of regulatory bodies and the number of programs and rules promulgated has continued to increase despite the lack of a consensus as to the benefits actually derived from these activities. It is estimated that at present more than 1,000 different federal programs are administered by more than seventy-seven federal agencies, of which at least fifty have been created during the past two decades.[3]

The burden of contending with various governmental rules and regulations, and the typically high cost of such compliance, tends to fall most heavily upon a few industries. The minerals and materials industries are among the most widely affected and, as noted elsewhere, "Every step in the materials cycle is controlled by federal agencies, which promulgated 19,366 new regulations in 1979."[4] At present, at least eighty different acts administered by twenty different federal agencies impact heavily upon these industries, including

- The National Environmental Policy Act;
- The Clean Air Act;
- The Clean Water Act;
- The Resource Conservation and Recovery Act;
- The Toxic Substance Control Act;
- The Safe Drinking Water Act;
- The Occupational Safety and Health Act;
- The Mine Safety and Health Act;
- The Wild and Scenic Rivers Act;

- The Endangered Species Act; and
- The Coastal Zone Management Act.[5]

The growth of federal rule making and regulatory activity inevitably has resulted in significantly increased costs for the industries regulated. Although estimates of such costs often tend to be somewhat incomplete or of doubtful validity, costs to specific companies or even to specific industries sometimes can be estimated fairly accurately. For example, a single copper company was shown to be subject to rules and regulations issued by fifty-four different federal departments and agencies, forty-two state boards and commissions, and thirty-nine local governmental units—a total of 135 different regulatory bodies, at an added cost of $0.10 to $0.15 per pound of copper produced.[6] Regulations also greatly increase the lead times necessary for expanding production capacity, resulting in the need for as much as three or four years to design and build a major new plant of any sort, and up to ten years to open any kind of new mining operation.

The Need for Regulatory Reform. Recognizing how greatly regulatory zeal had proliferated, the Reagan administration initiated attempts to restrict or eliminate regulations that it considered imposed unnecessary and unfairly expensive burdens on industrial institutions. Specifically, the objective was "to rationalize existing regulations and eliminate unnecessary regulations so that Government action does not increase industry costs without commensurate gains in public welfare" and to develop cost-effective approaches to regulations, including the consideration of competing national objectives in the regulation of industry.[7] Such pursuit of regulatory reform, however, is viewed with deep suspicion by many individuals and groups who fear that such changes may not be so much in the nature of reform as in permitting the recurrence of those very conditions that the rules and regulations were designed to prevent.

Responsibility for Regulation. Regulatory power and responsibility are constitutionally shared by Congress and the president and, indirectly, by the courts. Critics contend that Congress has enacted regulatory legislation without giving adequate attention to the needs of the industries being regulated, often setting extreme goals to be achieved in an unrealistically short time, and that the regulations contain ambiguities, inconsistencies, and provisions that sometimes overlap with, duplicate, or even conflict with existing laws. They maintain that the executive branch and regulatory agencies, acting through the authority of the president, tend to take an expansive view of their authority and a limited view of their mission, thus becoming single-purpose agencies responsive to narrow constituencies that are unable to consider other—and possibly less costly and disruptive—ways of achieving substantially the same results. Clearly, real progress toward the revision or elimination of unnecessary or unfairly restrictive rules and regulations affecting the materials industries necessarily will require joint action by the legislative and executive branches of government.

Government-Industry Adversarial Relationship

Expert observers of government-industry relationships often have noted that over approximately the last twenty-five years, an "adversarial" relationship has built up, in which each side views the attitudes and behavior of the other with considerable suspicion and distrust. This undesirable situation is said to be unique to the United States, since in virtually all other industrialized nations industry executives and advisors work rather closely and harmoniously with government policymakers. Political actions at all levels of government are sometimes seen as being particularly unfavorable to the materials industries. Indeed, this adversarial relationship has been described as one of the nation's most serious deficiencies and a major cause of materials supply problems.

In general, many industry representatives are agreed upon the need for an improved climate between government and industry, possibly along the lines set by the Japanese Ministry of International Trade and Industry, or the European Economic Community's Steel Commission, in which both sides jointly pool their efforts in seeking ways to promote industrial health and strength while paying appropriate attention to the national interest. These industry representatives suggest that in working within a more collaborative and less adversarial milieu, industry and government could help create a political, economic, and legal climate that would encourage investment in, and exploration and development of, domestic materials resources without the heavy cost in jobs, inflation, and supply disruptions experienced in the past. An atmosphere of trust, mutual respect, and confidence would place less emphasis upon regulation and more emphasis upon incentives and joint industry-government interchanges.[8]

Antitrust Laws

As the cost of producing materials increases, including the costs associated with conforming to government rules and regulations and carrying out necessary research and development, it becomes increasingly difficult for any one company to meet these costs by itself. Yet collective action among U.S. companies is frequently discouraged by U.S. antitrust laws, and collaboration that conceivably might be permissible under the laws often is shunned anyway for fear of possible adverse rulings and subsequent prosecution. As noted in the literature, "In the area of antitrust enforcement, one finds much the same narrow doctrinaire approach, the same tunnel vision, the same open disregard of national minerals policy as is found in other governmental arenas."[9] In particular, much evidence indicates that U.S. antitrust policies strongly discourage the pursuit of joint ventures made increasingly necessary because the capital costs of major new mining and mineral ventures have outgrown the financing capabilities of many independent U.S. mining concerns.

Faced with this same problem, many European nations as well as Japan have realistically liberalized their antitrust laws to permit significant pooling of company resources to common advantage. These efforts, especially by

Japan, involve the mounting of large-scale, government-subsidized efforts to seize or increase world market shares of new and rapidly growing industries by racing into new technologies and aggressively cutting prices to undermine foreign competition. Failure of the United States to do likewise has been said to reflect "serious misconceptions about the nature of competition in the world market in which American mining companies must operate."[10] In elaboration,

> The major focus of antitrust legislation has been concerned with competition within the United States. Today, the U.S. faces severe competition in the world market and domestically from foreign industries and even foreign government-owned or orchestrated industries. Thus, in light of changing trade patterns and economic conditions there is a pressing need to take appropriate action to modernize antitrust legislation in order to improve the competitive position of U.S. materials industries.[11]

Recent efforts have been initiated to convince federal policymakers and legislators that traditional U.S. antitrust policies have been unnecessarily restrictive, particularly so in discouraging industrial cooperation in research and development. Hence, the mining and mineral industries are actively promoting changes in federal antitrust laws to permit competing U.S. firms to cooperate in overseas joint ventures, a practice that currently is illegal.[12] Such cooperation is becoming increasingly necessary as world markets for raw materials become more dominated by nationally owned or controlled enterprises. In general, critics of current federal antitrust policy would like to see the two major enforcement agencies—the Department of Justice and the Federal Trade Commission—examine closely the way in which they currently administer the antitrust laws to, first, put an end to the destructive government-industry adversarial relationship and, second, revise and modify their enforcement policies to promote, wherever possible, cooperative industry projects, including those involving research and development. Such modifications possibly could enable companies to cooperate in jointly supporting massive capital-intensive ventures and would promote increased efficiency by permitting more horizontal and vertical integration of the materials industries.

Limited R&D Partnerships

Pending some of the suggested federal action with regard to antitrust laws, the Department of Commerce is encouraging the formation of limited partnerships to carry out research and development too expensive for individual companies to undertake alone, or too risky for such companies to finance from general operating revenues.[13] Under this procedure, several companies establish a general partner to manage one or more research and development projects funded by outside investors who hope to receive substantial tax benefits as well as sizable profits if the research proves successful. The founding companies are limited partners in the enterprise and not only derive benefits from the research and development, but also share in any profits in excess of those earned by the investors. Because the limited partners have no part in the management of the enterprise, theoretically they are not liable for antitrust violations. Nonetheless, most companies remain unconvinced of the safety of such limited partnerships from antitrust prosecution, and investors have no guarantee that anticipated tax benefits will be allowed by the Internal Revenue Service.

R&D Cooperatives

Similar to the limited partnerships described above are other cooperative arrangements designed to share the expense of research and development. Two types of arrangements are being considered by interested companies. Under the first arrangement, member companies form an independent corporation to conduct research and development of mutual interest to the companies. The research is carried out within the independent corporation by a relatively large staff consisting of employees on loan to the corporation from member companies, or hired outright by the corporation. Funding of the corporation is provided by a start-up entry fee paid by member companies and by their sharing of project expenses on a project-by-project basis.

Perhaps the most outstanding current example of such a cooperative is the Microelectronics and Computer Technology Corporation, formed by thirteen companies in the computer and electronics industries. Each member company pays a $200,000 entry fee and agrees to share expenses of particular projects for a minimum period of three years. In return, the member companies are entitled to the exclusive use of the results of these particular projects for three years following the completion of the projects, after which the corporation may license the technology to anybody, member or not. At present, MCC is conducting major research projects in artificial intelligence, new computer designs, database models and structures, software, computer-aided design and manufacturing for very large-scale integrated chips, and packaging for such chips.[14]

Under the second arrangement, member companies form a corporation essentially to manage research and development contracted out primarily to universities; consequently, the corporate staff is small. The corporation is financed through membership dues based upon some mutually agreed-upon scale, and members are automatically entitled to the results of all of the research conducted. Perhaps the most outstanding current example of this kind of arrangement is the Semiconductor Research Corporation, now involving nineteen member companies in the semiconductor industry, and carrying out generic research in microchip technology. Members' dues are assessed according to a sliding scale based upon the production or purchases of semiconductors.[15]

Although these examples illustrate some of the possibilities available to U.S. companies in forming "creative arrangements" that may permit multi-company pooling and sharing of research and development costs, still these arrangements fall far short of those available to foreign companies that need not fear adverse antitrust prosecution. As long as the possibility of such prosecution has existed, as well as the potential for triple-damage suits by private parties, many company executives have shunned meetings even to discuss the possibility of cooperative arrangements. Consequently, the Reagan administration early sought legislation that would exempt such arrangements from antitrust suits. As a result of this effort the National Cooperative Research Act (P.L. 98–642) was signed into law on 11 October 1984 to reduce the risk of research and development joint ventures running afoul of antitrust laws.

Public Lands

As discussed in Chapter 2, a major issue continues to be the extent to which the materials resources located on public lands should be exploited to increase domestic production and reduce U.S. materials import dependency. Through its control over access to these vast public lands, the government exercises considerable influence over the exploration for domestic materials and the development of materials resources that are found. This control over the public sector adds greatly to the government influence that otherwise results from the enforcement of federal rules, regulations, and antitrust and other policies in the private sector. Increasingly, therefore, the exploitation of domestic materials resources, both publicly and privately owned, has become more dependent upon government decision making. Consequently, mineral production often has been made more difficult, costly, and time-consuming as it has become more dependent upon the political process rather than upon free market forces.

Federal policy governing the use of public lands is complex and at times unclear. In general, it attempts to balance the need for utilization of public lands for materials development and other commercial uses, such as grazing, with the need to preserve such lands for recreational or wilderness purposes. Numerous laws attempt to maintain this delicate balance, including the following:

Access and Disposal:
    Mineral Leasing Act of 1920
    Acquired Lands Act of 1947
    Mining Law of 1972
Withdrawal and Restriction:
    National Forest Act of 1891
    Reclamation Act of 1902
    Antiquities Act of 1906
    General Withdrawal Act of 1910
    Recreation and Public Purposes Act of 1926
    Small Tract Act of 1938
    Defense Withdrawal Act of 1958
    Wilderness Act of 1964
    Classification and Multiple Use Act of 1964
    Wild and Scenic Rivers Act of 1968

Alaska Native Claims Settlement Act of 1971
Federal Land Policy and Management Act of 1976[16]

Unfortunately, some provisions of these various laws are sufficiently imprecise or difficult to interpret as to lead to overlapping land withdrawals or classifications that generate much controversy in their enforcement. Hence a need exists for a comprehensive review of the current status of all public lands to determine their present classification and status, including a review of existing withdrawals to determine whether any may be obsolete or no longer necessary, and to ascertain whether exploitation and development of their materials potential is in the public interest.

Ultimately, of course, it is up to Congress to resolve the problem of public lands classification and to determine legislatively the best way in which these lands can be used in the public interest.

Economics-Related Problems

In a very real sense, virtually all materials supply and demand problems have a strong economic component, including those already discussed above. However, some materials problems are much more intimately concerned with economic considerations than are others. For example, most environmental problems are essentially economic in nature, as are many of those problems associated with energy. Other economics-related kinds of materials problems include those concerned with the need for investment capital, those associated with taxation, and those having to do with productivity.

Environmental Quality

The desirability of a clean, healthy, and safe environment is recognized by virtually everybody. Likewise, few people question the very real economic benefits derived from the reduced sickness, decreased costs for general cleaning and maintenance, and inceased availability of food and water that accompany a clean environment. Many people also recognize the esthetic value of a clean environment and the increased potential for recreation and various outdoor pursuits. Despite this agreement on general principles, however, some of the most bitter and protracted battles are being waged over environmental policy, with no end or agreement yet in sight.

The reason for the conflict is almost entirely economic, with the battles being fought over the seemingly simple question, how much environmental quality can the nation afford? The answer to this question is complex.

Virtually any animal activity results in an environmental insult of some order of magnitude. In general, the environment exhibits great resiliency in responding to such insults and repairing the damage, providing the damage is not too great or is not inherently irreversible. In most cases it is a matter of degree, and nature tends to control the extent of naturally occurring damage by a system of built-in, self-correcting mechanisms that in time will restore the status quo. It is largely when human activity grossly overwhelms these mechanisms that permanent and often irreversible damage occurs.

As human populations grow and seek higher levels of comfort, security, and recreational opportunities, damage to the environment—at least in the near term—is unavoidable. Given the existing level of technology, there simply is no way at present that 5 billion people can live on the earth without inflicting a certain level of damage, a proportion of which may indeed be irreversible. The question is therefore not how environmental damage can be completely avoided, but rather to what extent the damage can be limited, constrained, and perhaps even ultimately repaired, consistent with other human goals.

Environmental controls generally take the form of externally imposed constraints, a large fraction of which affects the basic materials industries. The general purpose of the constraints is to reduce or, if possible, even eliminate pollution or undesirable by-products that these industries introduce into the environment, thereby reducing or eliminating the social costs—or "externalities"—borne by society rather than by the industries themselves. Typically, governmental controls, the usual form of such constraints, can be grouped into five categories:

- Limits upon the amount of some by-product of the firm's output that the firm can put into its external environment over a given period of time;

- Limits upon the total pollutant content that can be present in the firm's external environment;

- Imposition of emission or ambient controls on a firm's internal or external environment (for example, noise or dust controls on heavy equipment);

- Requirements that the land surface used by the firm during production be reclaimed in some specified manner at the end of production in that area; and

- Requirements that a bond to pay for such reclamation be posted at the beginning of the firm's operations.[17]

The costs of such controls can be staggering. It is estimated that capital expenditures for pollution control by the steel industry alone averaged about $530 million per year over the period 1976 to 1980, or about 17 percent of the total capital expenditures by the industry over those five years.[18] Estimates of the present cost of environmental protection range as high as $60 billion per year, for an estimated cumulative outlay of about $520 billion for the period 1979 to 1988 (in constant 1979 dollars).[19]

Unquestionably, much of this money is well spent and contributes to the prevention and control of unacceptable levels of environmental pollution. Nor is it surprising that much of this burden falls heavily upon the materials industries, because the extraction, processing, and fabrication of materials involves perhaps the most serious potential for environmental damage, as illustrated in Figure 7.1. Unfortunately, because the track record of these industries has not been especially memorable in the past, they now elicit little public sympathy for their plight. On the other hand, serious questions can be raised concerning whether "unacceptable" levels of pollution have been set too high, and whether part of this money might not be better spent elsewhere.

It is frequently pointed out that some government regulatory personnel seem responsive only to perfection. Although in other activities environmental and safety inspectors may recognize intuitively that perfection is rarely attainable in practice, in environmental and safety matters they often are accused of inability to evaluate an "acceptable risk." Those on whom the burdens fall are forced to point out that environmental controls, regardless of the desirability of their objectives, cannot indefinitely be pursued with disregard for the economic feasibility of their attainment. "The federal government, as a fundamental aspect of national minerals policy, must seek balance between the environmental, health and safety statutes and regulations and the need to ensure the reliable availability of strategic and critical materials."[20]

Clearly, what is needed is an acceptable compromise between those who are dedicated to preserving the maximum possible level of environmental quality, and those who at least to some extent degrade that quality in order to provide the material benefits that society wants and demands. Ultimately, it is up to society as a whole to determine approximately where this level should be set by modifying its demands for materials to a degree consistent with its environmental aspirations.

Energy

Energy is the capacity to do work, and much of the work that society requires is the conversion of raw materials to a more useful state.[21] Because each step from raw ore to refined material consumes energy and/or energy-intensive chemicals, energy represents a serious constraint on materials supply. Conversely, materials availability represents a serious constraint upon energy supply.

> Materials and energy are inextricably bound together. Industrial materials cannot be produced without energy, and energy cannot be produced and used without special materials. This interdependence has been increasing and holds true primarily for metals and common materials as well as for highly sophisticated materials.[22]

As energy becomes more costly, materials prices rise, and if energy supplies are disrupted, so also may be supplies of materials. Conversely, when materials become more costly, so also may the cost of energy, although in general the materials cost in producing energy (with a few notable exceptions) is far less than the energy cost in producing materials. The important

Figure 7.1 Examples of environmental effects of economic activities associated with minerals extraction and use

	Activities	Typical Environmental Effects

E X T R A C T I O N	**Mining**
	  – Deep tunnel and open pit
	
	  – Petroleum
	Agriculture – general
	
	  – plus, if practices are poor
	
	Forestry – thinning of growth
	
	  – plus, if clear cutting
		
		Tailings, leachates, mine acid drainage, underground fires, land surface disruption.
		Sludge ponds, oil spills, land subsidence.
		Land surface changes, disruption to pre-existing habitats, waterborne minerals get concentrated.
		Soil erosion and siltation, nutrient enrichment and eutrophication, toxic pesticides.
		Habitat disruption from logging, use of roads and increased human accessibility; pesticides.
		Habitat destruction, soil erosion.

P R O C E S S I N G	**Raw Materials Processing**
	  – Size classification and reduction
	  – Sintering, roasting and smelting
	  – Cooking
	  – Distilling
	  – Washing
	  – Separating
	Product Finishing, Converting and Assembly
		
		Noise, dust, tailings, sludges.
		Dusts, aerosols, gases, acid rains, slags.
		Pressings, sludges, aerosols, gases.
		Sludges.
		Suspended and dissolved solids in water.
		Sediments, elutriates, and sludges.
		Dusts, oils and other contaminants in water, noise, scrap (reusable), heavy metal plating wastes.

P O W E R	**Stationary**
	  – Fossil fuel power (steam, electricity, and direct drive)
	
	  – Nuclear power
	  – Electricity distribution
	
	Transportation
		
		Boiler ash, fly ash, low level radiation in ashes, aerosols, gases, acid rain, thermal pollution of waterways, steam plumes, flue gas desulfurization sludges, CO_2-induced weather modification.
		Radioactive waste fuel rods, nuclear fallout.
		Transmission right of ways.
		
		Emissions from internal combustion engines (CO, NOx, CO_2, hydrocarbons, lead), waste lubricating oils, land surface disruptions for road right of ways, oil and chemical spills.

P O S T C O N S U M E R	**Demolition (and Construction)**
	
	Commercial and Household
	  – Littering
	  – Land disposal
	  – Volume reduction
	Water and Sewage Treatment
		Dust, noise, scrap (reusable), debris, land surface disturbance, erosion, stream siltation.
		
		Litter
		Noise, land use disruption, noxious leachates, landfill gas.
		Incinerator emissions.
		Sludges, chlorine and other chemical residuals.

Source: Resource Conservation Committee, *Choices for Conservation* (Cincinnati, Ohio: U.S. Environmental Protection Agency, July 1979), p. 23.

consideration is that an intimate, two-way relationship exists between materials and energy.

This two-way relationship is complicated by the fact that a similar relationship exists between materials and the environment and between energy and the environment. Thus, in reality a "triad" relationship exists among materials, energy, and the environment.[23] Clearly, the production and consumption of energy, in whatever form, results in significant insults to the environment just as does the production of materials. A large fraction of energy is obtained through the burning of energy fuels, including fuel oil and gasoline, with the attendant pollution of the atmosphere. In another form of energy production, the potential hazards to the environment of nuclear power production are well known. Even relatively clean sources of energy like hydropower and solar power are not entirely without adverse environmental consequences. Thus, many of the same problems involving trade-offs between materials and the environment also apply, although in somewhat different measure, to energy and the environment.

There seems little likelihood that many consumers will be willing to accept voluntarily any reduction in either their materials or energy consumption for the foreseeable future when both are such strong determinants of our present life-style. Yet paradoxically, most consumers also will continue to sympathize more with the advocates of environmental control and preservation than with the producers of the materials and energy they consume. It is a no-win situation. The development of technology that may ultimately provide materials and energy at negligible cost to environmental quality is far off into the future. Hence it is imperative that consumers become better informed about the environmental costs of the materials and energy they consume in unprecedented quantities if they are to make intelligent choices in a world of rapidly expanding population but, at least temporarily, limited materials and energy availability.

Capital Formation and Taxation

The materials industries must continually raise substantial sums of capital to finance exploration to discover new ore bodies; to construct suitable facilities to mine and process these newly discovered resources; to develop, purchase, install, and operate equipment to improve worker health and safety and to limit environmental pollution to mandated levels; and to restore land that has been mined to a condition acceptable for further use. Because lead times for the development of new materials properties typically amount to five to ten years or more, capital often is tied up for considerable periods of time before any return is achieved on investment. Additionally, much capital is required to expand and modernize existing facilities and equipment, especially to meet new requirements for worker and environmental protection.

Overall, three features characterize the need for capital by the nonfuel materials industries: the relatively high-risk nature of investment, the long lead times before debt retirement, and the large amounts of capital required.

Mining is perhaps the most capital-intensive of all industries, with single projects costing as much as a billion dollars or more. Estimates of capital requirements for mineral exploration alone during the 1980s have ranged from $100 billion to $1,000 billion.[24] Total capital requirements for the minerals industries over the period from 1975 to 1985 may have been as high as $3,000 billion.[25] Large amounts of capital also are required for those industries that use raw materials to produce intermediates for general manufacturing. For example, to build a completely new steel-making facility (a "Greenfield" plant) including blast furnace, steel making and finishing, plus the necessary transportation infrastructure, now costs about $1,000 per annual ton of raw steel capacity. Since the minimum economic scale for such a plant is about 3 million tons per year, the least cost for such a steel-making facility is now about $3,000 million.[26]

High interest rates, increasing debt loads, and the inhibiting effect of government rules and regulations also have adversely affected the profitability of these industries. In general, their deteriorating financial condition has required them to rely increasingly upon debt financing for their capital needs. These factors, superimposed upon normal cyclical variations of materials prices, have served to increase the need of these industries for funds but decrease their ability to obtain financing.

The revitalization of the U.S. materials industries may require substantial changes in federal policies to help reduce costs and aid in raising necessary capital. Among the changes most frequently suggested are the following:

- Low-cost pollution control financing should be made more broadly available by permitting eligibility despite incidental recovery of mineral by-products.

- Industrial revenue bond financing should be made available for mineral activities costing more than $10 million.

- Percentage depletion allowances and expensing of exploration and development costs should be continued.

- Investment tax credit should be extended to include all buildings used in mining and manufacturing and should be made refundable or at least credited fully against a company's entire tax liability.

- Realistic, flexible capital cost recovery allowances for plant and equipment investments should be adopted in lieu of present depreciation allowances.

- The costs of environmental and other government-mandated requirements should be permitted to be written off over any period selected by the taxpaying company including the year of expenditure.

- Tax-exempt municipal bond financing should be available for non-productive pollution control equipment as well as for other government-mandated expenditures.[27]

Further suggestions have been made concerning changes in current tax policies that are said to place U.S. mining companies at a competitive disadvantage abroad as compared with mining companies of other major industrialized nations. Specifically, the following changes have been suggested as improvements in such tax laws:

- Ensure that a foreign tax credit is allowed for traditional income taxes to avoid international double taxation.

- Provide realistic deductions for all foreign exploration expenditures and foreign expropriation losses.

- Allow foreign assets to be treated the same as domestic assets for depreciation, investment tax credit, or capital recovery allowance purposes.

- Allow optional branch treatment for foreign corporate mining operations where the use of a local corporation is in conformance with the host country's policy.

- Provide equitable tax treatment of U.S. nationals employed abroad.[28]

At least some of these measures are being considered within the context of the current debate over the need for revitalization of the U.S. economy.

Productivity

Productivity remains one of the least understood elements of the economy. It is usually taken as a measure of the efficiency of production processes, or the rate of industrial output per unit of industrial input. In actuality it reflects the joint effects of many influences upon production, including new technology, capital investment, the capacity utilization of plants and equipment, energy use, and the skills of the labor force, including management, professional, and production workers. Many of the factors that help determine productivity are difficult to define in quantifiable terms, and their relative contributions are impossible to measure precisely.

Despite these difficulties, calculations of annual productivity growth are made by the U.S. Bureau of Labor Statistics, and attempts are made to relate these calculations to the economy as a whole. Such calculations show that over the period 1948 to 1978, U.S. productivity grew at an annual rate of about 2.4 percent, including periodic but temporary declines.[29] Since 1973, however, it has decreased more often than not and for several years now has virtually become stalled. This behavior stands in sharp contrast to that of other major industrialized nations. For example, over the past two decades, U.S. productivity has *averaged* only about 1.5 percent gain per year, as compared with 4.0 percent for West Germany and 7.1 percent for Japan.[30] Such low growth rates of productivity cause much concern in that they can represent some fundamental weaknesses in the nation's economy and can decrease the ability of U.S. industries to compete successfully with foreign industries in world markets. Not only does the U.S. world trading position become weakened, but frequently foreign-produced products are perceived as being better designed, better made, and more cost-effective and consumer-oriented than similar products made in the United States.

The recent decline in productivity has significantly affected almost all business sectors of the U.S. economy, including the basic materials industries. Materials policies and practices, as well as policies for science and technology in general, have long been recognized as important factors in productivity growth. Clearly productivity can be increased by incorporating advanced materials in innovative products with large improvements in performance. Those materials-related areas that show especially high promise include electro-optics and electronics, metastable (rapidly solidified) materials, composites, and synthetic polymers.[31]

A major difficulty often noted is that although the United States continues to lead the world in basic research in science and engineering, it continues to fall farther behind other nations, especially Japan, in applying such research to the development of new technologies. Thus, U.S. industries continue to neglect the middle ground between the discovery and development of new information and the practical application of such information to the output of manufactured goods. Two major reasons often cited for this neglect are, first, that product innovation lacks the same degree of public, professional, industrial, and social support that both basic science and fundamental engineering discoveries have received since World War II; and second, that innovation fails to appeal to U.S. businesses that remain primarily dedicated to short-range payoffs on investment.

Technical Problems

In addition to the institutional and economics-related problems so far discussed, materials supply and demand is also constrained by a number of scientific and technologically related problems. Perhaps the most fundamental of these problems are those related to materials research and development, long recognized as essential to the efficient production of adequate supplies of materials as well as to the discovery of new and improved methods of production. Less often recognized is the effect of materials research and development on demand, through its creation of new products and technologies with widespread consumer appeal. Furthermore, research and development that permits materials to be produced more cheaply helps promote increased demand.

A second problem clearly associated with those of materials research and development is that of maintaining an adequate supply of highly trained scientists and engineers, without whom research and development would be impossible. And third, once research and development has been successfully completed, technological innovation and technology transfer are required to bridge the gaps to successful commercial applications. Finally, materials supply and demand are also influenced by materials conservation and resource recovery and recycling.

Materials Research and Development Funding

An adequate level of materials research and development depends on adequate funding, which already has been cited as a shortcoming of businesses dedicated to short-range payoffs. Ongoing defense requirements have long made the federal government the major financial supporter of U.S. research and development efforts, the results of some of which have also benefited the private sector.

The federal government in recent years has averaged about $40 billion per year for research and development, including both efforts conducted within federal agency laboratories and efforts supporting private-sector laboratories. Funding specifically for *materials* research and development, spread throughout at least nineteen agencies, has amounted in the recent past to about 2 to 3 percent of overall federal research and development expenditures, or about $1 billion per year.

Because so many different federal agencies have responsibilities for various areas of materials research and development, coordination of their efforts is essential to avoid wasteful duplication of efforts and to assure that a proper balance is maintained overall. For many years, however, no single executive branch office or agency had responsibility for such coordination. More often than not, decisions were made by the Office of Management and Budget, which understandably chose to devote as little time as possible to so relatively minor a budget item, spread so diffusely over so many federal departments and agencies. Finally, the National Materials and Minerals Policy, Research and Development Act of 1980[32] directed the Office of Science and Technology Policy to serve as the primary coordinating agency for materials research and development. Responsibility for coordinating federal minerals and materials research and development activities is assigned to the office's Committee on Materials, under the direction of the Federal Coordinating Council for Science, Engineering, and Technology, and chaired by the office's assistant director for energy, natural resources, and international affairs. Among the current task forces of the committee is one specifically responsible for essential strategic and critical materials.

One of the first tasks of the Committee on Materials was to prepare an inventory of federal materials research and technology, which showed that six federal agencies have consistently provided the bulk of federal funding in this area, as shown in Table 7.1. A major portion of this funding was spent on research and development into the fundamental nature and behavior of materials, as well as in such areas as materials processing.[33]

Perhaps as important as the level of federal funding for materials research and development is the way in which such funds are allocated among the kinds of activities supported by the government. In general, widespread agreement exists among most analysts that government funding should be limited to long-term, high-risk technology of wide generic application to materials problems and thus unlikely to be pursued by private industry. This emphasis would fill the gap between what history has shown needs to be done and what private industry is willing to do and is able to afford.

Table 7.1   Federal Funding of Materials Research and Technology (data in thousands of dollars)

Agency	1976	1980	1982	1983[a]
Energy	332,897	514,100	285,262	276,207
Defense	131,881	160,200	147,000	162,200
Environmental Protection Agency	99,398	2,400	146,693	179,426
Interior	165,350	119,686	113,667	104,609
National Science Foundation	68,700	88,920	99,721	102,414
National Aeronautics and Space Administration	51,533	78,582	101,415	102,305
Health	16,625	6,070	31,920	34,260
Agriculture	38,254	64,598	29,759	28,551
Nuclear Regulatory Commission	7,028	13,674	17,710	18,740
Commerce	21,080	35,795	14,201	13,856
Transportation	6,153	3,442	5,682	6,854
Tennessee Valley Authority	9,226	9,650	2,792	2,607
Treasury	790	2,516	1,080	1,258
Smithsonian Institution	1,000	1,000	750	825
Federal Emergency Management Agency	0	50	107	0
Housing and Urban Development	6,669	0	0	0
State	540	0	0	0
Labor	4,063	3,000	0	0
General Services Administration	132	0	0	0
	961,320	1,103,683	998,329	1,034,112

a. Estimated.

Source: Committee on Materials, Federal Coordinating Council for Science, Engineering, and Technology, Research and Technology, fiscal year 1982 (Washington, D.C.: Office of Science and Technology Policy, June 1983), p. 11.

Scientific and Engineering Education and Manpower

Much concern has long been expressed over the scope and quality of scientific and engineering manpower in the United States, and particularly with regard to the education and training of men and women in these fields. Clearly, the issue of education underlies the entire spectrum of future civilian and defense research and development capabilities. Yet despite this admitted importance, much evidence suggests that a personnel shortage exists at nearly every degree level and specialty in the engineering, computer, and certain physical science fields, and that this shortage is likely to get worse. It has become popular to contrast the U.S. situation with that of the Soviet Union, which on the average graduates about 300,000 engineers each year compared with about 50,000 in the United States, and which already has at least three times as many engineers engaged in military research and development as does the United States.[34] Compounding the problem is the fact that for most of the 1980s, at least half of the nation's graduate students in science and engineering will be noncitizens, a large fraction of whom will return to their native countries after completing their educations. The only improvement visible in this otherwise gloomy picture is that science and engineering doctorate degrees, which had been declining for almost a decade, reversed this decline and increased slightly— by just over 2 percent—in 1981 and 1982.[35]

Among the steps most frequently suggested to improve the education and training of adequate numbers of physical scientists and engineers are the following:

- Strengthen science and mathematics at the secondary school level.

- Improve the technical personnel data base to permit more accurate forecasting of supply-demand requirements.

- Increase support and incentives for junior faculty and graduate students in materials science and engineering, and in technician training.

- Undertake an equipment modernization program at engineering schools with obsolete equipment and facilities.

- Educate materials scientists and engineers in the interaction of technology, society, and public policy.

- Emphasize industry-government-university cooperative materials- and minerals-related research programs.

Most analysts emphasize that funding to achieve such goals should be provided by both government and industry, both of which in the long run stand to benefit from the improvements gained. Ideally, cooperative efforts including government, industry, and the educational community itself can best approach the multitude of problems requiring solution.

Industrial Application of Research and Development

Research and development is of little practical value unless its results can be employed in useful applications to benefit society. Such applications are promoted through two somewhat diffuse processes generally identified as technological innovation and technology transfer. Both, through their impact upon all stages of the materials cycle, clearly exert a significant effect upon materials supply and demand.

Technological Innovation. Generally speaking, technological innovation is defined as the process of taking an idea, invention, or recognition of a market need and developing a useful product, technique, or service to its point of initial commercial acceptance. Innovation also is seen in the improvement or refinement of an existing product, technique, or service to render it more commercially acceptable. Typically, the innovative process "is characterized by the creative assimilation of seemingly disconnected and diverse elements into the development and user acceptance of a new product, process, or technique."[36]

Technological innovation draws upon the existing science and technology base, with research and development constituting an early and vital component of the innovative process. Other components include the commercialization of the original concept or idea, followed by a general diffusion of the innovation throughout the economy. This diffusion is enhanced by the effect of technology transfer, discussed separately below.

The status of industrial technological innovation in the United States has been of much concern and controversy for more than a decade, and its role in contributing to economic growth continues to be debated, largely because of the difficulty in attempting to measure its effects accurately. Usually analysts attempt to measure innovation by comparing such "input indicators" as funding for research and development and the level of employment in related occupations with such "output indicators" as the number of major innovations—as patents—that result from these inputs, or the effects of these innovations upon such economic parameters as company earnings, growth of productivity, and balance of trade. Very large effects, as during the 1960s, are readily detected, but exactly what is occurring at other times is less certain.

Whether federal government intervention to improve industrial innovation for commercial purposes is justified is a parameter that is much discussed. In a market-oriented economy such initiatives are typically considered as best left to the private sector. Yet the role of government in promoting innovation in a nation such as Japan has been very impressive. In the United States a government role in promoting increased industrial innovation conceivably could take many forms, but most analysts agree that whatever the form, the final decisions involved in the commercialization and marketing of new products, processes, and services that result should be made by the private sector. Much agreement exists for limiting federal involvement to providing incentives indirectly through the tax medium.

Technology Transfer. Broadly speaking, technology transfer is the application of existing technology to a new use, or the employment of the technology by a new user. Thus, technology transfer principally involves increased utilization of the existing science-technology base, as contrasted with expanding the base by means of further research and development. Technology transfer therefore provides a vital mechanism whereby elements of the existing science-technology base can be coupled more closely with the innovation process in order to stimulate productivity growth. The process can be quite short, possibly a matter of days if the technology that is transferred can be directly applied in its existing form to the new environment. On the other hand, the process may take place over a considerable number of years if extensive modification of the technology, or redesign or adaptive engineering, is required to make the technology useful in its new role.[37]

Technology transfer occurs through a wide variety of mechanisms, the most effective of which are person-to-person communications based upon personal relationships among students, scientists, businessmen, and managers. Not only is this the most direct means of transfer, it also appears to be the most efficient and reliable. Another primary mode of transfer is written communication, including letters, reports, the published professional literature, and unclassified technical data, reports, and patents. Commercial means of technology transfer include licensing, joint business ventures, technical exchanges, various forms of technical training, the sale of processing equipment, provision of engineering documentation and technical data, consulting proposals, and the sale of products that embody technology.

From the point of view of U.S. materials vulnerability, two aspects of technological transfer are of primary concern: first, the level of technology transfer to U.S. industry in general, usually criticized as grossly inadequate, and, second, the level of transfer of technology—including materials-related technology—to the Soviet Union, often criticized as potentially dangerous.

With regard to the first concern, although U.S. science is generally considered relatively strong, healthy, and productive, U.S. industry often is exceedingly slow in taking commercial advantage of the knowledge this science provides. Frequently foreign companies will capitalize upon U.S.-developed discoveries and utilize them to gain a competitive advantage over U.S. companies that failed to act. Especially frustrating has been the relative failure of U.S. industry to take advantage of discoveries made by the federal laboratories supported by taxpayers—including U.S. industry itself. To help redress this situation, the Stevenson-Wydler Technology Innovation Act of 1980 was enacted to (among other purposes) stimulate the transfer of federally owned or originated technology to the private sector.[38] The act directed each federal laboratory to establish an Office of Research and Technology Applications, and it directed each federal agency having one or more federal laboratories to devote at least 0.5 percent of its research and development budget to promoting technology transfer. Such efforts, for example, could help the private sector to implement the research findings of the U.S. Bureau of Mines to recycle strategic and critical materials.

With regard to the second aspect of technology transfer—to a new user— questions begin with the recognition that much modern technology is highly useful for military applications. Because the United States continues to maintain a considerable lead over the Soviet Union in the development of many kinds of technology, much effort is exerted to prevent the transfer of this technology to the Soviets. Of particular importance is the technology associated with computers, including systems design, concepts, and both hardware and software; microelectronics, including semiconductor processing, chip design and fabrication, and very large-scale integration; lasers, including optical, pulsed power, and other related components useful for laser weapons; and radars, especially air defense radars for missile systems. Despite the best efforts on the part of the United States, much of this sensitive technology continues to wind up in the Soviet Union.[39] It has been estimated that as many as several thousand technology-collection officers are currently involved in a "massive, well-planned and well-coordinated Soviet program to acquire Western technology through combined legal and illegal means," especially in the areas of guidance technology, rocket propulsion, missile defense, aircraft technology, computer-assisted design, anti-submarine warfare, submarine quieting, large carriers, computer equipment, and smart bombs.[40]

Recent Department of Defense estimates indicate that more than 150 Soviet weapons systems may now contain technology derived from Western sources, obtained by at least two dozen methods ranging from legal purchase to theft.[41] To the extent that the Soviet Union can make use of this technology for military purposes, U.S. strategic defense is compromised.

Continued efforts at excessively tight control of U.S. high technology limit exports to U.S. allies as well as to the Soviet Union, thereby making it even more difficult for U.S. companies to compete in world markets dominated by high technology. Furthermore, it aggravates the negative U.S. balance of payments and helps legitimize the charge that the United States is rapidly becoming a major importer rather than exporter of high technology. Clearly, an exceedingly delicate line must be tread in dealing with this particular problem.

International Problems

Materials supply and demand is increasingly subjected to major international constraints that may very well become the dominant constraints of the future. Worldwide competition for raw materials is increasing and is being made more difficult for U.S. companies by the assistance, direct and indirect, given many foreign companies by their governments. Increased foreign investment in the major developing and materials-producing nations, often accompanied by various forms of long-term trade agreements, places further limitations upon supplies of raw materials available on the free markets. Continued foreign investment in the United States, and particularly in the mines and mining sector, has raised questions regarding the unrestricted availability of future domestic materials supplies. Added to these difficulties are those associated with the desire of the materials-producing nations of the Third World to create a New International Economic Order that will give them more control over their own resources and a more powerful voice in foreign affairs. Finally, in their forward drive to join the industrial revolution, these countries have created new problems for the already-industrialized nations by their increased consumption of raw materials, their move toward exporting processed rather than raw materials, and their more frequent exhibitions of nationalism and protectionism. All of these elements affect supply and demand in a multitude of ways difficult to understand and virtually impossible to predict.

The Role of Foreign Governments

U.S. companies, including many within the materials industries, consistently maintain that they can compete effectively in world markets provided such competition is free from foreign government influence and intervention. However, their point of view is fast becoming historical in a rapidly changing world:

> International trade in metals is becoming less competitive day by day. Since the late 1960s central governments have interfered with international trade

in minerals for other-than-commercial motives. . . . It is no secret that international trade in metals was never an ideal example of a competitive market, even before central governments entered international markets. The long lead times needed to bring a metal mine or processing unit on stream, the capital intensiveness of metal projects, the worldwide vertical integration of many metal producers—all combined to prevent market forces from fully operating. Government interferences in the market place only diminish their competitiveness further, inducing investors to mine and produce metals uneconomically.[42]

Similar situations exist for many nonmetallic materials, as major consuming countries intensify their materials supply activities and adopt new measures to help assure their continued access to raw materials of all kinds. Cooperative arrangements between many foreign governments and their industries serve to enhance the economics, productivity, and effectiveness of those industries in competing with U.S. firms that lack similar arrangements with the U.S. government. In many cases, foreign firms may not only be government-subsidized, but may be government-owned or controlled. For example, in France and Japan minerals and materials policies are considered as necessary adjuncts to these nations' industrial policies. Even when such close inter-relationship is not intended, government policies toward private firms, often instituted for other purposes, may affect the supply of raw materials.

Foreign government influences upon the materials-related industries appear especially pervasive in major European nations and Japan. For example, the vital interest that most member nations of the Organization for Economic Cooperation and Development have in foreign sources of nonfuel materials has led certain European countries and Japan to intervene in world markets in support of their national companies in materials matters. These kinds of activities indicate a perspective in business-government relations quite different from that in the United States, and they underscore the increasing concern many nations have for assured supplies of key nonfuel materials. Among the measures taken to ensure and diversify their sources of supply are overseas insurance programs, direct financial assistance, technical assistance, tax concessions, and expansion of the role of government agencies in assisting the private sector.[43]

Japanese activities have perhaps received the most attention, and should be viewed in the light of that nation's scant resources of domestic materials and the rapid expansion of its economy since 1946. Japan has been characterized as the most formidable raw materials competitor in the world and has been described as pursuing tactics and strategies "based on concepts of sudden shock, secrecy, flexibility, deception, and above all the surprise of competitors and potential enemies."[44] Even prior to 1968, when the Japanese balance of payments could best be described as delicate, the Japanese government provided favored treatment to investment in the development of foreign materials resources. During the late 1960s and early 1970s, new corporations, formed to supply risk capital to Japanese firms engaged in foreign exploration and development projects, provided low-interest loans that could be forfeited in the event of failure of the project, or provided aid through equity participation.

At present, the Japanese conduct their pervasive global operations through private trading and operating companies that are highly competitive and often work jointly in developing foreign development projects. The Japanese government supports Japanese companies in these efforts through favorable foreign trade policies, tax incentives and low-interest funding, regulation of domestic production and trade, and suggestions of suitable stockpiling objectives. As noted by one observer, in comparison with other industrialized nations "Japan is like an armed fortress that is always expecting a siege" and, therefore, has sought to diversify its sources of essential raw materials as widely as possible.[45] Japan is now channeling almost one-half of its total foreign investment in the mining and smelting sector into facilities being built in the developing countries, where its direct investments in the materials sector have begun to exceed total annual European investment.

Among European nations, both France and West Germany directly subsidize the exploration for foreign minerals, providing tax incentives and in some instances depletion allowances. The French government has long provided the private sector with a variety of subsidies, guarantees, and loans to promote both domestic and overseas materials development. At least a decade ago, West German programs to guarantee or insure foreign private investment were already proliferating. Subsidies for West German companies for overseas exploration have been available since 1971 at the latest, and for domestic exploration since 1963.[46] As these programs have become more numerous and effective, the relative position of U.S. companies lacking such governmental support has steadily waned.

To what extent have foreign investments in the U.S. materials-related industries—in particular, the mines and mining sector—also grown? This question is outside the scope of the present discussion, but in general it appears that the current level of such foreign investment is still far less than similar U.S. investment abroad. On balance there appears little cause for alarm about this foreign investment in the U.S. materials-related industries, at least for the present. In the unlikely event that foreign investors should attempt to use such investment as a political tool to interfere with U.S. supplies of strategic and critical materials, the federal government already possesses ample authority to protect national security and other U.S. vital interests. Furthermore, Congress has provided the president with policy guidance and authority to control both exports and imports during any emergency. Hence, little success appears likely for any attempts by foreign investors, or foreign governments acting indirectly through such investors, to influence U.S. domestic materials supplies in such a way as to affect adversely U.S. security or well-being.

The New International Economic Order

The less-developed areas of the world possess a large fraction of the materials resources needed by the industrialized countries, and especially of materials considered to be the most strategic and critical. In the past, materials production in these areas was based largely upon private investment financed by capital from industrialized countries, under arrangements made with the local governing powers. The amount of capital involved was usually large, as was the risk, but frequently so was the rate of return. The mining ventures thus established were both owned and operated by private investors, usually foreign, except in the case of joint ventures for which the foreign partners typically were mining companies headquartered in one or more industrialized countries. Thus, the local nationals rarely had much part in these enterprises. On the other hand, the host countries usually benefited from such foreign investment, particularly in their extractive industries, by sharing in profits, by the proliferation of jobs, and by paid-for improvements in the local infrastructure, especially the transportation network.[47]

In time, however, these less than philanthropical—indeed sometimes exploitive—economic benefits increasingly appeared inadequate to local governments. Perhaps even more important, such governments considered it demeaning to play so passive a role in the development and exploitation of their own natural resources. Thus resource-rich nations began to demand a stronger voice in their materials affairs and, indeed, insisted upon a degree of ownership and control. From these demands emerged the call for a "New International Economic Order" that would include an increased role in processing and refining materials rather than being limited to only the extraction of raw materials. Accompanying this new awareness of the need and potential benefits of such changes was a rising tide of Third World nationalism, leading not infrequently to the expropriation of mining and mineral assets held by foreign investors.

The underlying rationale of the New International Economic Order is the generally agreed upon need to improve the quality of life in the developing nations, largely through achieving greater parity with the industrialized nations that depend upon them so heavily for materials resources.[48] The general concept of the organization was expressed in 1974 in a document that emerged from the 2229th plenary meeting of the U.N. General Assembly, "Declaration on the Establishment of a New International Economic Order."[49] Basic to this declaration is the intent of the developing nations to obtain higher revenues from their exports, more stable markets, and greater long-term control over the use of their natural resources. In addition to redistributing some of the world's wealth more equitably, the intent is to seize "the power to determine the rules that will govern the movement of goods, services, technology, and capital across international boundaries," thereby affecting such areas as "sovereignty over natural resources, raw materials, technology transfer, industrialization, and multinational corporations."[50] To a large extent, this declaration thus has become a means for expressing both the demands and expectations of the developing countries.

Materials Processing and Use. A major element of the New International Economic Order calls for the developing countries to move from primarily raw materials production to the export of processed materials, for several reasons. First, the export of processed materials can be expected to produce increased revenues for those countries equipped to do the processing, thereby accruing to these countries' benefit the revenues that in the past went to the industrialized nations that did the processing. Second, materials processing represents a more advanced stage of industrialization than does raw materials production, thus creating new jobs and contributing to a more advanced industrial infrastructure. Third, it contributes to a positive balance of payments because the developing nations can utilize their own processed materials rather than importing them from processors in industrialized nations. And fourth, it contributes to a more positive self-image in helping to erase the perceived stigma of a backward nation unable to produce anything of value except for raw matter dug from the ground—an image held over from the unhappy period of colonialism and its aftermath. Overall, the attitude on the part of the developing nations is that "unless they are able to industrialize, they will remain dependent upon the earnings they will receive from primary products, which means vulnerability, impoverishment, and continued loss of dignity."[51]

Thus far, the internal markets of developing nations for processed materials are much too small to sustain even a modest level of industrial production, so that foreign markets remain essential to make industrialization worthwhile. However, as the developing nations become more industrialized, they will consume larger quantities of the materials they produce and process. Unless they can increase production to accommodate their own growing needs as well as the increasing requirements of the rest of the world, it is conceivable—indeed, almost inevitable—that shortages of some materials may result.

Nationalism and Protectionism. The hopes, aspirations, and expectations of developing nations to achieve significantly higher standards of living have fueled a rising tide of nationalism and protectionism in many of those countries. At the same time, the proposals by the United Nations for a New International Economic Order have been taken by the leaders of some nations as a rationale for whatever actions they believe necessary to gain greater control over the production, processing, and marketing of their raw materials. Among the more popular actions that have thus become legitimized are the following:

- The regulation and exercise of authority over all foreign investment in accordance with local laws and national policies;

- The nationalization, expropriation, or transfer of ownership of all foreign property;

- The determination of compensation, if any, to foreign investors for expropriated properties in accordance with the relevant local laws or regulations and any other circumstances that may seem pertinent; and

- Settlement of all investment controversies in accordance with local laws and courts unless prior agreements for such settlement exist.[52]

Expropriation of foreign properties is, of course, one of the most extreme and aggressive actions a host country can take, and often it reflects the built-up resentment of past practices as much as it does a means for improving the value received for its natural resources. It is certainly the most direct way of obtaining greater control over the industries concerned. Because large, fixed capital investments constitute the bulk of the cumulative costs of most mining ventures, such ventures are particularly vulnerable to expropriation. Over the past two decades, local governments have taken over copper operations in Peru, Zambia, and Zaire; iron operations in Algeria, Liberia, Mauritania, and Venezuela; and bauxite operations in Guyana and Jamaica. Consequently, a large fraction of many materials now comes from state-owned or state-controlled mines located in developing countries.

Although expropriation of foreign holdings typically receives the most media attention, host country demands just short of expropriation often can be very effective in achieving nationalistic demands without creating the adverse publicity. Such demands can include higher prices for materials, whether raw or processed; increased domestic processing before export; training and employment of host country nationals in more highly skilled management and technical positions; and increased control over all phases of the exploration, production, and marketing of materials resources.

Unilateral actions such as those described obviously tend to discourage foreign investment in the developing nations, which, despite their desires for resource independence and control, have a growing appetite for foreign exchange and capital. Likewise, the industrialized countries continue to exhibit a growing appetite for the materials resources many developing nations so abundantly possess, many of which cannot be made available without the investment capital available from the industrialized nations. Thus, each side acutely needs what the other has to offer. The develop-for-import agreements discussed in Chapter 3 represent an attempt to reconcile these needs while reducing the risks incurred by the industrialized nations as the developing nations strive for a greater say in both their own and world affairs.

The Prospect for Future Materials Shortages

Few materials-related problems have received as much attention as that of the possibility of future materials shortages. In strictly economic terms, there is virtually no such thing as a materials shortage: when demand exceeds supply, the price rises until enough potential buyers are excluded from the market to again roughly equate supply with demand. What most observers mean by a shortage, therefore, is that not enough material is available at a price they can afford or wish to pay. Under these conditions, if the price of the material remains high, "displacement substitution" gradually takes place (as discussed in Chapter 6) until supply again meets demand at whatever price then prevails. In effect, a free market rations the demand for a material so that the demand exists in relative equilibrium with the amount available. Thus, in strictly economic terms, the world will never actually exhaust supplies of any material, because some will always be available at a price only a very few can afford to pay.

Likewise materials shortages in geological terms appear remote because supplies of materials in the earth's crust, oceans, and atmosphere are so huge that the prospect of actually exhausting any particular material in the foreseeable future is extremely implausible. Hence, as discussed earlier in this chapter, the future prospect is for the gradually increasing exploitation of marginally accessible materials deposits, at commensurately greater extraction and processing costs, resulting in ever-increasing materials prices that will automatically restrain demand and encourage the search for substitutes.

More practically, from the viewpoint of the materials purchasing agent or engineer, a materials shortage exists if one cannot obtain enough of a needed material at the specific time when one needs it, regardless of how much may be available elsewhere. Such a shortage may appear at any point in the materials supply cycle: a processor may lack adequate supplies of raw materials ore, a refiner may lack adequate quantities of processed ore, a fabricator may lack sufficient supplies of refined materials, and a manufacturer may lack adequate supplies of materials fabricated to that company's particular specifications. There may be no issue of price regarding any of these shortages, but rather a question of delivery, which may be measured in days, weeks, months, or perhaps even years depending upon particular circumstances. Thus, a shortage in this practical sense results more from a temporary failure of transportation, logistics, or production capacity than it does from any more fundamental economic or geological considerations.

Such practical problems for the most part can be solved, and shortages prevented, by adequate planning and foresight. Unfortunately, the planning and foresight often are lacking, not so much because policymakers are ignorant of what needs to be done, but because they lack the determination and, often, the economic means to prepare adequately for future needs and requirements for materials. Major materials users are generally reluctant on their own to stockpile or to create and maintain extensive inventories of the materials feedstocks they require because such inventories are expensive to acquire, store, and maintain and tie up scarce capital at a zero rate of return. Over the long term, most stockpiles acquire greater value, but over the shorter term, feedstocks acquired at today's prices may be more expensive than anticipated unless purchases can always be timed to coincide with an upswing in the business cycle. Materials producers also may fail to construct additional capacity, despite analyses that predict its future need, because such predictions may prove erroneous if economic conditions change or unforeseen technological developments occur. In the end, both materials users and producers are trapped in a system that, because it is inherently unable to predict future demand accurately and make available commensurate supplies, almost guarantees periodic materials shortages of one material or another.

Thus, the question is not so much whether materials shortages will occur in the future—for they almost inevitably will occur—but how the frequency of such shortages can be reduced and their deleterious effects minimized. This question leads to the topic of the next, and concluding, chapter—the need for a national materials policy.

Notes

1. Richard J. Barnet, *The Lean Years—Politics in the Age of Scarcity* (New York: Simon and Schuster, 1980), p. 122.

2. Jonathan R. T. Hughes, *The Governmental Habit* (New York: Basic Books, 1977), p. 3.

3. David C. Ridinger, "Cost of Regulation to the Mining Industry." *Mining Congress Journal*, February 1980, pp. 42–43.

4. "Critical Materials: How Big Is the Problem?" *Materials Engineering*, June 1981, pp. 54–55.

5. Ridinger, p. 43.

6. Stanley H. Dempsey, "Environmental Health and Safety Regulations." *Mining Congress Journal*, January 1980), p. 44.

7. *Critical Materials Requirements of the U.S. Aerospace Industry* (Washington, D.C.: U.S. Department of Commerce, October 1981), p. 303.

8. U.S. Congress, House Committee on Science and Technology, Subcommittee on Science, Research, and Technology, *Summary of Hearings on A National Policy for Materials—Research and Resources* (Washington, D.C.: U.S. Government Printing Office, September 1978), p. 12.

9. U.S. Congress, House Committee on Interior and Insular Affairs, Subcommittee on Mines and Mining, *U.S. Materials Vulnerability: National Policy Implications* (Washington, D.C.: U.S. Government Printing Office, 1980), p. 43.

10. Ibid., p. 43.

11. U.S. Congress, House Committee on Science and Technology, *Seventh Biennial Conference on National Materials Policy* (Washington, D.C.: U.S. Government Printing Office, March 1983), p. x.

12. Jerry Knight and Peter Behr, "In U.S., Strategic Minerals Acquire New Prominence," *Washington Post*, 15 March 1981, p. H-3.

13. Richard Corrigan, "Administration Pushes R and D Pooling to Maintain U.S. Lead in High Tech." *National Journal*, 1 October 1983, pp. 1992–1996.

14. "High Tech Companies Team Up in the R and D Race." *Business Week*, 15 August 1983, p. 95.

15. Ibid., p. 94.

16. *Critical Materials Requirements of the U.S. Aerospace Industry*, p. 251.

17. Gerhard Anders et al., *The Economics of Mineral Extraction* (New York: Praeger, 1980), p. 142.

18. *Critical Materials Requirements of the U.S. Steel Industry* (Washington, D.C.: U.S. Department of Commerce, March 1983), p. 17.

19. *Critical Materials Requirements of the U.S. Aerospace Industry*, p. 242.

20. U.S. Congress, *U.S. Materials Vulnerability: National Policy Implications*, p. 43.

21. Earl T. Hayes, "Energy Implications of Materials Processing." *Science*, 20 February 1976, p. 661.

22. D. G. Altenpohl, *Materials in World Perspective* (Berlin: Springer-Verlag, 1980), p. 197.

23. The significance of this "materials-energy-environment" triad was first emphasized in National Commission on Materials Policy, *Materials Needs and the Environment Today and Tomorrow* (Washington, D.C.: U.S. Government Printing Office, 1973), 308 pp.

24. Barnet, p. 118.

25. Eli Sani, "The Capital Shortage Phenomenon: Its Impact on the U.S. Mineral Industry." *Resources Policy*, December 1978, p. 263.

26. *Critical Materials Requirements of the U.S. Steel Industry*, p. 7.

27. U.S. Congress, *Seventh Biennial Conference on National Materials Policy*, p. 46.

28. American Mining Congress, "Declaration of Policy of the American Mining Congress." *Mining Congress Journal*, November 1980, p. 47.

29. Edward F. Denison, "Explorations of Declining Productivity Growth." *Survey of Current Business*, August 1979, p. 3.

30. Alton D. Slay, "Minerals and National Security." *Mining Congress Journal*, November 1980, p. 23.

31. U.S. Congress, *Seventh Biennial Conference on National Materials Policy*, p. xi.

32. U.S. Congress, *The National Materials and Minerals Policy, Research and Development Act of 1980* (Public Law 96–479, enacted 22 October 1980).

33. Committee on Materials, Federal Coordinating Council for Science, Engineering, and Technology, *Inventory of Federal Materials Research and Technology*, fiscal year 1982 (Washington, D.C.: Office of Science and Technology Policy, June 1983), 36 pp.

34. Slay, p. 22.

35. *Science and Engineering Doctorates, 1960–1981* (Washington, D.C.: National Science Foundation, 1983), pp. 7–20.

36. Sherman Gee, *Technology Transfer, Innovation, and International Competitiveness* (New York: John Wiley and Sons, 1981), p. 9.

37. Ibid., pp. 18–19.

38. *The Stevenson-Wydler Technology Innovation Act of 1980* (Public Law 96–480, enacted 21 October 1980).

39. "The High Tech Secrets Russia Seeks in the West." *U.S. News and World Report*, 3 May 1982, p. 44. For an overview of this subject, see: Office of Technology Assessment, *Technology and East-West Trade—An Update* (Washington, D.C.: U.S. Government Printing Office, May 1983), 106 pp.

40. *Soviet Acquisition of Western Technology* (Washington, D.C.: U.S. Central Intelligence Agency, April 1982), pp. 1–16.

41. Jack Anderson, "U.S. High Tech Drained Away by the Soviets." *Washington Post*, 19 March 1984, p. E20.

42. James I. Walsh, "Is Free Trade in Minerals A Myth?" *Materials and Society* 7:1 (1983), p. 13. For a more general discussion, see D. Beim, "International Mining Projects: Risks and Rewards." *Journal of International Trade Law and Economics* 12:2 (1978), pp. 223–225.

43. Amos A. Jordan and Robert A. Kilmarx, *Strategic Mineral Dependence* (Beverly Hills, Calif.: Sage Publications, 1979), p. 33.

44. Bohdan Szuprowicz, *How to Avoid Strategic Materials Shortages* (New York: John Wiley and Sons, 1981), p. 62.

45. Ibid., p. 62.

46. W.C.J. van Rensburg, "Global Competition for Strategic Mineral Supplies." *Resources Policy*, March 1981, pp. 9–10.

47. National Commission on Materials Policy, p. 9-12.

48. For a discussion of the New International Economic Order, see Edwin P. Reubins, ed., *The Challenge of the New International Economic Order* (Boulder, Colo.: Westview Press, 1981), 256 pp.

49. The complete declaration is given in Paul Rogers, ed., *Future Resources and World Development* (New York: Plenum Press, 1976), pp. 135–139.

50. Szuprowicz, p. 43.

51. Edward L. Morse, "Introduction: The International Management of Resources." In *Sharing Global Resources*, ed. Ruth W. Arad et al. (New York: McGraw-Hill, 1979), p. 9.

52. Jordan and Kilmarx, p. 29.

Debate over a National Materials Policy

The need for an overall, comprehensive national policy for materials has been under active consideration for more than three decades. Although a primary motivation underlying perceptions for the need for such a policy has been concern over the continued availability of strategic and critical raw materials, such concern has broadened over time to encompass materials in general and their influence, both directly and indirectly, upon virtually all areas of national policymaking.

The primary objective of a national materials policy, if one were established, would be to address the relationship of materials to human needs and purposes. Clearly, the role of policy is to set necessary goals or purposes and then determine those courses of action best suited to achieving the goals.[1] During much of the lengthy period throughout which the need for a national materials policy has been actively discussed and debated, participants have largely agreed upon the goals and purposes such a policy would serve, but they frequently have disagreed upon what courses of action would be needed to achieve those goals or, indeed, whether any deliberate course of action is desirable or feasible.

The Rationale for a National Materials Policy

The major argument in favor of a national policy for materials is that, over the past half-century, materials-related problems have increased in number, scope, and intensity and yet—lacking an effective, overall policy— little has been done about them. Over this period materials problems have become so enmeshed with other national problems, especially with those involving energy and the environment, that the future well-being of the nation could be placed in jeopardy. The general view of proponents is that an overall, coordinated materials policy could address materials-related problems within the context of other national policies—especially economic, environmental, energy, and strategic—to assure that solutions are found to these materials problems without exerting an adverse impact upon other national policies, and vice versa.

Centralization of Authority. Because materials-related problems are so intimately related to so many other kinds of national problems, advocates of a national materials policy maintain that only by centralizing policymaking for materials can a satisfactory balance be achieved among all problems in the best interests of the nation. In the absence of a centralized authority, materials-related problems become fragmented, and responsibility for their solution becomes dispersed. Responsibility for a particular problem invariably seems to fall within the jurisdiction of "some other" federal agency so that the problem becomes an orphan without hope of finding a home. Proponents of a national materials policy maintain that such difficulties could largely be avoided if policymaking for materials were centralized to provide a coherent, continuous mechanism for coordinating all aspects of materials policy and their interrelationships with other kinds of national policies.

The Materials-Energy-Environment Triad. Another reason for centralizing materials policymaking is to place all three elements of the materials, energy, and environment triad on an equal footing. Policymaking for environmental issues was centralized in 1970 by creation of the Environmental Protection Agency, and policymaking for energy issues was centralized in 1977 by creation of the Department of Energy.[2] Hence, proponents of a national materials policy contend that the centralization of policymaking for materials in an appropriate federal office or agency is long overdue. Indeed, creation of a formal mechanism for policymaking for materials can be seen as reflecting the prospect that, much as the 1960s was the decade of the environment and the 1970s the decade of energy, the 1980s could be the decade of materials—a period in which materials-related problems may become preeminent.[3] This likely preeminence demands that all three elements of the triad exist essentially on an equal footing, a condition in which laws, executive orders, and various administrative practices regarding these three areas complement, rather than conflict with, one another.

Conclusions of Study Groups. The logic of centralizing materials policymaking has been reaffirmed during the past thirty years by numerous high-level study groups that have assessed the question of need for a national policy for materials:

> It is significant that during this period, despite major changes in the U.S. posture in materials—in terms of usage patterns, external forces, and program priorities—the need for a national policy-forming institution has been expressed in each new assessment. . . . In sum, circumstances appear to call for a national policy for materials to serve domestic goals, to preserve the U.S. posture in a competitive world, and to anticipate the changing needs and pressures the future is certain to bring.[4]

The Case for the Status Quo

Those experts who, apart from the study groups, see no need for an overall national policy for materials or believe that such a policy would be impossible to achieve often cite a number of reasons in support of their view, as follows.

Pervasiveness of Materials. A basic argument against the concept of such a national policy, or even the possibility of devising one, is the fact that materials are so pervasive throughout today's society that it is virtually impossible to generalize regarding their role and how they can best be managed in the national interest. Various issues regarding materials arise in almost all areas of public policymaking, indicating that materials are much too diverse to permit their responsibility to be centralized in any single federal agency. Likewise, their diversity almost precludes their being specifically categorized in any national legislation, so that when such materials legislation is passed it is necessarily so comprehensive as to lack any operational significance.[5] The difficulty most often perceived is that only general statements concerning materials as a whole can be made, and such statements must in fact be so broad as to be relatively useless or meaningless. If specific statements are made, they can no longer encompass all materials. This difficulty also reflects that policy appropriate to one material is not necessarily appropriate to another, so that even a host of separate policies for individual materials would not add up to a cohesive national policy for all materials.

Lack of Economic Significance. Another argument used against the need for a national materials policy is that nonenergy materials are relatively unimportant with respect to the nation's economy as a whole. This unimportance is assumed because such materials contribute only modestly to the nation's GNP as contrasted with the contribution made by other economic sectors, including energy materials. For example, as noted in Chapter 1, nonfuel materials (at the mine) in 1982 amounted to only $27 billion as contrasted with $160 billion in energy materials. Such data, critics contend, demonstrate the relative economic insignificance of nonfuel materials to the economy and suggest that little need exists for any new national policy for such materials.

Adequacy of Existing Authority. Many analysts readily admit that important materials-related problems do exist, but maintain that such problems are still not as serious as other problems with which national policymakers must currently deal. Furthermore, they express conviction that federal policymakers already possess all of the statutory authority needed to deal with materials problems that do exist and, consequently, that no additional legislation is required to provide additional authority. This general theme has been consistently repeated in testimony before congressional committees, within the context of an already excessively large federal bureaucracy that should deter congressional attempts to enlarge it still further with unnecessary offices or agencies to deal specifically with strategic and critical materials problems.

Erroneous Predictions of Materials Scarcities. Critics of the need for a national materials policy often maintain that predictions of imminent materials scarcities, and the potential economic and strategic disasters that would result from them, are very much exaggerated and highly unlikely to occur. They note that the typical cycles of raw materials supply and demand, and the resulting fluctuations in materials prices and availability, are the natural consequences of global interactions of producers and consumers within a predominantly free economy. Despite such cycles, they maintain, national economies have almost always succeeded in righting themselves and preventing widespread or prolonged materials scarcities, contrary to predictions so often made in the past. They fear that a national materials policy ultimately might, through imposition of unnecessary and unwise controls upon the currently free economy, bring about the very conditions of materials scarcity that an overall national policy is intended to prevent.

Inaccurate Classification of Problems. Because of the complexity of many materials-related problems, the issues involved also invariably impact upon issues related to other national policy areas. Consequently, it is sometimes argued that at least some "materials problems" only superficially involve materials and are really problems of some other nature:

> It is clear that some problems are materials problems only on the surface. They really stem from social and economic factors such as relative labor costs, shifts in international competitiveness, relative changes in power costs, management decisions, and regulations. Therefore the remedial options do not fall neatly into a simple category of "materials policy."[6]

Lack of Action over Time. Some observers point out that despite all the high-level activity over the past thirty years and more by numerous professional task forces, working groups, congressional committees, and national commissions, the findings and recommendations of these various groups have largely been ignored. Nor has any great calamity befallen the nation as a consequence. This relatively extended experience is said to demonstrate that no need for a national materials policy actually exists.

Some General Observations

As briefly reviewed, many arguments are entertained both for and against the need for a national policy for materials. Yet unquestionably, serious problems do exist and are being questionably addressed. For much of the nation's history, a respected and predominantly effective approach to addressing problems of national importance, whatever their origin, has been the creation of an office or agency suitably empowered with both the authority and responsibility for seeking appropriate solutions. Furthermore, materials-related issues have long been sacrificed in favor of energy and environmental issues.

The expressed concerns about the pervasiveness of materials may arise from a basic misunderstanding on the part of critics as to what proponents of the need for a national materials policy are in fact proposing. Obviously it would be both undesirable and impractical to expect *every* decision related to materials, however small, to be made by a centralized federal materials agency. However, it appears entirely feasible to centralize responsibility for *major* policymaking in a single agency—a proposal by no means novel or new in other issue areas. And certainly at the uppermost policymaking levels, many materials problems reflect common or related issues that logically justify the need for a common materials policy.

Similarly, other criticisms also can be challenged. For example, the claim that materials are of relatively little importance to the nation's economy could indicate a lack of appreciation of the true role played by materials in the economy, when without them there would obviously be no economy. Similarly, the argument that adequate authority already exists to solve materials-related problems may stem from a failure to appreciate the problems and their potential for future harm; it begs the question of why such authority—if it indeed exists—has not been used effectively. In fact, such lack of effective action is a testament to the scope and complexity of the problems and, consequently, to the difficulty of dealing with them piecemeal, or leaving them to "the other" agency to handle. And finally, whether or not a specific problem has a relatively large or small materials component is of little consequence if nothing is done to find a solution. Materials analysts would be the first to agree that it is axiomatic that materials problems cannot be separated from industrial, social, strategic, political, environmental, and other major problem areas. Because the mix is necessarily complex, it is not always clear which particular area is uppermost in concern for each particular problem. Sometimes such a determination depends heavily upon a value judgment or the point of view taken in attempting to define and analyze the problem. Ideally an overall national policy for materials could make much easier the task of coordinating the materials aspects of problems with those other aspects that are not so directly related to materials.

Realistically, however, it remains the responsibility of those who advocate such a policy to convince others who are opposed that it is worth a try. Such a task has proved formidable, to say the least.

Problems with Which a National Materials Policy Could Deal

The establishment and pursuit of a national policy for materials could help shed light upon many of the nation's most pressing materials-related problems. In operation it could provide an "early warning" system to help anticipate changes in U.S. and global materials supply and demand, and to help foresee important global trends affecting the materials policies of other nations. It could help protect U.S. materials consumers from the potential impact of external changes in supplies or from the increased competition for dwindling world reserves of industrial raw materials. It could provide an "insurance policy" to cushion the potential adverse effects of supply disruptions or unnecessarily sharp increases in raw materials prices by anticipating such interruptions, thereby providing time during which orderly transitions could be made from one material to another. It could help focus attention upon the often-competing demands of materials, energy, environment, and other major national issues to illuminate the tradeoffs typically necessary in attempting to balance these demands in the overall national interest.

From the point of view of the present discussion, the major benefit of a national materials policy would be its influence in helping to assure the continued availability of adequate supplies of strategic and critical materials. At present, diverse national policies not infrequently have adverse impacts upon the materials area, thus working at cross purposes to the nation's vital materials interests. In the absence of an effective overall policy for materials, the nation's strategic and critical materials requirements will undoubtedly continue to be subordinated to other national interests. Some of the major problem areas that might be alleviated by a national materials policy are summarized below.

Lack of an Early Warning System

At present the government lacks any systematic mechanism for anticipating materials-related problems instead of merely reacting to them:

> The practice of waiting for the storms to strike and then, hurriedly, erecting shelters . . . is not only wasteful and an inefficient use of the resources of the nation but its cumulative effect may well be devastating. There is a need . . . to anticipate and, as far as possible, to act in an orderly fashion before the difficulties have descended upon us.[7]

The key to an early warning system, or to advanced contingency planning as it is often called, is reliable, complete, timely, consistent, and accessible information. In general, two kinds of information about materials are needed for such policymaking. First, technical information is required relating to the physical, chemical, electrical, optical, and other properties of materials; the uses of different materials for various applications; the substitution of one material for another; the management of materials to produce as well as conserve energy; the conservation and recycling of materials; and the psychological and environmental factors related to materials production and use. And second, quantitative information is required concerning trends in supply and demand for different materials, the sources and relative abundances of materials supplies, and the relative amounts of different materials employed in various uses.

Almost without exception, recent studies of present arrangements for the management of materials information in the United States have found them gravely inadequate.[8] Among the general criticisms have been the observation that available data are structured in ways that largely serve past needs and policy requirements, rather than present or prospective demands; that sufficient, reliable, and usable data concerning both the constituent parts of the materials system and the interactions of the system itself are not available; that an urgent need exists to improve the evaluation, condensation, presentation, and mechanized storage of materials information; and that major problems concerning proprietary information, statistical information relative to materials supply and demand, and lack of adequate information from foreign nations are not receiving the attention they deserve. In brief, the current status of materials-related information

- Is unsystematic;
- Is incompatible from one point to another;
- Employs different units for different materials;
- Covers various materials sources with different degrees of completeness;
- Tends to lag chronologically;
- Fails to make effective use of translations from foreign languages;
- Serves different classes of customers with different degrees of effectiveness;
- Provides inadequately for the dissemination of technical data from research and development paid for by tax dollars;
- Varies in degree of reliability; and
- Presents the information seeker with an unmanageably large volume of unevaluated literature more or less pertinent but of widely varying quality.[9]

It is not unusual for a federal policymaker to be unaware that the information he or she needs exists or, if it is suspected to exist, where it can be found in another federal agency. Even if it is found, differences in format and definitions often make the information difficult to understand and use. Incomplete coverage and lack of current data bases, inadequate analytical models and techniques for projecting the effects of changes in materials supply and demand, and agency-reporting formats that fail to meet the practical needs of decision makers all combine to inhibit the potential responses of policymakers to complex questions and situations, and to make it virtually impossible for them to plan ahead.

To help alleviate these difficulties, the National Commission on Supplies and Shortages has recommended, among other things, that data collection and analysis be upgraded, separated from policymaking, and made responsive to the needs of users with specific information on its limitations (including sampling error, uncertainty, and assumptions); that the credibility of data and analysis be maintained through open access, advisory committees, and other institutional safeguards; and that these activities and others be organized under high-level (preferably bureau-level) status independent of other government functions.[10]

Lack of Coordination in Decision Making

As noted frequently throughout this book, coordination of materials-related activities among various federal agencies, when it takes place at all, is woefully inadequate. Because responsibility for materials-related issues and problems is so scattered within both the executive and legislative branches, the tendency is to tackle problems piecemeal, with little regard for the effects that a decision made by one department may have upon the activities taking place in other departments. This ad hoc approach to policymaking for materials, usually conducted in reaction to problems that have become acute, frequently produces disappointing or counterproductive results. Existing federal programs rarely seem to pursue any central policy objectives or attempt to resolve the often conflicting demands imposed by the complexity of the problems the programs are designed to alleviate.

An example is provided by policymaking for chromium, one of the most strategic and critical materials:

> The United States has virtually no chromium indigenous to this country. . . . But at the same time we were in an accelerating, high level of consumption, we passed a group of environmental laws that virtually mandated an additional increase in the consumption of chrome to make the clean air and clean stream equipment and converters on our automobiles. We then unilaterally, in another part of government, placed an embargo on the importation of chrome from what was then our largest supplier, Rhodesia [Zimbabwe]. At the same time, we applied stricter environmental enforcement on the antiquated ferrochrome industry, reducing its productive capabilities. Also at the same time, we allowed unlimited export of stainless steel scrap, each ton of which contained 400 pounds of chrome.[11]

Lack of effective coordination has not resulted from a lack of trying, and indeed "a whole tangled spider's web of interagency committees . . . exists. But . . . each agency acts on the basis of its [own] responsibilities in relation to materials problems, without looking at the picture as a whole."[12] Typically, heads of departments or agencies who become members of such interdepartmental committees quickly designate lower level surrogates to attend in their place—surrogates who invariably lack the authority to do more than represent their agency heads in helping to define problems and identify options, with no means to set policy or make decisions.

Inadequate Materials Research and Development

Although an impressive amount of materials research and development is carried out within the United States, an overall national materials policy could be expected to improve both the quality and quantity of such efforts. For example, at the same time that real limitations exist economically in R&D in the private sector, it is difficult to assess the excessive duplication that takes place among various federal laboratories, or even between them and the private sector. A certain level of duplication ordinarily is inevitable and, indeed, is useful to the extent that it permits alternative approaches to specific problems or provides healthy competition among rival research teams. Unfortunately, however, excessive duplication and neglect appear to alternate with one another, partly as a result of inadequate coordination among laboratories throughout the federal establishment or because individual fiefdoms develop that refuse to recognize the legitimacy of similar research efforts elsewhere.

Although it is difficult to obtain an accurate assessment of the level of materials R&D funding in the private sector, estimates tend to cluster around a figure of about $4 billion per year, or approximately four times the federal level of funding. Yet such an estimate is meaningless in the context of the splintering of relatively lesser amounts of R&D funding among so many private corporations, or in the context of the actual kinds of activities included—because so much private-sector "research" in fact includes a good deal of technology and engineering.

A large fraction of all industrial research and development—however defined—is carried out by the chemical, electronics, and petroleum industries and probably does not duplicate federally funded activities to any large extent, although duplication (and secrecy) among companies is probably considerable. Much benefit could undoubtedly be derived from some form of overall coordinating mechanism that would serve to limit public and/or private duplication to the kind and degree that appears healthy and desirable in promoting and protecting industry prerogatives. It is possible that the research and development cooperatives and limited partnerships discussed in the previous chapter could serve as a vehicle to promote such coordination.

Areas of duplication and of neglect are important because the amount of funds available for research and development is always extremely limited. Although $1 billion in federal funding and another $4 billion in private-sector funding may seem like an immense expenditure for materials research and development each year, even that sum cannot begin to cover adequately all of the work that can be justified on the basis of scientific merit or technological need. At present there is no central focus of responsibility within the federal government for making choices in a rational manner. The Office of Management and Budget, as noted earlier, is theoretically charged with overall responsibility for weeding out unworthy projects or excessive duplication, but its relatively small staff encompasses little expertise in the many facets of materials research and development and, perhaps more important, considers current materials research expenditures as not warranting major attention. Hence, this office is also not concerned with lack of public-private coordination of R&D efforts. All in all, it is not surprising that many critics of the present system contend that substantially improved results might be obtained by coordinating materials research and development within the overall framework of a national materials policy.

Lack of Public Interest and Concern

One of the earlier arguments cited to support the view of critics of a national materials policy that such a policy is unnecessary is the relative lack of substantive progress made thus far by either the executive branch or Congress in recognizing the need for a policy despite numerous recommendations from major study groups. Among the reasons why progress has been so limited and so slow has been the relative lack of public interest and concern. The elected representatives have not been required by their constituents to work toward such a policy.

Although many government policies, including some environmental policies, have originated with public support and pressure, the populace has a right to expect that the government, too, can take the initiative on other policies and problems. Thus, from a popular perspective, government action can be expected in general on problems of which the populace is unaware.

This attitude takes the form of the often-heard expression that "if a problem exists, the government will say so and act on it."

Indeed the federal government does take the initiative on most national and international problems, aided or thwarted by various special-interest lobbying groups. The government also has the means to inform the public effectively about these problems after action has been contemplated or taken. Public interest and concern is aroused and thereafter continues to exist. One indicator that a national materials policy could be initiated in this way with subsequent popular support is the reluctance of critics of such a policy to predict that, even in the face of certain higher prices, the public would not go along with measures calculated to help keep the nation autonomous in as many ways as possible in the modern world.

A national materials policy, if established by the federal government, could count on the probability of good public relations and public support. The public support, in its turn, could be predicted to mature with better education of the public and a resulting balance in pressures to keep the materials policy dynamic and updated.

Need for an Improved National Defense Stockpile

The National Defense Stockpile remains the only effective near-term protection the nation has against disruptions in imports of materials considered strategic and critical—the only national "insurance policy" against their short supply. Since such stockpile "insurance" is expensive, it is important to know how the maximum insurance can be achieved, at minimum cost, against the contingency of disruptions in the nation's imports. One response follows:

> To answer that question one would have to have good information on two scores: the odds on occurrence of the contingency and the damage if it does occur. Attempts have been made to estimate both. All incorporate a great deal of subjective judgment, and none inspire much confidence. . . . There are, in fact, great and numerous difficulties. To name only a few:
>
> - Each mineral will have its own impact characterization;
> - The triggering event will set the dimensions of time and degree of severity;
> - The state of the economy will greatly shape the impact;
> - It will make a difference whether more than one country is affected, both on the supplier and on the consumer side;
> - Size of inventory will matter, and how it is used; and
> - Some minerals are more critical in more applications than others, or have a shorter or longer time horizon for adjustment.[13]

Each of these difficulties could be addressed more easily within the context of a national materials policy. For example, adequate knowledge concerning both the long- and short-term requirements for end use by the industrial users of strategic and critical materials could be promoted. The potential impact of new technologies upon future needs for strategic and critical materials could be better analyzed. Improved knowledge concerning processing requirements for utilizing stockpiled materials in an emergency, as well as knowledge concerning distribution problems in getting such materials to where they are most needed in an emergency, could be promoted. Likewise, the implications and extent of economic disruptions due to strategic and critical materials shortages, and the advance identification of potential materials substitutes, could be explored.

Need for a Systems Approach to Materials Management

Many materials-related problems undoubtedly could be alleviated by instituting a systems approach to the management of materials. A systems approach essentially consists of the breaking down of a system of some kind into its component parts, and suboptimizing each component for maximum performance, thereby optimizing the performance of the system as a whole. Although in practice the concept has been applied to physical systems—for example, optimizing the performance of a petrochemical plant or an automobile assembly line—there is no reason in principle why the approach cannot also be applied to nonphysical issues and problems.

A systems approach to the management of materials—and particularly to the management of strategic and critical materials—would seek to bring order to the bewildering maze of economic, political, international, strategic, industrial, and consumer materials-related issues that currently plague decision makers. At present, economic policies are implemented without due regard to their effect upon strategic issues, and international policies without regard to domestic issues, and both without regard to their effects upon materials issues. A systems approach to national materials policy would seek to optimize each relevant policy area consistent with its effects upon related areas while assuring that no particular policy area was optimized at the expense of any other. For example, an optimized materials policy would mesh as consistently as possible with both environmental policy and energy policy. A major difficulty at present is that, lacking an overall systems approach to national policymaking, individual policymakers often attempt to optimize their own policy areas without regard to others. One obvious consequence of this attempt at suboptimization has been the adverse impacts U.S. environmental, economic, and foreign policies frequently have had upon the materials sector.

Lack of Adequate International Materials Relationships

The importance of a U.S. foreign policy sensitive to the need for assuring the continued availability of strategic and critical materials has been emphasized throughout this book. In view of this importance, it could be expected that raw materials issues in general would be a significant factor not only in the development of an overall foreign materials strategy regarding key supplier nations, but also with regard to major U.S. allies.[14]

Certainly it seems reasonable to require that U.S. foreign policy reflect the importance of maintaining the independence and freedom of action of major U.S. supplier nations, as well as the importance of continued U.S.

access to key strategic and critical raw materials, whatever their source. This is not to say that the security of raw materials imports should be the sole aim of U.S. foreign policy, nor even that materials concerns should in all cases or in every circumstance override all other foreign policy considerations. However, it does suggest that such issues as national security, international trade, and cooperation and coordination of materials-related issues with other nations—including both U.S. allies and the various materials-producing nations—should be explicitly considered and given appropriate weight in formulating U.S. foreign policy.

National Security. Perhaps the most pertinent materials-related aspect of national security is the fact that true security is virtually impossible so long as it remains subordinate to foreign control of strategic and critical materials that the United States badly needs but does not have. It sometimes has been suggested that military action, although a drastic and potentially dangerous measure, nonetheless could be effective in assuring the continued supply of particular strategic and critical materials provided that such action were taken promptly enough in an emergency.[15] The obvious difficulty of such an approach, apart from the violence that it does to the underlying principles upon which the nation was founded, is that there can be no guarantee that such military action would necessarily prevail in all key materials-producing areas of the world. Furthermore, the likelihood of achieving a swift and decisive military victory even over relatively small and underdeveloped nations becomes less certain as such nations increasingly become more heavily armed with modern, sophisticated weapons largely supplied by the industrialized nations themselves. In the future these materials-supplying nations may possess tactical nuclear weapons.

More reasonable approaches to achieving national materials security are those discussed at considerable length in Chapter 6. Although a serious and realistic stockpiling program remains the only really effective short-term solution to the national security aspects of industrial raw materials supply, such approaches as conservation, substitution, recycling, and diversification of sources of supply all certainly could contribute to a long-term solution. Additionally, some analysts stress the need for a "new materials security" policy that would enable the nation to respond to an entire range of possible threats to supply rather than simply to the worse-case threats. Such a policy could deal with all possible economic, political, and military effects of supply interruptions and could address both short-term defensive measures and long-term remedial ones. More importantly, it could fix efforts to achieve materials security within the context of general foreign policy goals in Africa and around the world.[16]

Such a materials security policy, in addition to having the elements discussed earlier, could include, first, the encouragement and support of healthy domestic mining, processing, and fabricating industries to enable them to compete successfully both in domestic and international markets. Second, it could address the extent to which the export of strategic and critical raw materials, or of secondary materials containing significant percentages of them, may be harmful to the nation's security. Third, it could help determine the effect upon national security of such politically motivated government actions as "Buy America" clauses in defense-related purchasing, or sanctions against imports of strategic and critical materials from nations whose internal policies the United States disapproves. Fourth, it could include diplomatic initiatives to discourage or prevent military or terrorist activities that would interrupt materials production in producer nations. And lastly, it could make conscious use of the nation's foreign policy as a means for reducing the threat of foreign materials cartels or political blackmail as tools of international materials diplomacy.

International Trade Policy. In many respects, trade problems involving strategic and critical materials are much less soluble through the use of traditional trade policy instruments than are trade problems in general, for at least two reasons. First, the element of choice is missing. Such materials cannot at present be done without; they *must* be imported because of the lack of domestic production and reserves. Supplier nations are acutely aware of this U.S. weakness and may be inclined to take advantage of it. And second, in some respects the United States is its own worst enemy, consistently putting itself at a considerable disadvantage in trade relationships with the rest of the world:

> The U.S. government and business community in many cases continue to operate under the rules developed during a long period of self-sufficiency, although the economy is increasingly dependent on the whims of foreign politicians, suppliers, and manufacturers. In addition, the policies and objectives of business and government are not coordinated and often are unrelated to long-term national interests. What is more, business is increasingly suspicious of big government and its policies and would like to see less government interference and regulation. . . . Needless to say, the rest of the world, keenly competing for new markets, raw materials, and political influence, is quick to take advantage of these institutional weaknesses as it unbelievingly wonders at the naivete of much of the American political leadership.[17]

The federal government is long overdue in giving priority to correcting the adverse effects that many existing trade measures have upon U.S. strategic and critical materials supply. For example, U.S. materials producers—who are in effect the economy's procurement agents—need to be placed on an equal footing with their major world competitors, especially in Europe and Japan. This progressive step may require revision of current U.S. antitrust laws, and most certainly it requires a more enlightened view by the federal government of the realities of global materials competition. It suggests a need for intensive review of the cost effectiveness of current environmental, regulatory, and other policies that render U.S. materials producers less competitive than foreign producers in markets both at home and abroad.

Some mechanisms to assist U.S. firms in meeting foreign competition are already in place, including the U.S. Export-Import Bank, the Overseas Private Investment Corporation, and provisions of the Export Trading

Company Act.[18] However, in the aggregate, U.S. policies affecting international materials trade appear to discriminate against U.S. companies and, worse yet, often work at cross purposes to domestic materials production. For example, U.S. programs intended to promote the availability of low-cost foreign materials supplies (as in the Trade and Development Program, or through International Monetary Fund loans) often are in direct conflict with other programs seeking to maintain production and employment in the domestic mining and processing industries.

It has increasingly become urgent to resolve this conflict between the need to maintain healthy U.S. materials industries and the need to import low-cost materials from abroad. One suggestion is an international producer-consumer organization that would create some form of international network to control supplies of key industrial raw materials, in order to (1) provide a degree of stability in Third World export earnings, (2) reduce the uncertainty regarding future prices, (3) reduce uncertainties in Third World investments by industrialized nations, and (4) assure a steady flow of strategic and critical materials between producers and users.[19] Another suggestion is the establishment of more foreign-based mineral attachés—resource specialists in the regional bureaus of the State Department—who "could help to insure that U.S. resource needs are adequately taken into account in the formulation of day-to-day policy and that issues are flagged for higher level consideration as appropriate."[20] A third suggestion is the creation of a Department of Foreign Trade that could "provide the American businessperson operating in foreign countries much more specialized support in the form of up-to-date political and commercial intelligence and would be in a position better to confront foreign governments, most of which operate through highly specialized foreign trade ministries of their own." Such a department "should not simply promote foreign trade but also [should] analyze potential and real threats to domestic industries as a result of the policies and actions of foreign governments."[21] Although any particular approach is unlikely to provide a complete solution to current U.S. trade problems, clearly a beginning needs to be made somewhere in achieving a more realistic trade policy for strategic and critical materials.

International Cooperation and Coordination. International trade problems serve to emphasize the need for improved cooperation and coordination between the United States and its allies, some of which are also significant exporters of processed materials to the United States. It has been suggested that international markets cooperation and coordination could be enhanced "by establishing a permanent international materials institution to provide for continuity and ready exchange of information." Among the areas of special interest to such an institution would be "materials research and development, manpower, education and training, supply disruption mitigation, stockpiling, and access to resources."[22] Possibly such an institution could be built upon the foundation already provided by such groups as the Organization for Economic Cooperation and Development and the Raw Materials Commission of the Paris Conference on International Economic Cooperation.[23]

During periods of tight materials supply, the major industrialized nations may find themselves in competition for the limited resources that remain available. Although it seems unlikely that any nation would readily agree to sacrifice its trade autonomy in favor of allocating such resources, independent national approaches could result in a weakening of the bonds between the United States and its allies to the detriment of other common interests. The possibility of such a situation arising would be lessened to some extent if more nations would agree to the stockpiling of strategic and critical materials against the chances that materials scarcities may indeed occur.

The Role of the Federal Government

Unlike in such nations as Japan, the concept of economic planning has never been popular in the United States, especially among U.S. industrialists, who typically equate government intervention in the economy with arbitrariness, capricious decision making, excessive rules and regulations resulting in costly waste and inefficiency, and a tendency to convert technical considerations into matters of national concern and prestige. For the materials industries, a common fear is that "Turning concern over materials supplies and prices into affairs of state may worsen the state of affairs."[24]

However, decisions concerning the management of materials have become so complex, both domestically and internationally, that at least some degree of government participation and control appears inescapable. Left to the free marketplace, the frequent cycles in availability and price of raw materials result in serious social costs, including periodic unemployment, increased inflation, and the potential for market manipulation. Yet the consequences of deliberate actions taken by the government could in many instances become irreversible, depriving coming generations of their rights of decision in the future.

This irreversibility of some decision making dictates that government intervention in the marketplace always be carefully considered, and a key element in determining whether government intervention is necessary at all is the potential degree of damage that might result if the government fails to act. Two important caveats of government market activity are that, first, it should be undertaken only with adequate consultation with both the public sector and with private industry, and second, that once a course of action has been determined, private industry should be given as free a hand as possible in implementing that action in the most efficient and cost-effective manner.

The Executive Branch

Not only does the executive branch possess some policymaking responsibilities but, more importantly, it has the primary responsibility for implementing the policy decisions of Congress, as expressed through legislation. Yet the excuse is sometimes made—and in the absence of a continuous policy, with some substance—that presidents come and go over relatively short time periods, must often cope with hostile congresses of the opposite political party, and thus cannot give the executive branch the forceful continuity necessary to achieve consistent long-range success with many issues. However, this excuse fails to recognize that the federal government or bureaucracy itself, including the executive branch, remains remarkably stable over relatively long periods of time, even as the presidents come and go.

Past Activities. Most executive branch activities concerning strategic and critical materials management have focused upon the issue of stockpiling, as summarized earlier. However, the broader subject of general materials availability, as well as the role of the federal government in the management of all kinds of materials, has by no means been ignored. For example, two Hoover commissions addressed the subject following World War II. The first, in 1949, recommended the creation of a Department of Natural Resources, formed in part from the Department of the Interior, on the grounds that the nation had reached a point in its development requiring a new concept in relating its natural resources to the economy. As stated in the commission's report.

> To meet the needs of the future and to promote more orderly development and exploitation of the nation's resources, as well as to guard the heritage of the people, the unification of the responsibilities and services of the government dealing with such matters seems clearly called for.[25]

The second commission, in 1955, concerned itself largely with attempting to evaluate the effectiveness of the various technical advisory boards, committees, panels, and consultants employed by the executive branch to help it manage materials, especially strategic and critical materials for the national stockpile.

The Eisenhower administration, through a special cabinet committee appointed specifically for the purpose, undertook a study of the effect of national policies upon the production and utilization of materials. The study stressed the need for achieving a reasonable balance between domestic materials development and production, on the one hand, and assured access to overseas materials supplies, on the other. Significantly, the committee developed a new approach to strategic and critical materials that merged earlier concepts of strategic reserves with the new concepts of underwriting the market for surplus domestically produced materials and subsidizing new domestic sources of materials on a case-by-case basis.

National materials management was again reviewed under the Kennedy administration, with emphasis upon strategic and critical materials for the national stockpile. As a consequence of this review, the administration concluded that stockpile secrecy had been excessive, that objectives should be simplified, that stockpile holdings were unbalanced and required adjustment, and that stockpile purchases largely aimed at supporting domestic materials producers should be abandoned. At about the same time, a separate policy study called attention to the neglected roles of science and technology in the development of new, exotic materials and substitute materials, as well as in the conservation of materials. This study also pointed out the need for a balanced national materials policy, designed and orchestrated at a high level in government.[26]

Recent Activities. Two more recent attempts have been made to define and clarify the role of the executive branch in materials management. Both attempts were characterized by their broad scope in reaching virtually all major federal agencies and departments, by their extensive investment in both time and money, and by their relative failures to shed any significant light on the subject.

The domestic policy review of nonfuel minerals, a major review of executive branch materials activities, was the first such effort conducted under the Domestic Policy Review System instituted by the Carter administration to provide for full federal agency participation in developing administration positions on selected policy issues. The review was the administration's response to congressional concerns over U.S. vulnerability to potential supply interruptions of key strategic and critical raw materials, the declining health of the basic materials industries along with the effects of this decline on local and regional economies, and the rapid depletion of high-grade domestic ores. The review was launched in December 1977, and the advantage claimed for it over previous such studies was that the final product was legally and administratively intended directly for the president. Moreover, not only was the review requested by and being conducted directly for the president, but it was making use of a newly instituted administrative system—again the Domestic Policy Review System—that was specifically designed to insure that, where appropriate, presidential decisions would be forthcoming.[27]

The review examined the extent and seriousness of materials-related problems in nine specific areas, with a lead agency being assigned primary responsibility in each area, as follows:

- Major minerals supply problems (Minerals Review Committee);
- Availability of foreign minerals to the United States and its allies (State Department);
- Interrelationship of environmental quality, health and safety, and the price and availability of minerals (Environmental Protection Agency);
- Minerals resource potential of federal lands (Department of the Interior);
- Financing, capital formation, and tax policies (Treasury Department);
- Recycling, conservation, and substitution of materials (Department of Commerce);
- Competitiveness of U.S. minerals industries (Department of the Interior);
- Adequacy of minerals-related research and development (National Science Foundation); and
- Adequacy of existing government capabilities to support federal policy-making (Department of the Interior).

Twelve specific materials—aluminum, asbestos, chromium, cobalt, copper, iron ore and scrap, lead, manganese, nickel, phosphate, silver, and zinc—were reviewed from three perspectives: first, that minerals have particular characteristics that must be examined on a commodity-by-commodity basis; second, that certain materials issues are generic and cut across particular materials or groups of materials; and third, that issues relating to materials availability are international in scope.

From its initiation to the completion of a "phase one" report, the exercise took twenty-one months and involved approximately 13,000 days of cumulative individual work input at a cost of about $3.5 million.[28] Although four of the most strategic and critical materials were included—aluminum, chromium, cobalt, and manganese—several others were not, most notably columbium, tantalum, and the platinum-group metals. After the initial phase of problem analysis for the study had been completed, the second stage, policy analysis, seemed to fall apart. Despite the enormous scope of the first phase, little of real substance resulted from the study.

On 5 April 1982 the Reagan administration issued a National Materials and Minerals Program Plan and Report to Congress. The document, which quickly became known as the "Reagan Plan," had been due about six months earlier under requirements of the National Materials and Minerals Policy, Research and Development Act of 1980.[29] This act defined what Congress meant by "materials," declared what should be the nation's basic policy with regard to the management of materials, specified the essential elements to be observed in implementing this policy, and directed the executive branch to prepare a national materials program plan. The act assigned explicit responsibilities for certain aspects of materials management to the Departments of Commerce, Defense, and the Interior, but specified that the overall responsibility for "policy analysis and decision determination" regarding materials should be located within the executive office of the president.[30]

The report represented itself as the most significant presidential initiative for materials over the past thirty years and as signifying the administration's "serious concern and commitment" to reducing the nation's materials import dependency and restoring the health of the U.S. mining industry.[31] Although the report was indeed responsive to the requirements of the 1980 act in some respects, it fell far short in other critical respects. For example, it failed to address such issues as the nation's future needs for scientific and technical engineering manpower, shortcomings in current strategic and critical materials research and development, long-term materials needs assessments, and the need for an early warning system for materials—all of which were required by various provisions of the act. A disturbing feature of the report was that it appeared more designed to serve as a vehicle for promoting certain administration policies—including accelerated exploitation of materials on public lands, decreased environmental protection, and increased build-up of the nation's defense establishment—than a legitimate response to the act. However, perhaps a more serious flaw was the placement by the administration of materials policymaking and coordination within the Cabinet Council on Natural Resources and the Environment, under the direction of the secretary of the interior, rather than in the executive office of the president, as explicitly called for by the act.

Another flaw in the report was its inconsistency in attempting to deal with the nation's vulnerability to imports of strategic and critical materials. Although it clearly supported the need for improvements in national defense, and indeed stated that the administration would "rely primarily on the strategic stockpile as the primary means of providing for national defense objectives,"[32] it then proposed appropriations for the stockpile that were miniscule in comparison with actual needs.

Current Status. Although the prospect at present that the federal government will deal substantively with materials-related problems is not especially bright, neither is it as gloomy as it historically has been. No fewer than six administrations prior to the Reagan administration had attempted to deal to some extent with such problems, and none had achieved any substantive results. To its credit, the Reagan administration very early recognized the need to deal with these kinds of problems and, indeed, included a task force on its "transition team" to consider minerals and materials issues. Additionally, one of the administration's first initiatives was to appoint a Task Force for Regulatory Reform, headed by the vice president. And although its response to the 1980 Materials Policy Act fell short of expectations, nonetheless it is probably fair to say that the response did indeed represent the most detailed attention given the subject by any president over the past three decades. Likewise, the creation of an Office of Strategic Resources within the Department of Commerce, as well as derivative groups in other federal departments and agencies, at least gives an indication of positive ongoing activity.[33] Recent evidence of this continuing activity was the creation of a National Strategic Materials and Minerals Program Advisory Committee within the Department of the Interior to provide advice on both peacetime and defense mobilization responsibilities for strategic and critical materials.[34]

The Legislative Branch

In several important respects the legislative branch appears an unlikely body to assume a leading role in developing a unified national policy for materials. Unlike the executive branch, which theoretically is subject to the control of a single individual, Congress is composed of two autonomous but interdependent houses, each with representatives of two or more political parties. The 535 members of Congress all serve different constituencies. Furthermore, the large number of committees and subcommittees that carry out much of the major legislative work of Congress, with their inevitably overlapping jurisdictions when faced with complex materials issues, makes unified and coherent congressional action difficult to initiate or sustain.[35] Working to more advantage is the continuity achieved through senior members who may have twenty to thirty or more years of experience, committee staffs of equal length of service, and the long-range legislative "memory" provided by congressional support agencies.

Until the early 1970s, the legislative branch essentially relied upon the executive branch to take the lead in dealing with materials-related problems, so that congressional concern over strategic and critical materials largely mirrored that of the executive branch. However, it became increasingly evident to some members of Congress that the executive branch was negligent in its stewardship of materials management and, consequently, the leadership role gradually shifted to the legislative branch, where it remains. At present, Congress continues to push its initiatives for a national materials policy and the executive branch continues to resist, grudgingly giving way as little as possible and only when forced to do so. Although the major materials concerns of the legislative branch remain focused upon strategic and critical materials, Congress has been much more open than the executive branch to broadening its interests to include a wide spectrum of materials-related issues and problems.

Past Activities. Apart from congressional attention to the stockpiling of strategic and critical materials, broader congressional interest in materials dates at least as far back as the Malone hearings of 1947, which included detailed reports on the availability of selected materials, a review of the historical perspective of materials policy issues, and concern for the future outlook for materials. These hearings made clear that the nation could no longer afford to continue the de facto policy of simply letting nature take its course, but required a continued and authoritative appraisal of its natural resources if it was to look ahead and plan wisely for its future materials needs.[36]

Most major legislation has dealt specifically with strategic and critical materials stockpiling, as discussed earlier in this book.[37] However, much major legislation also has been enacted to address other areas of materials management. For example, the Resource Recovery Act of 1970[38] represented a dramatic shift in congressional concern from the disposal of materials as waste (the focus of the earlier Solid Waste Disposal Act) to the recovery and reuse of materials as part of an overall cycle of materials use. The act attempted to shift attention from waste disposal to the need to develop new technologies for reclaiming and recycling valuable materials from waste, and for conversion of waste materials to energy whenever more economically feasible than recycling.

The Mining and Minerals Policy Act of 1970[39] was another landmark congressional initiative, which dramatized such problems as the rapid depletion of high-grade domestic materials reserves; the increasing cost of producing materials from lower grade domestic ores in competition with foreign producers using relatively abundant, easily accessible, high-grade ores; shortages of highly trained mining and minerals scientists and engineers; and the lack of any consistent, long-range planning objectives on the part of the domestic materials-producing industries. Although the act reaffirmed that the responsibility for domestic mining and mineral activities lay within the private sector, it directed the Department of the Interior to monitor those activities carefully and to suggest any legislative initiatives that might prove necessary to complement them.

Recent Activities. One of the more outstanding examples of congressional leadership in attempting to develop a national policy for materials management was the National Materials and Minerals Policy, Research and Development Act of 1980, enacted despite continued resistance and opposition on the part of the executive branch that stopped just short of presidential veto. It was the first legislation to address directly the perceived need for a national materials policy and to attempt to define the role of the federal government toward that policy. The major purpose of the act was "to promote an adequate and stable supply of materials necessary to maintain national security, economic well-being, and industrial production with appropriate attention to achieving a long-term balance between energy needs, a healthy environment, natural resources conservation, and social needs."[40]

Subsequently, in reacting to perceived inadequacies in the administration of this act, Congress passed the National Critical Materials Act of 1984. This follow-up legislation established a mechanism for dealing with materials-related problems within the context of an overall national materials policy, by creating a National Critical Materials Council located under and reporting to the executive office of the president. The three members of the council, appointed by the president, require confirmation by the Senate. The legislation specifically requires the council to address a number of substantive issues and programs called for in the 1980 act but not addressed by the Reagan Plan. The major responsibility of the council is to assist and advise the president in establishing coherent national materials policies consistent with other federal policies, and in carrying out those activities necessary to implement such policies. Not only is the council to assist in establishing coordinating responsibilities for materials-related programs and research and technology activities, but it is to have the authority to review and appraise such programs and activities to oversee federal materials research and development policies and programs. However, as of this writing (April 1985, nine months after passage of the act), the president has yet to make any appointments to the council.

Congressional Support Agencies. By comparison with the enormous resources of the executive branch's many departments, bureaus, and agencies, the legislative branch has few support arms or agencies. This great disparity, however, has not proved a handicap to Congress in dealing with materials-related problems. As evident from earlier discussion, the sheer size and complexity of the executive branch has made extremely difficult, if not indeed impossible, agreement on any overall policy for materials management. The legislative branch has concentrated its much smaller resources for policy analysis into just four major support agencies, each with a different central focus.

The first of these agencies is the Congressional Research Service, located within the Library of Congress since about 1914, and the first agency created to assist Congress in considering a wide variety of problems. Initially it was known as the Legislative Reference Service. From the mid-1960s onward, the agency has been instrumental in providing much of the information and analysis upon which materials-related hearings and legislation have been based.

The second major agency, the General Accounting Office, was established in 1921 originally to assist Congress in carrying out its legislative and oversight responsibilities, especially with regard to legal, accounting, and claims settlement functions involved with federal programs and operations. However, over time the responsibilities of the office have been enlarged to include the conduct of studies and investigations on a wide range of subjects of congressional interest, including policy analysis for congressional committees. Such policy analyses have, since about the mid-1970s, also included the federal role in materials management and, increasingly, the issue of strategic and critical materials import dependency.

The third congressional support agency, the Office of Technology Assessment, was created by Congress in 1972 to help legislators anticipate and plan for the consequences of the widespread use of technology— especially its impacts, both beneficial and adverse, with its increasingly wide deployment in society. However, this originally envisioned role quickly became subordinated to the desire on the part of committee chairmen for major policy analysis studies of interest to their committees. Such studies, carried out under contract to private research organizations, typically are much larger in scope than those conducted by the other congressional support agencies and are conducted over a much more extended period of time.

The fourth agency, the Congressional Budget Office, was created in 1974 to provide Congress with basic budget data and analyses of alternative fiscal, budgetary, and programmatic policy issues, to enable it to achieve a legislative overview of the federal budget, including decision making regarding spending and taxing levels and the deficit or surplus such levels incur. Thus, the office helps Congress to weigh the priorities for national resource allocation and explicitly address issues of fiscal policy.

The Role of the Private Sector

It is clear that the federal government cannot assume sole responsibility for the development of a national policy for materials, nor should it. Since the management of strategic and critical materials poses potentially grave consequences for all industries and all citizens, responsibility likewise should be shared by all. Indeed, failure to make more significant progress in the management of strategic and critical materials may reflect the lack of strong grass-roots support from the private sector. It is probably safe to say that such support has been lacking not primarily because of opposition to the concept, but more because of inertia, apathy, and misinformation or ignorance. Yet if necessary government action is to take place to improve the nation's management of materials—and especially to reduce vulnerability to imports of strategic and critical materials—the private sector should greatly enlarge its role in the process.

The private or nongovernment sector typically is defined as consisting of four separate components: the general public, private industry, the professional community, and academe. Although useful, this definition is somewhat artificial in that the four components so greatly overlap; policy-making is done by individuals, whether alone or in concert, and individuals typically belong simultaneously to more than one component of the private sector. For example, a single individual may "wear three hats": one as a private citizen (the general public), one as a company president or official (private industry), and one as a member or officer of a technical or engineering society (the professional community). Although presumably the individual's personal views remain reasonably consistent regardless of which of the three hats is worn at any given moment, the point is that each hat gives its wearer a different platform from which to express these views—opportunities that should be exploited as fully as possible, even though the message may be the same.

The General Public

Although frequently neglected as a tool available to every citizen for influencing public policy, lobbying—both direct and indirect—can be as effective politically as voting, participating in local political organizations, or running for public office. The key is participation, which "is essential if ours is to be a government 'of the people, by the people, and for the people'—and not 'to the people, without the people, and despite the people.'"[41] Changes in government policy frequently reflect corresponding changes in the attitudes of citizens as made evident through lobbying.

Direct Lobbying. The most common form of individual citizen participation to influence public policy is by direct lobbying with elected representatives through letters, telegrams, or personal visits to congressional offices to talk directly with representatives, senators, and their staffs. To the extent that the concerns of Congress mirror those of the nation as a whole, such lobbying is indispensable to members in helping them determine the nature and extent of public views.

Unfortunately, the typical citizen acting alone is rarely an effective lobbyist. Too frequently an individual has failed to research an issue to raise it much above the purely emotional level. Although a legislator may sympathize with such emotional concern, congressional voting is more often than not a response to facts, logic, and carefully reasoned opinions rather than emotional arguments. Hence it is crucial for the citizen lobbyist to research and prepare a case properly in order to be certain that the information provided is accurate, complete, and effectively presented.

Effective preparation becomes even more important when one realizes that lobbying one's representative or senator is essentially the only direct input the individual has to the legislative process. An individual may attend congressional hearings, markup sessions, and floor debates, but only as a spectator who cannot speak. It may be possible to wrangle an appointment with a committee staffer, but in general such staff members are much too busy to meet with individuals representing only themselves. This situation must not be confused with meeting with a legislator's personal staff, who are normally readily accessible. However, it is the committee staff that normally exerts much more influence upon the legislative process than does the member's private staff, many of whom spend inordinate amounts of time dealing with constituents' nonlegislative needs.

Likewise, the individual citizen's opportunities to lobby the executive branch are very limited. He or she is highly unlikely to be successful in obtaining an interview with any high-level executive or, even in that event, to influence bureaucratic policies. A planned public hearing may be the only way, but the individual does not select the issues to be heard.

Group Participation. Because of the difficulties noted above, group participation in lobbying activities is essential in addition to private, individual efforts. By joining an existing organization or forming a new one, the individual will have an influence that is greatly multiplied. A strong grass-roots organization that is large, well organized, passionately dedicated to its cause, and focused on a single issue can be extremely effective in lobbying Congress, especially if it expands and becomes national in scope. It not only can lobby members of Congress directly, but also can be effective in enlisting the mass media—radio, television, and the press—to help keep an issue alive and in full public view. Equally important, its leaders frequently can exert influence at key points of the legislative process that are essentially closed to private individuals. For example, they can serve as witnesses at congressional hearings or may help committee staff in drafting legislation. In these respects, the private individual can achieve through collective group participation a measure of equality with the many industry and professional lobbying groups that exert considerable influence within Congress.

However, the key element in achieving such equality is active participation. Most private individuals participate passively, limiting their activity to contributing money. Although the importance of funding for such groups is unquestioned, money alone is surprisingly ineffective in influencing legislation. The "big stick" in legislative politics remains the head count, or sheer overwhelming number of active people vigorously and vocally supporting a particular issue being considered by Congress. Furthermore, successful lobbying of a legislator can exert a multiplier effect, as no one is better at lobbying a member of Congress than a fellow member.

Indirect Lobbying. Often overlooked by individuals is the impact that their actions in unilaterally instituting a policy ultimately may have upon achieving results at the national level. Many of the approaches discussed earlier in this book for reducing U.S. materials import vulnerability can be undertaken by individuals without waiting for development of a federal policy for materials. Admittedly the scope of such individual actions would be greatly enhanced if greater leadership were exhibited by federal officials, especially the president. However, it is not unusual for spontaneous grass-roots activity to promote action at the national level, which in turn can promote more grass-roots activity and public support. These materials initiatives can be undertaken either by private industry or by the general public. Those that might be pursued by the latter, possibly sponsored by nonprofit public groups, include discouraging wanton buying of unneeded products, emphasizing the long-term economy of buying well-made products that will provide extended useful service, eliminating the purchase of "throwaway" products, encouraging the purchase of products made from renewable or plentiful materials, and returning to service products that could be of use to others but that currently are abandoned in attics and basements.

A basic principle of wise materials use is materials conservation, and a basic principle of materials conservation is to be well informed. Unless one knows at least a rudimentary amount about the nature of materials and how this nature affects their performance and use, it is difficult to make wise materials choices. But it is not difficult to see that wise materials choices are *not* being made, and pressures ultimately could be brought against both industry and government on that account.

Private Industry

The individual and aggregated actions of the private industrial sector, as well as internal industry policies, represent an essential ingredient of a national policy for materials. Consequently, it is important that officers and other company officials effectively convey company views on legislation to members of Congress, who are inclined to give considerable weight to such views. Committee staff are also generally quite receptive to the views of company officials, who often are invited to testify at committee hearings. Such officials may present their own personal views or the views of their company, depending upon the specific agreement or arrangement. Whichever the case, such views typically carry considerably greater weight that those of an individual lacking any such industrial affiliation. Hearings testimony is extremely valuable as it provides an effective forum that has few parallels in Washington.

Industry leaders increasingly have come to appreciate the need for anticipating and helping to formulate national policymaking for materials, rather than reacting too late. A number of industry leaders learned an important and painful lesson in 1974 when widespread, ongoing shortages of many materials affected company productivity and profitability and in some instances threatened the very operations of certain companies. The lesson was twofold: first, that materials-related events in Washington cannot be ignored and, second, that more sophisticated management of materials has become a prime necessity.

Sophisticated Materials Management. One result of the 1974 materials shortages is that industry leaders know it is no longer sufficient for a company to limit its concern over raw and processed materials feedstocks simply to maintaining a normally adequate inventory from a preferred supplier. Prudent management, especially when dealing with strategic and critical materials, now demands more extended considerations such as the reliability of the primary supplier, its potential vulnerability to supply disruptions, other viable sources of supply, and potential substitute materials. Hence, it has become common for a company to develop a materials strategy as part of an overall strategic or contingency planning process that may include some variety of risk analysis or risk management.[42] Elements typical of such planning include the following:

- Economic and availability trends for major production materials, and the general conditions that might be expected to affect the supply of materials for the remainder of the twentieth century;

- Identification of critical problem areas in materials for future requirements;

- Elements of a design and supply strategy to minimize future materials availability risks, and contingency plans to adapt to changing supply situations;

- Research and development needs for new or substitute materials, and the potential for enhancing materials availability through recycling of scrap materials;

- Industrial facilities and capability needs with respect to future requirements and demand/supply balance; and

- Development of new manufacturing methods to minimize the waste of materials.[43]

Role of Industry Trade Associations. Efforts to promote industry views at the national level are considerably enhanced by the activities of numerous trade organizations and associations financially supported by particular industries. These organizations enhance the effectiveness of private companies through their group efforts, in much the same way that organized groups of individuals enhance the effectiveness of their members. A primary role of such organizations is to lobby Congress and federal departments and regulatory agencies, taking advantage of all the available inputs previously discussed.

A trade association is usually formed as a "nonprofit, cooperative, voluntarily joined organization of business competitors designed to assist its members and its industry in dealing with mutual business problems in several of the following areas: accounting practice, business ethics, commercial and industrial research, standardization, statistics, trade promotion, and relations with government, employees, and the general public."[44] Its ultimate goal is to increase income to its members from the products they make or the services they provide. In addition to promoting the views of its members through concerted action at the national level, it also helps solve other problems that they could not solve acting alone. Different such associations promote research on new products, new uses for by-products, and improved methods of manufacturing; develop market statistics; sponsor quality and certification standards and parts interchangeability; publish pamphlets, year-books, and articles about their industry; and compile statistics on all aspects of their industry. Importantly, these organizations thus represent a primary source of the vital statistics on their industry, as well as a source of information concerning the status of industry science and technology. Currently, such organizations have annual budgets that range from $25,000 to more than $5 million per organization, collectively employ from 500 to 600 people, and together represent about 25,000 separate companies.

Inputs to the Regulatory Process. As discussed earlier, some of the most difficult materials-related problems faced by private industry are those concerned with federal, state, and local rules and regulations. Much of the difficulty arises because of the surprising ignorance of many company officials about how regulations that affect their companies are proposed and developed. Often they miss entirely the available opportunities to participate in the process, and their protests afterwards tend to be relatively ineffective.

Briefly, upon enactment of a statute—whether related to the environment, transportation, energy, consumer product safety, or occupational health and safety—a specific agency is given the executive responsibility for implementing the law within some definite time frame, by developing effective regulation based upon, and responsive to, the policy mandated by the statute.[45] Often such development will require detailed technical knowledge of the processes and mode of operation of the industry being affected by the regulation. Either because of requirements set out in the original statute, or subsequently set by the Office of Management and Budget, cost and impact analyses will generally be required to make possible early public judgment of the cost/benefit effectiveness of the regulation and its underlying statute. After a reasonable period of time for public comment, the agency will consider this comment and may adjust the contents of the regulation accordingly.

Professional groups—whether representing themselves, their companies, or their trade associations or organizations—have essentially two major opportunities to provide helpful technical input to this regulatory process. The first stage is during the initial attempts to draft a suitable regulation, when extensive technical input is required. The second stage is during the public reaction phase when the proposed regulation is open for public comment. The first stage is preferable not only because it represents a period when technical inputs may be more helpful and persuasive, but also because it permits in-person inputs not possible during the second, open comment period. Needless to say, even more preferable are technical inputs at the time the original legislation is being drafted.

Current Status. Just as individuals must take the initiative in pursuing effective policies to curb unnecessary consumption and to more effectively utilize and conserve materials, so must private industry. Industry has been otherwise motivated historically, and yet it has done much to help improve its position with regard to strategic and critical materials. Many companies have adopted some form of materials risk analysis or risk management program for strategic materials planning. Such initiatives, and those concerning materials research and development discussed earlier, demonstrate that private industry is coming to recognize that it cannot delay addressing its own materials problems. But because few industry materials problems can really be isolated from national materials problems, it remains in the best long-term interests of industry to take a second and longer look at its distrust of government involvement and promote efforts at the national level to achieve an overall policy for materials management.

The Professional Materials Community

The professional materials community consists largely of various professional societies and scientific and technical organizations that have a direct or peripheral interest in materials. A very large majority of professional scientists and engineers, whether employed by industry, government, academe, or self-employed, are members of such organizations. Additionally, temporary commissions have been created from time to time to examine various materials problem areas. Such commissions have been staffed principally by professionals hired for the purpose or borrowed from industry, government, or academe.

Professional Societies. Many professional societies concerned with various aspects of materials properties, technology, availability, and use have contributed their expertise in various areas of national materials policy. Such contributions have included organization of symposia, workshops, and seminars; preparation of policy statements and position papers on various issues; testimony before congressional committees at hearings; and technical inputs to Congress. However, since its organization on 12 June 1972, the Federation of Materials Societies—consisting of thirteen professional member societies and one society with observer status, and representing about 750,000 professional scientists and engineers—has become the primary group to speak for the professional materials community on the subject of national materials policy.[46] The primary goals and activities of the FMS are grouped into three broad categories:

- To identify major materials activities of national and international scope and to summarize these activities;

- To identify opportunities for useful input to selected major national and international materials studies, and respond to such opportunities; and

- To define aspects of broad materials issues that need further attention, then promote additional study or dissemination of information as needed.[47]

The FMS has provided a mechanism for a continuing dialogue on national materials policy between the materials community and the federal government.

Both collective input from the materials community to the legislative and administrative policymaking process and feedback from the government to the materials community are parts of this process.

Scientific and Technical Organizations. Perhaps the most prestigious scientific and technical organization to become deeply involved in national materials policy issues is the National Academy of Sciences/National Academy of Engineering. Largely through the activities of its National Materials Advisory Board, the NAS/NAE has undertaken a number of important studies and has organized high-level materials-related conferences and symposia.

Commissions. Although not a formal part of the professional materials community, the various commissions that have been created from time to time have been staffed mainly by professionals with materials expertise. In addition to the two Hoover commissions already discussed, three major study commissions were created during the period from 1951 to 1976, one presidential and two congressional, to look into the possible need for better management and utilization of the nation's materials resources.

The President's Materials Policy Commission was created on 22 January 1951 by executive order of President Harry S. Truman and was administratively located within the executive office of the president. As noted in the president's letter to William S. Paley, chairman of the commission, the primary purpose of the commission was "to study the broader and longer range aspects of the nation's materials problem as distinct from the immediate defense needs, . . . to make an objective inquiry into all major aspects of the problem of assuring an adequate supply of production materials for our long-range needs, and to make recommendations which will assist me in formulating a comprehensive policy on such materials."[48] For its study, the president directed the commission to look into five major areas of interest: the long-range requirements outlook; the long-range supply outlook; the prospect and estimated extent of shortages; the consistency and adequacy of existing government policies, plans, and programs; and the consistency and adequacy of private industry practices.

The commission also considered the issue of the nation's growing reliance upon materials imports from abroad. It rejected the notion of materials self-sufficiency, even for reasons of national security, as "fallacious and dangerous," arguing instead in favor of the "least cost principle," that is, that "national materials policy should be squarely founded on the principle of buying at the least cost possible for equivalent values."[49] In so recommending, however, the commission recognized the strategic concerns of materials import dependency by also recommending the stockpiling of those specific strategic and critical materials without which an economically viable domestic industry could not be sustained.

The commission was especially impressed with the rate at which U.S. materials resources were being consumed and with how demands of new technology were enlarging the list of essential and therefore vulnerable imports. Accordingly, the commission made four more major recommendations: that materials supply and demand statistics be carefully maintained and watched closely; that resource conservation and development be encouraged, with emphasis placed upon new materials technology for substitute materials; that a nongovernmental institution be established to monitor the state of materials supply and demand; and that a new governmental institution be established located close to the president, for the purpose of formulating and directing national materials policy. The last of these recommendations was one of the earliest and most explicit acknowledgments of the need for a national policy for materials. As stated by the commission:

> There must be, somewhere, a mechanism for looking at the problem as a whole, for keeping track of changing situations and the interrelation of policies and programs. This task must be performed by a federal agency near the top of the administrative structure. . . . Such an agency, at the level of the Executive Office of the President, should review all areas of the materials field and determine how they can be best related to each other. It should maintain, on a continuing basis, the kind of forward audit which has been this commission's one-time function, but more detailed than has been possible here; collect and collate the facts and analyses of various agencies; and recommend appropriate action for the guidance of the President, the Congress, and the Executive agencies.[50]

The National Commission on Materials Policy, created on 26 October 1970 by the National Materials Policy Act of 1970, was intended to determine how "to enhance environmental quality and conserve materials by developing a national materials policy to utilize present resources and technology more efficiently, to anticipate the future materials requirements of the nation and the world, and to make recommendations on the supply, use, recovery, and disposal of materials."[51] On 27 June 1973 the commission transmitted to the president and to Congress its final report, *Materials Needs and the Environment Today and Tomorrow.* The major thrust of the report concerned eliciting ways in which the nation's current and future materials needs could be met while maintaining, or even improving where necessary, environmental quality. Indeed, one of the most noteworthy aspects of this study was that it introduced for the first time in formal materials policy literature the concept of the interconnectedness of materials, energy, and environment, a relationship that was to become more salient in future years.

In addressing U.S. materials import dependency, the commission took note of the fact that "the United States continues to be more autonomous than any major industrial country except the Soviet Union" and that the nation imported most materials not because of a lack of domestic resources, but because of "their availability at a price lower than domestic supplies." In essentially reaffirming the "least cost principle" of the Paley commission, the report stated that "Where the United States has had a choice of producing or importing certain materials, price has usually determined the mix" and "Pursuit of a policy of self-sufficiency is not possible in materials for which the United States lacks a resource base or for which no substitutes are available or economically feasible." In predicting that international competition for materials would grow both in variety and intensity, the commission concluded that national security considerations made it unwise to become dependent upon those specific strategic commodities for which no domestic resource base exists and which were obtained mainly from a small number of countries that might choose to restrict or cut off the flow of supply. Rather, the commission stated that national security interests would be best served by maintaining access to a reasonable number of diverse suppliers for as many materials as possible.[52]

To reduce materials import dependency, the commission then recommended that the United States attempt to foster the expansion of domestic production, diversify sources of supply, develop special relations with more reliable sources, find substitutes or develop synthetics, increase the dependence of supplying countries upon continuing U.S. goodwill, and allocate existing supplies through a priority use system.

The National Commission on Supplies and Shortages was created on 30 September 1974 to "facilitate more effective and informed responses to resources and commodity shortages and to report to the President and the Congress on needed institutional adjustments for examining and predicting shortages and on the existence or possibility of shortages with respect to essential resources and commodities."[53]

The establishment of the commission corresponded with the severe and at times widespread shortages of a variety of materials in 1973–1974 resulting from the oil embargo of 1973. U.S. import dependency was suddenly not only for petroleum but also for a wide variety of other materials.

As with the two previous commissions, this new commission in its final report, Government and the Nation's Resources, supported the concept of global interdependency. In noting that the United States imports many nonfuel materials because it and its citizens derive economic advantages from doing so—namely lower costs and higher real incomes—the report concluded that it would make no economic sense to forgo these advantages unless there were compelling national reasons for doing so. In other words, the commission held that import dependency was not a problem as such and that it was misleading to cite a U.S. "deficit" in the materials trade "as though this represented in some sense a national loss."[54]

The commission rejected materials cartel formation as a threat to growing U.S. import dependency but noted that military conflict, local wars, or civil disorders did pose significant prospects for supply disruptions and that strategic materials stockpiles represented what it termed a universal antidote to such risks. It therefore recommended that, first, if the existing defense stockpile were to be enlarged as proposed by the Ford administration, it should also be used for economic purposes. And second, that if the planned stockpile enlargement did not take place, then a completely separate stockpile should be created for purely economic purposes. Significantly, any such economic stockpile could also have served as an additional trade-off against the inherent risks of increased materials import dependency.

Conferences. Like commissions, professional conferences are not a formal aspect of the professional materials community. However, they do occur regularly and, indeed, the number of materials-related conferences that takes place each year is staggering. Unquestionably the most influential of these conferences has been the biennial series of National Materials Policy Conferences initiated in 1970, organized under the auspices of the Engineering Foundation and held at New England College, Henniker, New Hampshire. Beginning with the third conference in 1974, the series was also supported by the newly established Federation of Materials Societies, which assumed full responsibility for the series beginning with the seventh conference in 1982. Although each of the eight conferences held thus far has focused upon a particular materials policy area, each also has given specific attention to the continuing problem of strategic and critical materials import dependency.[55]

Academe

Members of the academic community play an important and often decisive role in the activities of the professional materials community. They derive considerable professional prestige from their association with their institutions, particularly those institutions that are well known and respected as centers of excellence. An important element of this association is a presumed objectivity and lack of bias with regard to controversial issues in that, unlike government or private industry, academicians theoretically have no personal axe to grind with respect to materials policy issues. Consequently, their views frequently are sought by both industry and government, and leaders of the academic community often are asked to testify at hearings before congressional committees.

Two major problems, however, beset the academic community. The first is that academicians are not entirely free from bias despite their academic credentials and reputation for scientific objectivity. Indeed, existence of bias is probably part of the human condition. Its existence is probably less important than its identification and characterization, but unfortunately, determining the biases of an academician who also may not have a clear picture of them can be very difficult.

The second problem has to do with the tendency of many academicians to seek perfect solutions in an obviously imperfect world. This "ivory tower" syndrome involves an excessive dedication to theory to the neglect of reality. Academicians are especially prone to exhibiting impatience with politicians, and vice versa, over the need for compromise on public issues. Often it is not difficult to see what course of action is best, and hence the academician may be opposed to any other course, which by definition is bound to be inferior. But most often the best course of action is impossible to achieve, and compromise is necessary. It is here that the politician recognizes the practical need to obtain the best result possible under the existing circumstances, rather than the best possible result.

Notes

1. U.S. Congress, House Committee on Science and Technology, Subcommittee on Science, Research, and Technology, *Materials Policy Handbook: Legislative Issues of Materials Research and Technology* (Washington, D.C.: U.S. Government Printing Office, June 1977), p. 3. Much of this chapter borrows heavily from this *Handbook*.

2. The Environmental Protection Agency was established as an independent agency within the executive branch pursuant to Reorganization Plan No. 3 of 1970, effective 2 December 1970. The Department of Energy was established by the Department of Energy Organization Act, approved 4 August 1977 and effective 1 October 1977, pursuant to Executive Order 12009 of 13 September 1977.

3. See the remarks of Stanley A. Margolin in "Minerals Supply Called Major Crisis of 1980s." *Chemical and Engineering News*, 26 April 1982, p. 5.

4. U.S. Congress, *Materials Policy Handbook*, pp. 5, 25.

5. *What Next for U.S. Minerals Policy?* (Washington, D.C.: Resources for the Future, October 1982), p. 3.

6. National Materials Advisory Board, *Assessment of Selected Materials Issues*, Report No. NMAB-381 (Washington, D.C.: National Academy of Sciences, September 1981), p. 5.

7. Advisory Committee on National Growth Policy Processes, *Forging America's Future: Strategies for National Growth and Development* (Washington, D.C.: U.S. Government Printing Office, 1976), p. 7.

8. See, for example, the following reports from the U.S. Government Printing Office: National Commission on Materials Policy, *Materials Needs and the Environment Today and Tomorrow* (June 1973); Office of Technology Assessment, *Requirements for Fulfilling a National Materials Policy* (1975) and *An Assessment of Information Systems Capabilities Required to Support U.S. Materials Policy Decisions* (December 1976); and National Commission on Supplies and Shortages, *Government and the Nation's Resources* (1976).

9. U.S. Congress, *Materials Policy Handbook*, p. 56.

10. National Commission on Supplies and Shortages, *Government and the Nation's Resources*, p. 79.

11. See the remarks of E. F. Andrews in "Critical Materials: How Big Is the Problem?" *Mechanical Engineering*, June 1981, p. 53.

12. Amos A. Jordan and Robert A. Kilmarx, *Strategic Mineral Dependence* (Beverly Hills, Calif.: Sage Publications, 1979), p. 53.

13. Hans H. Landsberg, "Key Elements Common to Critical Issues in Engineering Materials and Minerals." *Materials and Society* 7:1 (1983), p. 107.

14. For an analysis of materials-related aspects of foreign policy, see *American Foreign Economic Strategy for the Eighties* (Washington, D.C.: International Economic Policy Association, 1981), 62 pp.

15. Bohdan Szuprowicz, *How to Avoid Strategic Materials Shortages* (New York: John Wiley and Sons, 1981), pp. 217–218.

16. Michael Shafer, "Mineral Myths." *Foreign Policy*, Summer 1982, p. 163.

17. Szuprowicz, p. 243.

18. The Export Trading Company Act of 1982 (Public Law 97–290, enacted 8 October 1982).

19. Shafer, p. 169.

20. Timothy W. Stanley, *A National Risk Management Approach to American Raw Materials Vulnerabilities*, Contemporary Issues Paper No. 5 (Washington, D.C.: International Economic Studies Institute, January 1982), p. 20.

21. Szuprowicz, p. 245.

22. U.S. Congress, House Committee on Science and Technology, *Seventh Biennial Conference on National Materials Policy* (Washington, D.C.: U.S. Government Printing Office, March 1983), p. x.

23. *Critical Materials Requirements of the U.S. Aerospace Industry* (Washington, D.C.: U.S. Department of Commerce, October 1981), p. 257.

24. Hans H. Landsberg, "Materials: Some Recent Trends and Issues." *Science,* 20 February 1976, p. 640.

25. U.S. Congress, *Materials Policy Handbook,* p. 27.

26. W. Y. Elliott, "Materials Availability for the Free World." In *Washington Colloquium on Science and Society,* ed. S. F. Seymour (Baltimore: Mono Book Company, 1967), pp. 54–65.

27. James A. Holt, "The Domestic Policy Review of Nonfuel Minerals." In *Building a Consensus on Legislation for a National Materials Policy,* House Committee on Science and Technology, Subcommittee on Science, Research, and Technology (Washington, D.C.: U.S. Government Printing Office, December 1978), p. 56.

28. *Report on the Issues Identified in the Nonfuel Minerals Policy Review* (Washington, D.C.: U.S. Department of the Interior, August 1979), 42 pp.

29. The National Materials and Minerals Policy, Research and Development Act (Public Law 96-479, enacted 21 October 1980).

30. Ibid., Sec. 5(a)(1)(A).

31. *National Materials and Minerals Program Plan and Report to the Congress,* submitted by President Reagan to Congress on 5 April 1982, p. 2.

32. Ibid., p. 32.

33. See, for example, Office of Strategic Resources, *National Materials and Minerals Program Plan Implementation* (Washington, D.C.: U.S. Department of Commerce, April 1983), 40 pp.

34. News release: *Secretary Clark Names Chairman of National Strategic Materials and Minerals Program Advisory Committee* (Washington, D.C.: U.S. Department of the Interior, 25 April 1984).

35. For the 98th Congress, in session during 1983–1984, the count was as follows: Senate, sixteen standing committees with 103 subcommittees, and four select committees with four subcommittees; House, twenty-two standing committees with 132 subcommittees, and four select committees with seven subcommittees; hence a total, in both houses, of thirty-eight standing committees, eight select committees, and 248 subcommittees. Additionally, there were four joint committees having a total of six subcommittees.

36. U.S. Congress, Senate Committee on Public Lands, *Investigation of National Resources* (Washington, D.C.: U.S. Government Printing Office, 1947), 388 pp. The Malone hearings were chaired by George W. Malone, Nevada.

37. These legislative acts include The Strategic Materials Act of 1939 (P.L. 76-117, enacted 7 June 1939); The Strategic and Critical Materials Stock Piling Act of 1946 (P.L. 79-520, enacted 23 July 1946); The Defense Production Act of 1950 (P.L. 83-480, enacted 8 September 1950); and the Strategic and Critical Materials Stock Piling Revision Act of 1979 (P.L. 96-41, enacted 30 July 1979).

38. The Resource Recovery Act of 1970 (P.L. 91-512, enacted 26 October 1970).

39. The Mining and Minerals Policy Act of 1970 (P.L. 91-631, enacted 31 December 1970).

40. The National Materials and Minerals Policy, Research and Development Act of 1980.

41. Advisory Committee on National Growth Policy Processes, p. 53.

42. See, for example, Lousi J. Sousa, "Strategic Planning in the Minerals and Materials Industries in an International Era." *Materials and Society* 7:1 (1983), pp. 49–50. Additional papers on this subject are given on pages 51–86 of the same issue of *Materials and Society.*

43. J. J. Harwood and R. W. Layman, "Some Industrial Viewpoints on National Materials Policy." *Materials and Society* 7:1 (1983), p. 95. See also S. Victor Radcliffe, "World Changes and Chances: Some New Perspectives for Materials." *Science,* 20 February 1976, p. 704.

44. *National Trade and Professional Associations and Labor Unions of the United States and Canada* (Washington, D.C.: Columbia Books, 1982), p. 5.

45. This summary has been derived from an unpublished essay, "The Technical Professional and the Regulatory Process," by Stanley V. Margolin, Arthur D. Little Company, 1983.

46. The member societies are listed alphabetically here: American Association for Crystal Growth; American Ceramic Society, Inc.; American Chemical Society; American Institute of Chemical Engineers; American Institute of Mining, Metallurgical and Petroleum Engineers, Inc.; American Society of Mechanical Engineers; American Society for Metals; American Society for Testing and Materials; The Electrochemical Society, Inc.; Institute of Electrical and Electronic Engineers, Inc.; National Association of Corrosion Engineers; Society of Manufacturing Engineers; and Society of Plastics Engineers, Inc. The observer society is the Electric Power Research Institute.

47. Robert M. Goldhoff, *The Federation of Materials Societies: Its Role and Activities* (unpublished monograph), p. 3.

48. President's Materials Policy Commission, *Report to the President. Resources for Freedom. Vol. I. Foundations for Growth and Security* (Washington, D.C.: U.S. Government Printing Office, June 1952), p. 4. The commission's report was presented in five volumes and a summary, the remaining titles being II. *The Outlook for Key Commodities,* III. *The Outlook for Energy Sources,* IV. *The Promise of Technology,* V. *Selected Reports to the Commission,* and the summarizing *Resources for Freedom.*

49. President's Materials Policy Commission, *Resources for Freedom,* pp. 21–22.

50. Ibid., pp. 76–77.

51. Sec. 202, *National Materials Policy Act of 1970.*

52. National Commission on Materials Policy, *Materials Needs and the Environment Today and Tomorrow* (Washington, D.C.: U.S. Government Printing Office, June 1973), p. 9-26.

53. Sec. 5, *National Commission on Supplies and Shortages Act of 1974* (P.L. 93–426, *The Defense Production Act Amendments of 1974,* enacted 30 September 1974).

54. National Commission on Supplies and Shortages, *Government and the Nation's Resources,* pp. 30–31.

55. For additional information concerning these conferences, see the following references: Senate Committee on Public Works, *Problems and Issues of a National Materials Policy* (Washington, D.C.: U.S. Government Printing Office, December 1970), 272 pp.; Congressional Research Service, *Resolving Some Selected Issues of a National Materials Policy* (Washington, D.C.: U.S. Government Printing Office, December 1972), 101 pp.; Office of Technology Assessment, *Requirements for Fulfilling a National Materials Policy,* 194 pp.; Office of Technology Assessment, *Engineering Implications of Chronic Materials Scarcity* (Washington, D.C.: U.S. Government Printing Office, April 1977), 320 pp.; House Committee on Science and Technology, Subcommittee on Science, Research, and Technology, *Building a Consensus on

Legislation for a National Materials Policy (Washington, D.C.: U.S. Government Printing Office, December 1978), 384 pp.; House Committee on Science and Technology, *Innovation in the Basic Materials Industries* (Washington, D.C.: U.S. Government Printing Office, June 1981), 571 pp.; and House Committee on Science and Technology, *Seventh Biennial Conference on National Materials Policy,* 156 pp.

Acronyms

AID	Agency for International Development
ANMB	Army and Navy Munitions Board
CCC	Commodity Credit Corporation
CMI	Critical Minerals Index
COMECON	Eastern Europe Council for Mutual Economic Assistance
DOD	Department of Defense
DPA	Defense Production Act
EEC	European Economic Community
FEMA	Federal Emergency Management Agency
FMS	Federation of Materials Societies
GDP	gross domestic product
GNP	gross national product
GSA	General Services Administration
HIP	hot isostatic processing
IDCA	International Development Cooperation Agency
MNC	multinational corporation
NAS/NAE	National Academy of Sciences/National Academy of Engineering
NATO	North Atlantic Treaty Organization
NIEO	New International Economic Order
NSRB	National Security Resources Board
OECD	Organization for Economic Cooperation and Development
OPEC	Organization of Petroleum Exporting Countries
OPIC	Overseas Private Investment Corporation
RFC	Reconstruction Finance Corporation
R&D	research and development
RST	rapid solidification technology
TDP	Trade and Development Program (of IDCA)
USGS	U.S. Geological Survey

Index